The
Dumpling

The Dumpling

A SEASONAL GUIDE

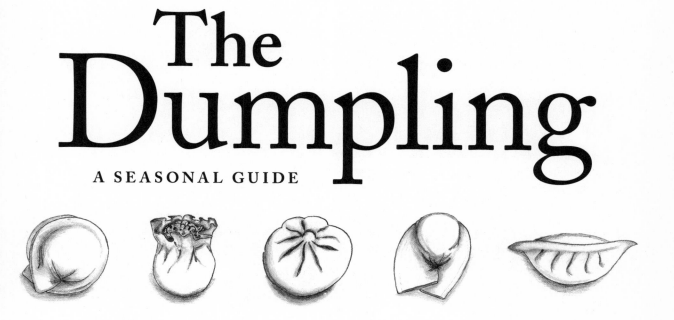

Wai Hon Chu and Connie Lovatt

WILLIAM MORROW
An Imprint of HarperCollins*Publishers*

Wai dedicates this book to his parents,
Wah and Sandra Chu

Connie dedicates this book to her parents, John H. Lovatt and
Margaret H. Lovatt, and to her husband, Ravi Nandan

. . . .

HarperCollins books may be purchased for educational, business, or sales promotional use. For information please write: Special Markets Department, HarperCollins Publishers, 10 East 53rd Street, New York, NY 10022.

FIRST EDITION

Designed by Kris Tobiassen
Photographs by Brandon Harman
Illustrations by Wai Hon Chu

Library of Congress Cataloging-in-Publication Data

Chu, Wai Hon.
    The dumpling: a seasonal guide / Wai Hon Chu and Connie Lovatt.—1st ed.
        p. cm.
    Includes index.
    ISBN 978-0-06-081738-1
    1. Dumplings. 2. Cookery, International. I. Lovatt, Connie. II. Title.
    TX769.H6475 2009
    641.8'15—dc22   2008013228

09   10   11   12   13   WBC/QW   10   9   8   7   6   5   4   3   2   1

Contents

Introduction 1

Glossary of Ingredients 5

Glossary of Equipment 25

Tips 33

Dumpling Fold Instructions and Illustrations 39

Recipes

January 63

Semolina Dumplings with Butter and Cheese Sauce • Butter-Tossed Spaetzle • Potato and Dumpling Boil-Up • Spiced Gingerbread • A Wealth of Steamed Rice Muffins • Steamed Bread Rolls • "Priest Stranglers" with Brown Butter and Sage • Potato Gnocchi • Marrow Dumplings in Beef Broth • Cassava "Tamales" Stuffed with Pork and Chickpeas • Pounded Rice Dumplings • New Year's Day Soup with Pounded Rice Dumplings

February 89

Spoon-Dropped Semolina Dumplings • Chocolate Bread Crumb Pudding • Milk-Steamed Buns with Vanilla Custard Sauce • Cloud-Shaped Bread Buns • Steamed Bread Loaves Stuffed with Sticky

Fried Rice • Potato Dumplings Stuffed with Ham • Silesian Potato Dumplings with Mushroom Sauce • Chestnut Gnocchi with Walnut Sauce • Panfried Dumplings Stuffed with Chicken and Mushrooms

March 113

Steamed Corn Bread • Sweet Potato Dumplings with a Melted Sugar Center • Tiny Gnocchi and Cranberry Bean Stew • Cauliflower Soup with Buttery Bread Crumb Dumplings • Cockles with Rice Dumplings in a Spicy Coconut Sauce • Chickpea Dumplings in Tomato Sauce • Kasha and Mushroom Pierogi • Rice Dumplings Stuffed with Pork and Kohlrabi

April 133

Masa Ball Soup • Chickpea Squares Topped with Mustard Seeds and Spiced Oil • Nine-Layer Coconut Tapioca Cake • Salty-Sweet Bean Puddings with Coconut Cream Topping • Matzo Balls in a Beef Broth • Chive-Stuffed Dumplings with Tomato Sauce and Minted Yogurt • Wheat Dumplings Stuffed with Turmeric-Stained Potatoes • Wheat Dumplings Stuffed with Beef and Onion • Spicy Lamb-Filled Dumplings in a Thick Yogurt Soup • Oven-Simmered Lamb-Filled Dumplings with Minted Yogurt • Dumplings Stuffed with Pork and Cabbage

May 163

Black Sesame Cupcakes • Boiled Fish with Okra and Dumplings • Slippery Rice Balls in Cabbage-Radish Soup • Pounded Cassava Dumpling • Mushroom-Asparagus Bread Dumplings in a Mushroom Sauce • Coconut and Rice Columns with Chickpea Curry • Small Pork Buns • Small Mushroom Buns • Pineapple-Pecan Tamales • Tamales Stuffed with Chicken and Tomatillo Sauce • Pounded Rice Dumplings Stuffed with Strawberries • Leaf-Wrapped Rice Packages Stuffed with Chicken and Bamboo Shoots

June 195

Flattened Rice Dumplings with Grated Coconut and Anise Sugar • Leaf Bread, a Fresh Corn "Tamale" • Taro Balls in a Sweet Coconut Soup • Canary Pudding with Lemon Curd • Black Sesame Roll-Ups • Lemony Lentil-Chard Soup with Bulgur Dumplings • Fish Ravioli with a Thinned Cream Sauce • Sticky Rice Dumplings Stuffed with Pork and Shrimp • Rice and Tapioca Dumplings

Topped with Shrimp and Bean Paste • Pork Tamales with Green Olives and Jalapeño • The Arm of the Queen Tamale • Leaf-Wrapped Rice Bundles Stuffed with Chicken and Peanuts

July...225

Banana Cupcakes • Plantain Dumplings in Chicken Broth • "Napkin" Bread Dumpling with Cherries • Fresh Corn and Coconut "Tamales" • Fresh Corn and Basil "Tamales" • Cabinet Pudding, a Cake and Almond Cookie Pudding • Sweet and Dark Pepperpot Stew and Dumplings • Bottle-necked Pork and Shrimp Dumplings • Rice Dumplings Stuffed with Peanut and Coconut • Lightly Soured Rice Cakes

August...253

Peach and Berry Grunt • Cassava Patties with Grated Coconut • Red Pea Soup with Spinners • Leaf-Wrapped Rice and Banana Bundles • Wontons with Red Chile Oil • Corn Tamales Stuffed with Stringy Cheese and Poblano • Leaf-Wrapped Black-Eyed Pea Dumplings • Leaf-Wrapped Rice Bundles Stuffed with Pork and Beans • Coconut-Filled Rice Dumplings • Tapioca Balls Stuffed with Minced Pork and Peanuts

September..275

Wild Grapes and Dumplings • Boston Brown Bread • Chicken Fricot with Dumplings • Chicken and Dumpling Soup • Bread and Semolina Loaf • Oat and Honey Pudding • Graham Potato Buns • Layered Apple and Bread Pudding • Beef and Oyster Stew with Suet Dumplings • Mild Yogurt Semolina Cakes • Buckwheat Dumplings Stuffed with Apples and Cheese • Potato Dumplings Stuffed with Sugar-Stuffed Plums • Leaf-Wrapped Rice Packages Stuffed with Peanuts and Sausage

October...303

No-Fuss Potato Dumplings • Spiced Carrot Pudding • Collard Greens with Corn Dumplings • Chicken Paprika with Dumplings • Bean Soup with Tiny Dumplings • Chickpea "Fish" in a Spicy Onion Sauce • Bacon and Sage Roly-Poly • Daikon Cake • Cheddar Cheese and Potato Pierogi • Lentil and Onion Pierogi • Potato "Tamales" Stuffed with Chicken and Jalapeño • Beef-Stuffed Plantain Balls in a Cassava-Corn Soup

November 331

Dumplings and Cocky's Joy • "Napkin" Bread Dumpling • Turkey Stew with Stuffing Dumplings • Cranberry Pudding • Lord Randall's Pudding, an Apricot Dessert • Sticky Toffee Pudding • Potato Dumplings with Crouton Centers • Country Cabbage Soup with Large Cornmeal Dumplings • Philadelphia Pepperpot Soup with Dumplings • Large Beef- and Spinach-Filled Dumplings in a Beef Broth • Dumplings Stuffed with Pears, Figs, and Chocolate • Pumpkin and Lentil Ravioli with Browned Butter and Rosemary • "Little Ear" Dumplings Stuffed with Mushrooms in a Beet Soup

December 363

Root Vegetable Bread Dumplings • Clootie Dumpling • Starchy Coconut Stew with Slippery Rice Balls • Guava Duff • Potato Dumplings with Cabbage Layers • John in the Sack • Classic Christmas Pudding • Chocolate Tamales • Siberian Meat Dumplings • Chestnut Ravioli with Sage Butter Sauce • Chicken-Filled Dumplings in an Escarole Soup • Dumplings Stuffed with "Stewed" Bread Crumbs

Broths 393

Chicken Broth • Pork Broth • Beef Broth • Beef and Chicken Broth

Acknowledgments 399
Dumplings by Region and Country 401
Dumplings by Type 406
Vegetarian Dumplings 411
Index 415

Introduction

This book is about traditional dumplings and the simple pleasures they can bring into your kitchen.

Dumplings embody the foundations of good cooking: ingredients that make the most of the seasons, time-honored techniques, and an open mind. Because most dumplings are made by hand, they pull you deeper into the craft of cooking by emphasizing the value of intuition and the benefits of learning through trial and error.

Much as with recipes for bread, pastry, pasta and noodles, pancakes, biscuits, and cakes, traditional dumpling recipes create delicious mainstays loaded with character and charm. What we hope to demonstrate with this book is the reality that, despite their similarities to other dough- or batter-based creations, dumplings are in a category all their own.

So, what makes a dumpling a dumpling? Is an empanada a dumpling? Is a fritter? Every definition we have come across presents a slightly different view. After exploring a thousand different dishes normally considered to be dumplings, it became clear to us that their identities revolved around two key traits: They are made out of some kind of dough, batter, or starchy plant foundation, and they are either steamed, simmered, or boiled.

It's the use of wet heat that gets to the heart of what a dumpling really is, even if the basic ingredients are similar to what makes up bread, pastry, and pancakes. Baking, frying, and other dry-heat methods of cooking bestow a distinctive crust, rich with caramelized flavors. In contrast, the characteristic softness and clean taste that dumplings develop through wet heat cooking is what makes them so distinctive and special.

In this light, we do not see empanadas or fritters as true dumplings, even if they are occasionally referred to that way, because they are baked or fried. And while fish balls, meatballs, and cheese balls look like dumplings, and are prepared by similar methods, they are not included in this book because they are not primarily based on starchy ingredients.

While dumplings come in many forms, not just "round" or "filled," they are not shaped as strands, or ribbons, as are pastas and noodles.

After working with hundreds of recipes for dumplings from around the world, our ideas of dumplings had expanded to include them in all their magnificent variety, and it also allowed us to refine our view into the following definition:

A dumpling is a portion of dough, batter, or starchy plant fare, solid or filled, that is cooked through wet heat, and is not a strand or ribbon.

. . . .

We prepared dumplings from well over eight hundred recipes before compiling this collection. We envisioned the book to include not only American favorites such as chicken and dumplings and blueberry grunt but also dumplings from Europe, South America, and every other part of the world where dumplings are enjoyed. We wanted layered tapioca dumplings from Thailand and lavishly topped rice dumplings from Vietnam. We wanted Middle Eastern dumplings smothered in rich sauces and oil-slicked chickpea dumplings from India. We could not leave out stuffed plantain dumplings found only in Peru, or freshly pounded *mochi* from Japan, with its marshmallow bite and sticky texture.

We bring you dumplings that are hallmarks of particular regions or cuisines, such as the generously spiced Christmas pudding from England, the tamale from Mexico, and the hearty *momo* from Tibet.

Nor have we neglected dumplings like matzo balls and pierogi, which transcend their regional origins and are eaten around the world. Our recipes for favorites such as these are popular but lesser-known versions, not often included in many cookbooks.

The 135 dumplings that follow, and the 60 soups, stews, and sauces in which they're cooked, are all traditional—adapted only as necessary for modern kitchen equipment and ingredients. You will find a detailed glossary of ingredients, equipment, tips, and diagrams to help simplify even the most demanding recipes. That being said, we strongly encourage you to use your hands, and not machines, when you roll out the dough that certain dumplings require. Of course, you can always use a pasta machine for dough that has to be rolled out thin, but using a rolling pin connects you more directly to the dough.

. . . .

Our month-by-month arrangement of the recipes is based on our experiences and preferences and is not meant to be a fixed timeline. Certainly an "August" dumpling can be made in February, but we think you might find it to be at its most excellent in August. One reason is that many of our recipes feature seasonal ingredients that are best at their natural peak, even if they may be available year-round in your market. Some dumplings are especially suitable for certain months when the weather mimics the climate or traditional serving season of the dumpling's home. Spicy dumplings from central Vietnam are great on hot days, while several rich dessert dumplings from England are best during the colder months. Of course, holiday dumplings are placed at the appropriate time of year.

Within each chapter, the recipes have been arranged in order from the easiest to the most challenging. The more demanding dumpling recipes require a degree of orderliness. Certain dumpling recipes have multiple components that must be prepared separately and then assembled together to create the final dish. Filling and folding several dozen dumplings is not a casual operation, but it can easily become a relaxing and enriching way to spend your time if your ingredients are sorted out, your workspace is clear, and you have allowed yourself plenty of time. No matter what your level of expertise is in the kitchen, we hope that these recipes will encourage you to try your hand at creating dumplings that are as enjoyable to make as they are to eat. There may be techniques and ingredients in this book that are unfamiliar to you, but this does not mean that you will not be able to understand them, apply what you already know as you work, and make a fantastic batch of dumplings.

Glossary
of Ingredients

This book is as much about quality ingredients as it is about dumplings. Shopping seasonally and as close as possible to the food's source ensures not only that you'll go home with a better product but also that you'll be more apt to support smaller, more sustainable farms. Farmers who provide their animals with a natural diet, and with plenty of light, air, and space, nurture not only the health of their animals but their customers' health as well. The following ingredients either play a central role in this book or make occasional appearances but merit further description.

BEANS: Dried beans are simple and sturdy and can be made into satisfying dumplings at any time of year. Bean dumplings are usually made by grinding soaked dried beans into a pasty batter before cooking. In India, spoonfuls are fried before being simmered in stews and sauces. Other, similar batters are steamed in molds and pans. Canned beans are too soft to make into dumpling doughs and batters, but they are perfectly acceptable when added to soups, stews, and sauces. Be sure to rinse canned beans thoroughly before adding them to other ingredients. Some of the beans used in this book include kidney beans, cranberry (or *borlotti*) beans, chickpeas, black-eyed peas, mung beans, and adzuki beans. Mung bean sprouts are also used in some Asian dumplings.

BREAD: Bread has long been incorporated into dumpling making throughout Europe, especially in England, Germany, Italy, and the Czech Republic. If you are new to dumpling making (or just learning how to cook in general), bread dumplings are good beginner's recipes because they are easy to make. The simplest ones involve little more than soaking bread cubes or bread crumbs in eggs and shaping them into balls to be boiled. Hardly any kneading is involved. Bread is a very flexible ingredient because there are so many kinds you can work with. While most of the bread dumplings in this book call for a standard loaf of eggless white bread, you can substitute whole grain bread if you want a different flavor or a less processed alternative.

Choosing your bread. When buying bread, try to find the freshest loaf possible that is free of preservatives. Preservative-filled doughs rob the loaf or bun of its natural cycle: a soft freshness, then a firm staleness, and then a brittle dryness. Breads made with preservatives, like those found at most supermarkets, are more likely to mold before changing texture for you, making them useless for most bread cubes or bread crumbs. All-natural loaves, or rolls that are freshly made, are not only better for eating but also better for dumpling recipes. Crusty breads, such as ciabatta or baguettes, will stay fresh for no more than a day. Sandwich loaves can last a day or two longer before they stale.

Cutting off the crusts: When using up leftover bread for dumplings, it is best to remove the crust for a more even texture and neutral taste. Use a serrated knife to trim off the crust while the bread is still somewhat soft. If the bread is already dry, grating off the crust, which can be messy, is a fast and somewhat satisfying project similar to sculpting or sanding.

Bread crumbs. Bread crumbs have a huge capacity to soak up liquids. There is a noticeable difference between a dough or batter of bread crumbs that has been soaking for 10 minutes and one that has soaked for 30 minutes. They also make soft, creamy dumpling fillings when flavored with rich broths or combined with other ingredients.

To make fresh bread crumbs: Remove the crust from a piece of stale bread and grate it through the medium or large holes of a box grater.

For dry bread crumbs: Allow the fresh bread crumbs to dry completely in a 200°F oven for 15 to 20 minutes or finely grate a dry piece of bread on a box grater.

Bread cubes. Small bread cubes (or croutons) are a useful ingredient in dumpling making, whether they are soaked and reshaped into balls, formed into loaves, or fried and stuffed into the center of a potato dumpling.

To make bread cubes: Remove the crust from a piece of fresh or stale bread and cut the bread into ½-inch to 1-inch cubes using a serrated knife.

For dry bread cubes: Arrange the bread cubes in a single layer on a baking sheet and allow them to dry completely in a 200°F oven for 20 to 25 minutes.

Fried bread crumbs. Bread crumbs fried in butter are used frequently as a topping or coating for pierogi and several other European dumplings. They add a satisfying crunch to soft, succulent dumplings.

To fry bread crumbs: For each ½ cup of dried bread crumbs, use 1 tablespoon of unsalted butter. Melt the butter in a skillet over medium heat. Add the bread crumbs and stir continuously until they are golden brown and crispy. Serve immediately or cool to room temperature on a paper-towel-lined plate.

CABBAGE: Cabbage is widely used in numerous European and Asian dumplings. Green cabbage, Savoy cabbage, bok choy, napa cabbage, and kohlrabi are all used as dumpling fillings, as are fermented cabbages such as sauerkraut and kimchee. Cabbage is often paired with dumplings in other ways, as a side or in soups.

CASSAVA: This yamlike root, also known as yuca or manioc, has a barklike skin (often coated in wax for market) and milky white flesh. It is a staple in African, South American, Philippine, and Caribbean cooking. Like the potato, cassava can be grated raw and cooked into dense, chewy dumplings, or it can be cooked, mashed, and made into softer, more cake-like dumplings.

Choosing your cassava. There are two main types of cassava (bitter and sweet), but only the sweet variety is sold whole in the United States. We use sweet cassava in all of our recipes and it is available at Caribbean or Asian food markets and in the produce section of some supermarkets. Peeled and frozen cassava can also be found at some supermarkets and can be used as a component in soups and stews, but we don't recommend using frozen cassava as a substitute for fresh cassava in dumpling dough or batter recipes. Bitter cassava is toxic when raw and is often made into flour or coarse meal, using a careful process that takes days, in which the root is soaked to leach out the toxins and then sun-dried and ground. It is generally not available in the United States.

Preparing the cassava: Since the cassava's skin is so thick and woody, you will need to peel it with a knife. Be sure you remove not only the waxy brown bark but also a barely distinguishable "second skin" that lies between the skin and the flesh of the cassava. This second skin is fine to eat, but it cooks up into an unappetizing shade of gray. After the cassava is peeled, quarter the flesh lengthwise and pull or cut out any tough or more fibrous strands from its center.

Tapioca. Tapioca pearls and tapioca flour (also called tapioca starch) are made from cassava and are used prominently in Southeast Asian dumplings. Tapioca pearls come in different sizes and colors and can be found at Asian food markets and supermarkets. Tapioca flour adds a distinctive jellied bite to dumplings and can be found in most supermarkets.

COCONUT: Coconut milk and grated coconut are used regularly in many Indian and Southeast Asian dumpling recipes. Grating your own coconut and making fresh coconut milk takes some time, but the results are stunning. Whole coconuts are available at different degrees of maturity. Young coconuts are valued for their soft, silky flesh and tantalizing light "coconut water," while mature coconuts offer up a firm, thick flesh with a much more concentrated flavor. Brown and hairy mature coconuts are the ones used for shredding and squeezing coconut milk. It's important to buy coconuts from stores that sell them often. Coconuts that sit around can turn moldy on the inside. Shake the coconut and listen for a faint sloshing sound. If the liquid sloshes conspicuously, or not at all, that may be a sign of a coconut that is just too old. We learned to buy two coconuts for every one called for in a recipe, in case one was a dud.

Cracking the coconut: There are many ways to crack open a coconut, and none of them is very elegant. This quick method works best for us: Wrap one coconut in three or four layers of paper towels (you could also use a kitchen towel and rinse it out afterward) and place it inside a sturdy plastic shopping bag or a comparable sack (double up on the bags if needed). Find a good hard surface to whack the coconut against, indoors or outdoors. Grip the bag a few inches above the coconut and slap it as hard as you can against the surface. Do this a few times, even after you hear it crack open, so you can loosen the meat and break the coconut apart into a few manageable pieces. Unwrap the pieces and rinse them off in a bowl of cool water.

Removing the flesh: Fold up a kitchen towel and use it to hold a shard of coconut in one hand. Slide a sturdy and—we cannot emphasize this enough—*blunt* knife in between the shell and the flesh as far as you can while still being able to twist the knife. This twisting motion should pop the coconut meat out. Some coconuts will be easier to work with than others. Take your time and use extra care in handling the sharp edges of the coconut shell. Once all the meat has been removed, peel off the brown skin with a vegetable peeler. Rinse off the peeled pieces in a bowl of cool water. If you are not using them immediately, peeled pieces of coconut can be kept in a bowl covered with a damp towel for up to 2 days in the refrigerator.

Grating the coconut: Grate the coconut pieces over a board or a cloth through the large or medium holes of a box grater. Measure out enough coconut for your recipe and keep the rest tightly packed and refrigerated for up to 2 days or frozen for up to a month. If making dried, grated coconut, spread the coconut out on a large sheet tray and bake in a 200°F oven for 15 to 20 minutes. One large coconut should make 4 cups of freshly grated coconut or, after baking, 2 cups of dried coconut.

Making fresh coconut milk: Put the meat of one grated coconut (or the meat of one coconut that has been cut into small chunks) into a blender. Pour in ¾ cup of room-temperature water, preferably nonchlorinated water, such as distilled or spring water, and blend for 1 minute. Add another ¾ cup of water and blend until it is mixed evenly and milky, about 1 minute longer. Strain the coconut milk through a sturdy sieve, pressing down on the coconut and squeezing out as much liquid as you can. You should have just about 2 cups of fresh coconut milk. Use coconut milk shortly after it has been made. If left to sit for an hour or two, it can begin to separate (see "Collecting the Coconut Cream," below).

Making the most out of your coconut: The squeezed-out coconut can be used for a second pressing by reblending it with the same amount of water. This second pressing will make a lighter coconut milk that can be used to cook rice or poach fish. The squeezed-out coconut can also be dried in an oven on low heat and used as a topping or as a breading in other recipes.

Collecting the coconut cream: Cover the freshly made coconut milk and place it in the refrigerator for at least 1 hour. The milk will separate into two distinct layers, a thick and creamy top layer and a watery bottom layer. Gently scoop out the top layer of coconut cream, being careful not to mix it back into the thin bottom layer. You should be able to gather about ½ cup of cream from every 2 cups of fresh coconut milk.

Using canned coconut milk. Canned coconut milk can be used when coconuts are not available or if there is not enough time to make coconut milk from scratch. Be sure to buy unsweetened, all-natural coconut milk that contains nothing but coconut, water, and a little guar gum. Canned coconut milk is thicker than fresh, so it must be blended with water before use in these recipes. In general, mix 5 parts canned coconut milk with 3 parts water to obtain a consistency comparable to fresh milk. (To use one 14-ounce can of coconut milk, stir in 1 cup of water.)

Using canned coconut cream. Canned coconut cream is found in a few Asian, Caribbean, Mexican, and South American markets. It can be difficult to find, so we use canned coconut milk in its undiluted form instead. Cream of coconut is a sweetened coconut product more specifically for blended drinks, and also should not be used as a substitute for coconut cream.

Using packaged frozen or dried grated coconut. Freshly grated coconut can be purchased frozen in some Asian or South American grocers or in specialty food markets. Look for packages in which the coconut appears firm, white, and free of ice crystals. Check the date if there is one. When buying dried, grated coconut, look for the all-natural, unsweetened variety. Most well-stocked health food stores carry a good-quality brand of dried, grated coconut. The packaged dried, grated coconut found on most supermarket shelves is heavily sweetened and full of preservatives and is not recommended for the recipes in this book.

Cooking with coconut milk. Coconut milk can separate when simmered for long periods of time or when brought up to a rolling boil. Once it separates, or curdles, there is really no way to stir or whisk it back together. This frustrating mishap is easily avoided by keeping your eye on the coconut milk as it simmers and making sure never to let it come to a full boil. And, while the flavors are not as superlative, canned coconut milk can withstand longer simmering times and higher temperatures.

CORN: A huge variety of dumplings is made from this grain. Nowhere is this more apparent than in Mexico, parts of South America, and the United States.

Fresh sweet corn. The simplest corn dumplings are made from freshly cut and pulped kernels, wrapped in the corn's own husks and steamed into tender, curdlike dumplings. Placing the reserved corn silk and the stripped cobs in the steaming water adds even more flavor and aroma.

Dried field corn for masa. Ground nixtamalized corn is the foundation of almost every Mexican tamale and tortilla. Dry kernels of field corn are boiled in a solution of water and slaked lime (calcium hydroxide or "cal") and soaked for up to 24 hours, creating nixtamalized or slaked corn. The corn is then cleaned and ground into a paste on a grinding stone called a *metate*. (We've adapted our recipe to work in a food processor; see page 189.) This ground paste, or masa, can then be made into different batters and doughs for tamales, flat breads, fritters, or pastries. Although making your own fresh masa can be a lengthy process, it's a procedure that imparts a balance to the flavor of corn in immeasurable ways. You can also find fresh or frozen masa at some Mexican markets and through mail-order suppliers. Calcium hydroxide is sold as a grainy white powder and can be found at some Mexican markets.

Masa harina. Masa harina is a processed meal made out of dried nixtamalized corn paste. It is the reliable, ready-to-use substitute for fresh masa and at times may be preferred, especially by those who appreciate a more cakelike tamale. Tamale recipes in this book allow the option of using either fresh masa or masa harina.

Cornmeal and corn flour. We recommend buying cornmeal that has been stone ground, which is somewhat coarse. When a finer consistency is called for, you can grind it further in a spice or coffee grinder by pulsing it a few times. Store coarsely ground corn and other whole grain flours in the refrigerator to prevent their natural oils from spoiling. Corn flour is much finer than cornmeal and should not be substituted for cornmeal.

EGGS: Eggs add both moisture and strength to dough that has to be rolled out until thin, and to batters that are dropped into boiling water. They bind together bread cubes and bread crumbs in dumplings that would otherwise crumble apart. Yolks add depth to fillings, and whipped whites add lightness to steamed cakes. Slices of hard-boiled egg are tucked into a number of dumplings. The recipes in this book were tested with large, organic, free-range eggs. These eggs taste much better and have richer yolks and less watery whites. Eggs are also very popular served up with leftover dumplings.

FATS AND OILS: Dumpling doughs and batters—just like those of breads, pastries, biscuits, and so on—often rely on some sort of oil or fat for tenderness and a richer flavor. Lard, suet, and butter are commonly used by dumpling makers around the world and appear many times in this book. A variety of oils is also used to make dumplings. Chemicals and toxins tend to be fat soluble, and because fats and oils are naturally dense or highly concentrated, their quality is paramount, making organic options more appealing.

Lard. Rendered pork fat or lard is used regularly in dumplings, especially in Mexico and China. Most of the lard called for in this book is used in tamales. All-natural lard has a slight meaty smell, an extremely creamy texture, and a certain indefinable quality that serious dumpling fans claim cannot be duplicated by substitutes. Leaf lard, the fat found around the kidneys, is considered the finest. Some butchers and well-stocked Mexican markets sell fresh as well as rendered lard. Commercially processed lard is deodorized, bleached, and often partially hydrogenated and is not used in this book. When making dessert tamales, we use lighter-tasting solid fats—either nonhydrogenated vegetable shortening or butter. Tamales can be made vegetarian with nonhydrogenated vegetable shortening.

To render lard: For 1 cup of lard, finely chop ½ pound of skinless pork fat into small pieces and place in a small pot. Place the pot over very low heat and allow the fat to melt slowly into an oily liquid. Do not cover. This step may take up to 1 hour. Stir occasionally to help the fat render evenly. Once the fat has melted completely, strain it through a sieve lined with several layers of cheesecloth. Once rendered, it should be kept refrigerated in a tightly sealed glass jar for up to 1 week or frozen for up to 1 year.

Suet. The stiff fat found around the kidneys of cows is the most commonly used form of suet. It is not used often in the United States, but it isn't too hard to track down. Butchers who sell more than steaks and chicken should be able to get their hands on some. Suet is used most often in England, most notably in steamed puddings and pastries. Its ability to melt slowly, even at high temperatures, makes it an ideal fat for the long cooking times of puddings. You can use suet straight from the butcher by chilling it and cutting it into small bits, or you can render it first for a smoother consistency. Rendering suet removes most of the meaty flavor and is suggested for the sweet steamed puddings. In most recipes, if suet is unavailable or not preferred, you can substitute grated frozen butter.

To chop raw suet: Peel off any membranes from around the fat and remove any noticeable bits of meat. Break the suet into smaller chunks and chop very fine. It helps to firm up the suet in the freezer for at least 1 hour for a cleaner chop. If the suet begins to get sticky, sprinkle with a little all-purpose flour and continue chopping. Don't worry if the chopped suet clings together in clumps, as you will be rubbing it into flour later.

To render suet: For 1 cup of rendered suet, clean and finely chop ½ pound of raw suet into small pieces and place in a small pot. Place the pot over very low heat and allow the suet to melt slowly into an oily liquid. Do not cover. This step may take up to 1 hour. Stir occasionally to help the fat render evenly. Once the suet has melted completely, strain it through a sieve lined with several layers of cheesecloth. Once rendered, it should be kept refrigerated in a tightly sealed glass jar for up to 1 week or frozen for up to 1 year.

Butter. Butter is the preferred fat for a great number of dumpling doughs and fillings, and melted butter may be the world's most common dumpling sauce. We use only unsalted (or sweet) butter and add salt when needed. All-natural butter of all types is easy enough to find, but the butter made from the milk of grass-fed cows tastes best. Avoid using margarine or artificially flavored spreads as a substitute for butter.

Ghee. Clarified—and then slightly caramelized—butter, or ghee, is used often to make dumpling fillings, along with stews, sauces, and soups for dumplings, throughout South Asia and the Middle East. Ghee, when liquid, is golden, thick, and silky. Once chilled it firms up and turns a milky, mild yellow. It has a nutty, buttery fragrance and outshines melted or clarified butter, keeps well at room temperature, and like clarified butter, has a high smoking point. Ghee can be found at Indian and some Middle Eastern markets, many health food stores, and well-stocked grocery stores. Keep an eye out for, and resist purchasing, ghee that is hydrogenated. If you are unable to find all-natural ghee, it is simple enough to make at home.

To make ghee: Place one pound of unsalted butter in a medium saucepan over medium heat. Do not cover. Once the butter has melted and has a foamy surface, reduce the heat to low and continue cooking for 8 to 10 minutes. Stir occasionally. Once the foam thins out and the milk solids at the bottom of the pot are golden brown, remove from the heat. The ghee will be a light to medium caramel color. Skim off any foamy bits from the surface and strain the ghee, leaving as many of the cooked solid bits as you can in the pot, through a sieve lined with several layers of cheesecloth. You should have about 1¾ cups. Keep refrigerated in a tightly sealed glass jar for up to 3 months or frozen for up to 1 year.

Grapeseed and other oils. When sautéing or frying ingredients for fillings or sauces, we use primarily grapeseed oil. It has a high smoking point and no discernible flavor. A neutral oil such as this can be used in recipes from around the world without changing signature flavors. Peanut, olive, and sesame oil are also used in this book. Coconut oil that has not been hydrogenated is a good cooking oil that works well in recipes where a light coconut flavor is welcomed.

FISH, SHRIMP, AND SHELLFISH: There are relatively few traditional dumplings made with fish or seafood, compared with meat, mushrooms, beans, and other savory fillings. More popular are fish balls (such as gefilte fish), fish cakes (such as crab cakes) or fritters (such as shrimp balls). Although dumplings are popular in places where people tend to eat a lot of fish, only a handful of traditional dishes combine fish with dumplings. The flavors of fish are perhaps too subtle to be paired with something as mild as a starchy dough or batter. Shrimp and shellfish, however, are popular in various Chinese and Vietnamese dumplings, especially those wrapped in rice or tapioca doughs. Cockles, oysters, sole, and shrimp are some of the seafood items that appear in these pages.

Dried or salted fish and shrimp. Seafood that is preserved by either of these means is used in dumplings from Vietnam, China, Japan, Africa, and the Caribbean. Dried shrimp powder is a popular topping for many Vietnamese dishes, but in China small dried shrimp are used to instantly flavor soups, rice, and many other foods. In Japan, the broth for many soups is flavored with dried fish shavings and pieces of dried seaweed. Fish is plentiful in the Caribbean and parts of Africa, and dried and salted fish are often used to provide a different texture and taste when served with, or stuffed into, dumplings.

Fruits: Dumplings are refreshing when made with fruit that's perfectly ripe and in season, while dried fruit dumplings are sticky, warming, and substantial in colder months.

Apples. There is a well-known dessert called an apple dumpling that is a dough-wrapped apple, stuffed with butter, sugar, spices, and often nuts and baked until golden brown. Because it is baked, it is not technically a dumpling in our eyes, and we've not included it in this book. We have included Layered Apple and Bread Pudding and Buckwheat Dumplings Stuffed with Apples and Cheese (both in September).

Stone fruit and berries. We used all sorts of plums, cherries, peaches, blueberries, and strawberries as we cooked our way through hundreds of dumplings. There is something special about these highly perishable fruits wrapped up and cooked to a jamlike perfection inside pockets of tasty dough. Thick, sticky batters dropped by the spoonful onto the surface of a bubbling stone fruit or berry stew create classic summer and early fall desserts. Recipes in this book use primarily fresh fruit, but there is no denying that these fruits also freeze well, and bags of blueberries or sliced peaches can be kept on hand for a quick dumpling dessert anytime.

Dried fruit. Raisins, dried plums (prunes), dried currants, dried apricots, and other dried fruits are more intense than fresh versions. They can be found in a number of steamed puddings from England—their innate stickiness helps to bind flours and bread crumbs together when used in large amounts—and to a lesser extent in steamed breads, cakes, and other dumplings throughout the rest of Europe, the Americas, Russia, and Asia. Dried fruit keeps well and is available for dumpling making year-round, but its darker, near-spicy richness is especially effective during the cold months. Many health food stores sell sugar-free and preservative-free dried fruit, which ensures character and exceptionally good taste. The flavor of treated dried fruit tends to melt away once the fruit is steamed or boiled within dumpling batters or dough.

HERBS, SPICES, SAUCES, AND PEPPERS: Certain dumplings aren't complete unless matched with fish sauce, soy sauce, hot sauce, or other condiments. Peppers, especially hot peppers, are vital to many Asian, Indian, Caribbean, Mexican, and African dumpling dishes. Spices, herbs, and peppers are used to intensify the flavor of both dumpling fillings and the soups, stews, sauces, and broths in which the dumplings are served.

Black pepper. Whole peppercorns are used to add an alluring spice and fragrance to many of the broths in which dumplings are served. Freshly ground pepper is also used to season a fair number of fillings, soups, sauces, and so on, throughout the book. We found ground black pepper to be used most indulgently as a topping for certain Eastern European and Russian dumplings, especially those slathered with melted butter, sour cream, or vinegar.

Chile peppers and powders. Spicy-hot dumpling fillings, stews, soups, and sauces are found predominantly in Asian, Mexican, African, and Caribbean kitchens. Whether the peppers are fresh, dried, or powdered, their use is completely to taste. Dumplings that are traditionally quite hot are prepared in this book in the medium-hot range. If you know your heat tolerance and know your peppers, you can definitely add more (or less). Whenever possible, try to use the peppers we recommend in the recipe. Regional favorites are favorites for a reason, and they have a role that is not easily replaced. You can find the peppers used in the following recipes at Indian, Thai, Chinese, Mexican, and African groceries and, depending on your location, some well-stocked supermarkets, health food stores, and specialty markets.

Fish sauce. Fermenting fish simply with salt or other spices creates an elaborately flavored and glossy sauce. Some are concocted from only one type of small oily fish, others are prepared from a specific ratio of two or more types of fish or fish parts, and still others are made of a seemingly random mixture of all things from the sea with scales or shells. The aroma of fish sauce is an acquired appreciation for some. Well-aged fish sauces smell mildly fishy and nutty compared to the sharp, dead-fish fragrance of some younger varieties. This addictive sauce is used regularly to season fillings and dipping sauces for an endless number of dumplings in the Philippines, Thailand, Vietnam, and other Southeast Asian countries.

Ginger. Dumplings from all regions of Asia depend on the refreshing, biting, and intriguing properties of freshly grated or chopped ginger. A grating of ginger adds immediate life to meat, vegetables, and mushrooms. It wakes up the mouth and, when not overused, calls direct attention to the flavors and fragrances of the other ingredients, including the dough. Ginger is temperamental. One piece will be mild, fruity, and basically fiber-free, while another piece will be hot, strong, and woody in texture. Look for sections that have smooth, thin skins pulled taut against the flesh. Avoid pieces that look shriveled or dried out in parts. If a recipe calls for chopped ginger and you find yourself with a particularly fibrous piece, grate it as best you can and add slightly less.

Herbs. Fresh herbs are used most often in this book, but dried herbs can usually be substituted, using about one-third of the amount. But when a recipe calls for ½ bunch of thyme or ½ cup of basil, such a large amount must be fresh and not replaced by the dried. Occasionally, when a recipe calls for dried herbs specifically, fresh should not be substituted.

Pandan (or screwpine) leaves. It is often said that *pandan* is to Asian cooking what vanilla is to European or Western cooking. But Westerners can't grow vanilla in their backyards and gardens the way *pandan* is grown throughout Thailand, the Philippines, and other countries. It adds both an aromatic essence to dumplings that we can only describe as sweet caramelized grass and, depending on how it is prepared, a natural shade of green. These tall, grassy-looking leaves are found, fresh or frozen, in good Thai, Philippine, and Vietnamese markets. *Pandan* extract is sold clear or artificially dyed green, resulting in a more electric type of color. If you have to use the extract, try to find the clear type. The extract can be found at the same Asian markets that carry the leaves and, at times, at well-stocked supermarkets or specialty food markets.

Sichuan (or Szechwan) pepper. This is not really a pepper but a tiny berrylike pod that opens up and gets extremely brittle as it dries. The seed inside is not what's used. It's the pod and the bit of stem that are ground into a powdery spice. It has a peppery, bitter, and slight lemony flavor that works brilliantly with most other spices as well as with sweet and savory ingredients. What makes the Sichuan peppercorn really unusual is its temporary, but nonetheless powerful, anesthetic properties. Sichuan pepper blankets the mouth with a mild to moderate numbness that may be off-putting if you don't expect it. You might think that a spice would have to be really hot to numb your tongue, but this "pepper" isn't hot at all. What it does quite well, though, is prime your mouth for the hotter, spicier peppers usually blended with it.

Soy sauce. Soy sauce is made from fermented soybeans and, aside from saltiness, adds a distinctive aged essence to dumpling fillings and dipping sauces. There are two main types of soy sauce, dark and light. Dark soy sauce, found at many Asian markets, is slightly thicker, darker, and less salty than light soy sauce. Light soy sauce is the type found at most supermarkets and is what we use in this book.

Spices. Grinding your spices fresh adds tremendous life to dumpling recipes that are, more often than not, quite simple. By grinding your own spices in a spice grinder or a small mortar with a pestle, you can add a fullness and a freshness that will benefit any dumpling. Toasting certain spices in a dry pan also helps to coax out their flavors.

MEATS: Making the most out of a piece of meat—taking hardly enough to fill a small bowl and turning it into enough dumplings to feed a family—is what meat-filled dumplings are all about. Dumplings also efficiently make use of just about all the parts of the animal. Tripe, knuckles, feet, tail, and marrow, as well as the less expensive cuts of meat, such as shoulder, neck, belly, and ribs, are all featured in the recipes that follow.

Choosing your meat. Despite the explosion of factory farms and the illusion of "cheap" chicken or beef, meat should be handled just as traditional dumpling recipes have long dictated—respectfully. Buy the best-quality meat you can, from trusted butchers, farmers' markets, or organic food markets. When purchasing meat, it's important to buy from sources that feed the animals a diet that is natural to them, allows them to move about, and does not falsely bulk up their bodies with hormones.

Chopping meat fine: In many dumpling fillings, if the meat isn't ground, it's chopped up pretty fine. Chopping meat into small bits allows you to make even the toughest cuts of meat tender without cooking it for hours. To make chopping an easier task, stiffen up the meat by chilling it for about 1 hour in the freezer just before chopping.

Salted, cured, smoked, or dried meat. Meats that are naturally preserved by one or more of these methods are the ideal accompaniment to dumplings. These meats have a heightened flavor that many find overwhelming. However, the same intense flavors become much lighter and utterly delectable when served with or within something bland and starchy, such as a dumpling. Recipes in this book make use of salt pork, corned or salt beef, bacon, pancetta, mortadella, dried Chinese sausage, and a variety of smoked and cured hams.

MUSHROOMS: A good cook knows that there are few ingredients as versatile as the mushroom. This certainly holds true when making dumplings, especially in kitchens throughout Asia, Russia, and Europe. Mushrooms add texture and good flavor and can be chopped fine, sliced thin or thick, or left whole. When not tucked into dumplings, mushrooms are great for sauces and gravies to pour over the top. Mushrooms are a great substitute for meat in many dumplings.

Choosing the right mushrooms. Consider personal preferences, cost, and availability when working with mushrooms, but keep in mind that one kind can often substitute for another. There are a few general rules: Strongly flavored porcini or portobello mushrooms are not good substitutes for mushrooms in Asian recipes, nor are the flatter flavors of white button or cremini mushroooms, which just get lost. It's best to substitute one Asian mushroom for another. Shiitake or *maitake* (hen-of-the-woods) will not always work as a substitute in European recipes, but they can make do, especially when they are mixed with a small handful of other mushrooms such as porcini or morels for a directional boost in flavor. We find that *maitake* and oyster mushrooms work well as a substitute for any type of mushroom, no matter the region. They are light but have just enough flavor to react with the other ingredients, resulting in a mild but perfectly flavored dumpling.

Dried mushrooms. Dried mushrooms are the premier pantry ingredient for dumplings because they can be kept fragrant in jars for months, if not seasons, at a time and make an excellent, satisfying filling, sauce, or soup. They have intense, provocative flavors that always range from good to exceptional. Dried shiitake or black mushrooms, for example, have an extra-firm texture that is meaty, chewy, and vastly different from the fresh. The bonus of working with dried mushrooms is the rich soaking liquid. It can add flavor and balance to broths, soups, sautéed filling ingredients, and much more.

Fresh mushrooms. Fresh mushrooms are lighter in texture and taste than dried mushrooms, which make them perfect for subtle sauces, soups, or stews. When intended for fillings, fresh mushrooms should be chopped and sautéed to cook off excess liquid, intensifying their flavor and density, before being added to other ingredients. No matter which mushrooms you are using, if they aren't in good shape, their flavors will be off. Avoid slimy surfaces and soggy-looking edges or the opposite problem—dried, shriveled tops, edges, or gills.

ONIONS: Onions are found in countless dumpling recipes. Not only basic yellow or white onions, but leeks, scallions, chives, garlic chives, and shallots are all used to make dumplings around the world. Onions are readily available and can add a natural sweetness and caramelization to anything cooked with them. They add moisture to fillings, break up denser ingredients, and work with all types of starches, seasonings, meats, and mushrooms.

PLANTAINS: Plantains are used in a couple of dumpling recipes in this book. Like potatoes, they can be grated when raw or cooked and mashed. Ripe plantains peel easily, but you may have to use a knife with green plantains because the skin is still fastened to the flesh. Their ripeness is indicated by the color of their skins: green (unripe), yellow with black spots (semi-ripe), and black (ripe).

To peel a green plantain: Score the skin four times down the length of the plantain in evenly spaced sections. Use your fingers to pry the skin free. Any bits of peel left behind will oxidize and turn black much faster than the flesh, so they are easy to spot and pick off.

POTATOES: The ever-dependable potato is the foundation for many tremendously filling dumpling dishes. You can make dumplings out of grated raw potatoes, cooked and riced (or mashed) potatoes, or a combination. When used in doughs and batters, potatoes add moisture and softness and act as a natural leavener. Potato dumplings are prevalent throughout Europe, especially Scandinavia, Germany, Poland, and northern Italy.

Baking (russet) potatoes. Because these potatoes are high in starch and relatively low in moisture, baking potatoes are the most common type of potato used for making dumpling doughs or batters. Dumplings made from grated raw russet potatoes are usually firm and chewy, whereas those made from cooked and riced potatoes are softer and more delicate.

Boiling (Yukon Gold and red-skinned) potatoes. Boiling (or waxy) potatoes have a higher moisture content and are seldom used for dumplings. They cook up firm, hold their shape, and are best in soups and stews alongside dumplings.

Riced vs. mashed potatoes. Using a potato ricer is the easiest way to turn cooked nonwaxy potatoes into a fluffy, floury mound of super-fine potato crumbs. Rice your potatoes whenever a smooth, lump-free dough is desired. A food mill does a good job too. Mashing potatoes with a potato masher can work for a less delicate dough or when the potato is meant for fillings. Rice or mash potatoes immediately after cooking while they are still hot, because they firm up considerably once cool.

Working with grated raw potatoes: Raw potatoes can hold a lot of juice. Squeezing grated potatoes in a cloth changes a potentially sloppy and wet ingredient into something much more manageable. This step also cuts down on the amount of flour needed when making a dough or a batter out of grated potato. The less flour you add, the more potato taste you will have. We like to grate the potatoes onto a kitchen towel, spread them out, roll the towel up like a jelly roll, and then twist it tightly to soak up excess moisture.

Peeling cooked potatoes: For doughs made with boiled potatoes, it is best to cook the potatoes whole, with their skins on, to help keep out unwanted water. Peeling a hot potato isn't hard if you let it cool slightly, hold it firmly with a kitchen towel, and peel away the skin with your fingers.

POULTRY: As with all kinds of meat, seek out chickens, turkeys, or other birds that are fed a natural diet, are free of growth hormones, and are allowed to walk around and use their muscles. A traditional recipe calling for chicken breast will be overwhelmed by the enormous size of today's factory-farmed chicken breast. A natural chicken breast is generally half the size of those jumbo-sized cuts and is what is used in this book.

RICE: Rice is used in more varieties of dumplings than any other grain in the world. There are thousands of different types of dumplings made from rice or rice flour throughout East Asia, Southeast Asia, and India, and they are a valued staple both in everyday cooking and at times of celebration. Rice dumplings are also found in parts of South America and Africa. Most of the dumplings in this book are made with either a short- or medium-grain sticky (or "sweet") rice popular throughout Asia. We also use basmati rice for some Indian dumplings and some basic rice flours for a number of other Asian dumplings.

Sticky rice. Delectable "sticky," "sweet," or "glutinous" rice (although actually there is absolutely no gluten in rice) is the most important ingredient within a wide range of leaf-wrapped dumplings. As these dumplings cook, the grains of rice soften and swell into each other, creating a chewy, glistening, and fragrant loaf within the leaf. In general, leaf-wrapped dumplings from China and Japan are made with a chubby short-grain rice, such as *botan* or *mochi*. This rice cooks up very moist and sticky and has a natural milky sweetness. It can be found at some supermarkets and at many specialty food markets. In Thailand and much of Southeast Asia, a medium-grain sticky rice is used, which cooks up quickly and is perfect for soaking up the subtle flavors from coconut and pandan. This rice can be found at Thai grocers and well-stocked Asian markets.

Basmati rice. The fragrant, irresistible long-grain rice of India, when used in the following recipes, is usually ground into a coarse or fine meal. Grinding the rice yourself creates perfectly nibbly and utterly fresh-tasting dumplings. We grind our rice in a clean spice or coffee grinder. Look for basmati rice at your supermarket, specialty food market, or Indian grocery store. Preground rice, also called rice *rava, idli rava,* or rice *sooji,* is available at many Indian groceries. It is sometimes sold as "cream of rice," but do not substitute cream of rice cereal for preground rice.

Regular rice flour and sweet (glutinous) rice flour. There are numerous rice flours available. The rice flour found at most specialty and health food stores tends to be gritty, and it frequently cooks up far too firm for most dumplings. Asian rice flours are finer and more powdery, and they come in two basic types, regular and sweet (or glutinous). Thai and Vietnamese flours are ground especially fine and can, in general, be used whenever rice flour is called for in a recipe. They are available at many Chinese and Thai groceries and at large Asian food markets.

Rinsing your rice: Most rice dumpling recipes ask that you give the uncooked rice a gentle (and often repeated) rinse to wash away some, but not all, of the powdery starch on its surfaces. To give your rice one full rinse, place it in a bowl, pour in enough cool water to cover the grains generously, and then swirl the rice around for a few seconds. Use one hand to hold back the grains as you tilt the bowl and pour out the starchy water.

SALT: Salt is used not only to season savory dumpling dishes but also as an ingredient to emphasize the sweetness of dessert dumplings. We recommend using sea salt for all general cooking needs. Pinch for pinch, sea salt has a deeper, more complex flavor, as well as vital nutrients not found in heavily processed table salts. Kosher salt is an economical alternative when salting large pots of water.

SUGARS, SYRUPS, AND HONEY: As with salt, too much sugar can flatten out flavors or stun the palate. White sugar is an all-purpose sugar that is used occasionally in the following recipes, but it's the fuller and more buttery-tasting unrefined sugars used traditionally in so many dumplings that figure prominently in this book. Unrefined cane and palm sugars are used in many Indian, Asian, and Mexican dumpling recipes. These sugars, with all their delicious undertones, add as much flavor as sweetness. Honey—a sweetener that varies widely in color, consistency, and flavor—also adds a unique sweetness to certain dumplings.

Palm sugar. Palm sugar, made from the sap of the date palm tree, can be found in solid bars, disks, or cones, or in jars as a soft, grainy paste. Blocks of hard palm sugar should be chopped and crushed fine, while soft palm sugar can easily be scooped out. The taste of this sugar is so inviting and appetizing that it is hard to find a proper substitute. If you can't find palm sugar, however, you can use panela or jaggery instead.

Panela and jaggery. Both *panela* and jaggery are unrefined cane sugars sold in bars or disks, although jaggery is sometimes sold in pebble-sized chunks. *Panela* is produced in South America and Mexico (where it is called *piloncillo*) and is used to sweeten many desserts and beverages. A similar hard sugar, jaggery is used in abundance in a host of Indian sweets. Like other bar sugars, these must be chopped and crushed in order to dissolve or melt into other ingredients.

Brown slab sugar. This semirefined cane sugar from China is sold in long 2-ounce slabs that can be broken off conveniently as needed.

Muscovado sugar. This soft brown sugar, also known as Barbados sugar, is made from natural sugarcane juice and is flavored with molasses. It has a deep, rich cane flavor and a warm, vibrant texture far superior to that of regular brown sugar. It is available in light and dark varieties at specialty food markets and health food stores. Light muscovado sugar is what we use most often and it has become our staple sugar in any recipe that calls for brown sugar.

Turbinado and Demerara sugar. These two unrefined granulated sugars can also be substituted in recipes calling for brown sugar. Because of their granulated texture, they are especially useful in coating pudding basins.

Golden syrup and treacle. These extremely sticky syrups from England are sold in containers that look like small paint cans (squeeze bottles are around too). Golden syrup, sometimes called light treacle, has a clean caramel taste that is key to a number of steamed puddings. Treacle is much darker in color and flavor and can be used as a substitute for molasses.

Molasses. Cane molasses is a by-product of sugar making and has a bitter, slightly medicinal taste. Molasses is not terribly sweet, as some people believe, since much of the sugar has already been extracted. Molasses is used to add color, depth of flavor, and stickiness to dumpling dough and batters.

Honey. We use raw honey. It tastes better, and has a much lower water content, than more refined honeys. It's thick and milky looking, tasty and tangy, and good straight off the spoon.

TOMATOES: Tomatoes flavor a good number of soups, stews, and sauces served with dumplings. We use plum tomatoes whenever possible. They're sweet, meaty, and delicate.

To peel and seed a tomato: This quick and easy technique is the surest way of peeling tomatoes without having to blanch them in boiling water: Cut the tomato into quarters lengthwise and place them skin side down on your cutting board, then run a sharp paring knife just above the skin of the tomato, separating flesh from skin. Give the tomato sections a gentle squeeze over a bowl to get rid of most of the seeds and the jelly that holds them in place.

WATER: People care about the taste or quality of their drinking water but pay less attention to its flavor and aroma when cooking. Because every one of the dishes in this book involves a wet-heat cooking method, water is the foremost ingredient in this book. Many dumplings are served in soups and broths, where water is the essential ingredient. Water is used to turn flours into dumpling doughs and batters. We also rely on water in smaller but essential ways, like using it to help seal the edges of a dumpling, to thin out a clumpy sauce, or to soak dried corn or beans.

Choosing your water. Water can have a unique connection to a place, depending on its source. It can have a high or low mineral content, it can be slightly salty or slightly acidic, and it can taste fresh or stale or even artificial. While writing this book, we tested a few recipes in a farmhouse where the water was supplied by a well surrounded by patches of onion grass. This gave the water a pronounced silvery onion flavor, especially in the summer. This water was delicious in chicken soups, vegetable broths, and other recipes that called for onions, but it overwhelmed the very delicate rice flavors in the Thai dessert dumplings we made. Whatever water you choose for cooking—whether tap water, filtered, distilled, or spring water—we encourage you to appreciate the full flavor of the water you are using and the impact it could have on the resulting dumpling.

Using a nonchlorinated water such as distilled or spring water. While there are a number of possible contaminants in tap water, chlorine has the strongest taste, the most obvious odor, and an undeniably harmful impact on cooking. Chlorine-free water is especially important when making any dumpling batter or dough that depends on fermentation. Chlorine in tap water can kill or weaken the "good" bacteria and yeast. Most filtering jugs or faucet attachments can remove a fair amount of chlorine, or you can let your water stand out in a wide-mouthed pitcher or bowl overnight, allowing the chlorine to dissipate. Chloramine, a chlorine/ammonia product used in some water systems, takes much more effort to filter out. To ensure success with recipes that require fermentation, we use distilled water or spring water. Because of the subtle flavors of coconut, we also use distilled or spring water when making fresh coconut milk or diluting canned coconut milk.

Replenishing with boiling water. When steaming dumplings with long cooking times, have ready a small pot of water you can bring to a boil quickly. Refilling water levels while dumplings cook can be done seamlessly only if you pour in water that is already boiling. Adding room-temperature or cold water will weaken, if not halt, the steaming process for at least a few minutes, and this could negatively affect the texture of your dumplings.

Making the most of your cooking water. Many dumplings are cooked in generous amounts of boiling or simmering water that's been salted lightly to generously. A ladleful of good starchy cooking liquid is a good way to prevent a bowl or plate full of dumplings from sticking. Starchy cooking liquid can also be used to improve the body of a sauce.

WHEAT: Every type of flour or meal that can be made from wheat is used to make dumplings. Wheat-based dumplings are most popular in Europe, Russia, the United States, and parts of Asia. Where there is bread and pasta, you will inevitably find an impressive array of dumplings made from wheat.

Whole wheat flour. Whole wheat flour is used in a number of traditional steamed dumplings. Made from grinding the entire wheat kernel (bran, endosperm, and germ), whole wheat flour retains nutrients that are lost in white flour. With stuffed dumplings like the *momo* (April), whole wheat flour is often mixed with a little white flour for a stronger, more elastic dough that can be rolled out thinly without breaking. Graham flour is similar to whole wheat flour, but it's processed differently, giving it a slightly gritty texture. Store whole wheat and other whole grain flours in the refrigerator to prevent their natural oils from spoiling.

Semolina flour. Semolina is perhaps best known for its use in dried Italian pasta, but it is also a popular dumpling ingredient in parts of India and Central and Eastern Europe. In India it is called *sooji* or *rava* and is sometimes toasted to enhance its flavor. In Europe it is used as a heartier alternative to all-purpose flour. Made from durum wheat, semolina flour is coarser and cooks up firmer than all-purpose flour. It is sometimes called farina, but do not confuse this with cream of wheat, which is a partially cooked and dried wheat product.

Pasta flour. For fresh pasta, Italians use a flour known as "00" flour. It is less glutinous than all-purpose flour and cooks up softer and with just the right amount of chew. If you can find this flour at your market, we recommend using it for all the dumplings made with pasta dough. If not, you can make your own "softer" flour by blending half all-purpose flour with half cake flour.

Unbleached all-purpose flour. A good portion of the dumplings in this book are made with all-purpose flour, including everything from the tiny spaetzle to all kinds of steamed breads and puddings. For all of these recipes, as well as for everyday use, we strongly recommend unbleached all-purpose flour. Unbleached flour has a more natural off-white color, a truer flavor, and it is just a healthier product. It is easy enough to find in most supermarkets, and there is really no need to use anything else.

YOGURT AND SOUR CREAM: The rich flavors of Russian, Eastern European and Middle Eastern dumplings are frequently balanced with sour, zingy, and creamy dairy toppings. A fine and affordable delicacy, strained yogurt is extra-thick and clings really well to the edges and bodies of dumplings. You can find strained yogurt (also called Greek yogurt) at some shops, but it's also easy to make in your own kitchen. Just be sure to buy plain yogurt that is free of emulsifiers, or the straining process will be pointless.

To make strained yogurt: Line a sieve with a couple of layers of cheesecloth and balance it across a deep bowl so that the whey can be collected as it drains out of the yogurt. Scoop the yogurt into the lined strainer, cover loosely with any overhanging ends of cheesecloth, and let sit in the refrigerator for 6 to 8 hours. The yogurt will lose volume as it drains, so if a recipe needs 1 cup of strained yogurt, start with 1½ to 2 cups of unstrained yogurt. This technique is also used to drain cottage cheese, farmer cheese, and ricotta.

Glossary
of Equipment

Every dumpling in the book was tested again and again in our kitchens at home. As we tested recipes, we collected a ridiculously large number of kitchen tools dedicated to dumpling making, most of which are not found in your average kitchen supply store, unless you happen to live in the particular region where one is used. Our fundamental goal, however, was to create each dumpling authentically, with equipment you probably own already or that is easy enough to find and inexpensive enough to buy.

With the exception of one recipe, the *Puttu Kadala* (May), all the dumplings in this book were simmered or boiled in an average pot or steamed in a standard steamer pot. In other words, we don't use tamale steamers, bamboo steamers, rice cookers, slow cookers, woks, or pressure cookers, but instead rely on just a few simple and common pieces of equipment.

There are some tools, however, that worked best for certain dumplings, such as an *idli* tree, which features distinctive round depressions riddled with tiny holes that let steam pass through the dumplings during cooking. We also use a spaetzle maker, the rotary type, for its sheer quickness and ease when making spaetzle. At times we altered the traditional shape of a dumpling to fit a standard piece of equipment. Some cakes that are customarily steamed into squares were made round simply because round cake pans fit more easily into standard-size pots. We adjusted the batch sizes of certain dumplings that are typically made in copious amounts.

We generally avoided tools that have only a single purpose (such as coconut scrapers or corn cutters) or tools that are hard to clean or handle, because inevitably we will never use them more than once or twice. With all that said, while there is nothing more helpful in the kitchen than an extra pair of hands, the following tools are a big help too.

BAKING CUPS: Some dumplings are steamed into muffin- or cupcake-size cakes. For these recipes you will need individual baking cups. You can line these cups with paper baking cup liners, just as you would for a muffin pan. Individual baking cups are available at many kitchen supply stores and are usually made of metal or silicone.

BAKING SHEET (TRAY): A 10×15-inch baking sheet lined with a clean kitchen towel may not seem like a necessary dumpling tool, but it can mean the difference between a batch of successful dumplings and a mound of little disappointments. Filled dumplings require multiple steps, and a tray keeps things organized during the process. Arranging dumplings in neat rows on a tray is the best way to keep them separated and easy to count. A tray also makes it easier to move dumplings from work surface to refrigerator to pot. A tray is necessary when freezing dumplings because they have to be spaced apart on a flat surface until frozen solid.

BOX GRATER: A sturdy box grater is a must when making dumpling batters or doughs that call for grated raw potato, cassava, carrot, or plantain. Because many fillings depend on finely chopped ingredients, a box grater is also a handy way to speed up—or replace in some cases—chopping. The finer, sharply toothed holes of the grater are effective when a dumpling recipe calls for grated nutmeg or ginger or hard cheeses such as Parmesan.

BRUSH: If you don't want to use your fingertips, a small clean paintbrush can be used to brush dough rounds or squares with a bit of water just before filling, folding, and sealing. Dampening the dough can make the dumplings easier to seal.

DIPPING BOWLS: Small dipping or condiment bowls are used when steaming certain dumplings that are typically small, flat, and round. Sometimes they are the mold of choice, as with the *Khanom Thuay* (April), while at other times they substitute for special molds that may be impractical to buy for a single recipe. These dipping bowls should be no more than 2 inches wide and about 1 inch deep. They can be found at many Asian markets that sell tableware or at department stores.

ELECTRIC SPICE OR COFFEE GRINDER: Of all the appliances to emerge as indispensable when making dumplings, this one surprised us. Not only is a spice grinder useful when handling familiar tasks such as grinding up spices, chunks of dry bread (into super-fine crumbs), and seeds and nuts, but it can also be used to grind whole grains of rice into a coarse or fine meal, mimicking the texture of wet-ground rice, and to mill coarse meals into a finer product. While grinding hard grains like rice can eventually wear down the blades, the incomparable qualities of dumplings made from freshly ground rice are worth it. We have used ours throughout the testing of this book and have had no problems. They need to be unplugged and cleaned well with a damp towel between ingredients. Having two on hand, one for spices and one for starches, is ideal.

FOOD PROCESSOR: We don't use a food processor often, but when we do it's essential. There is no faster, more convenient way to grind soaked corn for masa or beans for *Moyin Moyin* (August). It makes terrific bread crumbs in mere minutes and grinds vegetables into pulpy sauces. Occasionally we also grind chopped meat in a food processor to get a finer-textured filling.

GNOCCHI BOARD: A gnocchi board is a small paddle textured with straight, deep grooves. When you roll the soft dough pieces down the length of the paddle, you effortlessly work ridges into the dough. This ribbed texture gives sauces a surface that is easier to cling to. A similar effect can be managed by using the tines of a fork to indent the dough with subtle grooves.

KITCHEN STRING: All-cotton kitchen string is used to tie cloths to pudding basins, cinch up cloth-wrapped dumplings, and secure leaf-wrapped dumplings. Some leaf-wrapped dumplings may have a tendency to unfold if you do not keep a tight grip on them while tying. You can use a rubber band to hold down the leaves while tying your dumpling, but be sure to remove it before cooking.

KITCHEN TONGS: With tongs you can move leaf- or cloth-wrapped dumplings, no matter how heavy or oddly shaped, right out of boiling water and onto a towel without any trouble. Fishing out bones, pieces of meat, or vegetables from a big pot of soup is a cinch with a pair of tongs. You can pluck out dumplings, one by one, from a hot steamer basket. More delicate dumplings, especially filled ones, can tear or be pierced easily, so work with tongs that have rounded ends.

KITCHEN TOWELS: A supply of clean, thin kitchen towels is always useful when making dumplings. They can be used to line trays or squeeze excess liquid from ingredients like grated potatoes or wilted greens. A folded towel is a safe place to rest hot, dripping wet steamer baskets, pudding basins, and cloth- or leaf-wrapped dumplings. And needless to say, they help with cleanup.

LEAVES AND CORN HUSKS: Leaves and husks play a significant role in dumpling making. They provide not only structure but flavor and fragrance to an enormous collection of dumplings throughout Mexico, Central and South America, Asia, and the Pacific Islands. They hold together batters, grated roots, and grains that don't contain binders like gluten or eggs. When, for example, a thick smear of corn masa is wrapped snugly in a husk, it's provided with structure and shape long before the batter cooks into a solid dumpling. Leaves and husks have been used in cooking for thousands of years, and while there are leaf-wrapped dumplings that are mind-boggling feats of architecture, we've kept our folds pretty simple and worry-free.

Corn husks. Fresh husks pulled right off the cob are convenient and lightly scented wrappers for batters consisting entirely or partly of fresh corn kernels. Fresh husks from sweet corn are typically narrow and not too long, so you will need to overlap them in order to accommodate the batter or filling you're working with. Dried husks, however, are larger, because they are generally made from the husks of sizable field corn, not sweet corn. They can be found, usually folded up, in many markets, especially Mexican, Caribbean, or South American groceries, specialty food markets, and well-stocked supermarkets.

Preparing dried corn husks: Count out the number of husks needed for your recipe. Unfold them just enough to count out the number that you need, trying to avoid tearing or cracking them apart. Fill a pot large enough to fit the husks at least halfway with water and bring to a boil over high heat. Remove from the heat. Sink the husks in the hot water, cover, and soak for 1 to 2 hours, turning occasionally for a more even soak. Drain, unfold, rinse each husk under cool running water, and wipe dry. Keep covered under a damp towel until ready to use.

Banana leaves. Dark in color, yet surprisingly light in flavor, banana leaves are a delicious everyday culinary staple in many corners of the world. Difficult to find fresh, they are likelier to be found frozen at Asian, Mexican, and South American markets. Depending on the age of the leaves or how many times they may have thawed and refrozen in their packs during shipment, they can become brittle and tear easily. Be patient if this happens and prepare some extra leaves to patch up any gaps.

Preparing frozen banana leaves: Let the banana leaves thaw at room temperature. Cut the leaves to the required size until you have enough leaf squares (or rectangles) for your recipe. If your leaves are soft and pliable, rinse them well, wipe dry gently, and keep covered under a damp towel until ready to use. If they are brittle and tend to tear, you will need to blanch them. Fill a pot large enough to fit all of the leaf squares at least halfway with water and bring to a boil over high heat. Sink the squares into the hot water (keeping the bends and folds to a minimum), cover, reduce the heat to low, and simmer for 20 minutes. Drain, rinse each square under cool running water, and wipe dry. Keep covered under a damp towel until ready to use.

Bamboo leaves. These long, narrow leaves, used in this book for wrapping up Chinese and Vietnamese rice dumplings, are available at Chinese markets year-round, but especially around May and June, when these dumplings are celebrated. Bamboo leaves add a mild tea-smoked flavor to the rice.

Preparing dried bamboo leaves: Count out the number of leaves needed for your recipe. Trim off their woody stem ends. Fill a pot large enough to fit all of the leaves at least halfway with water and bring to a boil over high heat. Remove from the heat. Sink the bamboo leaves into the hot water, cover, and soak for 1 to 2 hours, turning them occasionally for a more even soak. Drain, rinse each leaf under cool running water, and wipe dry. Keep covered under a damp towel until ready to use.

Lotus leaves. Lotus leaves are the large umbrella-shaped leaves of the water lily plant. When dried and used in cooking, they impart a mossy, tealike flavor to food. The leaves are sold dried and folded in half, their shape resembling a fan. They are quite brittle when dry, but they soften and strengthen quickly in hot water. Lotus leaves can be found at well-stocked Chinese markets.

Preparing lotus leaves: Count out the number of leaves needed for your recipe. Fill a pot large enough to fit at least half the length of the leaves about three-quarters full with water and bring to a boil over high heat. Remove from the heat. Slide the lotus leaves into the hot water. As the leaves start to wilt and soften, push them entirely into the water, allowing them to fold over themselves. Cover and soak for 30 minutes, turning them occasionally for a more even soak. Drain, rinse each leaf under cool running water, and wipe dry. Cut off the woody stem end and open up the leaf, revealing its round shape. Cut each leaf in half along its central vein and keep covered under a damp towel until ready to use.

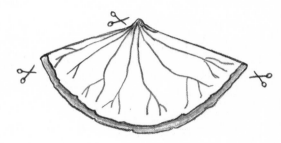

METAL RULER: Dumplings made out of squares of dough are much easier to fill and fold when the square is of the proper size. Having a metal ruler nearby makes cutting strips, squares, rectangles, or diamonds of dough more exact. Leaves—especially banana leaves that need to be cut to size—and lengths of string can be measured accurately if you have a ruler handy.

MORTAR AND PESTLE: We use a mortar and pestle when recipes call for quantities of spice that are too small to be ground in an electric spice grinder. Crushing a mound of spices on top of a hard flat surface with a meat pounder, a flat-bottomed bottle, or the bottom of a heavy pot also does a good job.

MUSLIN: It's incredible just how much of an impact this simple, inexpensive tool, with all of its myriad of uses, has had on us. We keep a collection of sizes on hand, but a standard 24-inch square is the only one used in the book. (When cutting a new piece of muslin, add an additional 4 inches per measurement, because the cloth will shrink permanently once it gets wet.) This cut of muslin can be used as a pudding bag, a cover for the pudding basin, a wrap for a number of boiled or steamed dumplings, a reliable liner for steamer baskets, a cloth for squeezing excess liquid out of grated potatoes or carrots, or a liner for sieves or colanders, capable of filtering out even the finest sediment from broths. Muslin cloth should not be used as a liner for a steamer basket unless the recipe specifically calls for it, however, because some dumplings will stick to the cloth. You can buy unbleached muslin at some kitchen supply stores, arts and crafts stores, and fabric stores. After each use, simply rinse it out in hot water, let it dry, and keep it tucked away until next time.

PARCHMENT PAPER: Parchment paper can be used to wrap dumplings when leaves or corn husks are too tattered or brittle. A square of this paper, lined with the imperfect leaf, will allow all of the leaf's flavors to sink into the dumpling while keeping it securely wrapped and contained. A round of parchment paper is also used in the Pudding Basin Setup (page 43) to separate the moist batter from the cloth covering the basin.

POTATO RICER: The easiest way to pulverize cooked potatoes into a light, evenly textured potato "snow," without overworking them, is with a potato ricer. Try to work with the potatoes while they are still quite warm, and therefore less dense, as they will stiffen as they cool. Attempting to get potatoes into a crumb that fine with a potato masher will almost always make the consistency of the potatoes pasty long before the last lump can be mashed out. A food mill can be used to the same effect as a ricer. A box grater makes a good substitute in a pinch. Place the grater on a flat surface and use your hands to press the chunks of potato through the smaller holes. It's quite messy, but it still creates a fluffier, more airy potato meal than a handheld potato masher.

PUDDING BASIN: Once you own a pudding basin, you can try all sorts of puddings, steamed breads, and cakes. A traditional pudding basin is a dome-shaped stoneware bowl with a flat base and a thick lip around the rim. This lip makes it possible to secure a cloth across the top of the basin with just a piece of string tied around the rim. A good pudding basin can double as a mixing bowl for just about anything and is also an excellent bowl for yeast doughs or fermented batters, because the heavy stoneware retains warmth.

ROASTING PAN FITTED WITH A RACK: To cook a large batch of dumplings, or for dumplings that are too long to fit into your steamer pot, it is helpful to have a covered roasting pan that can sit over two burners. These often come with a specially fitted rack that can double as a steamer rack, or you can place two of your own racks into the pan to create a suitable platform.

ROUND COOKIE CUTTERS: Different people roll out dough rounds in different ways. Many dumpling makers prefer to pinch or cut the dough into small, even pieces and then roll out each piece. Others prefer to roll out a long sheet of dough, place spoonfuls of filling on one side, fold over the other side, and stamp out rounds with a press. If you are not skilled at either one of those methods, we found that the best way to achieve satisfyingly flat and evenly shaped dough rounds was to roll out a manageable portion of the dough and then cut out rounds using a cookie cutter. Round cookie cutters are available, usually as a set, at any kitchen supply store. Cutters with a scalloped edge, often used for making biscuits, can give your dumplings a more decorated look.

SCISSORS: With scissors you can safely trim leaves and corn husks, cut kitchen string, and trim sheets of muslin or cheesecloth to size. Cutting the string off steamed puddings, tamales, or other tied-up dumplings is a much tidier task with scissors than with a knife.

SLOTTED SPOON: A wide slotted spoon with a long handle is the best and safest way to remove delicate dumplings—too delicate to dump into a colander—from a simmering pot of water or broth. Also, if you are cooking dumplings in batches, you don't want to drain off all the simmering water through a colander. You need that water for the remaining batches.

STEAMER POT (OR MULTICOOK POT): Most of the steamed dumplings in this book were cooked in an 8-quart stainless-steel steamer pot with a basket insert about 3 inches deep. It has a heavy bottom that can withstand long cooking times. Of course, you may already own a steamer pot of a different size or, if shopping for a steamer pot, feel that a different size is a better fit for your kitchen. In that case, adjust the dumpling counts we provide to fit your basket. Without the basket, the steamer pot can be used like any other large pot for cooking other types of dumplings, soups, and broths. The steamer basket can also double as a colander.

Multicook pots contain both a steamer basket insert and a pasta insert. The pasta insert is a much deeper basket that allows pastas and dumplings to boil freely in what is basically the entirety of the pot. We use a slotted spoon to remove dumplings from boiling water, but if you have a pasta insert, it can also be used to remove and drain dumplings. The pasta insert can also double as a steamer if there is enough space between the bottom of the insert and the simmering water. Alternatively, you can place a rack in the pasta insert, creating a platform for your dumplings. This setup works best with leaf- and cloth-wrapped dumplings.

If you have more than enough pots but don't have one specifically for steaming, all sorts of steamer basket inserts are sold separately. Be certain, before buying one, that it will fit properly into your selected pot.

The following pots and pans are essential when making a wide range of dumplings:
1- to 2-quart saucepan with cover
4- to 6-quart pot with cover
6- to 8-quart pot with cover
8- to 10-quart pot with cover (this can be your steamer pot)
8-inch-wide skillet with cover*
10-inch-wide skillet with cover*

---

*A "universal" lid (found at most kitchen supply stores) fits over a variety of pots and can be used if your skillet does not come with a lid.

The following pots and pans are good to have on hand but are not essential:

3- to 4-quart saucepan

10- to 12-quart pot with cover

14-quart roasting pan with cover

STEAMER RACKS AND COLLAPSIBLE STEAMERS: Inserting a steamer rack into a pot creates a platform for cloth- and leaf-wrapped dumplings, as well as for cake pans and other molds. The steamer racks we use look like, and can double for, round cooling racks. Racks can range in size, shape, and height, but you'll need one that is at least 2 inches high (to sit above 1½ inches of water) and large enough to sit comfortably in your pot without sliding around too much. Some racks have legs that fold up, both for storage purposes and for a quick change into a steamer plate. Collapsible steamers (made of overlapping petals of perforated metal) often stand a little lower than 2 inches but work fine for quick-to-cook dumplings or if you replenish the boiling water during longer cooking times. Because they are collapsible, they can fit into many different pots or pans. If you remove the center post on these steamers (most can be un-screwed), they can accommodate cake pans or single, larger dumplings.

WOODEN DOWEL ROLLING PIN: Dowel rolling pins (or French rolling pins) are our first choice for rolling out every type of dumpling dough. A dowel rolling pin is simply a rolling pin without distinct handles, though some versions do have tapered ends. Using a rolling pin with handles is more awkward compared with the direct pressure and maneuverability achievable with a dowel pin. When you're not caught up with gripping handlebars and trying to get the pin to roll consistently, you are able to feel every lump or unevenness in the dough. Also, the cylinder, or body, of a rolling pin with handles has a tendency to form deep grooves or lines with its edges, which can be troublesome when rolling out really thin sheets of dough.

....

There are three tools, used often in dumpling making, that we chose not to rely on—a pasta maker, an electric wet-grinder, and special dumpling molds. While pasta makers make it easy to roll dough out thin, learning how to roll out sheets of dough by hand is an indispensable skill we didn't want to step over. Electric wet-grinders are extremely heavy appliances. Even home versions—about the size of a large ice cream maker—weigh upward of 25 pounds. These are powerful machines that make short work of nixtamalizing corn, soaking rice and beans, and so on, and can produce high-quality pastes. If you want to produce a large amount of fresh, wet-ground pastes regularly, they are a worthwhile investment, but a food processor or a spice or coffee grinder fills in well enough. Dumpling molds and presses were created to make the work of stuffing or filling dumplings easier. They can do a pretty good job, but like any tool they take practice to learn how to use well, and we preferred spending our time learning how to fill and fold the dumplings by hand.

Tips

As we tested hundreds of dumplings, we kept a written log of observations, hard-earned lessons, fantastic successes, and mysterious quandaries. The following revelations and techniques are the result.

LEARN THROUGH EXAMPLE: Working alongside someone with experience is the best way to learn. If you know someone who already makes your favorite dumpling, take the time to cook up a batch together.

KNOW WHEN NOT TO SUBSTITUTE: While there are many, many versions of wontons, there are certain definitive ingredients and techniques that make a wonton a wonton. Alter a recipe too much and you're making another type of dumpling entirely, not a variation. We encourage you to experiment and adjust recipes to your tastes or diet, but pay attention to those ingredients or techniques that truly impart an essential flavor, texture, or aroma.

If you're a vegetarian and need to take the meat out of a recipe, try to work with the most appropriate alternative. When swapping out meat for other ingredients in fillings, soups, stews, sauces, and so on, we found certain options work better than others. Following is a list of our favorites:

For beef: seitan, mushrooms (cremini, shiitake, portobello, porcini), lentils, mung beans, tempeh, tofu, vegetarian "ground beef" (found in the frozen food section of health food stores and most supermarkets), whole-grain bread crumbs, eggplant, walnuts

For pork: seitan, tofu, white beans, mushrooms (porcini, shiitake, oyster, chanterelle), bread crumbs, eggplant, cashews, pumpkin seeds

For chicken: seitan, mushrooms (*maitake*, oyster, shiitake, chanterelle), chickpeas, white beans, bread crumbs, brown rice, artichoke hearts, eggplant, bamboo shoots, walnuts, peanuts, cashews, pine nuts

For seafood: mushrooms (oyster, shiitake, *maitake*), tofu, a few small pieces of kelp

For lard: nonhydrogenated vegetable shortening, oil

For suet: nonhydrogenated vegetable shortening, butter

If you are a vegan, you are probably already familiar with the array of substitutes available for milk, cheese, eggs, honey, meat, and animal fats. As you know, not all animal products can be replaced, but you can apply your experience with making cakes, pancakes, breads, and other foods to most dumpling recipes with good results. When we tailored recipes for vegan friends, we found that certain substitutes were often overlooked: fresh or canned coconut milk, which you can sweeten with sugar or sour with lemon juice, is an underutilized substitute for milk or cream, and agave is a light, slightly fruity syrup without the stronger flavors of honey, the concentrated flavors of maple syrup, or the too-subtle sweetness of brown rice syrup.

TIME: Before starting any recipe, read it through and consider how much time is involved. Be aware of what the recipe requires in terms of kneading, cooking, and so on, and take into account how long those steps will take. Set time aside for steps such as dough resting or fermentation. If it helps, see which steps can be done hours or even days in advance.

If you have not made a particular dumpling recipe before and it involves folding or wrapping, be sure to go over the instructions and the appropriate illustrations (see pages 39–61). A number of dumplings require folding and assembly. All goes quickly if things are organized.

Be aware of how dumplings are served. Some are pot-to-mouth dumplings, such as *Jiao Zi* (February) and *Mandu* (April), which must be served immediately after cooking. Other dumplings can rest or cool or be eaten the next day.

ORGANIZATION: Make sure you have all the ingredients and tools you need, a clean work space for assembly, and a place to organize the dumplings once they are assembled. Learn to prevent equipment surprises by making sure that things fit. For example, your pudding basin, when placed in a pot, must leave enough room to be covered.

EXTRA DOUGH AND FILLING: When making filled and folded dumplings, you will often have leftover scraps of dough or spoonfuls of filling. Dough scraps can be cut up and added to soups or frozen for future use. Leftover yeast dough can be steamed or baked into buns or tiny flat breads. Leftover filling can be added to soups, stirred into fried rice, cooked up and tossed into salads, cooked with eggs, or turned into a hash with some potato. Extra masa can be rolled into balls for Masa Ball Soup (April), thinned out and turned into a batter for corn pancakes, or frozen for later use.

ADJUSTING WET AND DRY INGREDIENTS FOR BETTER DOUGH AND BATTERS: Variations will result each time you make a batch of dough, no matter how carefully you follow the recipe. In general, it's easier to incorporate additional dry ingredients into a dough that is too wet than it is to incorporate additional wet ingredients into a dough that is too dry. All of the wheat-based dough recipes in this book have been adjusted so that you should never end up with a dough that is too dry. Instead, we ask you to measure out a certain amount of flour, add most of it, and keep the remaining flour handy, usually ¼ cup. After mixing, the dough will either be just right or if anything, a little wet and sticky. The remaining flour is there to be worked in, a little at a time, until the dough reaches its proper consistency.

ROLLING DOUGH: For the newcomer, rolling out dough can be a challenge. There are some tips, however, that can help make things easier. Prepare a work space that is larger than the anticipated area of the dough and leave yourself enough space to work. Roll the dough from the center outward and give the dough a quarter-turn every so often to keep things even. If the dough is snapping or shrinking back after you roll it out, let it rest in the half-rolled-out state, covered with a slightly damp cloth, until it relaxes further (about 5 minutes). Don't overflour your work space before you see just how the dough is reacting; you can always add more as you go. Finally, take your time. Remember that this is a skill that takes practice and that you will do better each time.

CUTTING DOUGH: How a dumpling is filled and folded depends on how the dough has been cut. Here are four typical approaches:

1. Divide the dough into two to four manageable pieces, roll out one piece, cut out your rounds or squares, fill and fold them, and then repeat with the remaining dough.

2. Roll out all the dough into one large sheet, cut out all the rounds or squares, then fill and fold them.

3. Pinch off a piece of dough large enough to create one dumpling round, roll it up into a ball, roll out the ball into a round, fill and fold it, and then repeat with the remaining dough (this technique doesn't apply to squares).

4. Roll out the dough or a portion of the dough, arrange spoonfuls of filling—evenly spaced apart—on the bottom half of the sheet of dough, fold the top half over, cut out stuffed rounds or squares with a cookie cutter, and then repeat with the remaining dough.

We found that option 1 was the simplest, easiest way to keep things organized and to prevent the dough rounds or squares from drying out. For dumplings where the dough must be warm to be rolled out successfully, we used option 3.

Cutting rolled-out dough into strips, diamonds, or squares large enough to fill and fold is not difficult. Rolling out the dough into the required dimensions is the key to success—you can't cut four 2-inch strips out of a 7-inch square. A ruler guarantees a better result and can also be used as a guide to trim off the outermost edges of the dough sheet conservatively for cleaner lines.

PROOFING POT SETUP: The two conditions for the proper proofing of dough are moderate heat and heavy humidity. For a reliable rise every time, we've come up with an easy setup that replicates the dependability of a professional proof box.

Setting up the proofing pot: You will need a bowl for the dough, a small rack, and a pot large enough to fit both the bowl and the rack when covered. Place the rack in the pot along with 3 cups of cool water. Boil an additional 3 cups of water in another pot and then pour it into the cool water in the first pot. Place the kneaded dough in the bowl and place it on the rack. (Because of the rack, the bowl should not have direct contact with the water. If for any reason the level of water is higher than the rack, place a plate or two on top of the rack to keep the bowl out of the water.) Cover the pot and allow the dough to double in size, 1 to 1½ hours. This setup can be repeated for a second rise if needed.

FREEZING DUMPLINGS: If you need to freeze extra dumplings, or want to make large batches and freeze them for later, there are a few things to consider. Almost all filled and folded dumplings can be frozen before cooking. They should be frozen in a single layer on a baking sheet or tray lined with parchment paper. If there is a second layer, separate the layers with another piece of parchment paper. Do not stack more than two layers of dumplings on one tray. Only after the dumplings have frozen solid should they be placed in bags or boxes, sealed tightly, and stored for up to 3 months. Fresh corn tamales, some wrapped rice dumplings, and steamed buns freeze well after cooking. Again, space them apart on a tray, let them freeze, then store in tightly sealed bags or boxes for up to 3 months.

BOILING AND SIMMERING: Certain dumplings cook best at a rolling boil, with lots of room, while others are more delicate and need only a simmer. Others are poached at a very gentle simmer. If dumplings are falling apart as they are being simmered or boiled, double-check the recipe to make sure you're cooking them at the proper heat.

TEST DUMPLING: It can be helpful, with more delicate or filled dumplings, to drop just one into the boiling or simmering water or soup to see how it cooks up and to identify any problems while there is still time to make adjustments.

TESTING FOR DONENESS: For dumplings that have a long cooking time, such as tamales or steamed puddings, there is usually no concern about doneness. For dumplings with a quick cooking time, the best way to check is just to pluck one out and taste it.

SETTING DUMPLINGS: Just as large cuts of meat need time to rest after cooking, many dumplings, both large and small, also benefit from a little resting time. Some filled dumplings may look slightly deflated after resting or cooling off a bit, but it's this slight shift in density that makes for a more toothsome texture. Resting can also give a dumpling a slight skin, which is important to dumplings like the *Clootie* (December) or the *Serviettenkloss* (November). The effect is greater in larger dumplings than in the small ones but even dumplings like gnocchi (February) have a better bite when they are allowed to rest and firm up a bit before being finished in a sauce. Some wrapped dumplings such as tamales are easier to open once they are allowed to cool slightly and pull away from the corn husk or leaf.

REHEATING DUMPLINGS: Boiling and steaming are the easiest ways to reheat the dumplings in this book. In general, for dumplings that are served in soups and stews, it is best to take out the dumplings and set them aside while you reheat the soup or stew in a pot over medium heat. You may need to add a little water if the soup or stew is too thick. When it comes to a simmer, add the dumplings, cover, and cook until the dumplings are heated through. Stand-alone dumplings, such as tamales, filled or wrapped dumplings, and puddings, are best reheated in a steamer pot or by using the Steamer Plate Setup (see below).

Setting up the steamer plate: Place a steamer rack in a large wide pot and fill the pot with enough water to reach just below the rungs. Find a small heatproof plate or a wide bowl large enough to hold the dumplings but small enough to fit in the pot and place it on top of the rack. Bring the water in the pot to a boil over high heat, then reduce the heat to medium for a steady simmer. Place the dumplings on the plate or in the bowl, cover, and simmer until the dumplings are heated through.

HAND-WILTING: Hand-wilting greens, herbs, and sliced or diced onion keeps their flavors ultra-fresh, and softens them considerably without adding extra water or oil, an important consideration when making dumpling fillings. Rinse the greens (or other similar ingredient), shake off excess water, place them in a bowl, and simply crumple, scrunch, and squeeze with your hand until the greens are soft and limp. Drain or squeeze off any excess liquid. Hand-wilted onions have a surprisingly diminished raw flavor and are soft, silky, and just right for fillings.

Dumpling Fold Instructions and Illustrations

We realize that for many people the process of folding or wrapping dumplings by hand can be unfamiliar or even a little daunting. The following illustrations, complete with step-by-step instructions, will take you through each of the folds in the book. With practice, you'll master even the most complicated folds with confidence and ease.

JELLY-ROLL SHAPE 41

DIAMOND IN THE SQUARE FOLD 42

PUDDING BASIN SETUP 43

FAN-KNOT FOLD 44

BOWL FOLD 45

PLEATED HALF-MOON FOLD 46

HALF-MOON FOLD 47

STANDING HALF-MOON FOLD 48

BELLY-BUTTON FOLD 49

BOTTLENECK FOLD 50

CANDY-WRAPPER SHAPE USING A CLOTH 51

PINCHED-TOP FOLD 52

SINGLE-HUSK TAMALE FOLD 53

LOTUS-LEAF FOLD 54

TWO-HUSK TAMALE FOLD 1 (WIDE) 55

ENVELOPE FOLD 56

CANDY-WRAPPER SHAPE USING A LEAF 57

PUDDING BAG FOLD 58

TWO-HUSK TAMALE FOLD 2 (LONG) 59

CURLED-LETTER FOLD 60

BAMBOO-LEAF FOLD 61

JELLY-ROLL SHAPE

The Jelly-Roll Shape is often used for pastries and baked goods (cinnamon rolls, rugelach, pinwheel cookies), but it is also used with both savory and sweet dumplings. Rolling up your dumpling into a jelly roll not only ensures that the filling is evenly distributed but also guarantees that each slice of the dumpling will have an attractive pinwheel swirl.

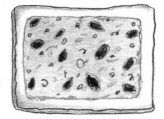

1. Arrange the filling on top of the dough rectangle, leaving a narrow border along all sides.

2. Starting on one of the longer sides, begin to roll up the dough, pinching the ends to seal as you go.

3. Pinch and press the far edge of the dough along the length of the log to seal.

DIAMOND IN THE SQUARE FOLD

The Diamond in the Square Fold is a simple package fold that has the advantage of having a double layer of leaves for a more secure hold. This fold can also be used instead of the Envelope Fold when dealing with leaves that are brittle or torn.

1. Lay flat the larger banana-leaf square, smooth side up (or parchment paper), and place the smaller banana-leaf square, smooth side up, diagonally on top of the first square.

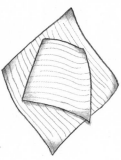

4. Fold over the opposite corner.

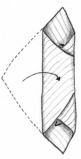

2. Center and arrange the cassava and filling or rice and filling on top of the stacked leaves.

5. Fold the ends of the leaves over as firmly as you can to create a neat, rectangular package.

3. Fold over one corner of the stacked leaves.

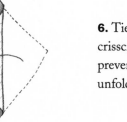

6. Tie the package in a crisscross pattern to prevent the leaves from unfolding.

PUDDING BASIN SETUP

You can make a great variety of steamed puddings flawlessly using this traditional technique. This setup is used for all the steamed puddings in this book and, in fact, is a wonderful way to steam pretty much any batter or quick bread. By cooking your pudding in a basin, you reap all the benefits of wet-heat cooking (a moist, soft texture) while still creating a light crust, as if the pudding were oven-baked.

1. Make sure the interior of the basin is dry before rubbing it with butter and coating it with sugar (and line the bottom of the basin with topping if called for).

2. Scoop the batter into the basin and give it a gentle shake to level it off. (If making a pudding with layers, arrange the layers within the basin without packing them down.)

3. Cut out a round of parchment paper and place it on top of the batter.

4. Cover the basin with the damp muslin and secure it tightly with string.

5. Tie opposite corners of the muslin into handles over the top of the pudding.

FAN-KNOT FOLD

This simple yet effective fold maximizes the way steam circulates around the dumpling, allowing it to cook faster and more evenly. All you have to do is stack up a few strips of dough, tie them into a knot, and fan out the edges. Truly, if you can tie a knot, you can master this fold.

1. Stack four dough strips on top of each other. The strips don't need to line up perfectly.

2. Bend the dough strips into a loop.

3. Push one end of the stacked strips through the loop, creating a simple knot.

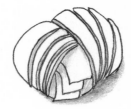

4. Tuck in any loose ends and gently fan out or nudge apart the strips of dough, making the layers more apparent.

BOWL FOLD

The Bowl Fold, the best way to center a portion of filling in a soft ball of dough, is better suited for dumplings that contain a chunky or crumbly filling. By forming the dough into a small bowl and then cupping it in your hand, you can easily scoop in the filling without its spilling over the sides. Closing the bowl may take some practice, but it is a skill that you can apply to a good number of dumplings.

1. Use your thumbs to shape the dough ball into a bowl just large enough to cradle the filling.

The shaped dough bowl

2. Place the filling in the dough bowl. This step can be made easier by cradling the dough bowl in your palm while spooning in the filling.

3. Close by pushing and pinching the edges of the dough around and over the filling until the filling is surrounded, pushing out any air. Dab a little water along the edges, if needed, for a better seal.

4. Reroll into a ball.

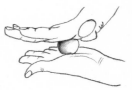

PLEATED HALF-MOON FOLD

This fold resembles the Standing Half-Moon Fold, but by pleating one side of the dough round you end up with a more elaborate appearance.

1. Pick up the dough round and begin to pleat and pinch one side.

2. Pull the round into a bowl shape.

3. Place the filling in the dough bowl. This step can be made easier by cradling the dough bowl in your palm while spooning in the filling.

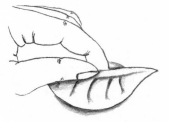

4. Bring together the edges, pushing out any air, and pinch to seal. Dab a little water along the edges, if needed, for a better seal.

The finished dumpling

HALF-MOON FOLD

There is no quicker or easier fold than the Half-Moon Fold, which is essentially a dough round folded in half over a mound of filling (or a dough square folded in half into a triangle). It's a great go-to fold for most filled dumplings if a traditional fold is too involved or time consuming.

1. Center the filling on top of the dough round.

2. Fold the round neatly in half, pushing out any air.

3. Pinch to seal. Dab a little water along the edges, if needed, for a better seal.

STANDING HALF-MOON FOLD

The Standing Half-Moon Fold, which is a slight variation of the Half-Moon Fold, is used for dumplings that need to sit upright in a steamer or a pan.

1. Center the filling on top of the dough round.

2. Fold the round neatly in half, pushing out any air.

3. Pinch to seal. Dab a little water along the edges, if needed, for a better seal.

4. Holding the dumpling by the seam, tap the filled base on your work surface until it has a flat bottom and can sit upright without tipping over.

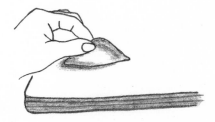

The finished dumpling

BELLY-BUTTON FOLD

The Belly-Button Fold is simply a variation on the Half-Moon Fold. By pulling together the ends of the half-moon below the base of the dumpling, you create a natural curl—a belly button—which squeezes the filling into a tight pocket, giving each dumpling a firmer, denser bite than simply pinching the two ends together over the dumpling.

1. Center the filling on top of the dough round or square.

2. Fold the round neatly in half, pushing out any air. (If using a dough square, fold it diagonally, over the filling, into a triangle.)

3. Pinch to seal. Dab a little water along the edges, if needed, for a better seal.

4. Join and seal the two ends together below the base of the dumpling. Dab a little water on the ends, if needed, for a better seal.

The finished dumpling

BOTTLENECK FOLD

The open pleats created by the Bottleneck Fold result in an especially pretty dumpling. The thinner you can roll out the dough, the more dramatic this effect. Creating the bottleneck is relatively easy, and you can make the opening as narrow or as wide as you like.

1. Center the filling on top of the dough round or square.

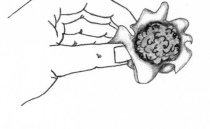

2. Gather up the sides of the round, creating a pouch around the filling, leaving an open neck in the center of the gathered dough.

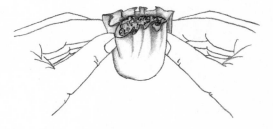

3. Pinch together, without closing the neck, the creases and pleats that formed naturally while the dough was gathered up. This gives the dumpling a loose and frilly top.

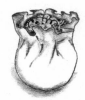

4. Gently squeeze the body of the dumpling until the filling pushes up a little through the neck. Holding the dumpling by the neck, tap the filled base on your work surface until it has a flat bottom and can sit upright without tipping over.

CANDY-WRAPPER SHAPE USING A CLOTH

Wrapping dumplings with a cloth in the Candy-Wrapper Shape is the surest way to cook a dumpling that is in the shape of a loaf or a log.

1. Rub one side of the damp muslin with butter, leaving a narrow border on all sides.

2. Arrange the dough log along one edge of the muslin.

3. Roll up the dumpling. The muslin should be slightly baggy so the dumpling can swell while it cooks.

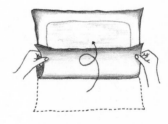

The rolled-up dumpling

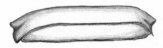

4. Tightly tie the two open ends, then tie the body of the dumpling to secure the seam.

PINCHED-TOP FOLD

The Pinched-Top Fold creates the look of a casually pleated top but is actually made by gathering and pinching up opposite sides of the dough round together to enclose the filling.

1. Center the filling on top of the dough round.

2. Gather up and pinch together the opposite sides of the round, creating a snug tent around the filling. Dab a little water along the edges, if needed, for a better seal.

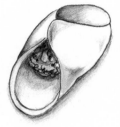

3. Gather and pinch together the remaining two sides to enclose the filling, pushing out any air.

4. Pinch any gaps to seal, and twist off the nub of dough that tends to form at the top of the dumpling.

SINGLE-HUSK TAMALE FOLD

The Single-Husk Tamale Fold shapes tamales into compact rectangular packages. Dried corn husks are often quite large and can easily wrap around big spoonfuls of batter and filling. If your husks are smaller or torn, however, you can overlap two husks and still complete the fold.

1. Lay flat one corn husk, smooth side up. Center the batter on top of the husk and spread it out toward the right side until you have a rectangle about 4 × 2½ inches.

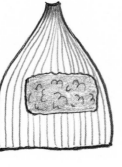

2. Arrange the filling on top of the left half of the batter, leaving the right half without any filling.

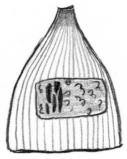

3. Fold the right side over, sandwiching the filling inside the batter.

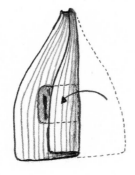

4. Fold over the left side.

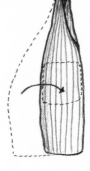

5. Fold the ends of the husk over as firmly as you can to create a neat rectangular package.

6. Tie the package in a crisscross pattern to prevent the husk from unfolding.

LOTUS-LEAF FOLD

The Lotus-Leaf Fold is ideal for large dumplings that are stuffed with rice and other chunky ingredients. The lotus plant has large leaves that are round or spade shaped. These leaves are dried and typically folded for sale in markets.

1. Lay flat two lotus-leaf halves (or two banana-leaf rectangles), smooth side up. Center and arrange the rice and filling on top of one leaf half.

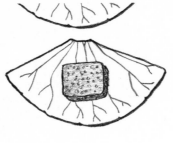

4. Fold over the ends of the leaf as tightly as you can to create a neat package. (If using banana leaves, know that they can be brittle and do your best to wrap the package as snuggly as you can.)

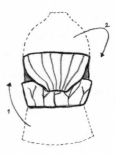

2. Fold over one side.

5. Place the package, folded side down, on the second leaf half (or banana-leaf rectangle). Wrap the package up in the second leaf half, using the same folds in steps 2 through 4. Keep the packages folded side down to prevent the leaves from unfolding. (If using banana-leaf rectangles, wrap and tie package in a criss-cross pattern to prevent the leaves from unfolding.)

3. Fold over the opposite side.

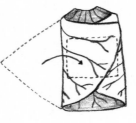

TWO-HUSK TAMALE FOLD 1 (WIDE)

The Two-Husk Tamale Fold 1 (Wide) is a common tamale fold. By overlapping the sides of two corn husks—fresh or dried—you create a wider surface area to hold the amount of batter and filling needed for an average-sized tamale.

1. Arrange two corn husks, smooth side up, next to each other lengthwise with the widest ends positioned on opposite sides. Overlap the husks by about 1½ inches.

4. Fold over the opposite side.

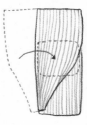

2. Center the dough or batter (and filling, if called for) on top of the overlapping husks.

5. Fold the ends of the overlapping husks over as tightly as you can to create a neat package.

3. Fold over one side.

6. Tie the package in a crisscross pattern to prevent the husks from unfolding.

ENVELOPE FOLD

The Envelope Fold is your basic rectangular leaf fold that is used in making a number of dumplings. If your banana leaves are cracked or torn, wrap your dumplings using the Diamond in the Square Fold (page 42) instead for a more secure hold.

1. Lay flat one banana-leaf square, smooth side up. Center the dough or batter (and filling, if called for) on top of the leaf.

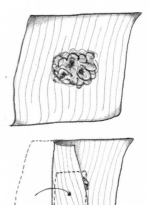

2. Fold over one side.

3. Fold over the opposite side.

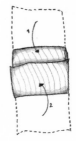

4. Fold the ends of the leaf over as tightly as you can to create a neat package.

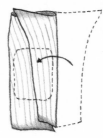

5. Tie the package in a crisscross pattern to prevent the leaf from unfolding.

CANDY-WRAPPER SHAPE USING A LEAF

The *Brazo de la Reina* (June) is the only dumpling that's wrapped in the Candy-Wrapper Shape Using a Leaf. This process is similar to the Candy-Wrapper Shape Using a Cloth (page 51), only instead of a cloth, here we use a large banana-leaf rectangle.

1. Lay flat the banana-leaf rectangle, smooth side up. Arrange the batter and filling on one of the longer edges of the leaf, leaving a 1-inch border in the front and a 2-inch border on each side.

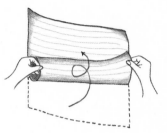

2. Roll up the dumpling, doing your best not to tear the leaf.

The rolled-up dumpling

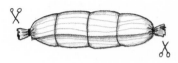

3. Tightly tie the two open ends, then tie the body of the dumpling to secure the seam. Using scissors, trim and neaten up the ends of the leaf.

PUDDING BAG FOLD

Boiling or steaming your food in a pudding bag has long been an economical and resourceful way to cook. A large amount of dough or batter, wrapped up in a sturdy cloth, is held together with just enough room to expand as it steams or boils up into a typically round, domelike, or even cylindrical shape. Clean your pudding cloth after each use and it can be used again and again.

1. Rub one side of the damp muslin with butter, leaving a narrow border on all sides (and coat with flour if called for).

2. Center the dough or batter on top of the muslin.

3. Gather up the corners of the muslin and arrange the folds neatly, creating a bag.

4. As you collect the muslin and prepare it for tying, it should be left slightly baggy so that the dumpling can swell as it cooks. Be certain, however, to grip the muslin low enough to leave no open gaps.

5. Tightly tie the gathered muslin.

TWO-HUSK TAMALE FOLD 2 (LONG)

Like the Two-Husk Tamale Fold 1 (Wide), this fold requires you to overlap two corn husks, only here the husks are positioned lengthwise instead of side by side. After the batter is added, the tamale is folded up and tied on both ends.

1. Arrange two corn husks, smooth side up, overlapping their wider ends by about 2 inches.

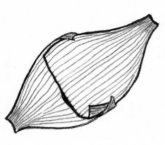

4. Fold over the opposite side.

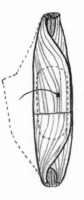

2. Center the batter on top of the overlapping husks.

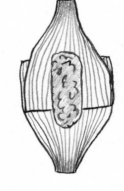

5. Tightly tie the two open ends, but leave a little room at each end for the dumpling to expand into while it cooks. Using scissors, trim and neaten up the ends of the husks.

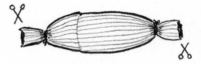

3. Fold over one side.

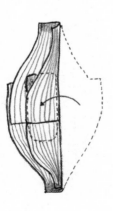

CURLED-LETTER FOLD

There are many ways you can fold the wontons in the *Hung You Chao Shou* (August), but the Curled-Letter Fold is deceptively easy. As with the Belly-Button Fold, you bring the ends of the folded dough square together, pushing the filling into a tight ball, which gives the dumpling a firmer, denser bite.

1. Center the filling on top of the square.

2. Fold one side over the filling.

3. Fold over the opposite side.

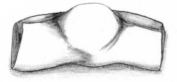

4. Now take both ends, pull them together, overlap them a bit, and pinch to seal. Dab a little water on the ends, if needed, for a better seal.

The finished dumpling

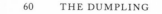

BAMBOO-LEAF FOLD

This fold may take some practice because you have to balance three bamboo leaves in one hand. If the bottom leaves begin to tear as you are folding them, carefully slide in a new leaf before removing the torn leaf. Bamboo leaves have a tendency to unravel if you do not keep a tight grip on them while folding. You can use a rubber band to secure the dumpling while you tie it, but be sure to remove the rubber band before cooking.

1. Place two bamboo leaves, smooth side up, lengthwise, and alongside each other in the palm of your hand. Overlap the leaves by about 1½ inches.

2. Center the rice on top of the overlapped bamboo leaves and spread out into a rectangle about the size of your palm. Arrange the filling on top of the rice and then top with additional rice. Lay a third bamboo leaf, smooth side down, on top of the mound of rice and filling.

3. Grip and curl the sides of the overlapped bottom leaves over the top leaf by closing your fingers and thumb around the mound of rice and filling.

4. Fold back the top ends of the leaves. Then fold back the bottom ends of the leaves as firmly as you can to create a neat and tight rectangular package.

5. Wrap and tie the package four or five times across the width of the dumpling and at least once lengthwise to prevent the leaves from unfolding.

January

SEMOLINA DUMPLINGS WITH BUTTER AND CHEESE SAUCE
Frascatelli (Italy) 65

BUTTER-TOSSED SPAETZLE
Spätzle (Germany) 67

POTATO AND DUMPLING BOIL-UP
Kartoffeln mit Mehlknödel (Germany) 68

SPICED GINGERBREAD
(United States) 70

A WEALTH OF STEAMED RICE MUFFINS
Fot Gao (China) 71

STEAMED BREAD ROLLS
Mantou (China) 72

"PRIEST STRANGLERS" WITH BROWN BUTTER AND SAGE
Strangolapreti (Italy) 74

POTATO GNOCCHI
Gnocchi di Patate (Italy) 76

MARROW DUMPLINGS IN BEEF BROTH
Markklösschensuppe (Germany) 79

CASSAVA "TAMALES" STUFFED WITH PORK AND CHICKPEAS
Pasteles de Yuca (Puerto Rico) 81

POUNDED RICE DUMPLINGS
Mochi (Japan)...84

NEW YEAR'S DAY SOUP WITH POUNDED RICE DUMPLINGS
Ozoni (Japan) 86

Semolina Dumplings with Butter and Cheese Sauce

Frascatelli (Italy)

SERVES 4

This is possibly the best technique in the world for making instant dumplings, and it is a liberating experience for both novices and experienced cooks. By raining droplets of water onto a mound of semolina, doughy morsels are formed of various sizes. These bits of dough are then dropped into simmering water, producing a fresh batch of dumplings in a matter of minutes. Like gnocchi or *spätzle*, these dumplings are full-bodied and stand up equally well in an impromptu butter and cheese sauce (as they are prepared here) as they do with a good broth to make a quick and satisfying soup. Semolina, made from durum wheat, is granular in nature, not powdery like all-purpose flour, and is available in both coarse and fine varieties. A fine semolina will give you softer, more tender dumplings as compared to the coarsely ground kind. You can experiment to see which type suits you best. If you can't find fine semolina, you can also pulse the coarser type in a clean spice grinder for a lighter consistency. *Frascatelli* can also be served with Oxtail Sauce (page 78) or Walnut Sauce from *Gnocchi di Castagne* (page 107).

For the Dumplings

3½ cups semolina, plus some extra for dusting

For the Sauce

4 tablespoons (½ stick) unsalted butter

1 cup freshly grated Romano or Parmesan cheese

Salt and freshly ground pepper to taste

Equipment

Colander with large (¼ inch) holes

Large, wide bowl to hold the dumplings cooked in batches

1. MAKE THE DUMPLINGS: Fill a large pot halfway with salted water, and bring it to a boil over high heat. Reduce the heat to low for a gentle simmer.

2. Meanwhile, spread the semolina out evenly on a work surface until about 1 inch deep. (You can also place it in a large, wide bowl. Using a bowl will reduce the surface area of the semolina, causing you to repeat the sprinkling and sifting steps a few more times.) Have ready two large plates.

3. Fill a medium bowl at least halfway with water and place it next to the semolina. Sink your fingers into the water, then flick them a few inches over the semolina, causing the water to splotch across its surface. Continue dipping and flicking until the saturated spots are visible and numerous. The goal is to create a generous amount of spots, not a surface that is soaked through. Dry your hands and gently swirl your fingers through the semolina until evenly coated clumps of dough form. Break apart any exceptionally large pieces into a more uniform size.

4. Gently scoop the dough pieces into the colander and sift over the semolina that remains on the work surface. Once the excess semolina and smaller bits have been sifted out, turn the dough pieces in the colander onto one of the plates. Gather up and spread the semolina out again. Repeat the sprinkling, swirling, and sifting steps until you have created as many dough pieces as you can, distributing them evenly between the two plates.

5. COOK THE DUMPLINGS: Bring the water back up to a strong boil over high heat. Carefully slide one plate of the dough pieces into the water and gently stir to prevent sticking. Cook until the dumplings become more buoyant and tumble around easily in the simmering water, about 1 minute, then cook for 1 minute longer.

6. Remove the *frascatelli* with a slotted spoon, place them in the large bowl, and drizzle with a ladle of the cooking liquid to prevent sticking. Cook the remaining dough pieces and put them in the bowl with another ladle of the cooking liquid. Reserve 1/2 cup of the cooking liquid.

7. MAKE THE SAUCE AND FINISH THE DUMPLINGS: Melt the butter in a large skillet over medium heat. Drain the *frascatelli* and turn them into the butter. Toss and stir gently to evenly coat the dumplings. Pour in the reserved cooking water and stir occasionally while the sauce comes to a simmer, about 1 minute. Remove from the heat, mix in the Romano, sprinkle with salt and pepper, and serve.

Butter-Tossed Spaetzle

Spätzle (Germany)

SERVES 4 TO 6

These small, quick-cooking dumplings are a welcome addition to soups, leftover vegetables, and fried eggs. *Spätzle* made from dough are firm and shapable, while batter-based recipes like this one create soft, squiggly dumplings that are spectacular with nothing but butter and a sprinkling of salt. A number of spaetzle-making tools are available at kitchen supply stores. A rotary *spätzle* press is the easiest type to handle because it requires very little effort to operate and cleans up fast and tidy.

For the Dumplings

 3 cups unbleached all-purpose flour

1½ teaspoons salt

 ¾ teaspoon freshly grated nutmeg

 3 large eggs, beaten

1½ cups milk or water

For the Sauce

3 tablespoons unsalted butter, cut into chunks

For Serving

Freshly ground black pepper to taste

Equipment

Spätzle maker, preferably a rotary one, or a food mill with ¼-inch holes

Large, wide bowl to hold the dumplings cooked in batches

1. MAKE THE BATTER: Fill a large pot halfway with salted water and bring to a boil over high heat. Reduce the heat to medium for a steady simmer.

2. Combine the flour, salt, and nutmeg in a large bowl. Add the eggs and milk and mix until just combined. Do not overmix.

3. COOK THE DUMPLINGS: Hold the *spätzle* maker over a bowl or a plate as you scoop in half of the batter. (This will catch any leaks and keep things cleaner while you work.) Quickly move the *spätzle* maker over the simmering water and crank the handle until the batter has been pushed through. Stir a couple of times to prevent sticking. Simmer until all the *spätzle* are floating, 1 to 2 minutes, then cook for 1 minute longer.

4. Remove the *spätzle* with a slotted spoon, place them in the large bowl, and drizzle with a ladle of the cooking liquid to prevent sticking. Cook the remaining batter and place the *spätzle* in the bowl with another ladle of the cooking liquid.

5. MAKE THE SAUCE AND FINISH THE DUMPLINGS: Melt the butter in a large skillet over high heat and swirl the pan around until it just begins to brown, about 1 minute. Drain the *spätzle* and turn into the hot butter. Toss and stir until the edges just begin to brown, about 2 minutes longer. Sprinkle with salt and pepper and serve.

Potato and Dumpling Boil-Up

Kartoffeln mit Mehlknödel (Germany)

SERVES 4 (MAKES ABOUT 20 DUMPLINGS)

We love this recipe because with just a few nice-sized potatoes and some flour you can pull together a dish that's both reliable and satisfying. Made out of a thick batter—similar to that used for *Spätzle* (preceding recipe)—these dumplings are cooked in a big pot of simmering potatoes. The dumplings and potatoes are then drained and tossed in a hot pan with a generous amount of butter. A topping of fried bread crumbs (see page 7) adds a salty, toasted crunch. This dumpling dish is good alone or as a side to meat or mushrooms.

For the Potatoes

3 large boiling potatoes, preferably German Butterball or Yukon Gold, peeled and cut into 1-inch cubes

For the Dumplings

1 cup unbleached all-purpose flour

½ teaspoon salt

¼ teaspoon freshly grated nutmeg

1 large egg, beaten

For Cooking

3 tablespoons unsalted butter, cut into chunks

1 small yellow onion, chopped fine

Salt and freshly ground black pepper to taste

¼ cup coarsely chopped fresh flat-leaf parsley

Equipment

Large, wide bowl to hold the cooked dumplings and potatoes

1. COOK THE POTATOES: Fill a large pot three-quarters of the way with salted water and bring to a boil over high heat. Add the potatoes, cover, reduce the heat to medium, and simmer until the potatoes are just tender, about 10 minutes.

2. MAKE AND COOK THE DUMPLINGS: While the potatoes are simmering, combine the flour, salt, and nutmeg in a medium bowl. Add the egg and ½ cup water and mix until combined. Don't overmix. You will have a very moist, sticky dough.

3. Once the potatoes have cooked for 10 minutes, scoop up a well-rounded teaspoon of dough. Use another spoon or your finger to move the dough gently off the spoon and into the simmering water with the potatoes. Continue with 10 more spoonfuls of dough, leaving as much space as you can around each, and stir to prevent sticking. Immediately spoon in the remaining dough and stir. Cook until all of the dumplings are floating, 2 to 3 minutes, then cook for 2 minutes longer.

4. Set aside a ladleful of the cooking liquid. Drain the dumplings and potatoes, place them in the large bowl, and drizzle with the reserved cooking liquid to prevent sticking.

5. PANFRY THE DUMPLINGS AND POTATOES: Melt the butter in a large skillet over medium heat. Add the onion and stir frequently until soft, about 4 minutes. Drain the dumplings and potatoes and turn them into the butter and onions. Sprinkle with salt and pepper. Raise the heat to high and toss and stir occasionally, until the edges of the dumplings begin to brown, about 3 minutes. Remove from the heat, stir in the parsley, and serve.

Spiced Gingerbread

(United States)

SERVES 6 TO 8 (MAKES 1 DUMPLING)

Steamed gingerbread is a classic. It's just as dark, moist, and rich as any baked version. While still warm, it can be spooned into a bowl and served with ice cream, or it can be cooled, sliced, and served with a good apple or pear butter.

For the Dumpling

⅔ cup graham flour

⅓ cup unbleached all-purpose flour

¾ teaspoon baking soda

¼ teaspoon salt

¾ teaspoon ground ginger

½ teaspoon ground cinnamon

¼ teaspoon freshly grated nutmeg

¾ cup milk

¼ cup light muscovado or other unrefined sugar (see page 20)

¼ cup molasses

1 large egg, beaten

4 tablespoons (½ stick) unsalted butter, melted

1 tablespoon finely grated fresh ginger

Grated zest of 1 small lemon

For Cooking

Unsalted butter to coat the cake pan

Equipment

2-inch-high steamer rack

Pot large enough to hold both the rack and the pan when covered

9-inch round cake pan

1. Place the steamer rack in the pot, add 1½ inches of water to the pot, and bring to a boil over high heat. Meanwhile, rub a little butter around the inside of the cake pan.

2. Combine the flours, baking soda, salt, ground ginger, cinnamon, and nutmeg in a large bowl. Mix together the milk, muscovado sugar, molasses, egg, melted butter, grated ginger, and lemon zest in a medium bowl. Pour the milk mixture into the flour mixture and stir until just combined. Pour the batter into the prepared cake pan and give it a gentle shake to level it off.

3. Carefully place the filled pan on the steamer rack, cover, reduce the heat to medium, and steam for 30 minutes.

4. Remove the pot from the heat. Carefully lift the pan out of the pot, place it on a folded kitchen towel, and allow the gingerbread to cool slightly. Slice and serve warm or at room temperature. Gingerbread can be refrigerated for up to 3 days. Reheat in a steamer pot or use the Steamer Plate Setup (page 37).

A Wealth of Steamed Rice Muffins

Fot Gao (China)

SERVES 6 TO 12 (MAKES 12 DUMPLINGS)

Fot gao means "fortune cake," and it's said that the more the tops of these tasty rice cakes bloom open during steaming, the greater your fortunes will blossom in the coming year. Chinese brown slab sugar is available at many Asian groceries, and is used to add a mild sweetness. If you have trouble finding it, you can add another ¾ cup of the muscovado sugar. These dumplings are associated primarily with the Chinese New Year, but we admit to making them anytime we want a light, sweet snack.

For the Dumplings

4 ounces Chinese brown slab sugar, chopped coarse, or ¾ cup other unrefined sugar (see page 20)

¼ cup light muscovado or other unrefined sugar

1¾ cups white rice flour, preferably from China or Thailand

2 tablespoons baking powder

Equipment

8- to 10-quart steamer pot

12 individual baking cups

12 paper baking cups

1. MAKE THE BATTER: Place the sugars in a small saucepan, pour in 1¼ cups water, and heat over medium heat. Stir, crushing apart any chunks of sugar with the back of a wooden spoon. Remove from the heat as soon as the sugar has dissolved, 3 to 4 minutes. Pour the sugar mixture into a bowl and allow it to cool to room temperature.

2. Combine the rice flour and the baking powder in a large bowl. Pour in the cooled sugar syrup and stir until the batter is completely smooth. It will be very thin. Pour the batter into a container with a spout for pouring.

3. STEAM THE DUMPLINGS: Remove the basket from the steamer pot, add 2 inches of water to the pot, and bring to a boil over high heat. Line the individual baking cups with the paper baking cups. Arrange as many of the lined cups in the basket as you can. Pour just enough batter into each cup to fill them two-thirds full. Place the basket in the pot, cover, and steam on high heat for 15 minutes.

4. Remove the pot from the heat. Carefully remove the basket, place on a folded kitchen towel, and allow the *fot gao* to cool slightly. Remove them from the individual baking cups and arrange them on a plate. Cook any remaining batter. Serve warm or at room temperature. *Fot gao* can be refrigerated for up to 3 days. Reheat them in a steamer pot or use the Steamer Plate Setup (page 37).

Steamed Bread Rolls

Mantou (China)

SERVES 3 TO 4 (MAKES 6 DUMPLINGS)

The ever-popular steamed bun of China is prized for its unique consistency and slightly sweet flavor. Bite into any well-made *mantou* and you'll notice a delicate balance of tenderness and chew. This pleasant bite is the result of a stretchy yeast dough that's been mellowed with baking powder and vegetable shortening. Traditionally, lard is used but vegetable shortening offers a cleaner, more neutral flavor. This same dough is used for other filled steamed buns in this book, including the *Zhu Rou Baozi* (May), *Xiang Gu Baozi* (May), and *Nuo Mi Juan* (February).

These dumplings are made using the Jelly-Roll Shape (page 41).

For the Dumplings

¾ cup warm milk or water

1¼ teaspoons active dry yeast (about ½ packet)

1½ tablespoons sugar

1¾ cups unbleached all-purpose flour, plus some extra for dusting

1 tablespoon nonhydrogenated vegetable shortening or lard

1 teaspoon baking powder

¼ teaspoon salt

For Cooking

Grapeseed or other neutral oil to coat the steamer basket

Equipment

8- to 10-quart steamer pot

1. PROOF THE YEAST: Pour the milk into a small bowl, stir in the yeast and the sugar, and proof for 15 minutes. The surface should become foamy. If not, start again with a new yeast packet.

2. MAKE THE DOUGH: While the yeast proofs, put 1½ cups of the flour in a large bowl and keep the remaining ¼ cup handy. Add the yeast mixture and mix until all the liquid has been absorbed. Work the dough with your hands into one manageable ball. If the dough is wet and sticky, work in some of the remaining flour, a little at a time, until it no longer sticks to your fingers.

3. Place the dough on a floured surface and knead for 4 to 5 minutes. The dough will be soft and tacky. Return the dough to the bowl, cover with a damp kitchen towel, and set aside in a warm place for 1½ to 2 hours. The dough will double in size. Use the Proofing Pot Setup (page 36) if the temperature of the room is not ideal.

4. Punch down the dough, place it on a floured surface, and knead once or twice. Sprinkle with flour if it gets a little sticky. Pat the dough into a small round, about 8 inches across.

Pinch the shortening into small bits and dot them across the surface of the dough round. Sprinkle the baking powder and salt over the top. Fold the dough over, enveloping the shortening, then roll it back into a ball. Knead until the shortening has been incorporated and the dough is smooth and elastic. If bits of the shortening ooze out, sprinkle that area with a little flour and continue kneading. Return the dough to the bowl, cover, and let the dough rest for 15 minutes.

At this point, the dough can also be used for the *Zhu Rou Baozi*, *Xiang Gu Baozi*, or *Nuo Mi Juan*.

5. ASSEMBLE THE DUMPLINGS: *Before assembling the* mantou, *review the Jelly-Roll Shape.*

6. Remove the basket from the steamer pot, add 2 inches of water to the pot, and set aside.

7. Knead the dough once or twice on a floured surface, shape it into a blunt log, then roll it out into an 8-inch square. Brush the surface of the square with a little water. Starting at any side, begin to roll up the dough. Pinch and press the far edge of the dough along the length of the log to seal. Use your hands to roll the log back and forth until it's 12 inches long. Cut the log into 6 equal pieces.

8. STEAM THE DUMPLINGS: Coat the bottom of the basket with oil and arrange as many of the dumplings as you can, seam side down, leaving about 1 inch of space around each. Cover any dumplings waiting to be cooked with a cloth.

9. Bring the water in the steamer pot to a boil over high heat. Place the basket in the pot, cover, reduce the heat to medium-high, and steam for 20 minutes.

10. Remove the pot from the heat. Carefully remove the basket, place it on a folded kitchen towel, and allow the *mantou* to cool slightly. Move them to a plate. Cook any remaining *mantou*. Serve warm or at room temperature. *Mantou* can be refrigerated for up to 3 days or frozen (see page 36) for up to 6 months. Reheat them in a steamer pot or use the Steamer Plate Setup (page 37). If reheating frozen *mantou*, allow them to thaw before steaming.

"Priest Stranglers" with Brown Butter and Sage

Strangolapreti (Italy)

SERVES 4 (MAKES ABOUT 48 DUMPLINGS)

Dumplings known as *strangolapreti* differ greatly throughout Italy. Spinach, chard, or other leafy greens worked into the dough are, however, often considered a defining characteristic. One popular type from northern Italy starts by soaking bits of day-old bread in spinach-water. Flour and spinach are then added to create a soft, easy-to-roll dough. The dumplings are vibrant in color and stand out as a special offering on any table.

For the Dumplings

1 large bunch spinach, stemmed, rinsed, and hand-wilted (see page 37)

10 cups ½-inch crustless white bread cubes (see page 6)

2 large eggs, beaten

2 teaspoons salt

½ teaspoon freshly grated nutmeg

¼ cup freshly grated Parmesan cheese

1 cup unbleached all-purpose flour, plus some extra for dusting

For the Sauce

3 tablespoons unsalted butter, cut into chunks

8 to 10 fresh sage leaves

1 garlic clove, chopped very fine

For Serving

½ cup freshly grated Parmesan cheese

Salt and freshly ground black pepper to taste

Equipment

Large plate or tray to hold the dumplings cooked in batches

1. MAKE THE DOUGH: Gather up half of the wilted spinach, hold it over the bowl, and squeeze out as much juice as you can. Place the squeezed spinach on a cutting board and repeat with the remaining spinach in the bowl. Pour the collected juice into a measuring cup. Add cool water to the juice until you have 1 cup of liquid.

2. Finely chop the spinach, place it back into the bowl, add the bread cubes, and pour in the spinach-water. Work the mixture together by squishing it through your fingers until all of the bread has been broken down into a pulp. Mix in the eggs, salt, nutmeg, and the ¼ cup of Parmesan. Add ¾ cup of the flour and keep the remaining ¼ cup handy. Work the mixture into one manageable ball. If the dough is wet and sticky, work in some of the remaining flour, a little at a time, until it no longer sticks to your fingers.

3. MAKE THE DUMPLINGS: Line a tray with a kitchen towel and sprinkle with a little flour.

4. Pinch off a small piece of dough and roll it into a ball about 1¼ inches around. Place the ball on a floured surface, roll into a rope about 4 inches long with tapered ends (a cigar shape), dust with flour, and place on the prepared tray. Repeat with the remaining dough, keeping the dumplings in a single layer on the tray.

5. COOK THE DUMPLINGS: Fill a large pot halfway with salted water and bring to a boil over high heat. Reduce the heat to medium for a steady simmer.

6. Carefully drop half of the dumplings, a few at a time, into the simmering water. Cook until all of them are floating, about 3 minutes, then cook for 2 minutes longer.

7. Remove the dumplings with a slotted spoon, scatter them around the large plate or tray, and drizzle with a few spoonfuls of the cooking liquid to prevent sticking. Cook the remaining dumplings and place them on the plate with another few spoonfuls of the cooking liquid.

8. MAKE THE SAUCE: Melt the butter in a large skillet over medium heat. Add the sage leaves and garlic and cook until the garlic just begins to brown, about 2 minutes. Drain the *strangolapreti* and add them to the butter sauce. Toss and stir gently until the edges just begin to brown. Remove from the heat, mix in the ½ cup of Parmesan, sprinkle with salt and pepper, and serve.

Potato Gnocchi

Gnocchi di Patate (Italy)

SERVES 4

Making gnocchi requires a light touch and the ability to be flexible, but once you master the recipe, you can easily make gnocchi anytime, in anyone's kitchen, without any instructions in front of you. We prefer gnocchi that are made without eggs so that less flour is needed to make the dough. The less flour you need, the more potato flavor there will be in each bite. If this dough is new to you, it may take a couple of tries to get it just right, but the gnocchi you produce while trying will still be perfectly good to eat.

For the Dumplings

4 medium baking potatoes, such as russet

1¼ cups unbleached all-purpose flour, plus some extra for dusting

½ teaspoon salt

For the Sauce*

4 tablespoons (½ stick) unsalted butter, cut into chunks

For Serving*

½ cup freshly grated Parmesan cheese

Salt and freshly ground black pepper to taste

Equipment

Potato ricer

Gnocchi board (optional)

Large plate or tray to hold the dumplings cooked in batches

1. MAKE THE DOUGH: Place the potatoes in a small pot, pour in enough water to cover them, and bring to a boil over high heat. Cover, reduce the heat to medium, and simmer until fork-tender, about 30 minutes. Drain and place the potatoes on a folded kitchen towel. When they're cool enough to handle, peel off their skins, break them into chunks, then press them through the ricer into a large bowl.

2. Add 1 cup of the flour to the riced potato, keeping the remaining ¼ cup handy, then add the salt and toss until mixed evenly. Work the dough with your hands into one manageable ball.

3. Place the dough on a floured surface and knead for 2 to 3 minutes. This dough needs to be firm enough to hold its shape when rolled into balls. If it is too soft or sticky, work in some of the remaining flour, a little at a time.

4. MAKE THE DUMPLINGS: Line a tray with a kitchen towel and sprinkle with a little flour.

---

*These amounts are for a full recipe. If you plan on freezing and storing some of the dumplings, reduce the amounts in proportion to the number you are serving.

5. Divide the dough into 8 equal pieces. Roll one piece of dough into a rope about ½ inch thick, sprinkling with flour if it gets a little sticky. Cut the rope into ¾-inch lengths.

6. If you don't want ridges on your gnocchi, place the cut dough pieces in a single layer on the prepared tray. If you do want ridges, roll each piece along the gnocchi board or along the tines of a fork. Roll the piece along the back of the fork to avoid catching it on the ends of the tines. Repeat with the remaining dough.

7. Set aside the number of gnocchi that you would like to cook and keep the rest frozen for up to 6 months (see page 36).

8. COOK THE DUMPLINGS: Fill a large pot halfway with salted water and bring to a boil over high heat. Reduce the heat to medium for a steady simmer.

9. Carefully drop up to a few dozen gnocchi into the simmering water, a few at a time. Cook until all of them are floating, about 2 minutes, then cook for 2 minutes longer. (If cooking frozen gnocchi, add them directly to the simmering water and increase the cooking time by 1 minute. Do not allow the gnocchi to thaw before cooking.)

10. Remove the gnocchi with a slotted spoon, scatter them on the large plate or tray, and drizzle with a few spoonfuls of the cooking liquid to prevent sticking. Resting the cooked gnocchi on a roomy plate prevents them from piling up while they set and firm up a bit. Cook the remaining gnocchi in batches, placing them on the plate with another few spoonfuls of the cooking liquid. Set aside ½ cup of the cooking liquid for the sauce.

11. Melt the butter in a large skillet over medium heat. Cook until the butter just begins to brown, about 2 minutes. Drain the gnocchi and add them to the butter. Toss and stir gently until the edges just begin to brown. Remove from the heat, mix in the Parmesan, sprinkle with salt and pepper, and serve.

POTATO GNOCCHI WITH OXTAIL SAUCE

Make the Oxtail Sauce (recipe follows). While the sauce is simmering, prepare the gnocchi and cook them in boiling water shortly before they need to be added to the sauce. Or you can make the sauce up to 3 days in advance, keeping it refrigerated in a tightly sealed container. Bring the sauce to a simmer before adding the cooked gnocchi.

OXTAIL SAUCE

MAKES ABOUT 4 CUPS

3 tablespoons olive oil

2 pounds meaty oxtail pieces

3 celery ribs with leaves, chopped fine

1 medium yellow onion, chopped fine

1 garlic clove, chopped fine

5 stems fresh thyme or 1 teaspoon dried

½ cup white wine

3 cups Beef Broth (page 396)

6 ripe plum tomatoes, peeled, seeded (see page 21), and crushed, or 6 canned plum tomatoes, drained and crushed (about 1½ cups)

1 teaspoon salt

½ teaspoon freshly ground black pepper

5 to 6 cremini mushrooms

1. Heat the oil in a medium pot over medium heat. Add the oxtail pieces in one layer and do not stir until the undersides are golden brown, about 10 minutes. Turn them over and brown the other sides, about 8 minutes longer. Using tongs, move the oxtail to a bowl, leaving behind the oily fat. Add the celery, onion, garlic, and thyme to the pot and cook, stirring occasionally, until the onion is soft, about 4 minutes. Pour in the wine and scrape up any sticky bits from the bottom of the pot with a wooden spoon.

2. Return the oxtail pieces and any drippings to the pot. Pour in the broth. Mix in the tomatoes, salt, and pepper. Cover, reduce the heat to low, and simmer for 2 to 2½ hours. Stir occasionally, adding a little water if the broth reduces below the halfway mark of the oxtail.

3. Using tongs, move the oxtail pieces to a bowl and allow them to cool as the sauce continues to simmer. Quarter the mushrooms, mix them into the sauce, cover, and cook for 20 minutes.

4. Meanwhile, pull the oxtail meat off the bones, discard the bones, and mix the meat back into the sauce. Immediately stir in the cooked gnocchi, cook for 1 minute to heat through, and serve.

Marrow Dumplings in Beef Broth

Markklösschensuppe (Germany)

SERVES 4 (MAKES ABOUT 24 DUMPLINGS)

Marrow gives these tender bread crumb dumplings a subtle beef flavor and a creamy texture. Beef marrow bones are frequently kept behind the butcher's counter. Ask for the freshest bones possible, approximately 1 inch thick. Once the bones have warmed to room temperature, you can easily scrape the marrow out with a butter knife or a small spoon. Work carefully and be mindful of the sharp edges or jagged points often found on saw-cut bones. For those who don't eat veal, know that when you ask for beef marrow bones, it's often veal bones that are handed over. Be specific if you want mature beef bones.

For the Dumplings

4 pounds beef marrow bones, at room temperature

2½ cups coarse dry crustless white bread crumbs (see page 6)

½ cup milk

1 large egg, beaten

¾ teaspoon salt

½ teaspoon freshly grated nutmeg

Unbleached all-purpose flour for dusting

For the Broth

1 recipe (2 quarts) Beef Broth with German Flavors (page 397)

Equipment

Sieve lined with 4 to 6 layers of cheesecloth

1. RENDER THE MARROW 1½ HOURS IN ADVANCE: Wipe down the marrow bones with a damp towel. Using a blunt knife, scoop and scrape the marrow out of the bones into a bowl. Place the collected marrow into a small saucepan, place over very low heat, and melt slowly into a clear, oily liquid, 25 to 30 minutes. As the marrow melts, foamy solid bits will naturally separate and become obvious. Remove the saucepan from the heat and strain the hot marrow through the cheesecloth-lined sieve into a glass bowl. Cover and refrigerate until solid, about 1 hour. (You can also render the marrow in advance and keep it refrigerated in a tightly sealed glass container for up to 1 week or frozen for up to 6 months.)

2. Remove the marrow from the refrigerator and let it rest until soft and creamy.

3. MAKE THE DOUGH: Place 1½ cups of the bread crumbs in a medium bowl and keep the remaining 1 cup handy. Stir in the milk.

4. Place the egg and the marrow in another bowl and whisk until the marrow has been distributed evenly throughout the egg. Mix in the salt and nutmeg. Pour the egg mixture over the milk-soaked bread crumbs and mix. You will have a slightly lumpy batter.

5. Work in some of the remaining bread crumbs, a little at a time, until you have a slightly sticky dough that just holds its shape when rolled into balls. Cover and refrigerate for 30 minutes.

6. COOK THE DUMPLINGS: Pour the beef broth into a medium pot and bring to a boil over high heat. Reduce the heat to low for a gentle simmer.

7. Line a tray with a kitchen towel and sprinkle with a little flour.

8. Pinch off a small piece of dough and roll it into a ball about 1 inch around, dust with flour, and place on the prepared tray. Repeat with the remaining dough.

9. Carefully drop the dumplings, one by one, into the simmering broth. Cook until all of them are floating, about 2 minutes, then cook for 2 minutes longer, and serve.

Cassava "Tamales" Stuffed with Pork and Chickpeas

Pasteles de Yuca (Puerto Rico)

SERVES 6 TO 12 (MAKES 12 DUMPLINGS)

At many Puerto Rican markets or restaurants you can find paper-wrapped *pasteles* soaking in pots of steaming liquid. They can be made from banana, plantain, taro, potato, pumpkin, rice, cassava, or a combination. *Pasteles de yuca*, made with cassava, are distinctly heavy and satisfying, with an intriguing texture, seeming to both crumble and melt around a savory and sweet filling of chickpeas, pork, and raisins.

These dumplings are wrapped using the Diamond in the Square Fold (page 42).

For the Achiote Oil

¾ cup grapeseed or other neutral oil

⅓ cup achiote (annatto) seeds or ½ teaspoon achiote powder

For the Filling

½ cup dried chickpeas, soaked in plenty of water for 6 to 8 hours, or 1 cup canned chickpeas, drained and rinsed

1 recipe *Sofrito* (recipe follows)

1 pound boneless pork shoulder, cut into ½-inch cubes

1 tablespoon tomato paste

¼ pound unsmoked brine-cured (or wet-cured) ham

1 tablespoon drained capers, rinsed

12 pimiento-stuffed green olives with 2 tablespoons of the brine

¼ cup raisins

Salt to taste

For the Cassava Mixture

4 pounds cassava (yuca)

½ cup milk

For Assembly

Twelve 10-inch prepared banana-leaf squares (see page 28)

Twelve 12 × 15-inch parchment paper sheets

Twelve 20-inch length of kitchen string for tying the *pasteles*

1. MAKE THE ACHIOTE OIL: If using achiote seeds, place the oil and the seeds in a small saucepan and cook over very low heat, stirring occasionally, for 15 minutes. The oil will gradually become dark red in color. Strain the oil through a sieve into a glass bowl and discard the seeds. Set the oil aside and let it cool to room temperature. If using achiote powder, mix it into the room temperature oil and set aside. (You can also make the achiote oil in advance and keep it refrigerated in a tightly sealed glass container for up to 1 month.)

2. MAKE THE FILLING: (Skip this step if using canned chickpeas.) Drain the chickpeas and place them in a small pot. Cover with water by 2 inches and bring to a boil over high heat. Cover, reduce the heat to low, and simmer until the chickpeas are just tender, 1 to 1½ hours.

3. While the chickpeas are simmering, add half of the achiote oil to a medium pot and heat over high heat. Quickly and carefully pour in the *sofrito*. Reduce the heat to medium and simmer, stirring frequently, until the sauce thickens and darkens in color, about 6 minutes. Stir in the pork, tomato paste, and ½ cup water. Cover, reduce the heat to low, and simmer for 30 minutes, stirring occasionally, and adding up to ½ cup water if the sauce starts to dry out around the edges of the pan.

4. Drain the chickpeas and stir them into the simmering pork along with the ham, capers, olives, and brine. Cover and cook for 10 minutes longer. Remove from the heat, stir in the raisins, and sprinkle with salt. Scoop everything, including all of the sauce, into a shallow bowl and allow it to cool to room temperature.

5. MAKE THE CASSAVA MIXTURE: While the filling is cooling, prepare the cassava (see page 7) and finely grate it onto a kitchen towel. Bring together the ends of the cloth and twist to squeeze out as much of the cassava juice as you can. The amount of liquid you are squeezing out won't be much and may simply be absorbed by the cloth. Do this step in batches if it seems more effective. Place the cassava in a bowl and break it up a little. Add in the remaining achiote oil and the milk and mix well.

6. ASSEMBLE THE DUMPLINGS: *Before assembling the* pasteles, *review the Diamond in the Square Fold. Instead of using two banana-leaf squares, replace the large square with a piece of parchment paper. The Diamond in the Square Fold is designed to make the most out of the strength of the banana leaf by crisscrossing its fibers.*

7. Line a tray with a kitchen towel. Have ready the cassava mixture, the filling, the parchment and banana-leaf squares, and their ties.

8. Lay flat 1 parchment paper square and place a banana-leaf square, smooth side up, diagonally on top of it. Center 2 rounded tablespoons of the cassava mixture on top of the leaf and spread it out into a 4-inch square. Place 2 rounded tablespoons of filling on top of the cassava mixture. Try to distribute the filling so that there is an olive in each package. Top with another 2 tablespoons of the cassava. Fold over one corner of the stacked paper and leaf, then fold over the opposite corner. Fold the ends over as firmly as you can to create a neat, rectangular package. Tie to secure the folds, place on the tray, and repeat the assembly until you have 12 packages.

9. COOK THE DUMPLINGS: Fill a large pot three-quarters of the way with water and bring to a boil over high heat. Reduce the heat to medium for a steady simmer. Gently drop the packages, one at a time, into the water. They will pile up, which is fine as long as the top layer is covered by at least 1 inch of water. Cover and simmer for 45 minutes.

10. Remove the *pasteles* with tongs and place in a colander to drain. Allow them to cool slightly, cut off the strings, and serve. It's best not to open the packages too soon, and to peel back the paper and leaf just before eating, so that they stay moist and warm. *Pasteles* can be refrigerated for up to 3 days or frozen (unopened) for up to 6 months (see page 36). Reheat the *pasteles* in a steamer pot or use the Steamer Plate Setup (page 37). If reheating frozen *pasteles*, allow them to thaw before steaming.

SOFRITO

MAKES ABOUT 1 CUP

1 large green bell pepper, chopped coarse

1 small yellow onion, chopped coarse

½ cup coarsely chopped fresh cilantro stems and leaves

3 garlic cloves, chopped coarse

2 small sweet *ajicito* chiles or 1 cubanelle chile, cored and seeded

4 culantro (*recao*) leaves, trimmed, or another ½ cup coarsely chopped cilantro

1 tablespoon fresh oregano leaves

3 tablespoons olive oil

Pulse all the ingredients in a food processor until the mixture is light and pulpy. Use immediately or store in a tightly sealed container for up to 1 week in the refrigerator or keep frozen for up to 6 months.

Pounded Rice Dumplings

Mochi (Japan)

SERVES 4 TO 8 (MAKES 8 SMALL DUMPLINGS)

Mochi is one of the great wonders of Japanese cooking and a New Year's tradition that requires impressive amounts of physical labor. Mounds of steamed sweet, sticky (glutinous) rice are pounded into a smooth, dense, marshmallowy textured treat. We've made the process easier by grinding the rice before steaming it, which shortens the pounding time considerably. There are electric *mochi*-making machines that are about the size of a bread maker, and they are a good investment if you plan to make it often. However, taking the time to pound the rice yourself is the best way to satisfy the occasional indulgence for *mochi*.

Because fresh *mochi* is so very soft and sticky, it is not recommended for small children.

For the Mochi

1 cup Japanese short-grain sweet (glutinous) white rice (*mochi gome*), coarsely ground in a clean spice or coffee grinder and soaked in plenty of water for 30 minutes

¼ cup potato starch (*katakuriko*)

For Serving

2 tablespoons soy sauce, sugar, or roasted soybean powder (*kinako*)

Equipment

8- to 10-quart steamer pot

24-inch square of muslin

Large sturdy wooden bowl and a large pestle or meat pounder for pounding the *mochi*

1. Remove the basket from the steamer pot, add 2 inches of water to the pot, and bring to a boil over high heat. Soak the muslin under running water, wring it out, then drape it inside the basket, creating a lining. Drain the ground rice, scoop it into the lined basket, and spread it out evenly. Place the basket in the pot, reduce the heat to medium, cover, and steam for 40 minutes.

2. Remove the pot from the heat and let the rice rest in the steamer for 5 minutes. Using the muslin liner, lift the rice out of the basket and turn it into the bowl. The bowl must be roomy enough for you to pound the rice freely without spilling. Using the pestle or meat pounder, begin to pound the rice steadily. Continue pounding until the rice is smooth (or mostly smooth), bouncy, and very sticky, about 10 minutes. If the *mochi* is too dry and firm to pound effectively, add some warm water and continue pounding.

3. Sprinkle the potato starch over a work surface. Wet your hands and move the *mochi* onto the starched surface. Now dry your hands and lightly knead the *mochi* into the starch until it is no longer exceedingly sticky to the touch. Divide into 8 equal pieces, roll into balls, and serve with a little soy sauce, sugar, or soybean powder.

If using the *mochi* to make *Ozoni* (recipe follows), divide it into 8 equal pieces, roll into balls, cover with a damp towel, and set aside until the dumplings are ready to be toasted.

If using the *mochi* to make *Ichigo Daifuku* (May), divide it into 12 equal pieces, roll into balls, and keep them covered with a damp towel until the dumplings are ready to be assembled.

New Year's Day Soup with Pounded Rice Dumplings

Ozoni (Japan)

SERVES 8 (MAKES 8 DUMPLINGS)

Ozoni is a New Year's seafood soup defined by the sweet rice dumplings that are toasted and added to the soup just before serving. These pounded rice dumplings, or *mochi*, offer a soft, taffylike chew and a clean, refreshing flavor within the aged, darker flavors of the broth. *Dashi* is not a time-consuming broth, made essentially by steeping pieces of kelp and bonito flakes in hot water. *Kamaboko* is also a vital component of the soup. Made from a white fish paste that's been steamed into slender loaves, *kamaboko* are firm fish cakes that can be sliced and added to soups and other dishes.

Because fresh *mochi* is so very soft and sticky, it is not recommended for small children.

For the Soup

Two 5-inch squares dried kelp (*kombu*), gently rinsed

1 cup loosely packed bonito flakes (*katsuobushi*)

4 skinless chicken breasts or thighs, trimmed of excess fat

1 small daikon radish, peeled and sliced into sixteen ⅛-inch rounds

1 teaspoon soy sauce

1½ teaspoons salt

1 small carrot, cut into ⅛-inch rounds

8 fresh shiitake mushroom caps

One 7-ounce fish cake (*kamaboko*), cut into 16 equal slices

1 small bunch *mizuna* or watercress, stemmed and rinsed

2 teaspoons dried *yuzu* rind or grated lemon zest

2 scallions, trimmed and sliced into thin rings

For the Dumplings

1 recipe *Mochi* (page 84), divided evenly into 8 pieces and rolled into balls (preferably made no more than 4 hours in advance)

Equipment

Sieve lined with 2 to 4 layers of cheesecloth

1. MAKE THE BROTH: Pour 10 cups water into a medium pot. Add the kelp and soak at room temperature for 15 to 20 minutes. Place the pot over high heat. As soon as the broth begins to simmer, stir in the bonito flakes and immediately remove from the heat. Cover and let the broth steep for 10 minutes. Strain the broth through the cheesecloth-lined sieve into a large bowl and clean the pot. Pour the broth back into the pot and set aside.

2. Pour 2 cups water into a medium pot and bring to a boil over high heat. Arrange the chicken in the pot in a single layer, cover, reduce the heat to low, and simmer for 10 minutes. Turn the chicken over, cover again, and cook for 5 minutes longer. Remove from the heat. Move the chicken with a slotted spoon to a plate to cool. Strain the chicken broth through the cheesecloth-lined sieve into a medium bowl.

3. MAKE THE SOUP: Pour the chicken broth into the kelp broth and bring to a boil over high heat. Add the daikon, soy sauce, and salt. Cover, reduce the heat to low, and simmer for 10 minutes.

4. Meanwhile, pull the chicken meat off the bones and tear it into bite-sized pieces. Once the daikon has finished cooking, stir in the chicken, carrot, mushrooms, and fish cake slices and cook for 5 minutes longer. Reduce the heat to very, very low to keep the soup hot while you toast the *mochi*. (You can also make the soup up to 3 days in advance and keep it tightly covered in the refrigerator.)

5. TOAST THE DUMPLINGS: Slowly heat a dry, heavy grill pan or skillet over medium heat. Arrange the balls of *mochi* in the pan, leaving about 1 inch of space around each. The *mochi* will soften and spread out as they cook. Toast until the bottoms are golden brown and crisp, about 5 minutes. You must let them brown before turning them or they might tear. Using a small spatula or a butter knife, carefully lift and turn them to toast the other sides. Place 1 toasted *mochi* in each soup bowl.

6. FINISH THE SOUP: Bring the soup back to a simmer over medium heat. Stir in the *mizuna* and the *yuzu* and cook for 2 minutes. Ladle the hot soup over the *mochi* along with a good mixture of the soup ingredients. Serve with a sprinkle of scallions.

February

SPOON-DROPPED SEMOLINA DUMPLINGS
Kletski (Russia) 90

CHOCOLATE BREAD CRUMB PUDDING
(England) 92

MILK-STEAMED BUNS WITH VANILLA CUSTARD SAUCE
Dampfnudeln (Germany) 95

CLOUD-SHAPED BREAD BUNS
Ting Momo (Tibet) 99

STEAMED BREAD LOAVES STUFFED WITH STICKY FRIED RICE
Nuo Mi Juan (China) 101

POTATO DUMPLINGS STUFFED WITH HAM
Kroppkakor (Sweden) 103

SILESIAN POTATO DUMPLINGS WITH MUSHROOM SAUCE
Kluski Śląskie (Poland) 105

CHESTNUT GNOCCHI WITH WALNUT SAUCE
Gnocchi di Castagne con Salsa di Noci (Italy) 107

PANFRIED DUMPLINGS STUFFED WITH CHICKEN AND MUSHROOMS
Jiao Zi (China) 110

Spoon-Dropped Semolina Dumplings

Kletski (Russia)

SERVES 4 (MAKES ABOUT 28 DUMPLINGS)

Kletski are soft, egg-rich dumplings full of buttery flavor. Lightly cooking the flour and fat as they are mixed together creates a tender, semicongealed paste into which the eggs are mixed. They are wonderful with melted butter and sour cream, but they are just as popular when served in a meaty broth or in a beet soup.

For the Dumplings

¾ cup milk

6 tablespoons (¾ stick) unsalted butter

½ cup semolina flour

½ teaspoon salt

2 large eggs, separated

2 tablespoons finely chopped fresh flat-leaf parsley, dill, tarragon, or a combination (optional)

For Serving

4 tablespoons (½ stick) unsalted butter, melted just before serving

½ cup sour cream

Equipment

Large, wide bowl to hold the dumplings cooked in batches

1. MAKE THE DOUGH: Pour the milk into a small pot and add the 6 tablespoons butter. Stir over medium heat until the milk just begins to bubble around the edges of the pot. Add the semolina flour and the salt all at once, stir vigorously until just combined, and immediately remove from the heat. Continue stirring until all the liquid has been absorbed and you have a thick, glossy, pasty batter.

2. Place the pan over low heat and stir continuously until the batter thickens into a soft dough that pulls away from the sides of the pot. Continue stirring until the pasty coating left on the bottom and sides of the pan begins to brown, about 2 minutes. Remove from the heat, scoop into a medium bowl, break it up a bit, and allow it to cool slightly.

3. While the dough is still warm, add one egg yolk. Mix it in completely with a wooden spoon, then mix in the second yolk.

4. Whisk the egg whites in a large bowl until they form soft peaks. Add half of the egg whites to the dough and mix until well combined. Now add and fold in the remaining egg whites and the parsley if using.

5. COOK THE DUMPLINGS: Fill a large pot halfway with salted water and bring to a boil over high heat. Reduce the heat to medium for a steady simmer. Scoop up a rounded tablespoon of the dough. Use another spoon or your finger to move the dough gently off the spoon and into the water. Try to drop in about 14 spoonfuls of dough, leaving as much space as you can around each dumpling, before the first one begins to float. Cook until all of them are floating, about 2 minutes, then cook for 3 minutes longer.

6. Remove the dumplings with a slotted spoon, place them in the large bowl with a ladleful of the cooking liquid to prevent them from sticking, and keep warm. Cook the remaining dough and place the dumplings in the bowl with another ladle of the cooking liquid.

7. Once all of the dumplings have been cooked, drain and place them in a large serving bowl. Drizzle with melted butter and serve with a side of sour cream. *Kletski* are also good the next day, fried in a little butter and served with eggs for breakfast or a light snack.

Chocolate Bread Crumb Pudding

(England)

SERVES 4 (MAKES 1 DUMPLING)

This steamed pudding looks like a traditional and elegant chocolate cake, but because it is made with bread crumbs it has a distinctive and denser texture. The slight saltiness of the bread accentuates the flavor of the sweet, dark chocolate. This pudding is excellent served warm or at room temperature.

The dumpling is made using the Pudding Basin Setup (page 43).

For the Dumpling

2 cups coarse fresh crustless white bread crumbs (see page 6)

1 cup unbleached all-purpose flour

½ cup sugar

2 teaspoons baking powder

¼ teaspoon salt

6 tablespoons (¾ stick) unsalted butter, cut into chunks

One 4-ounce bar semisweet or bittersweet chocolate, cut into small chunks, or ⅔ cup chocolate chips

2 large eggs, beaten

¼ cup milk

For Cooking and Serving

Unsalted butter and sugar to coat the pudding basin

1 recipe Cream Sauce or Sweetened Whipped Cream (recipes follow)

Equipment

24-inch square of muslin

35-inch length of kitchen string

4- to 5-cup pudding basin

Pot large enough to hold the basin when covered

Parchment paper

1. MAKE THE BATTER: Combine the bread crumbs, flour, sugar, baking powder, and salt in a large bowl.

2. Melt the butter and the chocolate in a double boiler or in a stainless-steel bowl set on top of a pot filled with 1 inch of simmering water. (The bowl should not touch the simmering water but should rest directly above it.) Stir constantly to avoid scorching the chocolate. Remove from the heat the moment the chocolate has melted completely, place on a folded kitchen towel, and allow the chocolate to cool slightly.

3. Pour the eggs into the bread crumb mixture along with the melted chocolate and mix well. Slowly stir in the milk. Do not overmix.

4. ASSEMBLE AND STEAM THE DUMPLING: *Before assembling the pudding, review the Pudding Basin Setup.*

5. Soak the muslin and the string under running water. Wring them out and set aside.

6. Place the empty pudding basin in the pot. Pour water into the space between the basin and the pot until it comes three-quarters of the way up the sides of the basin. Remove the basin and bring the water to a boil over high heat. Reduce the heat to low for a gentle simmer.

7. Meanwhile, make sure the interior of the basin is dry before rubbing it with butter and coating it with sugar. Scoop the batter into the basin and wiggle it gently to level it off. Cut out a round of parchment paper and place it on top of the batter. Cover the basin with the damp muslin and secure it tightly with the string. Tie the opposite corners of the muslin into handles over the top of the pudding.

8. Using tongs or a wooden spoon, push a folded cloth, such as a standard white cotton napkin, into the water and arrange it to lie flat on the bottom of the pot. Using the cloth handle, carefully lower the basin into the pot, cover, and simmer for at least 1½ hours or up to 2½ hours for a pudding that's even richer in flavor and texture. Check the water level every 30 minutes and replenish with boiling water as needed.

9. Remove the pot from the heat. Using a pot holder to grasp the cloth handle, carefully remove the basin from the pot, put it on a folded kitchen towel, and allow the pudding to cool for 5 minutes. Remove the string, cloth, and paper. Unmold by inverting it onto a plate. Slice and serve warm with Cream Sauce, Sweetened Whipped Cream, or vanilla ice cream. The pudding can be refrigerated for up to 3 days. Reheat in a steamer pot or use the Steamer Plate Setup (page 37).

CREAM SAUCE

MAKES ABOUT 1½ CUPS

¾ cup heavy cream

½ cup milk

¼ cup sugar

Pinch of salt

Combine all the ingredients in a small saucepan and heat over high heat. Stir continuously until the sugar has dissolved and the sauce just begins to bubble around the edges of the saucepan. Remove from the heat and let the sauce cool slightly before serving. You can also make the sauce up to 3 days in advance and keep it refrigerated in a tightly sealed container. Reheat the sauce over medium heat until warm, stirring constantly.

SWEETENED WHIPPED CREAM

MAKES ABOUT 1½ CUPS

¾ cup heavy cream

1½ tablespoons superfine sugar (or granulated sugar
    pulsed in a clean spice or coffee grinder for 1 to 2 minutes)

1. Chill a whisk and a medium metal bowl in the freezer for 5 minutes. If using an electric hand mixer, place the whisking attachment in the freezer.

2. Whisk the heavy cream in the chilled bowl until it forms soft peaks. Add half of the sugar and combine with a few strokes. Add the remaining sugar and whisk until firm peaks form. Serve immediately.

Milk-Steamed Buns with Vanilla Custard Sauce

Dampfnudeln (Germany)

SERVES 4 TO 8 (MAKES 8 DUMPLINGS)

These popular yeast buns go very well with meat and savory sauces, but they are also delicious as a snack or a dessert—as shown here—served with a good custard or fruit sauce. Simmering the buns in butter and milk makes them extra soft and moist, but once the liquid has cooked off, they're left in the pan a moment longer so that their bottoms can get crispy and brown. The prune sauce recipe that follows can be spooned over the top, or the buns can be cooked directly in the sauce.

For the Dumplings

- ¼ cup warm water, preferably nonchlorinated, such as distilled or spring water
- ⅓ cup plus 1 teaspoon sugar
- 1¼ teaspoons active dry yeast (about ½ packet)
- 2¼ cups unbleached all-purpose flour, plus some extra for dusting
- ¼ teaspoon salt
- 2 large eggs, at room temperature, beaten
- 6 tablespoons (¾ stick) unsalted butter, melted

For Cooking

- 2 cups milk
- 2 tablespoons unsalted butter, cut into chunks
- 1 tablespoon sugar
- ¼ teaspoon salt
- 1 vanilla bean or 1 teaspoon pure vanilla extract

For Serving

- 1 recipe Vanilla Custard Sauce or Prune Sauce (recipes follow)

Equipment

Large, deep skillet with cover

1. PROOF THE YEAST: Pour the warm water into a small bowl, stir in the yeast, and 1 teaspoon of the sugar, and proof for 15 minutes. The surface should become foamy. If not, start again with a new yeast packet.

2. MAKE THE DUMPLINGS: While the yeast proofs, place 2 cups of the flour into a large bowl and keep the remaining ¼ cup handy. Mix in the remaining ⅓ cup sugar and the salt. Pour in the yeast mixture, eggs, and melted butter and mix until all of the liquid has been absorbed. Work the dough with your hands into one manageable ball. If it is too wet and sticky, work in some of the remaining flour, a little at a time, until it no longer sticks to your fingers.

3. Knead the dough on a floured surface for 2 minutes. The dough will be soft and tacky. Return the dough to the bowl, cover with a damp kitchen towel, and set aside in a warm place until the dough doubles in size, 1½ to 2 hours. Use the Proofing Pot Setup (page 36) if the temperature of the room is not ideal.

4. Line a tray with a kitchen towel and sprinkle with a little flour.

5. Punch down the dough, place on a floured surface, and knead once or twice. Divide into 8 equal pieces. Roll each piece of dough into a ball and space them evenly on the prepared tray. Cover with a towel and allow them to rise for 20 minutes.

6. COOK THE DUMPLINGS: Put the milk, 2 tablespoons butter, 1 tablespoon sugar, and the salt in the skillet. Bring to a very gentle simmer over medium heat, being careful not to allow the milk to come to a full boil. Immediately reduce the heat to low.

7. Slice the vanilla bean open along its length with a sharp knife. Scrape out the gooey seeds and whisk them into the milk mixture. If using vanilla extract, stir it into the milk mixture. Using a spatula, gently lift and arrange the dumplings ½ inch apart in the simmering milk mixture. Cover and cook for 25 minutes.

8. Remove the cover to allow any remaining liquid to cook off. Continue cooking until you hear a strong sizzling sound and the undersides of the *dampfnudeln* become golden brown and crisp. Remove them with a spatula and place on a serving dish or individual plates. Serve with Vanilla Custard Sauce or Prune Sauce.

VANILLA CUSTARD SAUCE

MAKES ABOUT 1½ CUPS

1 cup milk

3 large egg yolks

¼ cup sugar

Pinch of salt

½ vanilla bean or ½ teaspoon pure vanilla extract

1 tablespoon brandy (optional)

1. Heat the milk in a small saucepan over medium heat until it just begins to bubble along the sides of pan. Do not allow the milk to come to a full simmer. Immediately remove from the heat and set aside.

2. Whisk together the egg yolks, sugar, and salt in a medium bowl until the sugar has mostly dissolved. Continue whisking while gradually drizzling in the warm milk.

3. Slice the vanilla bean open along its length with a sharp knife. Scrape out the gooey seeds and whisk them into the milk mixture. If using vanilla extract, stir it into the milk mixture.

4. Pour the mixture into a double boiler or a stainless-steel bowl set on top of a pot filled with 1 inch of simmering water. (The bowl should not touch the simmering water but should rest directly above it.) Whisk vigorously at all times until the mixture is thick and creamy, 4 to 5 minutes. Remove from the heat and place on a folded kitchen towel to cool slightly. Whisk in the brandy, if desired, just before serving. You can also make the sauce up to 3 days in advance and keep it refrigerated in a tightly sealed container. Reheat the sauce over medium heat until warm, stirring constantly.

PRUNE SAUCE

MAKES 2½ CUPS

1 cup pitted prunes (about 12 large prunes), chopped fine

2 tablespoons sugar

¼ teaspoon ground cinnamon

½ cup red wine

2 tablespoons fresh lemon juice, plus 1 tablespoon grated zest

1 tablespoon cold unsalted butter

1. Place the prunes, sugar, and cinnamon in a medium saucepan, pour in the wine, lemon juice, and 1½ cups water and bring to a boil over high heat. Cover, reduce the heat to low, and simmer for 15 minutes, stirring occasionally.

2. Remove the saucepan from the heat. Add the lemon zest and butter and stir until all the butter has melted into the sauce. Serve warm spooned over the *dampfnudeln*. You can also make the sauce up to 3 days in advance and keep it refrigerated in a tightly sealed container. Reheat the sauce over medium heat until warm, stirring constantly.

STEAMED BUNS COOKED IN PRUNE SAUCE

Instead of pouring the finished sauce over the *dampfnudeln*, thin it out with 1½ cups water. Use this in place of the milk mixture to cook the dumplings.

Cloud-Shaped Bread Buns

Ting Momo (Tibet)

SERVES 4 TO 8 (MAKES 8 DUMPLINGS)

These whole wheat buns can be found in several different shapes. We like the frilly Fan-Knot Fold because it steams up light and airy and also lets you tear into it layer by layer. The fold may look complicated, but it's really as simple as stacking a few strips of dough on top of one another and tying them off into a knot. Turmeric oil and a sprinkling of salt help to enhance the natural sweetness of the whole wheat.

These dumplings are made using the Fan-Knot Fold (page 44).

For the Dumplings

1 cup warm water, preferably nonchlorinated, such as distilled or spring water

¼ teaspoon sugar

1¼ teaspoons active dry yeast (about ½ packet)

1⅓ cups whole wheat flour

⅔ cup unbleached all-purpose flour, plus some extra for dusting

½ teaspoon baking powder

For the Glaze

½ teaspoon ground turmeric

½ teaspoon salt

2 tablespoons grapeseed or other neutral oil

For Cooking

Grapeseed or other neutral oil to coat the steamer basket

Equipment

8- to 10-quart steamer pot

1. PROOF THE YEAST: Pour the warm water into a small bowl, stir in the sugar and the yeast, and proof for 15 minutes. The surface should become foamy. If not, start again with a new yeast packet.

2. MAKE THE DOUGH: While the yeast proofs, combine the flours in a large bowl. Scoop out ¼ cup and set aside. Mix in the baking powder. Pour in the yeasty water and mix until all the liquid has been absorbed. Work the dough with your hands into one manageable ball. If the dough is wet and sticky, work in some of the reserved flour mixture, a little at a time, until it no longer sticks to your fingers.

3. Place the dough on a floured surface and knead for 4 to 5 minutes. The dough will be soft and tacky. Return the dough to the bowl, cover with a damp kitchen towel, and set aside in a warm place for 1½ to 2 hours. The dough will double in size. Use the Proofing Pot Setup (page 36) if the temperature of the room is not ideal.

4. ASSEMBLE THE DUMPLINGS: *Before assembling the* ting momo, *review the Fan-Knot Fold.*

5. Line a tray with a kitchen towel and sprinkle with a little all-purpose flour.

6. Punch down the dough, place on a floured surface, and knead once or twice. Sprinkle with flour if it gets a little sticky. Divide the dough in half, then shape one piece into a blunt log. Roll it out into an 8 × 12-inch rectangle about ⅛ inch thick. Cut the dough into strips every ¾ inch along the 8-inch side. You will have 16 strips.

7. Stack 4 dough strips on top of each other. They don't need to line up exactly. Bend the dough strips around into a loop, and push one end of the stack through the loop, creating a simple knot. Gently fan out or nudge apart the strips to make the layers more apparent, tuck in any loose ends, and place on the prepared tray. If you are short a strip or two, use what you have. Repeat with the remaining dough.

8. STEAM THE DUMPLINGS: Remove the basket from a large steamer pot, add 2 inches of water to the pot, and bring to a boil over high heat. Coat the bottom of the basket with oil and arrange as many of the knotted buns, about 1 inch apart, as you can.

9. Combine the turmeric, salt, and oil in a small bowl. Brush a thin coating of the turmeric oil over each bun. Place the basket in the pot, cover, reduce the heat to medium-high, and steam for 15 minutes.

10. Remove the pot from the heat. Carefully remove the basket, place it on a folded kitchen towel, and allow the *ting momo* to cool slightly. Place them on a plate and keep warm. Cook any remaining buns and serve. *Ting momo* can be refrigerated for up to 3 days or frozen (see page 36) for up to 6 months. Reheat them in a steamer pot or use the Steamer Plate Setup (page 37). If reheating frozen *ting momo*, allow them to thaw before steaming.

Steamed Bread Loaves Stuffed with Sticky Fried Rice

Nuo Mi Juan (China)

SERVES 4 TO 8 (MAKES 2 DUMPLINGS)

Stuffed inside this soft, slightly sweet dough is a filling of chewy sticky rice seasoned with bits of dried sausage, shrimp, and shallots. If it seems peculiar to you at first to eat a steamed bun that's stuffed with rice, you'll soon appreciate the unique balance of flavors and textures. Slices of this traditional dim sum offering also make an excellent snack.

For the Dough

1 recipe *Mantou* (page 72) dough, preferably made while the rice is steaming but no more than 2 hours in advance

Unbleached all-purpose flour for dusting

For the Filling

1 cup short-grain sweet (glutinous) white rice, preferably from China or Japan, rinsed (see page 18)

10 to 12 small or medium dried shrimp, soaked in hot water to cover for 30 minutes

¼ cup grapeseed or other neutral oil

1 link Chinese pork sausage (*la chang*), chopped fine

2 scallions, sliced into thin rings

1 tablespoon soy sauce

1 teaspoon salt

¼ teaspoon freshly ground white pepper

Equipment

8- to 10-quart steamer pot

24-inch square of muslin

1. STEAM THE RICE: Remove the basket from the steamer pot, add 2 inches of water to the pot, and bring to a boil over high heat. Soak the muslin under running water, wring it out, and then drape it inside the basket, creating a lining. Scoop the rice into the lined basket and spread it out evenly. Place the basket in the pot, cover, reduce the heat to medium, and steam for 40 minutes. Every 10 minutes, drizzle ⅓ cup water over the rice, mix gently, cover again, and continue steaming.

2. Remove the pot from the heat. Carefully remove the basket and place it on a folded kitchen towel and set aside to cool.

3. COOK THE FILLING: Drain and finely chop the shrimp. Once the rice has cooled, heat the oil in a large skillet over high heat. Add the sausage, shrimp, and scallion and stir continuously for 1 minute. Add the cooled rice and break up clumps with a wooden spoon. Immediately add the soy sauce and mix in the salt and pepper. Stir vigorously until combined. Move the rice onto a large plate and spread it out to cool to room temperature. (You can make the filling in advance and keep it tightly wrapped in the refrigerator for up to 3 days.)

4. ASSEMBLE THE DUMPLINGS: Line a tray with a kitchen towel and sprinkle with a little flour. Have ready the dough and the cooled rice.

5. Knead the dough once or twice on a floured surface and divide it in half. Shape one piece into a blunt log, then roll it out into a 6 × 9-inch rectangle. Sprinkle with flour if it gets sticky.

6. Divide the cooled rice mixture in half and, with wet hands, shape each half into an 8-inch-long log. Center the rice log, lengthwise, on top of the dough. Pick up one side of the dough, then the other, so that their edges can meet on top of the rice log. Pinch the edges of the dough together to seal while gently pressing out any air, then pinch and seal the loaf at each open end. The rice filling should be completely surrounded by dough. Place the assembled dumpling on the prepared tray and repeat with the remaining dough and rice.

7. STEAM THE DUMPLINGS: Remove the basket from the steamer pot, coat the basket with oil, and arrange the 2 loaves in the basket, seam side down, leaving at least 1½ inches of space between them. Set aside in a warm place and allow them to rise for 10 minutes.

8. Meanwhile, add 2 inches of water to the steamer pot and bring to a boil over high heat. Place the basket in the pot, cover, reduce the heat to medium-high, and steam for 20 minutes.

9. Remove the pot from the heat. Carefully remove the basket, place it on a folded kitchen towel, and allow the loaves to cool slightly. Move them to a large plate, cut them into 2-inch slices, and serve. *Nuo mi juan* can be refrigerated for up to 3 days or frozen (see page 36) for up to 6 months. Reheat them in a steamer pot or use the Steamer Plate Setup (page 37). If reheating frozen *nuo mi juan*, allow them to thaw before steaming.

Potato Dumplings Stuffed with Ham

Kroppkakor (Sweden)

SERVES 4 TO 8 (MAKES 8 DUMPLINGS)

These potato dumplings are a wonderful way to use up a small amount of leftover ham. Sautéed with onions and allspice, the ham becomes a flavorful stuffing inside a hearty potato shell made from a mixture of raw and cooked potatoes. Serve them up with the traditional side of lingonberry jam.

These dumplings are made using the Bowl Fold (page 45).

For the Filling

2 tablespoons unsalted butter

1 small yellow onion, chopped fine

½ pound unsmoked salt-cured ham, cut into ¼-inch cubes

½ teaspoon ground allspice

For the Dough

4 medium baking potatoes, such as russet

1 teaspoon salt

½ cup unbleached all-purpose flour or ¼ cup all-purpose flour mixed with ¼ cup barley flour

1 large egg, beaten

Unbleached all-purpose flour for dusting

For the Topping

4 tablespoons (½ stick) unsalted butter, melted just before serving

½ cup lingonberry jam

1. MAKE THE FILLING: Melt the 2 tablespoons butter in a medium skillet over medium heat. Add the onion and stir frequently until soft, about 4 minutes. Mix in the ham and allspice and continue stirring until both ham and onion are just beginning to brown, about 2 minutes. Remove from the heat, scoop the mixture into a bowl, and set aside to cool.

2. MAKE THE DOUGH: Place 2 of the potatoes in a small pot, pour in enough water to cover, and bring to a boil over high heat. Cover, reduce the heat to medium, and simmer until fork-tender, about 30 minutes. Drain and place the potatoes on a folded kitchen towel. Once they are cool enough to handle, peel off their skins and put the flesh in a large bowl. Mash until mostly smooth.

3. Peel the 2 raw potatoes and grate them through the finer holes of your box grater onto a kitchen towel. Bring together the ends of the cloth and twist to squeeze out as much of the potato juice as you can. Do this step in batches if it seems more effective.

4. Add the grated potato to the mashed potato along with the salt and ¼ cup of the flour or flour mixture, keeping the remaining ¼ cup of flour handy. Toss with your fingers until well mixed. Add the egg and work it into the mixture until you have a moist dough, about

2 minutes. This dough needs to be firm enough to hold its shape when rolled into balls. If it is too soft or sticky, work in some of the remaining flour, a little at a time.

5. ASSEMBLE THE DUMPLINGS: *Before assembling the* kroppkakor, *review the Bowl Fold.*

6. Line a tray with a kitchen towel and sprinkle with a little flour. Have ready the potato dough and the cooled ham mixture.

7. Fill a medium pot halfway with salted water and bring to a boil over high heat.

8. Meanwhile, place the dough on a floured surface. Use your hands to roll the log back and forth until it's 12 inches long. Cut the log into 8 equal pieces, roll each piece into a ball, dust with flour, and place on the prepared tray. Once the water is boiling, reduce the heat to very low to keep it hot while you assemble the dumplings.

9. Pick up one dough ball and use your thumbs to shape it into a bowl about 2 inches deep. This will be a wide bowl that is best supported in the palm of your hand. Place a rounded tablespoon of filling in the center of the dough bowl. Close by pushing and pinching the edges of the dough around and over the filling until the filling is surrounded, pushing out any air. Dab a little water along the edges, if needed, for a better seal. Reroll into a ball, dust with more flour, and place back on the tray.

10. COOK THE DUMPLINGS: Once all the dumplings have been assembled, bring the water back to a boil over high heat. Reduce the heat to medium for a steady simmer. Carefully drop the dumplings, one by one, into the water. Cover and simmer for 10 minutes, stirring occasionally to prevent sticking.

11. Remove the *kroppkakor* with a slotted spoon and place them in a shallow serving bowl. Drizzle with the melted butter and serve with lingonberry jam.

Silesian Potato Dumplings with Mushroom Sauce

Kluski Śląskie (Poland)

SERVES 4 (MAKES ABOUT 35 DUMPLINGS)

Kluski are potato dumplings with a unique shape that makes it possible for them to cook evenly despite their large size. A thumbprint is pressed deep into their centers to allow them to cook quickly. These dumplings are traditionally served with melted butter, fried bread crumbs, or a rich mushroom sauce.

For the Sauce

½ ounce dried mushrooms, preferably porcini, soaked in 1½ cups hot water for 30 minutes

3 tablespoons unsalted butter, cut into chunks

1 small yellow onion, chopped fine

4 ounces fresh mushrooms, such as cremini or oyster, sliced thin

1 tablespoon unbleached all-purpose flour

½ teaspoon salt

¼ teaspoon freshly ground black pepper

¼ cup sour cream

¼ cup finely chopped fresh chives

For the Dumplings

3 medium baking potatoes, such as russet

1½ teaspoons salt

1¾ cups unbleached all-purpose flour, plus some extra for dusting

1 large egg, beaten

Equipment

Potato ricer

Large, wide bowl to hold the dumplings cooked in batches

1. MAKE THE SAUCE: Fish out the soaked mushrooms with your fingers, squeezing the excess liquid back into the bowl. Set the liquid aside and finely chop the mushrooms. Strain all of the soaking liquid and set aside.

2. Melt the butter in a small pot over medium heat. Add the onion and stir until soft, about 4 minutes. Mix in the fresh and the soaked mushrooms and cook for 3 minutes longer, stirring occasionally. Sprinkle in the 1 tablespoon flour and stir until combined.

3. Pour in the reserved soaking liquid and scrape up any sticky bits from the bottom of the pot with a wooden spoon. Stir in the ½ teaspoon salt and the pepper. Cover, reduce the heat to low, and simmer for 30 minutes. Remove the pot from the heat and set aside. (You can make the sauce up to 3 days in advance and keep it refrigerated in a tightly sealed container.)

4. MAKE THE DOUGH: While the sauce is simmering, place the potatoes in a pot, pour in enough water to cover them, and bring to a boil over high heat. Cover, reduce the heat to medium, and simmer until fork-tender, about 30 minutes. Drain and place the potatoes on a folded kitchen towel. Once they're cool enough to handle, peel off their skins, cut the potatoes into chunks, and press them through the ricer into a large bowl.

5. Sprinkle the 1½ teaspoons salt and 1½ cups of the flour over the potato, keeping the remaining ¼ cup of flour handy, and toss with your fingers until mixed evenly. Add the egg and work the dough with your hands into one manageable ball. If the dough is wet and gooey, work in some of the remaining flour, a little at a time, until it no longer sticks to your fingers. Knead the dough in the bowl for about 1 minute. The dough will be soft and just a little sticky.

6. MAKE THE DUMPLINGS: Line a tray with a kitchen towel and sprinkle with a little flour.

7. Pinch off a small piece of dough and roll into a ball about 1½ inches around. Push your thumb into the center, without poking through, to create a deep dimple, and place on the prepared tray.

8. COOK THE DUMPLINGS: Fill a large pot three-quarters of the way with salted water, place over high heat, and bring to a boil. Reduce the heat to medium for a steady simmer. Gently drop half of the dumplings, a few at a time, into the water. Stir carefully to prevent sticking. Cook until all of them are floating, about 4 minutes, then cook for 2 minutes longer.

9. Remove the dumplings with a slotted spoon, place them in the large bowl, and drizzle with a ladle of the cooking liquid to prevent sticking. Cook the remaining dumplings and place in the bowl with another ladle of the cooking liquid.

10. Reheat the mushroom sauce, stirring occasionally, over medium heat. Reduce the heat to low, add the sour cream, and cook for 2 minutes, stirring continuously. Drain the *kluski* and turn them into the mushroom sauce. Toss and stir the *kluski* in the sauce, mix in the chopped chives, simmer for 1 minute to heat through, and serve.

Chestnut Gnocchi with Walnut Sauce

Gnocchi di Castagne con Salsa di Noci (Italy)

SERVES 4 TO 6

Chestnut flour gives these otherwise standard potato gnocchi a nutty and slightly bittersweet flavor that becomes mellow and fragrant when they are smothered in a walnut sauce. This particular walnut sauce is a plain white sauce (*besciamella*) flavored with fresh walnut paste. Peeling the membranelike skins off the walnut halves takes a couple of minutes, but it is well worth the extra effort and creates a sweeter sauce.

Chestnut flour is made from small garessina chestnuts, which are quite different from the larger, more common marroni chestnuts. It is a seasonal flour that is mostly available in the winter and is best kept in the freezer because of its high fat content.

For the Sauce*

- 1 cup raw walnut halves
- 4 garlic cloves, chopped coarse
- ¼ cup olive oil
- 1½ tablespoons unsalted butter
- 2 tablespoons unbleached all-purpose flour
- 1¾ cups milk
- ½ teaspoon salt
- ¼ teaspoon freshly ground black pepper
- ¼ cup coarsely chopped fresh marjoram leaves
- ½ cup freshly grated Parmesan cheese

For the Dumplings

- 3 medium baking potatoes, such as russet
- ¾ cup chestnut flour
- ½ cup unbleached all-purpose flour, plus some extra for dusting
- 1 teaspoon salt

Equipment

Potato ricer

Gnocchi board (optional)

Large plate or tray to hold the dumplings cooked in batches

1. PREPARE THE WALNUTS: Fill a small saucepan halfway with water and bring to a boil over high heat. Reduce the heat to low for a gentle simmer. Add the nuts and simmer for 10 minutes. Remove the nuts from the heat, drain, and run under cold water until cool. Peel off the skins as best you can. (We found starting in the center of the nut made it a little easier.) Place the peeled nuts in a bowl and set aside.

2. MAKE THE DOUGH: Place the potatoes in a small pot, pour in enough water to cover, and bring to a boil over high heat. Cover, reduce the heat to medium, and simmer until fork-tender, about 30 minutes. Drain and place the potatoes on a folded kitchen towel. Once they are cool enough to handle, peel off and discard their skins, break them into chunks, and then press through the ricer into a large bowl.

---

*These amounts are for a full recipe. If you plan on freezing and storing some of the dumplings, reduce the amounts in proportion to the number you are serving.

3. Combine the flours in a small bowl. Scoop out ¼ cup and set aside. Add the 1 teaspoon salt and the remaining flour mixture to the potato. Toss with your fingers until mixed evenly. Drizzle in ⅓ cup water and work the dough with your hands into one manageable ball. If the dough is too wet and sticky, work in some of the reserved flour mixture, a little at a time, until it no longer sticks to your fingers. Knead the dough in the bowl for about 1 minute. The dough will be soft and slightly sticky.

4. MAKE THE DUMPLINGS: Line a tray with a kitchen towel and sprinkle with a little flour.

5. Knead the dough once or twice on a floured surface, divide it into 8 equal pieces, and set 7 of them aside under a kitchen towel. Roll the remaining piece of dough into a rope about ½ inch thick. Cut the rope into ¾-inch lengths.

6. If you don't want ridges on your gnocchi, place the cut dough pieces on the prepared tray in a single layer. If you do want ridges, roll each piece along the gnocchi board or along the tines of a fork. Roll the piece along the back of the fork to avoid catching it on the ends of the tines. Arrange the gnocchi in one layer on the prepared tray. Repeat with the remaining dough.

7. Cover and place the tray of dumplings in the refrigerator while you make the sauce. Set aside the number of dumplings that you would like to cook and keep the rest frozen for up to 6 months (see page 36).

8. MAKE THE SAUCE: Fill a large pot halfway with salted water and bring to a boil over high heat. Once it comes to a boil, reduce the heat to low for a gentle simmer.

9. Meanwhile, pulse the walnuts and the garlic in a food processor until the walnuts are well broken apart. Continue to process while slowly drizzling in the oil until the mixture becomes a thick, grainy paste. Scrape down the sides of the processor bowl and scoop the paste into a bowl.

10. Melt the butter in a medium pot over low heat, add the 2 tablespoons flour, and stir continuously for 3 minutes. Pour the milk in slowly, whisking constantly. Once the mixture is smooth, raise the heat to medium and bring to a simmer. Mix in the walnut paste, ½ teaspoon salt, and the pepper and simmer for 1 minute longer. Cover and reduce the heat to very, very low to keep the sauce warm while cooking the gnocchi. (You can also make the sauce up to 3 days in advance and keep it refrigerated in a tightly sealed container.)

11. COOK THE DUMPLINGS: Bring the water back to a boil over high heat, then reduce the heat to medium for a steady simmer. Carefully drop a few dozen gnocchi, a few at a time, into the water. Cook until the gnocchi float to the surface of the water, about 2 minutes, then cook for 2 minutes longer. (If cooking frozen gnocchi, add them directly into the simmering water and increase the cooking time by 1 minute. Do not allow the gnocchi to thaw before cooking.

12. Remove the gnocchi with a slotted spoon, scatter them on the large plate or tray, and drizzle with a few spoonfuls of the cooking liquid to prevent sticking. Resting the cooked gnocchi on a roomy plate prevents them from piling up on each other while they set and firm up a bit. Cook the remaining gnocchi and place them on the plate with another few spoonfuls of the cooking liquid. Set aside ½ cup of the cooking liquid for the sauce.

13. Once all the gnocchi have been cooked, return the sauce to a simmer over medium heat. Drain the gnocchi, mix them into the sauce, and cook for 1 minute to warm through. If the sauce is a little thick, stir in some of the reserved cooking liquid. Remove from the heat, stir in the marjoram and the Parmesan, and serve.

Panfried Dumplings Stuffed with Chicken and Mushrooms

Jiao Zi (China)

SERVES 4 TO 8 (MAKES ABOUT 32 DUMPLINGS)

Most versions of these pot sticker dumplings are stuffed with a pork-based filling, but this one, made with chicken and mushrooms, is especially delicious. The pairing of dark-meat chicken and dried shiitake mushrooms is distinctly Chinese (see *Nuo Mi Juan*, February), and it gives these dumplings a fragrant, gamy taste. If the pork dumplings are what you crave, however, you can make this recipe using the filling from the *Zhu Rou Baozi* (May).

These dumplings are made using the Pleated Half-Moon Fold (page 46), but you can also use the simpler Standing Half-Moon Fold (page 48).

For the Dough

2¼ cups unbleached all-purpose flour, plus some extra for dusting

1 tablespoon grapeseed or other neutral oil

For the Filling

3 dried shiitake or black mushrooms, soaked in hot water to cover for 30 minutes

2 boneless, skinless chicken thighs (about ½ pound), chopped fine

5 to 6 fresh water chestnuts, peeled and chopped fine, or canned water chestnuts, drained and chopped fine

2 scallions, trimmed and sliced into thin rings

1 teaspoon grated fresh ginger

1 teaspoon cornstarch

2 tablespoons soy sauce

1 teaspoon rice wine

1 tablespoon toasted sesame oil

½ teaspoon salt

½ teaspoon freshly ground white pepper

For Cooking and Serving

Grapeseed or other neutral oil to coat a large skillet

1 cup water mixed with 1 teaspoon unbleached all-purpose flour

1 recipe Soy-Vinegar Sauce* (recipe follows)

Equipment

3¼-inch round cookie cutter

Large, preferably nonstick skillet with cover

1. MAKE THE DOUGH: Place 2 cups of the flour in a large bowl and keep the remaining ¼ cup handy. Add the oil and 1 cup water and mix until all the liquid has been absorbed. Work the dough with your hands into one manageable ball. If the dough is wet and sticky,

---

*This is for a full recipe. If you plan on freezing and storing some of the dumplings, reduce the amounts in proportion to the number you are serving.

work in some of the remaining flour, a little at a time, until it no longer sticks to your fingers.

2. Place the dough on a floured surface and knead for 2 to 3 minutes. The dough will be somewhat firm and elastic. Coat the dough with a little oil, return it to the bowl, cover with a clean kitchen towel, and let it rest for 30 minutes.

3. MAKE THE FILLING: While the dough is resting, drain the mushrooms and squeeze out any excess liquid. Remove and discard the stems, finely chop the mushroom caps, and place them in a medium bowl along with the other filling ingredients. Mix together well and keep refrigerated until you are ready to assemble the dumplings.

4. ASSEMBLE THE DUMPLINGS: *Before assembling the* jiao zi, *review the Pleated Half-Moon Fold.*

5. Line a tray with a kitchen towel and sprinkle with a little flour. Also have ready the dough and the filling.

6. Knead the dough once or twice on a floured surface, divide it into 4 equal pieces, and set 3 of them aside under a kitchen towel. Shape the remaining piece into a ball, then roll it out until about ⅛ inch thick. Sprinkle with flour if it gets sticky. Let the rolled-out dough relax for a couple of minutes before cutting out rounds.

7. Using the cookie cutter, cut out as many rounds as you can, usually 7 or 8. Collect the leftover dough and put it aside under a damp kitchen towel for later use.

8. Pick up 1 dough round and pleat and pinch one side. This will pull the round into a bowl shape. Place a rounded tablespoon of filling in the center. Bring together the edges, pushing out any air, and pinch along the top of the dumpling to seal. Place the dumpling, pleated side up, on the prepared tray. Repeat with the remaining rounds and filling. Keep the assembled dumplings in a single layer on the tray, covered with a kitchen towel as you work. Once you have assembled the first batch of dumplings, continue with the remaining dough and filling. Combine all the dough scraps, knead them into a ball, roll it out, cut out as many rounds as you can, and fill and fold those too.

9. Set aside the number of dumplings that you would like to cook and keep the rest frozen for up to 6 months (see page 36).

10. COOK THE DUMPLINGS: Generously coat a large skillet with oil and heat it over medium heat. Arrange the dumplings in the pan, pleated side up, leaving a little space around each. Cook until the bottoms just begin to brown. Choose an empty spot in the pan and pour in enough of the flour and water mixture to reach about a third of the way up the sides of the dumplings. Cover and simmer for 10 minutes. (If cooking frozen *jiao zi*, add them directly to the oil and increase the cooking time by 3 minutes. Do not allow the dumplings to thaw before cooking.)

11. Remove the cover so that any remaining liquid can cook off completely. Continue cooking until you hear a strong sizzling sound and the bottoms of the dumplings are golden brown and crisp.

12. Remove the *jiao zi* with a small spatula and place them on a plate. Serve immediately while you cook any remaining *jiao zi*. Serve with the Soy-Vinegar Sauce.

SOY-VINEGAR SAUCE

MAKES ABOUT ½ CUP

¼ cup soy sauce

3 tablespoons rice vinegar

2 teaspoons sugar

1 teaspoon toasted sesame oil

1 tablespoon finely chopped scallion

Combine the soy sauce, rice vinegar, sugar, and sesame oil in a small bowl. Stir until the sugar has dissolved. Pour into small dipping bowls and add the scallion just before using. This sauce will keep for up to 1 week in the refrigerator in a tightly sealed container.

March

STEAMED CORN BREAD
(United States) 114

SWEET POTATO DUMPLINGS WITH A MELTED SUGAR CENTER
Onde-Onde (Malaysia)..115

TINY GNOCCHI AND CRANBERRY BEAN STEW
Pisarei e Faso (Italy) 118

CAULIFLOWER SOUP WITH BUTTERY BREAD CRUMB DUMPLINGS
Květáková Polévka s Knedlíky (Czech Republic) 121

COCKLES WITH RICE DUMPLINGS IN A SPICY COCONUT SAUCE
Kube Mutli (India) 123

CHICKPEA DUMPLINGS IN TOMATO SAUCE
Chana Vada ki Tomatochi Bhaji (India) 125

KASHA AND MUSHROOM PIEROGI
Pierogi z Kaszą Gryczaną (Poland) 127

RICE DUMPLINGS STUFFED WITH PORK AND KOHLRABI
Fen Guo (China)...130

Steamed Corn Bread

(United States)

SERVES 6 TO 8 (MAKES 1 DUMPLING)

Steaming corn bread instead of baking it makes it especially moist and flavorful. You can stir some corn kernels into the batter for a chunkier texture and an even deeper corn taste. Serve it up with some butter for a scrumptious side dish or snack. And as with baked corn bread, any leftovers can be used to make stuffing or bread pudding.

For the Dumpling

1 cup coarse yellow cornmeal

⅓ cup unbleached all-purpose flour

1 teaspoon baking powder

¾ teaspoon baking soda

1 teaspoon salt

½ teaspoon freshly grated nutmeg

1 large egg, beaten

1 cup milk

2 tablespoons light muscovado or other unrefined sugar (see page 20)

2 tablespoons unsalted butter, melted

½ cup fresh corn kernels or frozen, thawed (optional)

For Cooking

Unsalted butter to coat the cake pan

Equipment

2-inch-high steamer rack

9-inch round cake pan

Pot large enough to hold both the rack and the pan when covered

1. Place the steamer rack in the pot, add 1½ inches of water to the pot, and bring to a boil over high heat. Meanwhile, rub a little butter around the inside of the cake pan.

2. Combine the cornmeal, flour, baking powder, baking soda, salt, and nutmeg in a large bowl. In another bowl, whisk the egg, milk, sugar, and melted butter until the sugar has mostly dissolved. Pour the egg mixture into the cornmeal mixture, add the corn kernels, if desired, and stir until just combined. Pour the batter into the prepared cake pan and wiggle it gently to level it off.

3. Carefully place the filled cake pan on the steamer rack, cover the pot, reduce the heat to medium, and steam for 25 to 30 minutes.

4. Remove the pot from the heat. Carefully lift the pan out of the pot, place it on a folded kitchen towel, and allow the corn bread to cool slightly. Slice and serve warm or at room temperature.

Sweet Potato Dumplings with a Melted Sugar Center

Onde-Onde (Malaysia)

SERVES 4 TO 8 (MAKES ABOUT 40 DUMPLINGS)

These modest-looking dessert dumplings will surprise you. Inside each strawberry-sized dumpling is a warm sugar center that floods your mouth with a lush, buttery flavor. Making these dumplings may seem like a challenge, but it is surprisingly easy. The balls of dough are stuffed with a small piece of tasty palm sugar, and as the dumplings cook, the sugar melts slowly into syrup. If you can't find palm sugar, use jaggery or *panela* (see page 20) instead. Adding mashed sweet potato to the dough gives the *onde-onde* its pale orange color and a mild fruit flavor.

These dumplings are made by pushing a piece of sugar into a dough ball, but they can also be made using the Bowl Fold (page 45).

For the Filling

2 ounces hard palm sugar or ¼ cup soft palm sugar or other unrefined sugar (see page 20)

For the Dough

1 small sweet potato (about ½ pound)

1¼ cups sweet (glutinous) rice flour, preferably from Malaysia or Thailand, plus some extra for dusting

3 tablespoons pandan water (recipe follows) or ¼ teaspoon pandan extract mixed into 3 tablespoons water

For Serving

1 cup freshly grated coconut (see page 8), or 1 cup frozen grated coconut, thawed

¼ teaspoon salt

Equipment

Potato ricer

Large, wide bowl to hold the cooked dumplings

1. MAKE THE FILLING: Depending on the type of palm sugar you are using, you will need to cut or roll the sugar into small ½-inch pieces. If using hard palm sugar, cut the sugar into small pieces and pick out as many ½-inch chunks as you can. Collect any crumbs or loose bits of sugar and pack them into balls about the size of a pea by pressing and rubbing them between damp fingers. If using soft palm sugar, use a small spoon to scoop up about ¼ teaspoon sugar and compress the sugar into a ball with your fingers. When you have 40 sugar pieces or balls, place them on a plate and set aside.

2. BOIL THE SWEET POTATO: Place the sweet potato in a small saucepan, pour in enough water to cover, and bring to a boil over high heat. Cover, reduce the heat to medium, and simmer until fork-tender, about 20 minutes. Drain and place the sweet potato on a folded kitchen towel. Once it's cool enough to handle, peel off its skin, break it into chunks, and press through the ricer into a small bowl.

3. Move the sweet potato onto a clean kitchen towel and pat it down into a circle about 6 inches wide. Fold the towel over or use a paper towel to soak up as much excess liquid as you can. Turn the sweet potato back into the bowl.

4. MAKE AND ASSEMBLE THE DUMPLINGS: *This is a very soft dough, and often the sugar piece can be pushed into the center of the dough ball. Using the Bowl Fold can help make centering the sugar even easier.*

5. Line a tray with a kitchen towel and sprinkle with a little rice flour. Also have ready the sugar pieces and all the dough ingredients.

6. Place 1 cup of the rice flour in a large bowl and keep the remaining ¼ cup handy. Add the sweet potato and toss with your fingers until well mixed. Add the pandan water and use your hands to work the mixture into a dough. This dough needs to be firm enough to hold its shape when rolled into balls. If it is too soft and sticky, work in some of the remaining flour, a little at a time.

7. Pinch off a very small piece of dough and roll it into a ball about ¾ inch around. Keep the remaining dough covered with a kitchen towel as you work. Use your thumbs to shape it into a bowl, just large enough to cradle a piece of sugar. Place one piece of sugar in the center of the dough bowl. Close by pushing and pinching the edges of the dough around and over the filling until the sugar is surrounded, pushing out any air. Dab a little water along the edges, if needed, for a better seal. Reroll into a ball, dust with flour, and place on the prepared tray. Repeat with the remaining dough and filling.

8. COOK AND COAT THE DUMPLINGS: Spread the grated coconut out on a large plate and sprinkle it with the salt.

9. Fill a large pot halfway with water and bring to a boil over high heat. Reduce the heat to medium for a steady simmer. Add the dumplings to the water a few at a time and stir gently. Cook until all of them are floating, 2 to 3 minutes, then cook for 2 minutes longer.

10. Remove the pot from the heat. Use a slotted spoon to remove the dumplings, place them in the large bowl, and drizzle with a ladle of the cooking liquid to prevent sticking.

11. Pick up 2 to 6 *onde-onde* and roll them around on the grated coconut. If they are at all dry, dampen their surfaces with your fingers to ensure an even coating. Place them on a plate and continue with the remaining *onde-onde*. Serve warm or at room temperature. *Onde-onde* can be refrigerated for up to 2 days. Allow them to come back to room temperature before serving.

PANDAN WATER

MAKES ½ CUP

20 large fresh pandan leaves, or frozen, thawed, chopped coarse

1. Pulse the pandan leaves once or twice in a food processor to start breaking down their fibers. Add ½ cup water and process for 2 minutes, scraping down the sides as you go. The pureed pandan bits will be very fibrous, and the water will turn a deep olive green.

2. Strain the pandan liquid through a sieve into a small bowl. Squeeze out any excess water from the pandan leaves. Measure out what you need for your recipe and keep the rest frozen for up to 6 months.

Tiny Gnocchi and Cranberry Bean Stew

Pisarei e Faso (Italy)

SERVES 4

A pot of stewed beans becomes an unusual and delectable dish when mixed with an equal quantity of tender yet chewy bean-sized dumplings. You can serve this dish as a side or as a meal with a simple salad. Such a large number of dumplings may take a little extra time to roll out and cut, but they're worth the effort. You may choose to curl the *pisarei* by gently pressing and slightly squishing each one along your work surface. This optional step gives the dumpling a dimple, which allows more sauce to cling to it.

For the Stew

1½ cups dried cranberry beans *(borlotti)* or pinto beans, soaked in plenty of water for 6 to 8 hours or 3 cups canned

2 tablespoons olive oil

¼ pound pancetta or 4 strips bacon, chopped fine (about ½ cup)

1 medium yellow onion, chopped fine

1 medium carrot, chopped fine

1 celery rib, chopped fine

1 tablespoon coarsely chopped fresh rosemary or 1 teaspoon dried

½ cup coarsely chopped fresh flat-leaf parsley leaves

3 garlic cloves, chopped fine

4 ripe plum tomatoes, peeled (see page 21) and crushed, or 4 canned plum tomatoes, drained and crushed (about 1 cup)

1 tablespoon tomato paste

1 teaspoon salt

½ teaspoon freshly ground black pepper

¼ cup coarsely chopped fresh basil leaves

½ cup freshly grated Parmesan cheese

For the Dumplings

2 cups unbleached all-purpose flour, plus some extra for dusting

¾ cup coarse dry crustless white bread crumbs (see page 6)

½ teaspoon salt

Equipment

Large, wide bowl to hold the dumplings cooked in batches

1. MAKE THE STEW: Drain the beans. Heat the oil in a medium pot over medium heat and add the pancetta. Stir occasionally and cook until just beginning to crisp, about 2 minutes. Mix in the onion, carrot, celery, and rosemary and stir frequently until the onion is soft, about 4 minutes. Stir in the parsley and garlic and cook for 2 minutes longer. Pour in 5 cups water. Immediately stir in the beans, tomatoes, tomato paste, 1 teaspoon salt, and the pepper. Raise the heat to high and bring to a boil. Cover, reduce the heat to low, and cook, stirring occasionally, until the beans are fork-tender, 1½ to 2 hours. (You can also make the stew up to 3 days in advance and keep it refrigerated in a tightly sealed container. If the stew is too thick to stir easily, add a little water to thin it out.)

2. MAKE THE DOUGH: While the stew is simmering, place 1¾ cups of the flour in a large heatproof bowl and keep the remaining ¼ cup handy. Add the bread crumbs and the ½ teaspoon salt and mix well.

3. Heat ¾ cup water in a small saucepan over medium heat until it is hot to the touch but not close to simmering. Pour the hot water into the flour mixture and mix until all the liquid has been absorbed. Let the dough cool slightly.

4. Carefully work the dough with your hands. If this is uncomfortable in any way, let it cool for another minute or two, but keep in mind that you need to work with this dough while it is still very, very warm. Work the dough in the bowl into one manageable ball. If the dough is too wet and sticky, work in some of the remaining flour, a little at a time, until it no longer sticks to your fingers.

5. Place the dough on a floured surface and knead for 3 to 4 minutes. Cover and let rest for 15 minutes at room temperature.

6. MAKE THE DUMPLINGS: Line a tray with a kitchen towel and sprinkle with a little flour.

7. Knead the dough once or twice on a floured surface, divide it into 8 equal pieces, and set 7 of them aside under a kitchen towel. Roll the remaining piece into a rope about ¼ inch thick, and cut it into ½-inch pieces.

8. If you don't want to curl the dumplings, place the cut dough pieces in a single layer on the prepared tray. If you do want to curl them, push your finger into the center of a cut piece of dough and gently squish and roll it toward you just long enough to create a deep dimple or a fat "C" shape. Place in a single layer on the prepared tray. Repeat with the remaining dough. Once all the *pisarei* have been cut, cover them with a kitchen towel and refrigerate until you are ready to add them to the stew.

9. Once the stew has cooked for 1½ to 2 hours, the level of the sauce should be slightly below the beans. Give it a good stir and mix in a little water if there is not enough sauce. Cover and reduce the heat to very, very low to keep the stew hot until it's time to add the dumplings.

10. COOK THE DUMPLINGS: Fill a large pot halfway with salted water and bring to a boil over high heat. Reduce the heat to medium for a steady simmer.

11. Move half of the dumplings onto a plate, slide them into the simmering water, and stir gently to prevent sticking. Cook until all of the dumplings are floating, about 2 minutes.

12. Remove the dumplings with a slotted spoon, place them in the large bowl, drizzle them with a ladle of the cooking liquid to prevent sticking. Cook the remaining dumplings and place them in the bowl with another ladle of the cooking liquid. Reserve 1 cup of the cooking liquid.

13. Drain the dumplings and mix them into the stew. If the stew is too thick to stir easily, mix in some of the reserved cooking liquid. Raise the heat to medium and heat through for 1 to 2 minutes. Remove from the heat, stir in the basil and Parmesan, and serve.

Cauliflower Soup with Buttery Bread Crumb Dumplings

Květáková Polévka s Knedlíky (Czech Republic)

SERVES 4 (MAKES ABOUT 40 DUMPLINGS)

This easy, no-frills cauliflower soup is grand when it's cold outside. The grape-sized bread dumplings cook up quickly and soak up a good amount of flavor. They're firm but not chewy, like soft meatballs, and they add a certain robust character to the soup.

For the Soup

- 3 tablespoons unsalted butter, cut into chunks
- 2 medium leeks, white and light green parts only, rinsed and chopped coarse
- 2 large parsnips, peeled and cut into ½-inch rounds
- 1 small turnip, peeled and cut into ½-inch cubes
- ½ teaspoon freshly grated nutmeg
- 2 tablespoons unbleached all-purpose flour
- 1½ teaspoons salt
- 1 small cauliflower, cored and cut into small florets
- 1 tablespoon finely chopped fresh dill

For the Dumplings

- 1¼ cups fine dry crustless white bread crumbs (see page 6)
- 1 tablespoon unbleached all-purpose flour, plus some extra for dusting
- ¼ teaspoon salt
- 2 tablespoons unsalted butter, melted
- 2 large eggs, beaten
- 2 tablespoons milk or water
- 2 teaspoons finely chopped fresh dill

1. MAKE THE SOUP: Melt the 3 tablespoons butter in a medium pot over low heat. Add the leeks and stir frequently until very soft, about 10 minutes. If the leeks look dry or begin to sizzle as they cook, stir in a little water to prevent them from browning. Mix in the parsnips, turnip, and nutmeg, then sprinkle in the 2 tablespoons flour and cook for 2 minutes, stirring constantly.

2. Pour in 6 cups water, add the 1½ teaspoons salt, and bring to a boil over high heat. Cover, reduce the heat to low, and simmer for 30 minutes, stirring occasionally.

3. MAKE THE DOUGH: While the soup is simmering, place 1 cup of the bread crumbs in a medium bowl and keep the remaining ¼ cup handy. Mix the 1 tablespoon flour and the ¼ teaspoon salt into the bread crumbs. In another bowl, whisk together the melted butter, eggs, milk, and 2 teaspoons of the dill. Add the egg mixture to the bread crumb mixture and mix until all the liquid has been absorbed. This dough needs to be firm enough to hold its shape when rolled into balls. If the dough is too soft or sticky, work in some of the remaining bread crumbs, a little at a time. Cover and refrigerate for 20 minutes.

4. Once the soup has simmered for 30 minutes, stir in the cauliflower, cover, and simmer for 30 minutes longer. Reduce the heat to very, very low to keep the soup hot until it's time to add the dumplings. (You can also make the soup in advance and keep it refrigerated in a tightly sealed container for up to 3 days.)

5. MAKE AND COOK THE DUMPLINGS: Line a tray with a kitchen towel and sprinkle with a little flour.

6. Fill a medium pot halfway with salted water and bring to a boil over high heat. Reduce the heat to low for a gentle simmer.

7. While waiting for the water to come to a boil, start rolling your dumplings. Pinch off a very small piece of dough, roll it into a ball about ¾ inch around, dust it with flour, and place on the prepared tray. Repeat with the remaining dough. This is a soft dough, so balls may not hold their shape perfectly, especially as the butter in the dough begins to warm.

8. Drop the dumplings, a few at a time, into the simmering water. Stir occasionally. Cook until all of them are floating, about 1 minute, then cook for 1 minute longer.

9. Remove the dumplings with a slotted spoon and place them directly in the soup. Remove from the heat, stir in the remaining 1 tablespoon dill, and serve.

Cockles with Rice Dumplings in a Spicy Coconut Sauce

Kube Mutli (India)

SERVES 4 (MAKES ABOUT 40 DUMPLINGS)

This outstanding shellfish stew is utterly sumptuous because it is full of plump, nibbly dumplings made from freshly ground basmati rice. Making these dumplings from scratch involves three separate steps: grinding the rice in a spice grinder, partially cooking the rice in just enough liquid to form a sticky dough, and finally, rolling the dough into balls and steaming them before dropping them into the stew. It sounds like a lot of work, but every one of these steps is easy and nearly impossible to mess up. If cockles are not available, you can use any other type of small clam.

For the Coconut Spice Mixture

⅔ cup freshly grated and dried coconut (see page 9) or unsweetened dried grated coconut

1½ tablespoons coriander seeds

1 teaspoon cumin seeds

1 teaspoon black or brown mustard seeds

1 teaspoon black peppercorns

2 to 3 small dried hot red chiles, such as *Kashmiri* or *lal mirch*, tougher top ends cut off

For the Dumplings

1½ cups white basmati or other long-grain rice, finely ground in a clean spice or coffee grinder, or 1½ cups preground rice (rice *sooji*, rice *rava*, or *idli rava*)

1 teaspoon salt

White rice flour for dusting

For the Stew

2 tablespoons ghee (page 12) or a neutral oil, such as grapeseed

1 large yellow onion, cut in half and sliced thin

2 garlic cloves, chopped very fine

2 cups fresh coconut milk (see page 8) or 2 cups measured from one 14-ounce can coconut milk mixed with 1 cup water

2 teaspoons ground turmeric

1 tablespoon tamarind paste

½ teaspoon salt

3 pounds fresh cockles or other very small clams, scrubbed clean under cold running water and kept on ice (discard any cockles that do not close when you tap them)

Equipment

Clean spice or coffee grinder

8- to 10-quart steamer pot

24-inch square of muslin

Large plate or tray to hold the dumplings cooked in batches

1. MAKE THE COCONUT SPICE MIXTURE: Combine all the ingredients for the coconut spice mixture in a medium skillet over medium heat. Shake and stir the coconut mixture continuously until the coconut is lightly browned, 5 to 6 minutes. Remove from the heat, scoop into a shallow bowl, and allow it to cool to room temperature. Once cooled, grind in the spice grinder until you have a coarse powder and set aside. (You can make the coconut spice mixture in advance and keep it refrigerated in a tightly sealed glass container for up to 1 month.)

2. MAKE THE DUMPLINGS: Place the ground rice and the 1 teaspoon salt in a large saucepan. Pour in 2 cups water and place over medium heat. Cook, stirring continuously, until all the liquid has been absorbed and the mixture thickens into a soft dough that pulls away from the sides of the pot, about 5 minutes. Remove from the heat, move the dough into a bowl, and allow it to cool slightly.

3. Line a tray with a kitchen towel and sprinkle with a little rice flour.

4. While it is still warm, pinch off a small piece of dough and roll it into a ball about 1 inch around, dust with flour, and place it on the prepared tray. Repeat with the remaining dough.

5. STEAM THE DUMPLINGS: Remove the basket from the steamer pot, add 1 inch of water to the pot, and bring to a boil over high heat. Soak the muslin under running water, wring it out, then drape it inside the basket, creating a lining. Arrange as many dumplings in the lined basket as you can fit without their touching. Place the basket in the pot, cover, reduce the heat to medium, and steam for 15 minutes.

6. MAKE THE STEW: While the dumplings are steaming, melt the ghee in a medium pot over medium heat. Add the onion and stir frequently until soft, about 4 minutes. Add the garlic and the coconut spice mixture and stir until the mixture is golden brown. Pour in the coconut milk and 2 cups water, then stir in the turmeric, tamarind paste, and ½ teaspoon salt. Bring to a simmer over medium-low heat, then reduce the heat to low, and keep covered until the dumplings are ready to be added. If using fresh coconut milk, do not let it come to a boil, or it will separate into what looks like a superfine curdle and you will have to start the stew over.

7. Once the dumplings have cooked, remove the steamer pot from the heat. Carefully remove the basket and place it on a folded kitchen towel. Arrange the dumplings in a single layer on the large plate or tray, lightly sprinkle them with a few spoonfuls of water to prevent sticking, and cover with a kitchen towel. Cook any remaining dumplings and place them on the plate with another few spoonfuls of water. Once all the dumplings have been cooked and arranged on the plate, keep them covered until it's time to add them to the stew.

8. FINISH THE STEW: Bring the stew back to a simmer over medium heat. Stir in the dumplings, then gently stir in the cockles, cover, and cook until all the cockles have opened, about 5 minutes, and serve.

Chickpea Dumplings in Tomato Sauce

Chana Vada ki Tomatochi Bhaji (India)

SERVES 2 TO 4 (MAKES ABOUT 20 DUMPLINGS)

Made from a small chickpealike bean (*chana dal*), these dumplings, like many other dumplings from North India, are fried before being added to a simmering sauce. Containing no egg, flour, or other binder, they would fall apart without the crispy skin that frying gives them. Once they have been simmered in this mild and tangy tomato sauce, they become tender and more delicate.

For the Dumplings

½ cup *chana dal* (a type of dried split chickpea), soaked in plenty of water for 6 to 8 hours

2 to 3 small hot green chiles, such as *Kashmiri* or *lal mirch*, seeded and chopped fine

1 tablespoon finely chopped fresh cilantro leaves

⅛ teaspoon baking powder

1 teaspoon salt

8 to 10 large fresh spinach leaves, stemmed

For Cooking

Grapeseed or other neutral oil with a high smoking point for shallow frying

For the Sauce

¼ cup grapeseed or other neutral oil

1 large onion, cut in half and sliced thin

1 teaspoon freshly ground cumin

2 teaspoons coriander seeds, freshly ground

1 tablespoon finely grated fresh ginger

3 garlic cloves, chopped fine

3 plum tomatoes, chopped coarse

1 teaspoon ground turmeric

½ teaspoon chile powder, preferably from India

1½ teaspoons salt

For Serving

3 tablespoons finely chopped fresh cilantro leaves

1. MAKE THE BATTER: Drain the *chana dal*, place in a food processor, and process until broken into bits, about 4 minutes, scraping down the sides as you go. Continue to pulse while adding up to 5 tablespoons water, a little at a time, until you have a gritty paste.

2. Scoop the batter into a medium bowl. Stir in the chiles, 1 tablespoon cilantro, the baking powder, and 1 teaspoon salt. Stack the spinach leaves and roll them up into a cigar shape. Thinly slice the rolled leaves and mix them into the batter.

3. MAKE THE DUMPLINGS: Line 2 large plates with a couple layers of paper towels. Fill a large, deep skillet with 1 inch of grapeseed oil and heat over medium heat. To check the temperature of the oil, dip the end of a dry wooden spoon into the center of the pan. The oil is ready when it bubbles actively around the edges of the spoon.

4. Scoop up a rounded teaspoon of batter. Use another spoon or your finger to move the batter gently off the spoon and into the oil. Drop in spoonfuls of the remaining batter, leaving as much space as you can around each. Cook until lightly browned, 3 to 4 minutes. Carefully turn the fritters over with a fork and cook until golden brown, 1 to 2 minutes longer.

5. Remove the fritters with a slotted spoon, place them in a single layer on one of the prepared plates, and allow them to cool to room temperature.

6. Fill a large bowl three-quarters of the way with cold water. Slide the cooled fritters into the water and soak for 1 minute. Using your hand, scoop them up one by one and gently jiggle off the excess water. Place the soaked fritters in a single layer on the other prepared plate and set aside.

7. MAKE THE SAUCE AND COOK THE DUMPLINGS: Heat the oil in a medium pot over medium heat. Add the onion. Stir occasionally until the onion begins to brown, about 5 minutes. Add the cumin, coriander, ginger, and garlic and stir for 1 minute longer. Mix in the tomatoes, turmeric, chile powder, and 1½ teaspoons salt. Reduce the heat to low and stir frequently until the tomato softens and breaks apart, about 10 minutes. Pour in 1 quart water, raise the heat to high, and bring to a boil. Cover and reduce the heat to low for a gentle simmer.

8. Carefully arrange the soaked fritters in the simmering sauce, leaving a little space between them. Cover and cook for 10 minutes, occasionally shaking the pan to prevent sticking. Remove from the heat. Sprinkle with the 3 tablespoons of cilantro and serve.

Kasha and Mushroom Pierogi

Pierogi z Kaszą Gryczaną (Poland)

SERVES 4 TO 8 (MAKES ABOUT 40 DUMPLINGS)

The meaty taste of these vegetarian pierogi would lead you to think the filling included some amount of beef, but it's the combination of kasha (toasted buckwheat groats) and mushrooms that creates such rich flavors. Kasha has a warm nutty essence, but by toasting it once again in your own kitchen you revive it and bring out an even deeper flavor. It's important to use dried mushrooms in this recipe because they have a more intense flavor than fresh.

These dumplings are made using the Half-Moon Fold (page 47).

For the Dough

2 cups unbleached all-purpose flour, plus some extra for dusting

1 large egg, beaten

3 tablespoons sour cream

2 tablespoons unsalted butter, melted

¼ cup warm water

½ teaspoon salt

For the Filling

⅓ cup coarse kasha

½ ounce dried porcini mushrooms, soaked in 1 cup hot water for 1 hour

2 tablespoons unsalted butter, cut into chunks

1 small yellow onion, chopped fine

1 teaspoon salt

½ teaspoon freshly ground black pepper

For Serving*

3 tablespoons unsalted butter, melted just before serving

½ cup fried bread crumbs (see page 7)

Sour cream

Equipment

2½-inch round cookie cutter

Large, wide bowl to hold the dumplings cooked in batches

1. MAKE THE DOUGH: Place 1¾ cups of the flour in a large bowl and keep the remaining ¼ cup handy. In another bowl, whisk together the egg, 3 tablespoons sour cream, 2 tablespoons melted butter, warm water, and ½ teaspoon salt. Add the egg mixture to the flour and mix until all the liquid has been absorbed. Work the dough with your hands into one manageable ball. If the dough is wet and sticky, work in some of the remaining flour, a little at a time, until it no longer sticks to your fingers.

2. Place the dough on a floured surface and knead for 2 to 3 minutes. The dough will be somewhat firm and smooth. Return the dough ball to the bowl, cover, and let it rest for 30 minutes.

---

*These amounts are for a full recipe. If you plan on freezing and storing some of the dumplings, reduce the amounts in proportion to the number you are serving.

3. MAKE THE FILLING: Place the kasha in a small skillet over medium heat. Toast the grains, stirring frequently, until they are noticeably darker in color and fragrant, 8 to 10 minutes. Immediately move to a small bowl to cool.

4. Fish out the soaked mushrooms with your fingers and squeeze the excess liquid back into the bowl. Set the liquid aside and finely chop the mushrooms. Strain and reserve ¾ cup of the soaking liquid. (If you have less than ¾ cup, add just enough water to make ¾ cup.) Pour the soaking liquid into a small pot and bring to a boil over high heat. Stir in the toasted kasha, cover, reduce the heat to low, and simmer until all the liquid has been absorbed, about 10 minutes. Remove from the heat, keep covered, and set aside.

5. Melt the 2 tablespoons butter in a large skillet over medium heat. Add the onion and stir frequently until soft, about 4 minutes. Add the mushrooms and stir until the onion is golden brown, about 5 minutes. Scoop into a food processor, add the kasha, the 1 teaspoon salt, and the pepper and pulse until it becomes a coarse mash. Scoop into a bowl and allow it to cool to room temperature.

6. ASSEMBLE THE DUMPLINGS: *Before assembling the pierogi, review the Half-Moon Fold.*

7. Line a tray with a kitchen towel and sprinkle with a little flour. Have ready the dough and the filling.

8. Knead the dough once or twice on a floured surface, divide it into 4 equal pieces, and set 3 of them aside under a kitchen towel. Shape the remaining piece into a ball and roll it out until it's about ⅛ inch thick. Sprinkle with flour if it gets sticky.

9. Using the cookie cutter, cut out as many rounds as you can, usually 8 to 10. Collect the scraps from around the rounds and put aside under a damp kitchen towel for later use.

10. Lay flat 1 to 5 dough rounds. Brush each round with a very thin coating of water to make it sticky enough to seal. Center a rounded teaspoon of filling on top of each round, fold each neatly in half, pushing out any air, and pinch to seal. Dab a little water along the edges, if needed, for a better seal. Place the assembled dumplings in a single layer on the prepared tray and keep them covered with a kitchen towel while you work. Once you have assembled the first batch of dumplings, continue with the remaining dough and filling. Combine all the dough scraps, knead them into a ball, roll it out, cut out as many rounds as you can, and fill and fold those too.

11. Cover the tray of assembled dumplings and place in the refrigerator for 30 to 60 minutes before cooking. Chilling them helps to set the dough, making the dumplings firm and toothsome when cooked instead of puffy and soft. Set aside the number of dumplings that you would like to cook and keep the rest frozen for up to 6 months (see page 36).

12. COOK THE DUMPLINGS: Fill a large pot halfway with salted water and bring to a boil over high heat. Reduce the heat to medium for a steady simmer.

13. Gently drop up to 20 dumplings, a few at a time, into the simmering water. Stir gently to prevent sticking. Cook until all of them are floating, about 3 minutes, then cook for 2 minutes longer. (If cooking frozen pierogi, add them directly to the simmering water and increase the cooking time by 2 minutes. Do not allow the pierogi to thaw before cooking.)

14. Remove the dumplings with a slotted spoon, place them in the large bowl, and drizzle them with a ladle of the cooking liquid to prevent sticking. Cook the remaining dumplings and place them in the bowl with another ladle of the cooking liquid and keep warm.

15. Once all the pierogi have been cooked, drain and place them in a large, shallow serving bowl. Drizzle with the 3 tablespoons melted butter and top with fried bread crumbs. Serve with sour cream.

Rice Dumplings Stuffed with Pork and Kohlrabi

Fen Guo (China)

SERVES 4 TO 8 (MAKES ABOUT 32 DUMPLINGS)

Fen guo can be made with different fillings, but their common feature is a delicate round of rice dough wrapped around the freshest ingredients available. This recipe includes pork, mushrooms, and kohlrabi. Kohlrabi, which looks very much like a turnip, has a mild and clean flavor similar to napa cabbage and absorbs other flavors very well. It is often available at supermarkets, as well as at certain Asian markets, but if not, you can easily substitute a small turnip, a small jícama, or a large carrot. Once these dumplings are cooked, they should be served immediately, because they tend to stiffen up once cool.

These dumplings are made using the Standing Half-Moon Fold (page 48), but you can also use the more detailed Pleated Half-Moon Fold (page 46).

For the Filling

4 dried shiitake or black mushrooms, soaked in hot water to cover for 30 minutes

15 to 20 small or medium dried shrimp, soaked in hot water to cover for 30 minutes

3 tablespoons grapeseed or other neutral oil

½ pound boneless pork loin, chopped fine

1 link Chinese pork sausage (*la chang*), chopped fine (about ⅓ cup)

1 small kohlrabi or small turnip, peeled and chopped fine (about 1½ cups)

2 tablespoons rice wine

1 tablespoon soy sauce

¼ teaspoon sugar

⅛ teaspoon salt

Pinch of freshly ground white pepper

¼ cup finely chopped fresh cilantro stems and leaves

For the Dough

2¼ cups regular white rice flour, preferably from China or Thailand, plus some extra for dusting

For Cooking and Serving

Soft lettuce leaves, such as Boston, to line the steamer basket and serving plate

1 recipe Soy-Vinegar Sauce (page 112)

Equipment

8- to 10-quart steamer pot

1. MAKE THE FILLING: Drain the mushrooms and squeeze out any excess liquid. Remove and discard the stems and finely chop the mushroom caps. Drain and finely chop the shrimp.

2. Heat the oil in a medium skillet over high heat. Add the pork, sausage, and shrimp. Stir frequently until the pork is just beginning to brown, about 2 minutes. Add the kohlrabi and mushrooms and stir until well combined. Add the rice wine and scrape up any bits from the bottom of the pan with a wooden spoon. Add the soy sauce, sugar, salt, and pepper and stir vigorously for 1 minute longer. Remove from the heat and stir in the cilantro. Scoop into a shallow bowl and allow it to cool completely. (You can also make the filling in advance and keep it tightly covered in the refrigerator for up to 2 days.)

3. MAKE THE DOUGH: Place 2 cups of the rice flour in a large heatproof bowl and keep the remaining ¼ cup handy.

4. Heat 1 cup water over medium heat until it is hot to the touch but not close to simmering. Add the hot water to the flour and mix until all the liquid has been absorbed. Let the dough cool slightly.

5. Carefully work the dough with your hands. If this is in any way uncomfortable, let it cool for another minute or two, but keep in mind that you need to work with this dough while it is still very, very warm. Work the dough in the bowl into one manageable ball. If the dough is wet and sticky, work in some of the remaining flour, a little at a time, until it no longer sticks to your fingers. Keep the dough covered with a towel while assembling the dumplings.

6. ASSEMBLE THE DUMPLINGS: *Before assembling the* fen guo, *review the Standing Half-Moon Fold.*

7. Line a tray with a kitchen towel and sprinkle with a little rice flour. Have ready the very warm dough and the cooled filling.

8. Pinch off a small piece of dough and roll it into a ball about 1¼ inches around. Flatten the ball into a thick disk and dust each side with rice flour. Place the disk on a floured surface and roll it out into a 3-inch round. Center a rounded tablespoon of filling on top of the round, fold it neatly in half, pushing out any air, and pinch to seal. Dab a little water along the edges, if needed, for a better seal. Holding the dumpling by the seam, tap its base on your work surface until it is flat enough on the bottom to sit upright. Place it on the prepared tray. Repeat with the remaining dough and filling. Keep the dumplings in a single layer on the tray covered with a kitchen towel as you work.

9. STEAM THE DUMPLINGS: Remove the basket from the steamer pot, add 2 inches of water to the pot, and bring to a boil over high heat. Line the basket with lettuce leaves. Arrange as many dumplings in the basket as you can, spacing them about ½ inch apart. Place the basket in the pot, cover, reduce the heat to medium, and cook for 15 minutes.

10. Remove the pot from the heat. Carefully remove the basket, place it on a folded kitchen towel, and allow the *fen guo* to cool slightly. Arrange a few lettuce leaves on a plate. Use a spoon or a small spatula to move the *fen guo* to the prepared plate. Serve immediately while you cook any remaining *fen guo*. Serve with Soy-Vinegar Sauce.

April

MASA BALL SOUP
Sopa de Bolitas de Masa (Mexico) 135

CHICKPEA SQUARES TOPPED WITH MUSTARD SEEDS AND SPICED OIL
Khaman Dhokla (India) 137

NINE-LAYER COCONUT TAPIOCA CAKE
Khanom Chan (Thailand) 139

SALTY-SWEET BEAN PUDDINGS WITH COCONUT CREAM TOPPING
Khanom Thuay (Thailand) 141

MATZO BALLS IN A BEEF BROTH
Fleischsuppe mit Matzoknepfle (France) 143

CHIVE-STUFFED DUMPLINGS WITH TOMATO SAUCE AND MINTED YOGURT
Ashak (Afghanistan) 145

WHEAT DUMPLINGS STUFFED WITH TURMERIC-STAINED POTATOES
Shogo Momo (Tibet) 148

WHEAT DUMPLINGS STUFFED WITH BEEF AND ONION
Sha Momo (Tibet) 151

SPICY LAMB-FILLED DUMPLINGS IN A THICK YOGURT SOUP
Sheesh Barak bi Laban (Lebanon) 153

OVEN-SIMMERED LAMB-FILLED DUMPLINGS WITH MINTED YOGURT
Manti (Turkey)..156

DUMPLINGS STUFFED WITH PORK AND CABBAGE
Mandu (Korea) 159

Masa Ball Soup

Sopa de Bolitas de Masa (Mexico)

SERVES 4 (MAKES ABOUT 24 DUMPLINGS)

These masa harina dumplings, flavored with cheese and jalapeños, are delectable in a bowl of spicy chicken soup. Masa harina is a processed meal available at Mexican markets and many supermarkets. Because the dough is made without any binders, the masa harina balls must be fried before being cooked in the soup. A number of recipes call for deep-frying, but similar results can be achieved by rolling the balls around in a skillet with only a small amount of oil. *Queso añejo* is an aged Mexican cheese that is also available at Mexican markets and at some supermarkets.

For the Dumplings

1 cup masa harina, plus some extra for dusting

¼ teaspoon baking powder

¼ teaspoon salt

3 tablespoons nonhydrogenated lard or vegetable shortening, at room temperature

⅓ cup Chicken Broth with Mexican Flavors (page 394)

⅔ cup freshly grated *queso añejo* or Romano cheese

2 tablespoons finely chopped fresh cilantro leaves

1 to 2 jalapeño chiles, seeded and chopped fine

For the Soup

6 cups Chicken Broth with Mexican Flavors

1 medium white onion, chopped coarse

1 garlic clove, peeled

2 plum tomatoes, peeled, seeded (page 21), and chopped coarse

1 tablespoon dried Mexican (not Mediterranean) oregano

1 teaspoon ground cumin

1 teaspoon ground *pasilla* or *ancho* chile

1 cup fresh corn kernels, or frozen, unthawed

¾ teaspoon salt

3 fresh cilantro sprigs, chopped coarse

For Cooking

Grapeseed or other neutral oil with a high smoking point for shallow frying

1. MAKE THE DOUGH: Combine 1 cup masa harina with the baking powder and the ¼ teaspoon salt in a large bowl. Add the lard and mix until well combined. Pour in half of the ⅓ cup broth and stir until all the liquid has been absorbed. Mix in more broth, one spoonful at a time, until you have a thick, pasty batter. This batter will just hold its shape when scooped up with a spoon. Mix in the *queso añejo*, 2 tablespoons cilantro, and the jalapeño. Cover and refrigerate for at least 30 minutes. The batter will firm up as it cools, and you will have a soft, easy-to-shape dough. (You can also make the dough 1 day in advance and keep it tightly wrapped in the refrigerator.)

2. MAKE THE DUMPLINGS: Line a tray with a kitchen towel and sprinkle with a little masa harina.

3. Pinch off a small piece of dough, roll it into a ball about 1¼ inches around, dust with a little masa harina, and place it on the prepared tray. Repeat with the remaining dough.

4. Line a large plate with a couple of layers of paper towels. Add ½ inch oil to a medium skillet and heat over medium heat. To check the temperature of the oil, dip the end of a dry wooden spoon into the center of the pan. The oil is ready when it bubbles actively around the edges of the spoon.

5. Carefully place 8 masa harina balls in the oil. Gently and constantly shake the pan to keep the balls rolling. This constant movement helps these soft balls keep their shape and brown evenly. Keep the pan moving until they're golden brown, 4 to 5 minutes. Using a slotted spoon, carefully move them to the prepared plate. Cook the remaining masa harina balls, adding more oil after each batch. As soon as the last batch has been browned and placed on the plate, discard all but 1 tablespoon of the oil from the pan. Set the pan aside for later use. The browned masa harina balls can be kept at room temperature while you prepare the soup.

6. MAKE THE SOUP AND COOK THE DUMPLINGS: Pour the 6 cups chicken broth into a medium pot and bring to a boil over high heat. Cover and reduce the heat to medium for a steady simmer.

7. While the broth is coming to a boil, pulse the onion, garlic, and tomatoes in a food processor until light and pulpy. Heat the pan with the reserved oil over high heat. Carefully and quickly scoop in the onion mixture. When the onion mixture begins to simmer, reduce the heat to medium and stir in the oregano, cumin, and chile powder. Cook, stirring frequently, until most of the liquid has cooked off and you have a brownish paste, 5 to 6 minutes.

8. Stir the cooked onion mixture, corn, and ¾ teaspoon salt into the simmering broth. Cover and simmer for 10 minutes. Add the masa harina balls to the soup a few at a time. Cover and simmer for 3 minutes longer. Sprinkle with the chopped cilantro sprigs and serve.

Chickpea Squares Topped with Mustard Seeds and Spiced Oil

Khaman Dhokla (India)

SERVES 4 TO 8 (MAKES 1 DUMPLING)

This savory steamed cake, made from semolina flour and *chana dal,* a type of dried split chickpea, is a delicious midday snack. A scoop of yogurt added to the batter guarantees that the cake will cook up extra smooth and tender. Topped with cilantro and grated coconut, and drizzled with an oil that's been seasoned with spices and seeds, this savory cake possesses an aromatic and complex freshness.

For the Dumpling

- ¾ cup *chana dal,* soaked in plenty of water for 6 to 8 hours
- ½ cup plain whole-milk yogurt
- ⅓ cup finely ground semolina flour (*sooji* or *rava*)
- 2 to 3 small dried hot red chiles, such as *Kashmiri* or *lal mirch,* seeded if you want less heat and chopped very fine
- ½ teaspoon finely grated fresh ginger
- ⅛ teaspoon ground turmeric
- 1 teaspoon salt
- 1 tablespoon fresh lemon juice
- 2 teaspoons grapeseed or other neutral oil
- 1 teaspoon baking soda

For the Topping

- 2 tablespoons grapeseed or other neutral oil
- ½ teaspoon black or brown mustard seeds
- ½ teaspoon sesame seeds
- 2 tablespoons coarsely chopped fresh cilantro leaves
- 2 tablespoons freshly grated coconut (see page 8) or frozen grated coconut, thawed (optional)

For Cooking

Grapeseed or other neutral oil to coat the cake pan

Equipment

2-inch-high steamer rack

9-inch round cake pan

Pot large enough to hold both the rack and the pan when covered

1. MAKE THE BATTER 1 TO 2 HOURS IN ADVANCE: Place the steamer rack in the pot, add 1½ inches of water to the pot, and set aside. Rub a little oil around the inside of the cake pan.

2. Drain the *chana dal* and place it in a food processor with the yogurt. Process until the mixture is frothy and slightly gritty, about 3 minutes, scraping down the sides as you go.

3. Scoop the batter into a large bowl and stir in ¾ cup water. Mix in the semolina flour, chiles, ginger, turmeric, salt, and lemon juice. Cover with a cloth and let rest at room temperature for 1 to 2 hours, stirring occasionally. The batter will swell slightly and look softer.

4. Combine the 2 teaspoons oil with the baking soda in a small bowl and set aside until the *khaman dhokla* is ready to be steamed.

5. STEAM THE DUMPLING: Bring the water in the pot to a boil over high heat.

6. Add the oil and baking soda mixture into the batter and stir until combined. Pour the batter into the prepared cake pan and wiggle it gently to level it off.

7. Carefully place the filled pan on the steamer rack, cover, and steam for 15 minutes.

8. Remove the pot from the heat. Carefully lift the pan out of the pot and place it on a folded kitchen towel, allowing the *khaman dhokla* to cool slightly. Unmold the *khaman dhokla* and place it right side up on a large plate.

9. MAKE THE TOPPING: Heat the 2 tablespoons oil in a small skillet over medium heat. Add the mustard seeds and sesame seeds and stir until the sesame seeds are golden brown, about 3 minutes. Spoon the oil mixture evenly over the *khaman dhokla* and sprinkle with cilantro and coconut. Slice and serve warm.

Nine-Layer Coconut Tapioca Cake

Khanom Chan (Thailand)

SERVES 4 TO 6 (MAKES 1 DUMPLING)

This dense coconut cake made in nine noodle-thin layers is popular at weddings and other celebrations because the number nine is believed to symbolize luck and progress. The layers serve a practical purpose too. Steaming this dumpling in layers allows it to cook quickly and evenly, a feat that would be nearly impossible if the *khanom chan* were steamed as a solid cake. Sometimes each layer is given its own vibrant color, creating a rainbow effect, but those that glow with only the natural tint of the ingredients are also alluring and beautiful. You can bite into a slice of this firm, jellylike cake and feel your teeth pop satisfyingly through each layer, but it is hard to resist peeling off the layers one by one.

For the Dumpling

1¼ cups tapioca flour (tapioca starch)

⅓ cup white rice flour, preferably from Thailand

1¾ cups fresh coconut milk (page 8) or 2 cups measured from one 14-ounce can coconut milk mixed with 1 cup water

6 ounces hard palm sugar or ¾ cup soft palm sugar or other unrefined sugar (see page 20)

¼ cup pandan water (page 113) or ¼ teaspoon pandan extract mixed into ¼ cup water

For Cooking

Grapeseed or other neutral oil to coat the cake pan

Equipment

2-inch-high steamer rack

8-inch round cake pan

Pot large enough to hold both the rack and the pan when covered

1. MAKE THE BATTER: Combine the tapioca flour and rice flour in a large heatproof bowl.

2. Place the steamer rack in the pot. Keeping the cake pan level is key for such a thin batter, so take the time now to check for any tilts or leanings with your rack or pot and try to even things out as best you can. Add 1½ inches of water to the pot, and bring to a boil over high heat. Meanwhile, rub a little oil around the inside of the cake pan.

3. Pour the coconut milk into a small saucepan, add the palm sugar, and heat over medium-low heat. Stir until all the sugar has dissolved. The mixture should be hot to the touch but not close to simmering. Immediately pour the coconut milk into the flour mixture and whisk until smooth. This is a very thin batter that cooks up into a firm jellylike texture.

4. DIVIDE THE BATTER: Measure out 1⅓ cups of the batter and set aside. Stir the pandan water into the batter remaining in the bowl, giving it a light green color.

5. STEAM THE DUMPLING: Measure out ⅓ cup of the green pandan batter and pour it into the prepared cake pan. Tilt the pan until the batter spreads out to coat the bottom of the pan evenly.

6. Carefully place the pan on the steamer rack, making sure that it is level. Cover and steam over high heat for 3 minutes.

7. Uncover and slowly pour in ⅓ cup of the white batter mixture evenly over the steamed layer, cover, and steam for 3 minutes longer. Continue adding and steaming alternating layers of batter every 3 minutes, ending with a ninth and final layer of the green pandan batter.

8. Remove the pot from the heat. Carefully remove the cake pan from the pot. Place it on a folded kitchen towel and allow the *khanom chan* to cool to room temperature. Unmold by inverting it onto a plate, slice, and serve. *Khanom chan* can be kept tightly covered in the refrigerator for up to 3 days. Allow it to come back to room temperature before serving.

Salty-Sweet Bean Puddings with Coconut Cream Topping

Khanom Thuay (Thailand)

SERVES 4 (MAKES 16 DUMPLINGS)

These striking coconut dumplings are a popular street snack in Thailand. Like the *Khanom Chan* (preceding recipe), these dumplings are made from a batter flavored with palm sugar, pandan leaves, and coconut milk. They're steamed in small bowls, topped with a rich coconut cream, and steamed again. Just enough salt is added to the creamy topping to make them extra tasty and totally satisfying. Traditionally they are eaten at room temperature, but we can't keep from eating one or two the moment they are plucked from the steamer.

For the Dumplings

3 tablespoons mung bean starch

1 tablespoon white rice flour, preferably from Thailand

½ cup fresh coconut milk (see page 8) or ⅓ cup canned coconut milk mixed with 3 tablespoons water

2 tablespoons pandan water (page 117) or ⅛ teaspoon pandan extract mixed into ¼ cup water

2 ounces hard palm sugar or ¼ cup soft palm sugar or other unrefined sugar (see page 20)

For the Coconut Cream Topping

¼ cup white rice flour, preferably from Thailand

¾ teaspoon sugar

⅛ teaspoon salt

⅓ cup fresh coconut cream (see page 9) mixed with ⅔ cup fresh coconut milk or 1 cup canned coconut milk

Equipment

8- to 10-quart steamer pot

Four to sixteen 2-inch-wide dipping bowls (see page 26)

1. MAKE THE BATTER: Combine the mung bean starch and the 2 tablespoons rice flour in a medium heatproof bowl.

2. Mix together the ½ cup coconut milk, the pandan water, and palm sugar in a small saucepan. Heat over medium-low heat, stirring constantly, until the sugar has dissolved and the mixture is hot to the touch but not close to simmering, about 2 minutes. Pour into the mung bean starch mixture and whisk until smooth. This is a very thin batter that cooks up into a puddinglike texture.

3. MAKE THE COCONUT CREAM TOPPING: Combine the ¼ cup rice flour, sugar, and salt in a medium heatproof bowl.

4. Mix together the coconut cream mixture in a small saucepan. Heat over medium-low heat, stirring constantly, until it is hot to the touch but not close to simmering, about 2 minutes. Pour into the rice flour mixture and whisk until smooth.

5. STEAM THE DUMPLINGS: Remove the basket from the steamer pot, add 2 inches of water to the pot, and bring to a boil over high heat. Arrange as many small dipping bowls as you can in the basket. Give the mung bean batter a good stir before spooning a tablespoon of it into each bowl. Carefully place the basket in the pot, cover, and cook for 10 minutes. The batter will thicken into a puddinglike consistency.

6. Once the first layer has cooked, stir the coconut cream mixture and spoon a tablespoon into each filled bowl, covering the mung bean layer. Cover and steam for 15 minutes longer. The coconut topping is not supposed to be firm, though it will set slightly as it cools.

7. Remove the pot from the heat. Carefully remove the basket and place it on a folded kitchen towel. Carefully remove the bowls and allow the *khanom thuay* to cool slightly. Slip them out of their bowls with a butter knife and arrange them, top side up, on a plate. Repeat the steaming steps with the remaining batter. Serve at room temperature. *Khanom thuay* can be kept tightly wrapped in the refrigerator for up to 3 days. Allow them to come back to room temperature before serving.

Matzo Balls in a Beef Broth

Fleischsuppe mit Matzoknepfle (France)

SERVES 4 TO 6 (MAKES ABOUT 12 DUMPLINGS)

There is a beef matzo ball soup from the Alsace region of France that stands as a good contrast to the more familiar chicken-based Central European and American versions. These dumplings start with whole matzo crackers that are broken into pieces and soaked. Precooking the dough in a pan with some onions gives these matzo balls an aromatic sweetness and a more toasted flavor.

For the Soup

3 pounds small beef marrow bones

3 pounds beef stew meat, such as shank or rump

6 to 8 fresh thyme sprigs

2 bay leaves

5 whole cloves

1 teaspoon black peppercorns

1 small yellow onion, quartered (unpeeled)

1 large whole leek, split in half, rinsed clean, and chopped coarse

1 large carrot, cut into 1-inch rounds

1 celery rib with leaves, cut in half

1 medium turnip, peeled, cut in half, and sliced thick

1 tomato, quartered

½ small green cabbage, cored, quartered, and sliced into 1-inch ribbons

2 teaspoons salt

For the Dumplings

Two 6-inch square matzo crackers, broken into small pieces and soaked in plenty of cold water for 30 to 60 minutes

1 tablespoon rendered duck fat or neutral oil, such as grapeseed

½ small yellow onion, chopped fine

¾ teaspoon salt

½ teaspoon ground ginger

¼ teaspoon freshly grated nutmeg

2 large eggs, beaten

¼ cup matzo meal

2 tablespoons finely chopped fresh flat-leaf parsley leaves

Equipment

Colander lined with 6 to 8 layers of cheesecloth

1. MAKE THE SOUP 2½ TO 3 HOURS IN ADVANCE: Place the beef bones, beef stew meat, thyme, bay leaves, cloves, and peppercorns in a large pot. Pour in 3 quarts water and bring to a boil over high heat. Skim the froth off the surface with a spoon. Add the quartered onion, the leek, carrot, celery, turnip, tomato, cabbage, and 2 teaspoons salt. Cover, reduce the heat to low, and simmer for 2½ to 3 hours. (You can also make the soup in advance and keep it refrigerated in a tightly sealed container for up to 3 days.)

2. MAKE THE DOUGH: While the soup is simmering, drain the matzo crackers in a colander or sieve and gently press out excess water. The matzo will be mushy, so be careful not to push it through the holes of the colander or sieve while pressing out the water. Place the drained matzo crackers in a small bowl and set aside.

3. Melt the duck fat in a small pot over low heat. Add the chopped onion, ¾ teaspoon salt, the ground ginger, and nutmeg and cook, stirring frequently, until the onion is very soft but not brown, about 8 minutes. Add a little water if the onion starts to darken around the edges. Add the matzo mush and stir vigorously until the mixture begins to turn into a doughy ball and the pasty coating on the bottom and sides of the pan begins to brown, about 2 minutes. Remove from the heat, scoop into a medium bowl, break it up a bit, and allow it to cool slightly.

4. While the dough is still warm, mix in the eggs. Mix in the matzo meal and the parsley. Cover and refrigerate for 2 to 8 hours. For especially tender dumplings, let the dough chill for the full 8 hours.

5. MAKE AND COOK THE DUMPLINGS: Remove the meat from the broth using a slotted spoon, place in a bowl, and cover to keep warm. Do the same with the carrots. Remove the marrow bones and discard. Strain the broth into a medium pot through the cheesecloth-lined colander. Discard the rest of the vegetables. Bring the broth to a steady simmer over medium heat.

6. Refresh the chilled dough by giving it a quick stir. Scoop up a rounded tablespoon of dough. Use another spoon or your finger to move the dough gently off the spoon and into the broth. Drop in spoonfuls of the remaining dough, leaving as much space as you can around each. These dumplings will sink at first but will float to the surface as they cook. Cover, reduce the heat to low, and cook for 10 minutes. Turn the dumplings over, cover, and cook for 5 minutes longer. Once the dumplings have cooked, gently stir in the cooked meat and carrots, cook for 1 minute longer, and serve.

Chive-Stuffed Dumplings with Tomato Sauce and Minted Yogurt

Ashak (Afghanistan)

SERVES 4 TO 8 (MAKES ABOUT 48 DUMPLINGS)

Ashak are traditionally filled with an aromatic, grassy green called *gandana,* also known as garlic chive or Chinese chive (not to be replaced by onion chives). If garlic chives aren't available, you can substitute equal parts chopped parsley and scallion mixed with a spoonful of chopped garlic. Leeks or ramps are also common substitutes. Whatever greens you use, hand-wilting them instead of blanching will keep their flavor fresh and intense. Topped with a thick and meaty tomato sauce and garlic-infused yogurt, the dumplings themselves are surprisingly light and refreshing and make this dish suitable for any meal.

These dumplings are made using the Half-Moon Fold (page 47).

For the Yogurt Sauce*

- 4 cups plain whole-milk yogurt, drained (see page 23) for 12 hours (about 2 cups)
- 2 garlic cloves, chopped very fine

For the Filling

- 2 cups finely chopped and hand-wilted (see page 37) garlic chives (*gandana*), or 1 cup finely chopped fresh flat-leaf parsley, plus 1 cup finely chopped scallion mixed with 1 tablespoon very finely chopped garlic
- ½ teaspoon salt
- 1 teaspoon ground turmeric
- ½ teaspoon ground cumin
- ½ teaspoon ground cinnamon
- 2 teaspoons freshly ground black pepper

For the Dough

- 1 recipe *Shao Mai* (page 242) dough, preferably made no more than 1 hour in advance
- Unbleached all-purpose flour for dusting

For the Tomato Sauce*

- ¼ cup grapeseed or other neutral oil
- 1 small yellow onion, chopped fine
- ¼ pound lean ground beef
- 6 ripe plum tomatoes, peeled, seeded (see page 21), and crushed, or 6 canned plum tomatoes, drained and crushed (about 1½ cups)
- 1 teaspoon grated fresh ginger
- 1 garlic clove, chopped fine
- ½ teaspoon salt
- ¼ teaspoon freshly ground black pepper
- ¼ cup finely shredded fresh mint

Equipment

2½-inch round cookie cutter

Large, wide bowl to hold the dumplings cooked in batches

1. MAKE THE YOGURT SAUCE 2 TO 8 HOURS IN ADVANCE: Combine the yogurt and the 2 cloves of chopped garlic in a medium bowl and mix well. Cover and refrigerate for at least 2 hours.

---

*These amounts are for a full recipe. If you plan on freezing and storing some of the dumplings, reduce the amounts in proportion to the number you are serving.

2. MAKE THE FILLING: Combine all the filling ingredients in a medium bowl.

3. ASSEMBLE THE DUMPLINGS: *Before assembling the* ashak, *review the Half-Moon Fold.*

4. Line a tray with a kitchen towel and sprinkle with a little flour. Have ready the dough and filling.

5. Knead the dough once or twice on a floured surface, divide it into 4 equal pieces, and set 3 of them aside under a kitchen towel. Shape the remaining piece into a ball, then roll it out until it's 1/16 inch thick. (For tips on how to roll dough out thin, see page 35.) Sprinkle with flour if it gets sticky. Let the rolled-out dough relax for a couple of minutes before cutting out rounds.

6. Using the cookie cutter, cut out as many rounds as you can, usually 10 to 12. Scraps cannot be reused because dough rolled out this thin is too dry to recombine.

7. Lay flat 1 to 5 dough rounds. Brush each round with a very thin coating of water to make it sticky enough to seal. Center a rounded teaspoon of filling on top of each round, fold each neatly in half, pushing out any air, and pinch to seal. Dab a little water along the edges, if needed, for a better seal. Place the assembled dumplings in a single layer on the prepared tray and keep them covered with a kitchen towel while you work. Once you have assembled the first batch of dumplings, continue with the remaining dough and filling.

8. Cover the tray of assembled dumplings and place in the refrigerator for 30 to 60 minutes before cooking. Chilling them helps to set the dough, making the dumplings firm and toothsome when cooked instead of puffy and soft. Set aside the number of dumplings that you would like to cook and keep the rest frozen for up to 6 months (see page 36).

9. MAKE THE TOMATO SAUCE: Heat the oil in a small pot over high heat. Add the onion and stir consistently until the onion just begins to brown, about 4 minutes. Add the beef and stir frequently. Break up clumps with a wooden spoon as the beef begins to brown, 5 to 6 minutes.

10. Mix in the tomatoes, ginger, the clove of chopped garlic, the salt, and 1/4 teaspoon pepper. Reduce the heat to low and cook until the tomatoes break down into the sauce, about 5 minutes. Remove from the heat and keep warm.

11. COOK THE DUMPLINGS: Spread half of the yogurt sauce across a large plate or individual serving plates and set aside. Fill a large pot halfway with salted water and bring to a boil over high heat. Reduce the heat to medium for a steady simmer. Gently drop a few dozen dumplings, a few at a time, into the simmering water. Cook until all of them are floating, about 3 minutes, then cook for 2 minutes longer. (If cooking frozen *ashak,* add them directly to the simmering water and increase the cooking time by 1 minute. Do not allow them to thaw before cooking.)

12. Remove the dumplings with a slotted spoon, place them in the large bowl, drizzle with a ladle of the cooking liquid to prevent sticking, and keep warm. Cook the remaining dumplings, place them in the bowl with another ladle of the cooking liquid, and keep warm.

13. Drain the *ashak* and arrange them on top of the yogurt sauce on the plate. Spoon the remaining yogurt sauce over the *ashak*, spoon the tomato sauce over everything, sprinkle with fresh mint, and serve.

Wheat Dumplings Stuffed with Turmeric-Stained Potatoes

Shogo Momo (Tibet)

SERVES 4 TO 8 (MAKES ABOUT 40 DUMPLINGS)

The *shogo momo* is a whole wheat dumpling stuffed with mashed potato. The texture of the potato can be as smooth as you like, but we prefer it when it's a little lumpy. Leftover boiled or baked russet potatoes are great for this dumpling, but don't use potatoes that have been mixed with cream or cheese. A half cup of fresh or frozen baby peas may be added to the potatoes for color and flavor.

These dumplings are made using the Standing Half-Moon Fold (page 48), but you can also use the more detailed Pleated Half-Moon Fold (page 46).

For the Dough

1½ cups whole wheat flour

¾ cup unbleached all-purpose flour, plus some extra for dusting

For the Filling

1 teaspoon cumin seeds

1 medium baking potato, such as russet

1 scallion, sliced into thin rings

½ teaspoon ground turmeric

½ teaspoon salt

⅛ teaspoon freshly ground white pepper

1 tablespoon finely chopped fresh cilantro leaves

For Cooking and Serving

Soft lettuce leaves, such as Boston, to line the steamer basket

1 recipe Soy-Vinegar Sauce* (page 112)

Equipment

3-inch round cookie cutter

8- to 10-quart steamer pot

1. MAKE THE DOUGH: Combine the whole wheat flour and the all-purpose flour in a large bowl. Scoop out ¼ cup and set aside. Add 1 cup water and mix until all the liquid has been absorbed. Work the dough with your hands into one manageable ball. If the dough is wet and sticky, work in some of the reserved flour mixture, a little at a time, until it no longer sticks to your fingers.

2. Place the dough on a floured surface and knead for 4 to 5 minutes. The dough will be smooth and elastic. Return the dough to the bowl, cover with a clean kitchen towel, and let rest for at least 30 minutes, but no longer than 1 hour.

---

*This is for a full recipe. If you plan on freezing and storing some of the dumplings, reduce the amounts in proportion to the number you are serving.

3. MAKE THE FILLING: Toast the cumin seeds in a small skillet over medium heat, stirring constantly until they are lightly browned, about 2 minutes. Immediately move them to a small bowl to cool.

4. Place the potato in a small saucepan, pour in enough water to cover, and bring to a boil over high heat. Cover, reduce the heat to medium, and simmer until fork-tender, about 30 minutes. Drain and place the potato on a folded kitchen towel. Once it's cool enough to handle, peel off its skin and put the flesh into a medium bowl. Mash until mostly smooth. Mix in the remaining filling ingredients and set aside to cool.

5. ASSEMBLE THE DUMPLINGS: *Before assembling the* shogo momo, *review the Standing Half-Moon Fold or the Pleated Half-Moon Fold.*

6. Line a tray with a kitchen towel and sprinkle with a little all-purpose flour. Have ready the dough and the chilled filling.

7. Knead the dough once or twice on a floured surface, divide it into 4 equal pieces, and set 3 of them aside under a kitchen towel. Shape the remaining piece into a ball, then roll it out until it's about ⅛ inch thick. Sprinkle with flour if it gets sticky.

8. Using the cookie cutter, cut out as many rounds as you can, usually 8 to 10. Collect all the scraps from around the rounds and put them aside under a damp kitchen towel for later use.

9. Lay flat 1 to 5 dough rounds. Brush each round with a very thin coating of water to make it sticky enough to seal. Center a rounded teaspoon of filling in the center of each round, fold each neatly in half, pushing out any air, and pinch to seal. Dab a little water along the edges, if needed, for a better seal. Holding each dumpling by its seam, tap its filled base on your work surface until it has a flat bottom and can sit upright without tipping over. Place the assembled dumplings in a single layer on the prepared tray and keep them covered with a kitchen towel while you work. Once you have assembled the first batch of dumplings, continue with the remaining dough and filling. Combine all the dough scraps, knead them into a ball, roll it out, cut out as many rounds as you can, and fill and fold those too.

10. Set aside the number of dumplings that you would like to cook and keep the rest frozen for up to 6 months (see page 36).

11. STEAM THE DUMPLINGS: Remove the basket from the steamer pot, add 2 inches of water to the pot, and bring to a boil over high heat. Line the basket with the lettuce leaves and arrange as many dumplings in the basket as you can fit without their touching. Place the basket in the pot, cover, reduce the heat to medium-high, and steam for 15 minutes.

(If steaming frozen *shogo momo*, place them directly in the basket and cook them in the steamer pot for 20 minutes. Do not allow the *shogo momo* to thaw before cooking.)

12. Remove the pot from the heat. Carefully remove the basket and place it on a folded kitchen towel. Gently lift up the *shogo momo* using tongs and place them on a large plate. Serve immediately while you cook any remaining *shogo momo*. Serve with a side of Soy-Vinegar Sauce.

Wheat Dumplings Stuffed with Beef and Onion

Sha Momo (Tibet)

SERVES 4 TO 8 (MAKES ABOUT 40 DUMPLINGS)

The *sha momo* is revered in Nepal and Tibet for its austerity of ingredients and its ability to feed many with what seems like so little. Yak meat is the traditional filling of choice for this *momo*, but beef is a common substitute. The whole wheat dough adds a kind of sweetness and chew that complements and enhances the meaty filling.

These dumplings are made using the Standing Half-Moon Fold (page 48), but you can also use the more detailed Pleated Half-Moon Fold (page 46).

For the Filling

½ pound lean ground beef

½ small yellow onion, chopped fine and hand-wilted (see page 37)

2 scallions, sliced into thin rings

2 garlic cloves, chopped very fine

1 teaspoon grated fresh ginger

2 tablespoons finely chopped fresh cilantro leaves

½ teaspoon salt

⅛ teaspoon freshly ground white pepper

For the Dough

1 recipe *Shogo Momo* dough (preceding recipe), preferably made no more than 2 hours in advance

Unbleached all-purpose flour for dusting

For Cooking and Serving

Soft lettuce leaves, such as Boston, to line the steamer basket

1 recipe Soy-Vinegar Sauce* (page 112)

Equipment

3-inch round cookie cutter

8- to 10-quart steamer pot

1. MAKE THE FILLING: Combine all the filling ingredients in a medium bowl. Cover and refrigerate for 10 minutes.

2. ASSEMBLE THE DUMPLINGS: *Before assembling the* sha momo, *review the Standing Half-Moon Fold or the Pleated Half-Moon Fold.*

3. Line a tray with a kitchen towel and sprinkle with a little all-purpose flour. Have ready the dough and the chilled filling.

4. Knead the dough once or twice on a floured surface, divide it into 4 equal pieces, and set 3 of them aside under a kitchen towel. Shape the remaining piece into a ball, then roll it out until it's about ⅛ inch thick. Sprinkle with flour if it gets sticky.

---

*This is for a full recipe. If you plan on freezing and storing some of the dumplings, reduce the amounts in proportion to the number you are serving.

5. Using the cookie cutter, cut out as many rounds as you can, usually 8 to 10. Collect all the scraps from around the rounds and put them aside under a damp kitchen towel for later use.

6. Lay flat 1 to 5 dough rounds. Brush each round with a very thin coating of water to make it sticky enough to seal. Center a rounded teaspoon of filling in the center of each round, fold each neatly in half, pushing out any air, and pinch to seal. Dab a little water along the edges, if needed, for a better seal. Holding each dumpling by its seam, tap its filled base on your work surface until it has a flat bottom and can sit upright without tipping over. Place the assembled dumplings in a single layer on the prepared tray and keep them covered with a kitchen towel while you work. Once you have assembled the first batch of dumplings, continue with the remaining dough and filling. Combine all the dough scraps, knead them into a ball, roll it out, cut out as many rounds as you can, and fill and fold those too.

7. Set aside the number of dumplings that you would like to cook and keep the rest frozen for up to 6 months (see page 36).

8. STEAM THE DUMPLINGS: Remove the basket from the steamer pot, add 2 inches of water to the pot, and bring to a boil over high heat. Line the basket with the lettuce leaves and arrange as many dumplings in the basket as you can fit without their touching. Place the basket in the pot, cover, reduce the heat to medium-high, and steam for 20 minutes. (If steaming frozen *sha momo*, place them directly in the basket and cook them in the steamer pot for 25 minutes. Do not allow the *sha momo* to thaw before cooking.)

9. Remove the pot from heat. Carefully remove the basket and place it on a folded kitchen towel. Gently lift up the *sha momo* with tongs and place them on a large plate. Serve immediately while you cook any remaining *sha momo*. Serve with Soy-Vinegar Sauce.

Stirring the rice batter

Filling the baking cups

Lining the steamer pot with a
damp towel for a tighter seal

A Wealth of Steamed Rice Muffins
Fot Gao (China), page 71

Cockles with Rice Dumplings in a Spicy Coconut Sauce
Kube Mutli (India), page 123

The ground rice

Stirring the cooked ground
rice to form the dough

Rolling the dough into balls

The chickpea-yogurt mixture

Stirring the spices and lemon juice into the batter

Filling the cake pan

Chickpea Squares Topped with Mustard Seeds and Spiced Oil
Khaman Dhokla (India), page 137

Pounded Rice Dumplings Stuffed with Strawberries
Ichigo Daifuku (Japan), page 190

Pounding the rice into *mochi*

Wrapping the strawberry
with bean paste

Wrapping the enclosed
strawberry with *mochi*

Filling the pudding basin with layers of apple and bread

Pouring in the custard sauce

Tying the muslin cover to create a handle

Layered Apple and Bread Pudding
(United States), page 291

Potato Dumplings Stuffed with Sugar-Stuffed Plums
Švestkové Knedlíky (Czech Republic), page 299

Filling the plum with
cinnamon sugar

Wrapping the plum
with dough

Pinching the dough to seal

Centering the rice and filling on top of the leaves

Folding the leaves to form a package

Wrapping and tying the package with string

Leaf-Wrapped Rice Packages Stuffed with Peanuts and Sausage
Zhong Zi (China), page 301

Chicken Paprika with Dumplings
Csirke Paprikas Galuskaval (Hungary), page 311

Combining the dough ingredients

Mixing the moist dough

Dropping the dough into simmering water

Spicy Lamb-Filled Dumplings in a Thick Yogurt Soup

Sheesh Barak bi Laban (Lebanon)

SERVES 4 TO 6 (MAKES ABOUT 60 DUMPLINGS)

Yogurt soup is a soothing contrast to these spicy, meat-filled dumplings. The lamb filling in these dumplings is well seasoned with allspice, cinnamon, and paprika. The spicier the dumplings, the more aromatic and outlandish their flavor in this silky soup. Some people like to fry the dumplings before simmering them in the soup, but that makes them firm and kind of brittle. The yogurt has a way of tenderizing the raw dough, making the dumplings lush and slippery as they cook. The dried mint in the soup, with its deeper, more tealike flavors, should not be replaced with fresh mint.

These dumplings are made using the Belly-Button Fold (page 49).

For the Dough

2 cups unbleached all-purpose flour, plus some extra for dusting

1 tablespoon grapeseed or other neutral oil

For the Filling

⅓ cup pine nuts

2 tablespoons ghee (page 12)

1 small yellow onion, chopped fine

2 garlic cloves, chopped very fine

1 teaspoon ground allspice

¼ teaspoon ground cinnamon

¼ teaspoon sweet paprika

½ pound ground lamb

½ teaspoon salt

¼ teaspoon freshly ground black pepper

For the Soup*

1 tablespoon ghee or a neutral oil, like grapeseed

4 garlic cloves, chopped very fine

⅓ cup coarsely chopped fresh cilantro leaves

¾ teaspoon salt

4 cups plain whole-milk yogurt, drained (see page 23) for 12 hours (about 2 cups)

2 teaspoons unbleached all-purpose flour mixed into 3 cups water

1 large egg white, beaten

2 tablespoons dried mint

Equipment

2-inch round cookie cutter

1. MAKE THE DOUGH: Place 1¾ cups of the flour in a large bowl and keep the remaining ¼ cup handy. Add the oil and ¾ cup water and mix until all the liquid has been absorbed. Work the dough with your hands into one manageable ball. If the dough is wet and sticky, work in some of the remaining flour, a little at a time, until it no longer sticks to your fingers.

---

*These amounts are for a full recipe. If you plan on freezing and storing some of the dumplings, reduce the amounts in proportion to the number you are serving.

2. Place the dough on a floured surface and knead for 2 to 3 minutes. The dough will be somewhat firm and elastic. Coat the dough with a little oil, return it to the bowl, cover with a clean kitchen towel, and let it rest for 30 minutes.

3. MAKE THE FILLING: Toast the pine nuts in a small skillet over medium heat, stirring constantly, until they just begin to brown, 2 to 3 minutes. Turn them into a bowl immediately and set aside.

4. Heat the 2 tablespoons ghee in a large skillet over medium heat. Add the onion and stir frequently until soft, about 4 minutes. Mix in the 2 cloves of chopped garlic, the allspice, cinnamon, and paprika. Add the lamb and break up clumps with a wooden spoon as it begins to brown. Stir in the pine nuts, ½ teaspoon salt, and the pepper and continue cooking until the lamb is golden brown, about 4 minutes longer. Remove from the heat, scoop into a shallow bowl, and set aside to cool.

5. ASSEMBLE THE DUMPLINGS: *Before assembling the* sheesh barak, *review the Belly-Button Fold.*

6. Line a tray with a kitchen towel and sprinkle with a little flour. Also have ready the dough and the filling.

7. Knead the dough once or twice on a floured surface, divide it into 4 equal pieces, and set 3 of them aside under a kitchen towel. Shape the remaining piece into a ball and roll it out until it's 1⁄16 inch thick. (For tips on how to roll dough out thin, see page 35.) Sprinkle with flour if it gets sticky. Let the rolled-out dough relax for a couple of minutes before cutting out rounds.

8. Using the cookie cutter, cut out as many rounds as you can, usually 12 to 15. Scraps cannot be reused because dough rolled out this thin is too dry to recombine.

9. Lay flat 1 to 5 dough rounds. Brush each round with a very thin coating of water to make it sticky enough to seal. Place 1 scant teaspoon of filling in the center of each round, fold neatly in half, pushing out any air, and pinch to seal. Pick up one of the half-moons and join and pinch its two ends together behind the base or "belly" of the dumpling. Dab a little water on the ends, if needed, for a better seal. Repeat this step with the remaining half-moons. Place the assembled dumplings in a single layer on the prepared tray and keep them covered with a kitchen towel while you work. Once you have assembled the first batch of dumplings, continue with the remaining dough and filling.

10. Cover the tray of assembled dumplings and place in the refrigerator for 30 to 60 minutes before cooking. Chilling the dumplings helps to set the dough, making them firm and toothsome when cooked instead of puffy and soft. Set aside the number of dumplings that you would like to cook and keep the rest frozen for up to 6 months (see page 36).

11. MAKE THE SOUP: Heat the 1 tablespoon ghee in a small skillet over medium heat. Add the 4 cloves of chopped garlic and stir until it just begins to brown. Mix in the cilantro and stir until the garlic is golden brown. Scoop into a bowl, sprinkle with the ¾ teaspoon salt, and set aside.

12. Whisk together the yogurt, flour and water mixture, egg white, and mint in a medium pot. Slowly bring it to a simmer over low heat, 10 to 15 minutes, stirring frequently.

13. COOK THE DUMPLINGS: Once the soup comes to a simmer, stir in the garlic and cilantro mixture. Gently drop in the *sheesh barak* a few at a time. Simmer, stirring occasionally, for 6 to 8 minutes, and serve. If cooking frozen *sheesh barak,* add them directly to the simmering yogurt soup and increase the cooking time by 4 minutes. Do not allow the dumplings to thaw before cooking.

Oven-Simmered Lamb-Filled Dumplings with Minted Yogurt

Manti (Turkey)

SERVES 4 TO 6 (MAKES ABOUT 64 DUMPLINGS)

What makes lamb-filled *manti* exceptional is that once they are assembled, they are placed in a baking dish, flooded with a savory broth, and simmered in the oven with their tops exposed just long enough to turn crispy and golden brown. Like *Shao Mai* (July), these dumplings are made with a very thin dough that requires practice. Take your time, enjoy the process, and try to roll out the dough a little thinner each time.

These dumplings are made using the Bottleneck Fold (page 50).

For the Sauce*

4 cups plain whole-milk yogurt, drained (see page 23) for 12 hours (about 2 cups)

4 garlic cloves, chopped very fine, mixed with ½ teaspoon salt and ground into a paste

1 teaspoon dried mint

For the Dough

1¼ cups unbleached all-purpose flour, plus some extra for dusting

1 large egg yolk

1 tablespoon olive oil

½ teaspoon salt

For the Filing

½ pound ground lamb

1 medium yellow onion, chopped fine

2 tablespoons dried oregano

1 tablespoon dried mint

1 teaspoon salt

½ teaspoon freshly ground black pepper

For Cooking and Serving*

Olive oil to coat the baking pan

1½ cups Chicken Broth (page 394)

Equipment

9 × 13-inch baking pan or 10-inch round ovenproof skillet

1. MAKE THE YOGURT SAUCE 2 HOURS IN ADVANCE: Place all of the sauce ingredients and 1 cup water in a large bowl and mix well. Cover and refrigerate for at least 2 hours but no more than 8 hours.

2. MAKE THE DOUGH: Place 1 cup of the flour in a medium bowl and keep the remaining ¼ cup handy. Add the egg yolk, ⅓ cup water, the oil, and the ½ teaspoon salt and mix until all of the liquid has been absorbed. Work the dough with your hands into one manageable

---

*These amounts are for a full recipe. If you plan on freezing and storing some of the dumplings, reduce the amounts in proportion to the number you are serving.

ball. If the dough is wet and sticky, work in some of the remaining flour, a little at a time, until it no longer sticks to your fingers.

3. Place the dough on a floured surface and knead for 5 to 7 minutes. Sprinkle with flour if it gets a little sticky. The dough will be somewhat firm and elastic. Coat the dough with a little oil, return it to the bowl, cover, and let it rest for 30 minutes.

4. MAKE THE FILLING: Meanwhile, combine all the filling ingredients in a medium bowl and keep refrigerated until the dumplings are ready to be assembled.

5. ASSEMBLE THE DUMPLINGS: *Before assembling the* manti, *review the Bottleneck Fold. Instead of a round piece if dough, you will be using a square.*

6. Line a tray with a kitchen towel and sprinkle with a little flour. Have ready the dough and the filling.

7. Knead the dough once or twice on a floured surface, divide into 4 equal pieces, then set 3 of them aside under a kitchen towel. Shape the remaining piece into a blunt log and roll it out into an 8-inch square. This dough should not be thicker than $\frac{1}{16}$ inch, even thinner would be ideal. (For tips on how to roll dough out thin, see page 35.) Take your time and sprinkle with a little flour if it gets sticky. Let the rolled-out dough rest for a couple of minutes.

8. Trim the edges, creating a cleaner square shape. Cut the dough into 2-inch strips, then cut again going across to form 16 squares. Place the squares in a single layer on the prepared tray. Repeat with the remaining dough pieces, separating layers with kitchen towels. Keep the squares covered as you work. Scraps cannot be reused because dough rolled out this thin is too dry to recombine.

9. Line another tray with a kitchen towel and sprinkle with a little flour. Have ready the dough squares and the filling.

10. Lay flat 1 to 5 dough squares. Brush each square with a very thin coating of water to make it sticky enough to seal. Place a heaping teaspoon of filling in the center of each square. Gather up the sides of the square, creating a pouch around the filling, leaving an open neck in the center of the gathered dough. Pinch together the creases and pleats that formed naturally while the dough was gathered up without closing the open neck. This gives the dumpling a loose and frilly top. Gently squeeze the body of the dumpling until the filling pushes up through the neck a little. Holding the dumpling by the neck, tap its base on your work surface until it is flat enough on the bottom to sit upright. Place the assembled dumplings in a single layer on the prepared tray and continue with the remaining squares and filling. Keep the dumplings covered with a kitchen towel as you work.

11. Set aside the number of dumplings that you would like to cook and keep the rest frozen for up to 6 months (see page 36). Cover and place the dumplings to be cooked in the refrigerator while you preheat the oven.

12. COOK THE DUMPLINGS: Preheat the oven to 400°F. Bring the yogurt sauce to room temperature.

13. Coat the inside of the baking pan with oil and arrange the dumplings in the pan. Place the pan in the oven and bake until the tops of the dumplings are just beginning to brown, 10 to 15 minutes. (If cooking frozen *manti,* place them directly in the pan and then immediately into the oven, increasing the cooking time by 5 minutes. Do not allow the *manti* to thaw before cooking.)

14. Meanwhile, pour the chicken broth into a small saucepan and bring it to a boil over high heat. When the tops of the dumplings have just browned, choose an empty spot in the pan and pour in the broth. Return the pan to the oven and continue to cook until the tops of the dumplings are golden brown and most of the broth has cooked off or been absorbed, about 10 minutes.

15. Remove the pan from the oven, place on a folded kitchen towel, and allow the *manti* to cool slightly. Scoop up the *manti* with a spoon or a small spatula, place right side up on a large serving plate, spoon the yogurt sauce over the top, and serve.

Dumplings Stuffed with Pork and Cabbage

Mandu (Korea)

SERVES 4 TO 8 (MAKES ABOUT 48 DUMPLINGS)

At first glance, these Korean dumplings appear to be no different from Chinese *Jiao Zi* (February). Both are filled with meat and seasoned with scallions and ginger, soy sauce and sesame oil, but *mandu* fillings are lighter because they include lots of juicy, crispy vegetables such as cabbage and bean sprouts. If you want vegetarian *mandu,* you can make the mushroom and tofu variation that follows.

These dumplings are made using the Standing Half-Moon Fold (page 48), but you can also use the more detailed Pleated Half-Moon Fold (page 46).

For the Dough

2 cups unbleached all-purpose flour, plus some extra for dusting

¼ cup cornstarch

1½ tablespoons grapeseed or other neutral oil

For the Filling

8 large napa cabbage leaves, chopped fine and hand-wilted (see page 37), or one 18-ounce jar cabbage kimchee, drained

1 pound lean boneless pork loin, chopped very fine, or freshly ground pork

¾ pound mung bean sprouts, hand-wilted and chopped fine

6 garlic cloves, chopped very fine

4 scallions, sliced into thin rings

1 tablespoon finely grated fresh ginger or ¾ teaspoon ground

2 tablespoons toasted sesame oil

1 tablespoon cornstarch

1 teaspoon soy sauce

2 teaspoons salt (reduce the salt by half if using kimchee instead of fresh napa cabbage)

½ teaspoon freshly ground white pepper

For Cooking and Serving

Soft lettuce leaves, such as Boston, to line the steamer basket and serving plate

1 recipe Soy-Vinegar Sauce* (page 112)

Equipment

3¼-inch round cookie cutter

8- to 10-quart steamer pot

1. MAKE THE DOUGH: Place 1¾ cups of the flour in a large bowl and keep the remaining ¼ cup handy. Add the ¼ cup cornstarch and mix well. Add the oil and ¾ cup water and mix until all of the liquid has been absorbed. Work the dough with your hands into one manageable ball. If the dough is wet and sticky, work in some of the remaining flour, a little at a time, until it no longer sticks to your fingers.

---

*This is for a full recipe. If you plan on freezing and storing some of the dumplings, reduce the amounts in proportion to the number you are serving.

2. Place the dough on a floured surface and knead for 2 to 3 minutes. The dough will be somewhat firm and elastic. Coat the dough with a little oil, return it to the bowl, cover with a clean kitchen towel, and let rest for at least 30 minutes but no more than 1 hour.

3. MAKE THE FILLING: While the dough is resting, combine the cabbage with the rest of the filling ingredients in a medium bowl.

4. ASSEMBLE THE DUMPLINGS: *Before assembling the* mandu, *review the Standing Half-Moon Fold or the Pleated Half-Moon Fold.*

5. Line a tray with a kitchen towel. Have ready the dough and the filling.

6. Knead the dough once or twice on a floured surface, divide it into 4 equal pieces, and set 3 of them aside under a kitchen towel. Shape the remaining piece into a ball, then roll it out until it's 1/16 inch thick. (For tips on how to roll dough out thin, see page 35.) Sprinkle with flour if it gets sticky. Let the rolled-out dough relax for a couple of minutes before cutting out rounds.

7. Using the cookie cutter, cut out as many rounds as you can, usually 10 to 12. Scraps cannot be reused because dough rolled out this thin is too dry to recombine.

8. Lay flat 1 to 5 dough rounds. Brush each round with a very thin coating of water to make it sticky enough to seal. Center a rounded tablespoon of filling in the center of each round, fold each neatly in half, pushing out any air, and pinch to seal. Dab a little water along the edges, if needed, for a better seal. Holding the dumpling by its seam, tap the base on your work surface until it is flat enough on the bottom to sit upright. Place the assembled dumplings in a single layer on the prepared tray and keep covered with a kitchen towel as you work. Once you have assembled the first batch of dumplings, continue with the remaining dough and filling.

9. Set aside the number of dumplings that you would like to cook and keep the rest frozen for up to 6 months (see page 36).

10. STEAM THE DUMPLINGS: Remove the basket from the steamer pot, add 2 inches of water to the pot, and bring to a boil over high heat. Line the basket with the lettuce leaves and arrange as many dumplings in the basket as you can fit without their touching. Place the basket in the pot, cover, reduce the heat to medium, and steam for 15 minutes. (If steaming frozen *mandu*, place them directly in the basket and cook them in the steamer pot for 20 minutes. Do not allow the *mandu* to thaw before cooking.)

11. Remove the pot from the heat. Carefully remove the basket, place it on a folded kitchen towel, and allow the *mandu* to cool slightly. Arrange a few lettuce leaves on a plate. Use a spoon or a small spatula to move the *mandu* to the prepared plate. Serve immediately while you cook any remaining *mandu*. Serve with Soy-Vinegar Sauce.

TOFU AND MUSHROOM MANDU

Leave out the cornstarch and ground pork, instead adding:

4 ounces firm tofu, finely crumbled and folded up in a kitchen towel for 30 minutes to soak up excess water

3 dried shiitake or black mushrooms, soaked in hot water to cover for 30 minutes, then stemmed and chopped fine

May

BLACK SESAME CUPCAKES
Kurogoma Mushipan (Japan) 165

BOILED FISH WITH OKRA AND DUMPLINGS
(Caribbean) 167

SLIPPERY RICE BALLS IN CABBAGE-RADISH SOUP
Tang Yuan (China) 169

POUNDED CASSAVA DUMPLING
Fufu (West Africa) 171

MUSHROOM-ASPARAGUS BREAD DUMPLINGS IN A MUSHROOM SAUCE
Schwammerl Knödel mit Spargel (Austria) 173

COCONUT AND RICE COLUMNS WITH CHICKPEA CURRY
Puttu Kadala (India) 176

SMALL PORK BUNS
Zhu Rou Baozi (China) 179

SMALL MUSHROOM BUNS
Xiang Gu Baozi (China) 181

PINEAPPLE-PECAN TAMALES
Tamales Dulces (Mexico) 184

TAMALES STUFFED WITH CHICKEN AND TOMATILLO SAUCE
Tamales de Pollo (Mexico) 186

POUNDED RICE DUMPLINGS STUFFED WITH STRAWBERRIES
Ichigo Daifuku (Japan) 190

LEAF-WRAPPED RICE PACKAGES STUFFED WITH CHICKEN AND BAMBOO SHOOTS
Nuo Mi Ji (China) 192

Black Sesame Cupcakes

Kurogoma Mushipan (Japan)

SERVES 4 TO 8 (MAKES 8 DUMPLINGS)

Mushipan are a collection of steamed Japanese cakes inspired in part by French pastries and British puddings. They come in an array of flavors and densities, and some even have fillings. *Kurogoma mushipan* are made with a ground black sesame seed batter and have a beautiful, richly speckled look. These dumplings are as light as angel food cake, and make a tasty dessert or snack.

For the Dumplings

¼ cup cake flour

¼ cup superfine sugar (or granulated sugar pulsed in a spice or coffee grinder for 1 to 2 minutes)

½ teaspoon baking powder

Pinch of salt

¼ cup black sesame seeds

3 large eggs, separated, plus 1 large egg white

2 tablespoons grapeseed or other neutral oil

¼ teaspoon cream of tartar

Equipment

Clean spice or coffee grinder

8 individual baking cups

8 paper baking cups

8- to 10-quart steamer pot

1. MAKE THE BATTER: Sift the cake flour, sugar, baking powder, and salt through a fine sieve into a bowl. Sift 2 more times, then set aside.

2. Toast the black sesame seeds in a small skillet over medium heat, stirring continuously, for 2 minutes. Immediately move them to a small bowl to cool. Finely grind in the spice grinder.

3. Mix together the ground sesame seeds, the 3 egg yolks, and the oil in a large bowl and set aside.

4. In a medium bowl, whisk the 4 egg whites until very light and foamy. Add the cream of tartar and continue whisking until the mixture forms soft peaks.

5. Add half of the flour mixture to the sesame and egg yolk mixture and stir until combined. Scoop in half of the whipped egg whites and stir until it forms a thick batter. Stir in the remaining flour mixture, then add the remaining egg whites and fold until just combined.

6. STEAM THE DUMPLINGS: Line the individual baking cups with the paper baking cups. Remove the basket from the steamer pot, add 2 inches of water to the pot, and bring to a boil over high heat. Arrange the lined baking cups in the basket. Spoon in enough batter to fill each cup to just over three-quarters full. Carefully place the basket in the pot, cover, and cook for 20 minutes.

7. Remove the pot from the heat. Remove the basket, place on a folded kitchen towel, and allow the *kurogoma mushipan* to cool slightly. Remove them from the individual baking cups, arrange the dumplings on a plate, and serve warm or at room temperature.

Boiled Fish with Okra and Dumplings

(Caribbean)

SERVES 4 (MAKES 12 DUMPLINGS)

The flavors of Caribbean cooking are apparent in this simply prepared seafood dish. The dumplings, purposely dense and chewy, are smothered in a spicy tomato sauce with chunks of okra and green pepper and a generous helping of fish. Cod, snapper, and grouper are commonly used, but alarmingly, all of these fish have been depleted to dangerously low levels. You can use any firm white-fleshed fish that is more abundant, whole or cut into fillets.

For the Dumplings

2 cups unbleached all-purpose flour, plus some extra for dusting

½ teaspoon salt

For the Fish

3 tablespoons grapeseed or other neutral oil

1 small yellow onion, chopped coarse

3 garlic cloves, sliced thin

1 large green bell pepper, cored and chopped coarse

1 small Scotch bonnet chile,* cored and quartered (or left whole if you want a less spicy sauce)

5 okra pods, trimmed of their tops and cut into ½-inch rounds (about 1 cup)

1 tablespoon fresh thyme leaves

¾ teaspoon salt

1½ tablespoons tomato paste

4 firm white-fleshed fish fillets such as tilapia (about 1 pound)

1 scallion, trimmed and sliced into thin rings

1 lime, cut in half

Equipment

Large, wide pot or skillet with a cover

Large, wide bowl to hold the cooked dumplings

1. MAKE THE DOUGH: Place 1¾ cups of the flour in a large bowl and keep the remaining ¼ cup handy. Add the ½ teaspoon salt and 1 cup water and mix with a fork until all the liquid has been absorbed. Work the dough with your hands until you have one manageable ball. If the dough is wet and sticky, work in some of the remaining flour, a little at a time, until it no longer sticks to your fingers.

2. Place the dough on a floured surface and knead for 3 to 4 minutes. Sprinkle with flour if it gets a little sticky. The dough will be soft and stretchy. Return the dough to the bowl, cover, and let it rest for 30 minutes.

3. MAKE AND COOK THE DUMPLINGS: Line a tray with a kitchen towel and sprinkle with a little flour.

---

*To ensure safe handling of hot chiles, wear rubber gloves and wash your hands thoroughly afterward.

4. Knead the dough once or twice on a floured surface and divide into 12 equal pieces. Roll 1 piece into a 5-inch rope, flatten it with your fingers into a bar about ¼ inch thick, and place on the prepared tray. Repeat with the remaining pieces of dough.

5. Fill a medium pot halfway with water and bring to a boil over high heat. Carefully drop the dough bars, a few at a time, into the water and stir. Cook until all of them are floating, about 2 minutes, then cook for 5 minutes longer. Remove with a slotted spoon, place in the bowl with a ladle of the cooking liquid to prevent sticking, and keep warm.

6. COOK THE FISH: Heat the oil in the large pot over high heat. Add the onion and garlic and stir until the onion just begins to soften, about 2 minutes. Mix in the bell pepper and chile and cook until the onion and peppers are lightly browned, about 3 minutes. Add the okra, thyme, ¾ teaspoon salt, the tomato paste, and 1 cup water, stir, and bring to a boil.

7. Clear some space in the pot by moving the vegetables to the side. Arrange the fish in the center of the pan and spoon some of the sauce and vegetables on top. Cover, reduce the heat to low, and simmer for 2 minutes. Gently turn the fish pieces over and simmer uncovered until they are cooked through, about 1 minute. Drain the dumplings, add them to the fish, shake the pan to coat the dumplings, cook for 1 minute longer, and serve.

Slippery Rice Balls in Cabbage-Radish Soup

Tang Yuan (China)

SERVES 4 (MAKES ABOUT 20 DUMPLINGS)

Tang yuan, or "soup balls," are very basic rice flour dumplings. They have a clean, light flavor, a chewy and almost bouncy texture, and a silky, slippery feel. Variations of these small dumplings are found throughout Asia, both savory and sweet, and a couple of others are featured in this book (*Guinataan at Bilo-Bilo* in December and *Onde-Onde* in March). The broth used in this recipe is delicious on its own and can also be used with other Chinese soup dumplings, such as *Hung You Chao Shou* (August).

For the Soup

4 small dried shiitake or black mushrooms, soaked in 1 cup hot water for 30 minutes

½ pound lean boneless pork butt, cut into 8 equal pieces

6 to 8 small or medium dried shrimp

4 large napa cabbage leaves, sliced into 1-inch ribbons

1 small daikon radish, peeled and coarsely grated, or 1 medium carrot, sliced into thin rounds

1 link Chinese pork sausage *(la chang),* cut diagonally into thin slices

1 teaspoon salt

For the Dumplings

1¼ cups sweet (glutinous) rice flour, preferably from China or Thailand, plus some extra for dusting

½ cup warm water

1. MAKE THE SOUP: Fish out the soaked mushrooms with your fingers, squeezing excess liquid back into the bowl. Remove and discard the stems and set the mushroom caps aside. Strain the soaking liquid.

2. Place the pork, dried shrimp, mushrooms, and their soaking liquid in a medium pot. Pour in 5 cups water and bring to a boil over high heat. Cover, reduce the heat to low, and simmer for 30 minutes. Skim the froth off the surface with a spoon.

3. MAKE THE DOUGH: While the soup is simmering, place 1 cup of the rice flour in a medium bowl and keep the remaining ¼ cup handy. Pour in the warm water and mix until all the liquid has been absorbed. Knead the dough in the bowl for a minute. This dough needs to be firm enough to hold its shape when rolled into balls. If it is too soft or sticky, work in some of the remaining flour, a little at a time.

4. Once the soup has simmered for 30 minutes, mix in the cabbage, daikon, sausage, and salt, cover, and simmer for 10 minutes longer. Reduce the heat to very, very low to keep the soup hot until it's time to add the dumplings.

5. MAKE AND COOK THE DUMPLINGS: Line a tray with a kitchen towel and sprinkle with a little rice flour.

6. Fill a medium pot halfway with salted water and bring it to a boil over high heat.

7. As the water comes to a boil, pinch off a small piece of dough and roll it into a ball about 1 inch around. Dust with a little rice flour and place on the prepared tray. Repeat with the remaining dough.

8. Lower the heat under the boiling water for a gentle simmer. Carefully drop the dumplings, a few at a time, into the water. Cook until all of them are floating, about 2 minutes, then cook for 2 minutes longer.

9. Remove the *tang yuan* with a slotted spoon, place them in the hot soup, cover, steep for 3 minutes, and serve.

Pounded Cassava Dumpling

Fufu (West Africa)

SERVES 4 (MAKES 1 LARGE OR 4 SMALL DUMPLINGS)

Fufu is a family of pounded dumplings that are a staple throughout the central and western regions of Africa. Making *fufu* the traditional way, communally and in big batches, requires hours of work akin to chopping wood. A starch (like yam, cassava, plantain, or a combination) is boiled and then pounded in a large mortar with a big flat-bottomed pestle until smooth and stretchy. *Fufu* is meant to be pinched off and then dipped into a hearty sauce, stew, or soup. *Fufu* made out of cassava has a very clean taste and can be quite soothing when paired with a bowl of spicy Groundnut Soup.

We've adapted the traditional method of pounding *fufu* into a 15-minute effort. By grating the cassava before steaming, you eliminate a great portion of the pounding time. For a more tender, mildly fruity *fufu*, try the cassava and plantain version.

For the Dumplings

2 pounds cassava, prepared (see page 7) and grated coarse

For the Soup

1 recipe Groundnut Soup (recipe follows)

Equipment

8- to 10-quart steamer pot

24-inch square of muslin

Large, sturdy wooden bowl and large pestle or meat pounder for pounding the *fufu*

1. Remove the basket from the steamer pot, add 2 inches of water to the pot, and bring to a boil over high heat. Soak the muslin under running water, wring it out, then drape it inside the basket, creating a lining. Scoop the cassava into the lined basket and spread it out evenly. Place the basket in the pot, cover, reduce the heat to medium, and steam for 45 minutes.

2. Remove the pot from the heat. Carefully remove the basket and place it on a folded kitchen towel. Using the muslin liner, lift the cassava out of the basket and turn it into the bowl. The bowl must be roomy enough for you to pound the cassava freely without spilling. Using the large pestle, begin to pound the cassava steadily. Continue pounding until the cassava is smooth (or mostly smooth), stretchy, and very sticky, about 10 minutes. If the *fufu* is dry and too firm to pound effectively, add some warm water and resume pounding.

3. Wet your hands and shape the *fufu* into a big ball or divide and shape it into 4 equal balls and serve slightly warm or at room temperature with the Groundnut Soup. If making the *fufu* in advance, wrap the balls in wax paper to prevent them from forming a skin and keep at room temperature for no more than 4 hours.

CASSAVA AND PLANTAIN FUFU

Add 1 coarsely chopped green plantain to the cassava (for a fluffier and plain *fufu*) or ripe plantain (for a gooier and fruitier *fufu*) during the last 10 minutes of cooking. Continue with steps 2 and 3 and serve.

GROUNDNUT SOUP

MAKES 3 QUARTS

One 3- to 4-pound chicken, cut into serving pieces

2 cups all-natural unsweetened peanut butter

¼ cup peanut oil or a neutral oil, such as grapeseed

1 small yellow onion, chopped fine

3 plum tomatoes, peeled (see page 21) and chopped fine

2 tablespoons tomato paste

1 small Scotch bonnet chile,* cored, seeded, and chopped fine

1 small eggplant, peeled and chopped fine

1 to 2 ounces fried or preserved (dried, smoked, or salted) white fish, shredded

Salt to taste

1. Place the chicken pieces in a large pot, pour in 9 cups water, and bring to a boil over high heat. Cover, reduce the heat to low, and simmer for 30 minutes. Skim the froth off the surface with a spoon.

2. Remove the chicken with a slotted spoon or tongs and place in a bowl to cool. Using your hands, pull off bite-sized pieces until all the chicken meat has been removed. Place back in the bowl and set aside. Discard the bones.

3. Thin out the peanut butter by mixing it with 1 cup of the simmering broth, then stir it into the broth.

4. Heat the oil in a medium pot over medium heat. Add the onion and cook, stirring occasionally, until soft, about 4 minutes. Stir in the tomatoes, tomato paste, chile, and eggplant and cook until the tomatoes have broken apart, about 5 minutes. Add the tomato and eggplant mixture to the broth and simmer for 10 minutes. Stir in the chicken and the fish and cook for 10 minutes longer. Sprinkle with salt and serve with cassava *fufu*. Groundnut soup can be made in advance and kept in a tightly sealed container for up to 3 days.

---

* To ensure safe handling of hot chiles, wear rubber gloves and wash your hands thoroughly afterward.

Mushroom-Asparagus Bread Dumplings in a Mushroom Sauce

Schwammerl Knödel mit Spargel (Austria)

SERVES 6 TO 12 (MAKES 2 DUMPLINGS)

These long, tender bread dumplings are chock-full of sautéed mushrooms and asparagus. This dumpling is fun to cut into when the stalks of asparagus are left whole and nestled into the dough, but you can just as easily chop the asparagus and mix it directly into the dough along with the mushrooms. This recipe can be fashioned into one very long dumpling or two more manageable dumplings, as we do here. Serve as a side to any meal that goes well with mushrooms or asparagus.

These dumplings are made using the Jelly-Roll Shape (page 41) and then wrapped using the Candy-Wrapper Shape Using a Cloth (page 51).

For the Dough

¼ cup grapeseed or other neutral oil

1 large yellow onion, chopped fine

10 ounces whole white button mushrooms, cut in half

3 tablespoons finely chopped fresh oregano leaves

6 cups ½-inch crustless white bread cubes (see page 6)

¾ cup milk

1 large egg, plus 2 large egg yolks

1½ teaspoons salt

1 cup unbleached all-purpose flour, plus some extra for dusting

For the Filling

16 thin asparagus spears, trimmed and blanched in boiling water for 3 minutes, then cooled under cold running water

For the Sauce

1½ tablespoons unsalted butter

1½ tablespoons unbleached all-purpose flour

1½ cups Beef Broth (page 396)

½ teaspoon salt

¼ teaspoon freshly ground black pepper

For Cooking

Unsalted butter to coat the muslin

Equipment

Two 24-inch squares of muslin or white cotton napkins

8- to 10-quart steamer pot

1. MAKE THE DOUGH: Cook the mushrooms in 2 batches as follows. Heat 2 tablespoons of the oil in a large skillet over high heat. Add half of the onion and stir until it just begins to soften, about 2 minutes. Add half of the mushrooms and cook, stirring occasionally, until the mixture is golden brown, about 6 minutes. Scoop into a bowl and set aside. Wipe the skillet clean and heat the remaining 2 tablespoons of oil. Repeat the cooking steps with the remaining onion and mushrooms. Once the second batch of mushrooms is golden brown, return the first batch to the pan, add the oregano, and mix well. Scoop a third of the mushroom mixture back into the bowl and set aside. Keep the remaining two-thirds in the pan.

2. Place the bread cubes in a medium bowl and pour in the milk. Work the mixture together by squishing it through your fingers until all the bread has been broken down into a pulp. Beat together the egg and the egg yolks. Add the egg and the 1½ teaspoons salt to the bread mixture and stir vigorously until well mixed. Add the mushroom mixture from the pan and the 1 cup flour and work the paste into a soft dough. Cover and refrigerate for 20 minutes.

3. ASSEMBLE THE DUMPLINGS: *Before assembling the* schwammerl knödel mit spargel, *review the Jelly-Roll Shape and the Candy-Wrapper Shape Using a Cloth. The Jelly-Roll Shape begins with a sheet of dough covered with a sweet or savory filling. Starting at one end, the dough and filling are rolled up into a solid log, which gives a characteristic swirl of filling throughout the body of the dumpling. The Candy-Wrapper Shape is a quick and easy way to wrap up a portion of dough or batter in a cloth or a leaf, creating or supporting the shape of a log.*

4. Soak both pieces of muslin under running water, wring them out, and set aside. Have ready the chilled dough, the asparagus, and a large plate.

5. Divide the dough in half and place one piece on a well-floured surface. Wet your hands and gently press it into a rectangle about 9 inches long (or about the length of the asparagus) and 7 inches wide. Arrange half of the asparagus in parallel lines on top of the dough, making sure they are spaced evenly apart. Gently press down on each stalk until it has been pushed about halfway into the dough. Starting with one of the longer sides, roll up the dough, pinching the ends to seal as you go. Sprinkle with flour if it gets sticky. Pinch and press the far edge of the dough along the length of the loaf to seal.

6. Spread one piece of muslin out on a flat surface and rub it generously with butter, leaving a narrow border on all sides. Place the loaf along one edge of the prepared muslin, seam side down. Roll up the loaf in the muslin. The muslin should be slightly baggy so that the loaf can swell while it cooks. Tie the two open ends, then tie some string around the body of the wrapped loaf to secure the seam. Repeat with the remaining dough, asparagus, and cloth. When both loaves have been wrapped and tied, place them on the plate, and refrigerate for at least 15 minutes. (You can also assemble the dumplings in advance and keep them tightly wrapped in the refrigerator for up to 8 hours.)

7. STEAM THE DUMPLINGS: Remove the basket from the steamer pot, add 2 inches of water to the pot, and bring to a boil over high heat. Arrange the loaves in the basket, then place the basket in the pot. Cover, reduce the heat to medium, and steam for 1 hour. Check the water level halfway through cooking and replenish with boiling water as needed.

8. MAKE THE SAUCE: Shortly before the dumplings have finished cooking, melt the butter in a small saucepan over medium heat. Add the 1½ tablespoons flour and stir until the mixture is well browned, about 3 minutes. Pour in the broth, stirring constantly, until combined. Once the sauce begins to simmer, 2 to 3 minutes, add the ½ teaspoon salt, the pepper, and the remaining cooked mushrooms to the sauce and simmer for 3 minutes longer.

9. Remove the steamer pot from the heat. Carefully lift the *schwammerl knödel mit spargel* out of the basket, place them on a folded kitchen towel, and allow them to cool slightly. Remove the strings, unwrap, slice, and serve with the mushroom sauce poured over the top. *Schwammerl knödel mit spargel* can be refrigerated for up to 3 days. Reheat using the Steamer Plate Setup (page 37) or by frying the slices in a little butter or oil.

Coconut and Rice Columns with Chickpea Curry

Puttu Kadala (India)

SERVES 4 TO 8 (MAKES 2 DUMPLINGS)

To make this breakfast dumpling in its traditional pillar shape, you need a *puttu* steamer, available at most Indian markets. This metal *puttu* maker resembles a small saucepan with a chimneylike top. You assemble this dumpling by packing layers of moist ground rice and freshly grated coconut loosely inside the mold. As the steam builds up, it makes its way through the rice and coconut layers, cooking everything flawlessly. This dumpling is delicate and tender and is typically served smothered in a spicy chickpea stew.

For the Stew

1½ cups dried chickpeas, preferably black chickpeas (*kala chana*), soaked in plenty of water for 6 to 8 hours or 3 cups canned chickpeas, drained and rinsed

2 teaspoons ground turmeric

2 tablespoons ghee (page 12) or a neutral oil, such as grapeseed

1 teaspoon black or brown mustard seeds

5 fresh curry leaves

1 medium yellow onion, cut in half and sliced thin

2 garlic cloves, chopped very fine

1 tablespoon grated fresh ginger or ¾ teaspoon ground

1 to 2 small fresh green or red chiles, such as *lal mirch,* seeded and chopped fine

¼ cup Coconut Curry Masala (recipe follows) or 2 tablespoons garam masala mixed with 2 tablespoons unsweetened dried grated coconut

½ teaspoon sugar

2 teaspoons salt

1 teaspoon freshly ground black pepper

For the Dumplings

1¼ cups white basmati or other long-grain rice, ground fine in a clean spice or coffee grinder, or 1¼ cups preground rice (rice *sooji,* rice *rava,* or *idli rava*)

1 teaspoon salt

½ cup fresh coconut milk (see page 8) or ⅓ cup canned coconut milk mixed with 3 tablespoons water

1 cup freshly grated coconut (see page 8) or 1 cup frozen grated coconut, thawed

Equipment

Puttu steamer with cylinder mold (a standard steamer will hold about 1½ cups)

1. MAKE THE SAUCE: (If using canned chickpeas, place them in a bowl and set aside. Stir the turmeric into 5 cups of water and set aside.) Drain the chickpeas and place in a small pot. Add the turmeric and 5 cups water and bring to a boil over high heat. Reduce the heat to low, cover, and simmer until the chickpeas are just tender, 1 to 1½ hours. Remove from the heat. Reserve the cooking liquid by draining the chickpeas over a bowl, then set both the chickpeas and the cooking liquid aside.

2. Melt the ghee in a medium pot over medium heat. Stir in the mustard seeds and curry leaves and cook for 1 minute. Add the onion, garlic, ginger, and chile and stir frequently until the onion is soft, about 4 minutes. Mix in the Coconut Curry Masala and stir frequently until the onion is golden brown, about 2 minutes longer. Stir in the cooked chickpeas, the sugar, the 2 teaspoons salt, and the pepper. Immediately pour in just enough of the reserved cooking liquid (or turmeric water) to cover the chickpeas. If there is not enough cooking liquid, use water. Cover and simmer until the chickpeas are tender, about 10 minutes. Remove from the heat and set aside. (You can make the sauce in advance and keep it refrigerated in a tightly sealed container for up to 3 days.)

3. MAKE AND STEAM THE DUMPLINGS: Combine the ground rice and the 1 teaspoon salt in a medium mixing bowl. Stir in just enough coconut milk to make the ground rice moist enough to form a loose clump when you squeeze it. This is not a dough but more of a gritty, loose mixture.

4. Remove the cylinder mold from the *puttu* steamer, fill the *puttu* pot halfway with water, and bring to a boil over high heat.

5. Make sure the bottom end of the mold has its steaming plate in place. Fill the mold with 1 heaping tablespoon of coconut, followed by 3 heaping tablespoons of the rice mixture. Tap the mold gently to settle the layers. Continue with another layer of coconut, then the rice mixture, then a final layer of coconut. You will have used half of the coconut and half of the rice mixture. Place the cover on the top of the mold and insert the mold into the pot. Reduce the heat to medium and steam for 10 to 12 minutes. Steam will start vigorously streaming out the top of the mold when the dumpling has cooked through.

6. Remove the pot from the heat. Using pot holders, remove the mold from the pot, lay it on a folded kitchen towel, and allow the *puttu* to cool slightly. Lift the cover off the mold and use the end of a wooden spoon to push the steaming plate, and the *puttu* along with it, up through the mold and onto a serving plate. Cover and keep warm. Assemble and steam the second *puttu*.

7. While the second *puttu* is steaming, reheat the sauce. Once the second *puttu* has been cooked and placed on the plate, spoon the sauce over both and serve.

COCONUT CURRY MASALA

MAKES ABOUT ¾ CUP

⅔ cup freshly grated and dried coconut (see page 8) or unsweetened dried grated coconut

2 tablespoons coriander seeds

2 tablespoons peeled black gram (*urad dal*)

1 teaspoon cumin seeds

1 teaspoon fennel seeds

1 teaspoon fenugreek seeds

1 teaspoon black peppercorns

1 to 2 small dried red chiles

10 fresh curry leaves

One 1-inch cinnamon stick

4 whole cloves

Equipment

Clean spice or coffee grinder

1. Heat a large skillet over medium heat and add all the ingredients. Stir continuously until the mixture is golden brown, about 5 minutes. Remove from the heat, place in a bowl, and set aside to cool.

2. Pulse the mixture in batches in the spice grinder until it is a coarse powder. Measure out what you need for your recipe and keep the rest in a tightly sealed glass container in the refrigerator for up to 3 months.

Small Pork Buns

Zhu Rou Baozi (China)

SERVES 4 TO 8 (MAKES ABOUT 24 DUMPLINGS)

Zhu rou baozi may be the best-known Chinese dumpling. Made out of the same yeast dough as *Mantou* (January), *Xiang Gu Baozi* (recipe follows), and *Nuo Mi Juan* (February), these steamed dumplings are a type of supremely soft and perfectly seasoned pork sandwich. These smaller versions are the most popular: one is a snack, while two or three make a light meal.

These dumplings are made using the Pinched-Top Fold (page 52).

For the Filling

½ pound boneless pork loin, chopped fine, or freshly ground pork

1 large carrot, finely grated

2 scallions, sliced into very thin rings

2 teaspoons finely grated fresh ginger or ¼ teaspoon ground

1 teaspoon cornstarch

¼ teaspoon salt

¼ teaspoon freshly ground white pepper

¼ teaspoon sugar

2 tablespoons grapeseed or other neutral oil

1½ tablespoons soy sauce

For the Dough

1 recipe *Mantou* (page 72) dough, preferably made no more than 2 hours in advance

Unbleached all-purpose flour for dusting

For Cooking

Soft lettuce leaves, such as Boston, to line the steamer basket

Equipment

2¾-inch round cookie cutter

8- to 10-quart steamer pot

1. MAKE THE FILLING: Combine all the filling ingredients in a medium bowl. Cover and refrigerate for at least 20 minutes. (You can make the filling in advance and keep it tightly covered in the refrigerator for up to 1 day.)

2. ASSEMBLE THE DUMPLINGS: *Before assembling the* zhu rou baozi, *review the Pinched-Top Fold, which produces natural pleats when you simply gather up the sides and pinch off the top.*

3. Line a tray with a kitchen towel and sprinkle with a little flour. Also have ready the dough and the filling.

4. Knead the dough once or twice on a floured surface, divide it in half, and set one piece aside under a kitchen towel. Shape the remaining piece into a ball, then roll it out until it's about ⅛ inch thick. Sprinkle with flour if it gets sticky.

5. Using the cookie cutter, cut out as many rounds as you can, usually 10 to 12. Collect the scraps from around the rounds and put them aside under a damp kitchen towel for later use.

6. Lay flat 1 to 5 dough rounds. Brush each round with a very thin coating of water to make it sticky enough to seal. Place a rounded teaspoon of filling in the center of each round. Gather up the sides of the round, joining the edges to form a casually pleated top. Pinch and squeeze the gathered dough at the top of the dumpling to seal. Dab a little water along the edges, if needed, for a better seal. There is usually a little nub of the dough at the top of the dumplings assembled using the Pinched-Top Fold that you can twist off for a neater look. Place the assembled dumplings in a single layer on the prepared tray and keep them covered with a kitchen towel while you work. Once you have assembled the first batch of dumplings, continue with the remaining dough and filling. Combine all the dough scraps, knead them into a ball, roll it out, cut out as many rounds as you can, and fill and fold those too. Allow the dumplings to rise at room temperature on the tray for 30 to 45 minutes before steaming.

7. STEAM THE DUMPLINGS: Remove the basket from the steamer pot, add 2 inches of water to the pot, and bring to a boil over high heat. Line the basket with the lettuce leaves. Gently arrange as many dumplings as you can, spacing them about ½ inch apart, on top of the leaves. Place the basket in the pot, cover, and steam on high heat for 20 minutes.

8. Remove the pot from the heat. Carefully remove the basket, place it on a folded kitchen towel, and allow the *zhu rou baozi* to cool slightly. Using a spoon or a small spatula, move them to a plate and serve. Cook any remaining *zhu rou baozi*. These are best eaten hot but are also good at room temperature. *Zhu rou baozi* can be refrigerated for up to 3 days or frozen for up to 6 months (see page 36). Reheat them in a steamer pot or use the Steamer Plate Setup (page 37). If reheating frozen *zhu rou baozi*, allow them to thaw before steaming.

Small Mushroom Buns

Xiang Gu Baozi (China)

SERVES 4 TO 8 (MAKES ABOUT 24 DUMPLINGS)

The intensely flavored filling for these steamed buns can be made from several different types of dried mushrooms. The thin, dense wood ear mushrooms are excellent, but they must be chopped very fine. You can use dried maitake mushrooms if you can't find wood ear mushrooms, or you can just add more dried shiitake. You can also make the lighter, fresh mushroom variation that follows. *Xiang gu baozi* are a terrific snack, light breakfast, lunch, dinner, or appetizer.

These dumplings are made using the Pinched-Top Fold (page 52).

For the Filling

8 large dried shiitake or black mushrooms

2 ounces dried wood ear mushrooms or dried maitake, soaked with the shiitake mushrooms in 2 cups hot water for 30 minutes

1 tablespoon soy sauce

1 teaspoon cornstarch

¼ teaspoon salt

¼ teaspoon freshly ground white pepper

¼ teaspoon sugar

2 tablespoons grapeseed or other neutral oil

2 teaspoons finely grated fresh ginger or ¼ teaspoon ground

1 small carrot, finely grated

½ cup finely chopped fresh garlic chives or cilantro

1 scallion, sliced into thin rings

For the Dough

1 recipe *Mantou* (page 72) dough, preferably made no more than 2 hours in advance

Unbleached all-purpose flour for dusting

For Cooking

Soft lettuce leaves, such as Boston, to line the steamer basket

Equipment

2¾-inch round cookie cutter

8- to 10-quart steamer pot

1. MAKE THE FILLING: Fish out the soaked mushrooms with your fingers, squeezing the excess liquid back into the bowl. Set the liquid aside. Remove and discard the stems and finely chop the mushroom caps. Strain and pour 1 cup of the soaking liquid into a bowl. Stir the soy sauce, cornstarch, salt, pepper, and sugar into the reserved soaking liquid and set aside.

2. Heat the oil in a large skillet over high heat. Add the mushrooms and ginger and stir for 1 minute. Bits of the mushroom and ginger will stick to the pan. This is fine for now. Mix in the carrot and garlic chives and cook for 1 minute longer, stirring continuously. Pour in the soaking liquid mixture and scrape loose any sticky bits from the bottom of the pan with a wooden spoon. Simmer until most of the liquid has cooked off but the filling is still moist and sticking together. Remove from the heat and stir in the scallion. Scoop into a bowl, break it up a bit, and and allow it to cool to room temperature. (You can make the filling in advance and keep it tightly wrapped in the refrigerator for up to 1 day.)

3. ASSEMBLE THE DUMPLINGS: *Before assembling the* xiang gu baozi, *review the Pinched-Top Fold, which produces natural pleats when you simply gather up the sides and pinch off the top.*

4. Line a tray with a kitchen towel and sprinkle with a little flour. Also have ready the dough and the filling.

5. Knead the dough once or twice on a floured surface, divide it in half, and set one piece aside under a kitchen towel. Shape the remaining piece into a ball, then roll it out until it's just under ⅛ inch thick. Sprinkle with flour if it gets sticky.

6. Using the cookie cutter, cut out as many rounds as you can, usually 10 to 12. Collect the scraps from around the rounds and put them aside under a damp kitchen towel for later use.

7. Lay flat 1 to 5 dough rounds. Brush each round with a very thin coating of water to make them sticky enough to seal. Place a rounded teaspoon of filling in the center of each round. Gather up the sides of the round, joining the edges to form a casually pleated top. Pinch and squeeze the gathered dough at the top of the dumplings to seal the top. Dab a little water along the edges, if needed, for a better seal. There is usually a little nub of dough at the top of the dumplings assembled using the Pinched-Top Fold that you can twist off for a neater look. Place the assembled dumplings in a single layer on the prepared tray and keep them covered with a kitchen towel while you work. Once you have assembled the first batch of dumplings, continue with the remaining dough and filling. Combine all the dough scraps, knead them into a ball, roll it out, cut out as many rounds as you can, and fill and fold those too. Allow the dumplings to rise on the tray at room temperature for 30 to 45 minutes before steaming.

8. STEAM THE DUMPLINGS: Remove the basket from the steamer pot, add 2 inches of water to the pot, and bring to a boil over high heat. Line the basket with the lettuce leaves. Gently arrange as many dumplings as you can, spacing them about ½ inch apart, on top of the leaves. Place the basket in the pot, cover, and steam on high heat for 15 minutes.

9. Remove the pot from the heat. Carefully remove the basket, place it on a folded kitchen towel, and allow the *xiang gu baozi* to cool slightly. Using a spoon or a small spatula, move them to a plate and serve. Cook any remaining *xiang gu baozi*. These are best eaten hot, but they are also good at room temperature. *Xiang gu baozi* can be refrigerated for up to 3 days or frozen for up to 6 months (see page 36). Reheat them in a steamer pot or use the Steamer Plate Setup (page 37). If reheating frozen *xiang gu baozi*, allow them to thaw before steaming.

FRESH MUSHROOM BUNS

Replace the dried shiitake and wood ear mushrooms with 8 ounces fresh shiitake mushrooms, stemmed.

Pineapple-Pecan Tamales

Tamales Dulces (Mexico)

SERVES 4 TO 8 (MAKES 16 DUMPLINGS)

The combination of corn and fresh pineapple creates a flavor that is well balanced and irresistible. The Mexican brown sugar *panela* (see page 20) rounds off the flavors of this sweet tamale. Most of the tang from the pineapple disappears, and the level, creamlike flavor of the corn becomes more pronounced. Chopped pecans, raisins, and small chunks of pineapple add extra texture and a burst of flavor.

These dumplings are wrapped using the Single-Husk Tamale Fold (page 53).

For the Batter

⅔ cup nonhydrogenated vegetable shortening, at room temperature

2 cups masa harina

1 teaspoon baking powder

⅛ teaspoon salt

1 ounce *panela*, chopped fine (about ½ cup), or other unrefined sugar (see page 20)

½ cup warm water

½ small pineapple, peeled, cored, and pureed (about 1½ cups)

For the Filling

1¾ cups roasted or raw unsalted shelled pecans

½ small pineapple, peeled, cored, and cut into ½-inch pieces

1 cup raisins

For Assembly

20 to 25 prepared dried corn husks (see page 28)

Sixteen 12-inch lengths of kitchen string for tying the tamales

Equipment

Electric hand mixer

8- to 10-quart steamer pot

1. MAKE THE BATTER 30 MINUTES IN ADVANCE: Whip the shortening in a medium bowl with the hand mixer at medium speed until light and glossy, about 5 minutes.

2. Combine the masa harina, baking powder, and salt in a large bowl.

3. Combine the *panela* and the warm water in a medium bowl, crushing any hard-to-dissolve bits with the back of a wooden spoon. Once the sugar has dissolved, add it to the masa harina mixture along with the pineapple puree and mix with the hand mixer at low speed to combine. Raise the speed to high and mix in the shortening, one spoonful at a time. Continue to mix at high speed until the batter is very light and fluffy, about 10 minutes. Cover and refrigerate for at least 30 minutes before using. (You can also make the batter 1 day in advance and keep it refrigerated in a tightly sealed container.)

4. PREPARE THE PECANS: If using roasted pecans, coarsely chop them. If using raw pecans, roast them in a 375°F oven until they just begin to brown, 6 to 8 minutes. Once the pecans have cooled completely, coarsely chop and set them aside.

5. ASSEMBLE THE TAMALES: *Before assembling the tamales, review the Single-Husk Tamale Fold.*

6. Line a tray with a kitchen towel and have ready the batter, the pineapple, pecans, the raisins, the husks, and the ties.

7. Loosen up the chilled batter by whisking it for 2 to 3 minutes. The consistency should be something similar to a grainy and dense mousse. If the batter is too stiff to whisk easily, mix in some cold water, a little at a time, until it is softer and fluffier.

8. Pick out the best 16 husks. Lay flat 1 husk, smooth side up. Center 2 rounded tablespoons of the batter on top of the husk and spread it to the right until it forms a rectangle about 4 × 2½ inches. Arrange 3 to 4 pieces of pineapple, a tablespoon of the pecans, and a tablespoon of the raisins on top of the left half of the rectangle only. Fold the right side of the husk over, sandwiching the filling between the batter. Fold the left side of the husk over the top. Fold the ends of the husk over as firmly as you can to create a neat rectangular package. Tie the package in a crisscross pattern to prevent the husk from unfolding and place on the lined tray. Repeat until you have 16 tamales.

9. Set aside the number of tamales that you would like to cook and keep the rest frozen for up to 6 months (see page 36).

10. STEAM THE TAMALES: Remove the basket from the steamer pot, add 2 inches of water to the pot, and bring to a boil over high heat. Meanwhile, arrange the packages upright, leaning, or wedged loosely against each other in the basket. Ball up and stick in any extra husks or parchment paper to keep the tamales propped up if needed. Blanket them with any remaining husks. Place the basket in the pot, cover, reduce the heat to medium, and steam for 1½ hours. Check the water level every 30 minutes and replenish with boiling water as needed. (If steaming frozen tamales, place them directly in the basket and cook them in the steamer pot for 2 hours. Do not allow the tamales to thaw before cooking.)

11. Remove the pot from the heat. Carefully remove the basket and place it on a folded kitchen towel. Let the tamales cool slightly, cut off the strings, and serve. It's best not to open the tamales too soon and to peel back the husks just before eating so that they stay moist and warm.

Tamales Stuffed with Chicken and Tomatillo Sauce

Tamales de Pollo (Mexico)

SERVES 4 TO 8 (MAKES 16 DUMPLINGS)

The tangy and refreshing qualities of tomatillo seem to work best with chicken, and they are often paired to form the base for a large variety of tamale fillings. Tomatillos instantly invigorate leftover chicken, even meat that's been cooked a long time to make a broth. If you already have some chicken broth on hand for the batter, you can also use leftover roasted chicken or, of course, fresh chicken, as long as you cook it before mixing it into the tomatillo sauce.

These dumplings are wrapped using the Single-Husk Tamale Fold (page 53).

For the Filling

6 medium tomatillos, papery husks removed and fruit rinsed

2 to 3 serrano chiles or 1 large jalapeño chile

1 small white onion, chopped coarse

3 garlic cloves, crushed

¼ cup finely chopped fresh cilantro stems and leaves

½ teaspoon salt

2 tablespoons nonhydrogenated lard or a neutral oil, such as grapeseed

1 cup bite-sized pieces of cooked chicken (if you are making fresh chicken broth for the tamale batter, this will provide you with more than enough chicken)

For the Batter

1 recipe Tamale Batter from Fresh Masa or Tamale Batter from Masa Harina (recipes follow) made with chicken broth

For Assembly

20 to 25 prepared dried corn husks (see page 28)

Sixteen 12-inch lengths of kitchen string for tying the tamales

Equipment

8- to 10-quart steamer pot

1. MAKE THE SAUCE AND THE FILLING: Preheat the oven to 400°F.

2. Place the tomatillos and chiles on a baking sheet and roast until they are soft and charred in spots, about 20 minutes. Once they are cool enough to handle, pick off or rub off the patches of charred skin as best you can. Trim the tomatillos and the peppers of their firmer stem ends. For less heat, core and seed the chiles.

3. Pulse the onion, garlic, and roasted tomatillos and chiles in a food processor until the mixture is light and pulpy. Add the cilantro and salt and pulse once or twice to combine. There will be about 1½ cups of sauce.

4. Melt the lard in a small pot over high heat. Carefully and quickly pour in the tomatillo sauce. Reduce the heat to medium and simmer, stirring frequently, until the sauce thickens and darkens in color, about 8 minutes. (You can also make the sauce in advance and keep it refrigerated in a tightly sealed container for up to 3 days.)

5. Pour half of the cooked tomatillo sauce into a small bowl and set aside to cool. Mix the chicken into the sauce that remains simmering in the pot and cook for 3 minutes longer. Remove from the heat, scoop into a medium bowl, and set aside to cool.

6. ASSEMBLE THE TAMALES: *Before assembling the tamales, review the Single-Husk Tamale Fold.*

7. Line a tray with a kitchen towel and have ready the batter, the cooked chicken, the tomatillo sauce, the husks, and the ties.

8. Loosen up the batter by whisking it for 2 to 3 minutes. The consistency should be something similar to a grainy and dense mousse. If the batter is too stiff to whisk easily, mix in some cold water, a little at a time, until it is softer and fluffier.

9. Pick out the best 16 husks. Lay flat 1 husk, smooth side up. Center 2 rounded tablespoons of the batter on top of the husk and spread it to the right until it forms a rectangle about 4 × 2½ inches. Arrange a generous forkful of the chicken mixture and then a spoonful of the sauce on top of the left half of the rectangle only. Fold the right side of the husk over, sandwiching the filling between the batter. Fold the left side of the husk over the top. Fold the ends of the husk over as firmly as you can to create a neat rectangular package. Tie the package in a crisscross pattern to prevent the husk from unfolding and place on the lined tray. Repeat until you have 16 tamales.

10. Set aside the number of tamales that you would like to cook and keep the rest frozen for up to 6 months (see page 36).

11. STEAM THE TAMALES: Remove the basket from the steamer pot, add 2 inches of water to the pot, and bring to a boil over high heat. Meanwhile, arrange the packages upright, leaning, or wedged loosely against each other in the basket. Ball up and stick in any extra husks or parchment paper to keep the tamales propped up if needed. Blanket them with any remaining husks. Place the basket in the pot, cover, reduce the heat to medium, and steam for 1½ hours. Check the water level every 30 minutes and replenish with boiling water as needed. (If steaming frozen tamales, place them directly in the basket and cook them in the steamer pot for 2 hours. Do not allow the tamales to thaw before cooking.)

12. Remove the pot from the heat. Carefully remove the basket and place it on a folded kitchen towel. Let the tamales cool slightly, cut off the strings, and serve. It's best not to open the tamales too soon and to peel back the husks just before eating so that they stay moist and warm.

TAMALE BATTER FROM FRESH MASA

MAKES 3½ CUPS

½ cup nonhydrogenated lard or vegetable shortening

2 cups Fresh Masa (recipe follows)

½ teaspoon salt

¼ teaspoon baking powder

¾ cup Chicken Broth with Mexican Flavors (page 394) or Pork Broth with Mexican Flavors (page 395), lukewarm

Equipment

Electric hand mixer

1. Place the lard in a large bowl and whip with the hand mixer at medium speed until light and creamy, about 5 minutes.

2. Slowly add about half of the corn masa while continuing to whip at medium speed. Once combined, whip in the salt, baking powder, and remaining masa.

3. Slowly drizzle in the broth as you continue whipping the batter, scraping down the sides as you go. Once all the broth has been added, raise the mixer speed to high and continue to mix until the batter is light and fluffy, about 10 minutes, scraping down the sides as you go. Cover and refrigerate for at least 30 minutes. You can also make the batter in advance and keep it refrigerated in a tightly sealed container for up to 1 day.

FRESH MASA

MAKES ABOUT 2 POUNDS (6½ CUPS)

2 tablespoons slaked lime (calcium hydroxide or "cal")

1½ pounds dried field corn kernels (about 4 cups), sorted and rinsed

Equipment

Colander with small holes (about 2mm)

1. Fill a large pot with 2 quarts water, stir in the slaked lime, and bring to a boil over high heat. Stir in the corn kernels, which will immediately turn a brighter yellow. Cover, reduce the heat to medium, and simmer for 30 minutes. Remove from the heat and allow the kernels to soak for at least 3 hours, but no more than 8 hours. Drain and return the kernels to the pot.

2. Place about a third of the kernels in a medium bowl and add enough water to cover them by a couple of inches. Rub the kernels against each other between your palms to work off their skins. Swirl the bowl around occasionally, encouraging the loosened skins to float to the top of the water so they can be collected or poured out of the bowl. Add fresh water and continue rinsing and rubbing the kernels until most of them have been peeled. Drain the skinned corn and place it in a large bowl. Repeat with the remaining kernels.

3. Pinch off the tougher, pointy tip from the end of each kernel. Rinse the kernels in a colander under cool running water and wipe them dry as best you can between two kitchen towels.

4. Place a third of the kernels in a food processor and process into a grainy meal, about 5 minutes, scraping down the sides as you go. Sift the meal through the colander into a bowl, scooping out the coarser bits and placing them in a small bowl. Repeat with the remaining kernels. Scoop the collected coarser bits back into the food processor, process, and sift again.

5. Measure out the amount of masa you need for your recipe. You can also make the masa in advance and keep it refrigerated in a tightly sealed container for up to 3 days or frozen for up to 6 months. Frozen masa must be thawed before using.

TAMALE BATTER FROM MASA HARINA

MAKES 3½ CUPS

⅓ cup nonhydrogenated lard or vegetable shortening, at room temperature

1 cup masa harina

¼ teaspoon baking powder

¼ teaspoon salt

1¼ cups Chicken Broth with Mexican Flavors (page 394) or Pork Broth with Mexican Flavors (page 395), lukewarm

Equipment

Electric hand mixer

1. Place the lard in a small bowl and whip with the hand mixer at medium speed until light and creamy, about 5 minutes.

2. Combine the masa harina, baking powder, and salt in a large bowl. Pour in the broth and whip at medium speed until all the liquid has been absorbed. Continue whipping as you slowly add the lard, a spoonful at a time.

3. Once the last spoonful of lard has been added, raise the mixer speed to high and continue to mix until the batter is light and fluffy, about 10 minutes, scraping down the sides of the bowl as you go. Cover and refrigerate for at least 30 minutes. You can also make the batter in advance and keep it refrigerated in a tightly sealed container for up to 1 day.

Pounded Rice Dumplings Stuffed with Strawberries

Ichigo Daifuku (Japan)

SERVES 4 TO 6 (MAKES 12 DUMPLINGS)

Daifuku is a classic Japanese confection made with *mochi* and sweetened adzuki bean paste. *Ichigo daifuku* includes the inspired addition of whole fresh strawberries. The combination of fresh berries, bean paste, and *mochi* is an unusual juxtaposition of flavors and tastes like an unusually mellow nut paste and berry candy. The sweetest element, by far, is the bean paste, but because it's sandwiched between the *mochi* and the fruit, it doesn't overwhelm the way some bean paste fillings can. You will need to work with small strawberries for the dumplings to end up the right size. Cutting large berries in half or trimming them to size will only make them slippery and impossible to wrap the bean paste around.

Because fresh *mochi* is so very soft and sticky, it is not recommended for small children. These dumplings are made using the Bowl Fold (page 45).

For the Filling

½ cup dried adzuki beans, soaked in plenty of water for 6 to 8 hours

⅓ cup sugar

¼ teaspoon salt

12 small strawberries (about 1 inch around), stemmed and caps removed

For the Mochi

1 recipe *Mochi* (page 84) dough, divided into 12 equal pieces and rolled into balls, preferably made while the bean paste is cooling, but no more than 1 hour in advance

¼ cup potato starch (*katakuriko*) for dusting and coating the dumplings

1. **MAKE THE FILLING:** Drain the beans and place them in a small saucepan. Fill the pot with enough water to cover the beans by about 2 inches and bring to a boil over high heat. Cover, reduce the heat to low, and simmer until the beans are soft and just beginning to split apart, 45 to 60 minutes. Drain the beans and set them aside.

2. Place the sugar and salt in the same saucepan, pour in ¼ cup water, place over medium heat, and stir until all the sugar has dissolved. Place over medium heat and continue stirring until all the sugar has dissolved. Mix in the beans and simmer for 5 minutes.

3. Turn the beans and all of the cooking liquid into a food processor (don't rinse the saucepan) and process until the mixture becomes a grainy paste, about 3 minutes, scraping down the sides as you go. Scoop the bean paste back into the same saucepan. Place over medium heat and stir continuously until the paste begins to turn into a doughy ball, 3 to 5 minutes. Remove from the heat, scoop into a wide bowl, break it up a bit, set aside, and allow it to cool to room temperature. (You can also make the bean paste in advance and keep it wrapped tightly in the refrigerator for up to 3 days.)

4. ASSEMBLE THE DUMPLINGS: *Before assembling the* ichigo daifuku, *review the Bowl Fold.*

5. Have ready the cooled bean paste, the strawberries, the *mochi*, and a tray dusted with potato starch.

6. Pinch off a small piece of bean paste and roll it into a ball about 1 inch around. Pat it out into a 2-inch round. If it's a little crumbly, put it back into the bowl and work in a little water. Hold the round in the palm of your hand and place a strawberry in the center. Close by pushing and pinching the edges of the bean paste around and over the strawberry until it is surrounded, pushing out any air. Place on the prepared tray and repeat the assembly steps with the remaining bean paste and strawberries. Cover with a towel and set aside.

7. Pick up one ball of *mochi* and use your thumbs to shape the ball into a bowl about 2 inches deep. This will be a wide and floppy bowl that is best supported in the palm of your hand. Place a wrapped strawberry in the center of the *mochi* bowl. Close by pushing and pinching the edges of the *mochi* around and over the wrapped strawberry until it's surrounded, pushing out any air. Reroll into a ball, dust with some potato starch, and place back on the tray. Repeat with the remaining *mochi* and wrapped strawberries. Serve immediately or keep them covered at room temperature for no more than 5 hours.

Leaf-Wrapped Rice Packages Stuffed with Chicken and Bamboo Shoots

Nuo Mi Ji (China)

SERVES 4 TO 8 (MAKES 4 DUMPLINGS)

The name *nuo mi ji* means "glutinous rice chicken," because the rice is thought of as a moist, chewy extension of the chicken pieces it surrounds. This dumpling often includes bamboo shoots and whatever meaty extras are around. Mushrooms, dried shrimp, Chinese sausage, and hard-boiled eggs are favorite additions, but any of these things can be left out or substituted. You must, however, use dried lotus leaves to wrap *nuo mi ji,* because the leaves infuse a dry, tealike flavor into the rice.

These dumplings are wrapped using the Lotus-Leaf Fold (page 54).

For the Marinade

1 tablespoon grapeseed or other neutral oil

1 tablespoon soy sauce

1 tablespoon oyster sauce

1 teaspoon cornstarch

⅛ teaspoon sugar

¼ teaspoon salt

¼ teaspoon freshly ground white pepper

For the Filling

2 chicken thighs with skin, cut in half across the bone, or 4 chicken wings

4 small dried shiitake or black mushrooms, soaked in 1½ cups hot water for 30 minutes

1 teaspoon cornstarch

10 to 12 small or medium dried shrimp, soaked in hot water to cover for 30 minutes

2 tablespoons grapeseed or other neutral oil

¼ pound boneless pork loin, chopped very fine or coarsely ground

½ medium fresh bamboo shoot, trimmed and sliced thin, or one 8-ounce can sliced bamboo shoots, drained

2 tablespoons rice wine (optional)

1 link Chinese pork sausage (*la chang*), cut diagonally into 4 equal pieces

1 large hard-boiled egg, quartered

For the Rice

2 cups short-grain sweet (glutinous) white rice, preferably from China or Japan, rinsed (see page 19)

2 teaspoons salt

For Assembly

8 prepared lotus-leaf halves (see page 29)

Equipment

8- to 10-quart steamer pot

24-inch square of muslin

Large skillet with a cover

1. PREPARE THE FILLING 1 TO 8 HOURS IN ADVANCE: Whisk together all the marinade ingredients in a medium bowl. Add the chicken and turn until coated evenly. Cover and refrigerate for at least 1 hour.

2. STEAM THE RICE: Remove the basket from the steamer pot, add 2 inches of water to the pot, and bring to a boil over high heat. Soak the muslin under running water, wring it out, then drape it inside the basket, creating a lining. Scoop the rice into the lined basket and spread it out evenly. Sprinkle the 2 teaspoons salt over the rice. Place the basket in the pot, cover, reduce the heat to medium, and steam for 25 minutes. Every 10 minutes or so, drizzle ½ cup water over the rice, mix gently, cover again, and continue steaming.

3. Remove the pot from the heat. The rice will be slightly undercooked. Move the rice to a large plate or tray, spread it out to cool, and then divide it into 8 equal piles.

4. COOK THE FILLING: Fish out the soaked mushrooms with your fingers, squeezing the excess liquid back into the bowl. Remove and discard the stems and set the mushroom caps aside. Measure out ¼ cup of the soaking liquid, stir in the cornstarch, and set aside. Drain the shrimp and set aside. Have the marinated chicken ready.

5. Heat the 2 tablespoons oil in a large skillet over high heat. Shake off excess marinade from the chicken pieces (set the marinade aside for later use), place them in the pan, and immediately stir until the chicken just begins to brown, about 3 minutes. Add the pork, shrimp, mushrooms, and bamboo shoot and cook for 1 minute longer, stirring constantly.

6. Add the rice wine and scrape up any sticky bits from the bottom of the pan with a wooden spoon. Mix the mushroom and cornstarch liquid into the chicken marinade, pour it over the chicken mixture, and stir until the sauce begins to simmer. Cover, reduce the heat to low, and cook for 5 minutes. Remove from the heat. Divide the filling evenly among 4 small bowls. Each bowl should have a mushroom and a piece of chicken.

7. ASSEMBLE THE DUMPLINGS: *Before assembling the* nuo mi ji, *review the Lotus-Leaf Fold.*

8. Have ready the prepared lotus leaves, the preportioned rice and the filling, sausage, and the hard-boiled egg. Also have a large plate to place the dumplings once they have been assembled.

9. Lay flat 2 of the leaf halves, smooth side up. Center 1 portion of rice on one of the leaf halves. Moisten your hands with water and pat the rice into a 6-inch round patty. Spoon a bowl of filling onto the rice. Nestle a piece of sausage and egg into the filling. Pick up another portion of rice and form another 6-inch round patty as best you can. Place this patty on top of the filling, creating a loose, slightly messy sandwich. Use your hands to pack the pile inward just gently enough to neaten the edges.

10. Fold one of the longer sides of the leaf snugly over the pile of rice and filling. Fold the opposite side over just as snugly. Fold over the 2 ends as tightly as you can to create a neat package. Center this package, seam side down, on the second leaf half. Using the same folding pattern, wrap the package as tightly as you can. Keep this bundle folded side down on your plate to prevent the leaves from unfolding. Repeat the assembly steps until you have 4 bundles.

11. STEAM THE DUMPLINGS: Remove the basket from the steamer pot, add 2 inches of water to the pot, and bring to a boil over high heat. Arrange the bundles, seam side down, in the basket. They can be wedged against each other if the space in the steamer is tight. Place the basket in the pot, cover, reduce the heat to medium, and steam for 30 minutes.

12. Remove the pot from the heat. Carefully remove the basket, place it on a folded kitchen towel, and let the *nuo mi ji* cool slightly. Remove the outer leaves (unless you are freezing the dumplings), place the dumplings seam side up on a plate, and serve. It's best not to open the packages too soon, and to peel back the leaves only just before eating, so that they stay moist and warm. *Nuo mi ji* can be refrigerated for up to 3 days or frozen (unopened) for up to 6 months (see page 36). Reheat them in a steamer pot or use the Steamer Plate Setup (page 37). If reheating frozen *nuo mi ji,* allow them to thaw before steaming.

June

FLATTENED RICE DUMPLINGS WITH GRATED COCONUT AND ANISE SUGAR
Palitao (Philippines) 197

LEAF BREAD, A FRESH CORN "TAMALE"
(United States and Canada) 199

TARO BALLS IN A SWEET COCONUT SOUP
Bua Loi Phuak (Thailand) 201

CANARY PUDDING WITH LEMON CURD
(England) 203

BLACK SESAME ROLL-UPS
Hei Zi Ma Juan (China) 205

LEMONY LENTIL-CHARD SOUP WITH BULGUR DUMPLINGS
Kibbet Raheb (Lebanon) 207

FISH RAVIOLI WITH A THINNED CREAM SAUCE
Ravioli di Pesce (Italy) 209

STICKY RICE DUMPLINGS STUFFED WITH PORK AND SHRIMP
Bánh Ít Trán (Vietnam) 212

RICE AND TAPIOCA DUMPLINGS TOPPED WITH SHRIMP AND BEAN PASTE
Bánh Bèo (Vietnam)...215

PORK TAMALES WITH GREEN OLIVES AND JALAPEÑO
Tamales de Puerco (Mexico)..217

THE ARM OF THE QUEEN TAMALE
Brazo de la Reina (Mexico)...220

LEAF-WRAPPED RICE BUNDLES STUFFED WITH CHICKEN AND PEANUTS
Juanes de Arroz (Peru)..222

Flattened Rice Dumplings with Grated Coconut and Anise Sugar

Palitao (Philippines)

SERVES 4 (MAKES ABOUT 20 DUMPLINGS)

These small oval dumplings are made of sweet rice flour and water. This easy dough can be made in a matter of seconds, for dumplings that are gooey, chewy, and surprisingly fragrant. A topping of grated coconut and anise sugar adds a necessary sweetness. Many recipes use sesame seeds instead of anise, but the licorice flavor of anise provides a much more unexpected flavor.

For the Dumplings

1¼ cups sweet (glutinous) rice flour, preferably from the Philippines or Thailand, plus some extra for dusting

⅔ cup warm water

For the Coating

1 cup freshly grated coconut (see page 8) or frozen grated coconut, thawed

2 teaspoons anise seeds or 1 tablespoon sesame seeds

2 tablespoons sugar

Equipment

Large, wide bowl to hold the cooked dumplings

Mortar and pestle

1. MAKE THE DUMPLINGS: Place 1 cup of the rice flour in a medium bowl and keep the remaining ¼ cup handy. Pour in the warm water and mix until all the liquid has been absorbed. Knead the dough in the bowl for a minute. This dough needs to be firm enough to hold its shape when rolled into balls. If it is too soft or sticky, work in some of the remaining flour, a little at a time.

2. Fill a large pot halfway with lightly salted water and bring to a boil over high heat. Reduce the heat to medium for a steady simmer.

3. Line a tray with a kitchen towel and sprinkle with a little rice flour. Spread the grated coconut out on a large plate and have another plate ready to hold the dumplings once they've been coated.

4. Pinch off a small piece of dough and roll it into a ball about 1¼ inches around. Gently flatten and shape it between your hands into an oval patty about ¼ inch thick, place it on the prepared tray, and continue with the remaining dough.

5. COOK AND COAT THE DUMPLINGS: Carefully drop the dumplings, a few at a time, into the simmering water. Cook until all of them are floating, about 2 minutes, then cook for 2 minutes longer.

6. Remove the dumplings with a slotted spoon, place them in the large bowl, and drizzle with a ladle of the cooking liquid to prevent sticking.

7. Working quickly, remove one dumpling from the bowl, and if it is at all dry, dampen its surface with wet fingers to ensure an even coating. Place it on the grated coconut, gently press both sides into the coconut, then place on the other plate. Repeat with the remaining dumplings and set aside.

8. Toast the anise seeds in a small skillet over medium heat, stirring constantly for 2 minutes. Immediately move them to a bowl to cool, then grind in the mortar with the pestle. Mix together the ground anise seeds and the sugar in a small bowl. Serve the *palitao* at room temperature with a sprinkling of anise sugar.

Leaf Bread, a Fresh Corn "Tamale"

(United States and Canada)

SERVES 4 TO 6 (MAKES 12 DUMPLINGS)

Leaf bread, sometimes called Iroquois leaf bread, includes no fat and is made only from freshly cut corn and a little cornmeal. Once the corn has been pulped and mixed with the cornmeal, the batter is scooped back into the husks, wrapped into small packages, and steamed. Serve these dumplings with melted butter and a sprinkling of salt for an appealing snack or side.

These dumplings are wrapped using the Two-Husk Tamale Fold 1 (Wide) (page 55).

For the Dumplings

6 large ears of corn with husks

⅔ cup coarse yellow cornmeal

For Assembly

Twelve 20-inch lengths of kitchen string for tying the leaf bread

For Serving

4 tablespoons (½ stick) unsalted butter, melted just before serving

Equipment

8- to 10-quart steamer pot

1. MAKE THE BATTER: Remove the husks from the corn and separate them from the silk. Set aside the silk and a handful of the smaller husks for later use. Count out 24 of the largest husks, rinse them, pat dry, and set aside.

2. Cut the kernels off the cobs over a large board or a towel-lined tray to make the kernels easier to collect. You will need 5 cups of kernels.

3. Process the kernels in a food processor until almost smooth, about 3 minutes, scraping down the sides as you go. Pour into a large bowl and add half of the cornmeal. Continue mixing as you add more cornmeal, a little at a time, until the batter is stiff enough just to hold its shape when scooped up with a spoon.

4. ASSEMBLE THE DUMPLINGS: *Before assembling the leaf bread, review the Two-Husk Tamale Fold 1 (Wide). This fold makes it possible to create wrappers for generous portions of batter by overlapping fresh corn husks. Dried husks are typically much larger than fresh husks so there's no need to overlap, but they will slightly alter the flavor of the dumplings.*

5. Line a tray with a kitchen towel and have ready the batter, the 24 husks, and the ties.

6. Arrange 2 husks, smooth side up, next to each other lengthwise with the widest ends on opposite sides. Overlap the husks by about 1½ inches. Center about ½ cup of batter on top of the overlapping husks. Fold over one side. Fold over the opposite side. Fold the ends of the overlapping husks over as tightly as you can to create a neat package. Tie the package in a crisscross pattern to prevent the husks from unfolding and place it on the lined tray. Repeat until you have 12 packages.

7. STEAM THE DUMPLINGS: Remove the basket from the steamer pot, add 2 inches of water to the pot, and stir in the reserved corn silk. Meanwhile, arrange the packages in flat layers inside the basket. Blanket them with the smaller, reserved husks. Place the basket in the pot, reduce the heat to medium, cover, and steam for 1 hour. Check the water level halfway through the cooking and replenish with boiling water as needed.

8. Remove the pot from the heat. Carefully remove the basket and place it on a folded kitchen towel. Let the leaf bread cool slightly. Cut off the strings (unless you are freezing the dumplings) and serve with melted butter and a sprinkle of salt. It's best not to open the packages too soon, and to peel back the husks just before eating, so that they stay moist and warm. Leaf bread can be refrigerated for up to 3 days or frozen (unopened) for up to 6 months (see page 36). Reheat them in a steamer pot or use the Steamer Plate Setup (page 37). If reheating frozen leaf bread, allow it to thaw before steaming.

Taro Balls in a Sweet Coconut Soup

Bua Loi Phuak (Thailand)

SERVES 4 TO 8

Bua loi phuak, like *Onde-Onde* (March), is made out of a rice flour dough that's been combined with a mashed root vegetable to give these dumplings a softer texture and a subtle fruity flavor. It takes only about 15 minutes to roll up two hundred of these small dumplings, and they don't need to be strictly equal in size. Taro can be found at many well-stocked Chinese grocery stores and Asian food markets. Look for the large root, not the smaller, goose egg–sized root.

For the Dumplings

1 pound taro, peeled and quartered

2 cups sweet (glutinous) rice flour, preferably from Thailand, plus some extra for dusting

For the Coconut Soup

6 cups fresh coconut milk (see page 8) or two and a half 14-ounce cans coconut milk mixed with 2 cups water

¼ pound hard palm sugar or ½ cup soft palm sugar or other unrefined sugar (see page 20)

Pinch of salt

2 fresh or frozen pandan leaves, each folded in half and tied into a knot for easier handling, or ⅛ teaspoon pandan extract (optional)

Equipment

8- to 10-quart steamer pot

Potato ricer

1. STEAM THE TARO: Remove the basket from the steamer pot, add 1 inch of water to the pot, and bring to a boil over high heat. Place the taro in the basket, then place the basket in the pot. Cover, reduce the heat to medium, and steam until the taro is fork-tender, 20 to 25 minutes. Remove from the heat, carefully remove the basket, place it on a folded kitchen towel, and allow the taro to cool slightly.

2. MAKE THE SOUP: While the taro is steaming, pour the coconut milk into a medium pot. If using hard palm sugar, chop it into small pieces. Add the palm sugar, salt, and pandan leaves to the coconut milk and bring to a very gentle simmer over medium-low heat, stirring continuously with a wooden spoon. Crush apart any bits of sugar with the back of the spoon. If using fresh coconut milk, be careful not to let it come to a boil, or else it will separate into what looks like a superfine curdle and you will have to start over. Remove from the heat as soon as the sugar has dissolved and set aside.

3. MAKE THE DOUGH: Cut the taro into small chunks and press them through the ricer into a large bowl. Add 1½ cups of the rice flour to the taro, keeping the remaining ½ cup handy. Rub with your fingers until the mixture is well combined and looks like a coarse meal. Pour in ¾ cup water and work the mixture with your hands into one manageable ball. This dough needs to be firm enough to hold its shape when rolled into balls. If the dough is too soft and sticky, work in some of the remaining flour, a little at a time.

4. MAKE AND COOK THE DUMPLINGS: Line a tray with a kitchen towel and sprinkle with a little rice flour.

5. Pinch off a very small piece of dough and roll it into a ball about ½ inch around. Sprinkle with rice flour if it gets sticky. Place the ball on the prepared tray and continue with the remaining dough. Cover with a kitchen towel and set aside.

6. Fill a large bowl halfway with cold water. Fill a large pot halfway with water and bring to a boil over high heat. Reduce the heat to low for a gentle simmer. Carefully drop the dumplings, a few at a time, into the water and stir gently to prevent sticking. Cook until all of them are floating, about 2 minutes, then cook for 2 minutes longer. Remove the dumplings with a slotted spoon, place them in the cold water for 1 minute, drain, and move them to a large bowl. Cook, cool, and drain the second batch of dumplings and place them in the bowl.

7. Bring the coconut soup back to a gentle simmer over low heat, add the dumplings, and cook for 2 minutes to warm through. Remove from the heat, remove the pandan leaves, and serve.

Canary Pudding with Lemon Curd

(England)

SERVES 4 TO 6 (MAKES 1 DUMPLING)

There is a large variety of lemon puddings from England, but the canary pudding is simple to make, exceptionally lemony, and cooks up flawlessly each time. Lining the basin with thin slices of lemon gives this pudding a lacy and glistening cap once it is unmolded. If you want to skip making the curd, you can place a large spoonful or two of lemon marmalade in the bottom of the basin (unlined with lemon slices) before pouring in the batter.

This dumpling is made using the Pudding Basin Setup (page 43).

For the Lemon Curd

1 large egg plus 1 large egg yolk

3 tablespoons fresh lemon juice and 1 tablespoon grated zest

½ cup sugar

2 tablespoons (¼ stick) cold unsalted butter, cut into 4 equal pieces

For the Dumpling

6 tablespoons (¾ stick) unsalted butter, at room temperature

½ cup sugar

3 large eggs, at room temperature

3 tablespoons fresh lemon juice and 1 tablespoon grated zest

1 cup unbleached all-purpose flour

¾ teaspoon baking powder

¼ teaspoon freshly grated nutmeg

Pinch of salt

For Assembly and Cooking

Unsalted butter and sugar to coat the pudding basin

1 large lemon for decorating the top of the pudding (optional)

Equipment

24-inch square of muslin

35-inch lengths of kitchen string

4- to 5-cup pudding basin

Pot large enough to hold the basin when covered

Parchment paper

1. MAKE THE LEMON CURD: Whisk the egg, egg yolk, lemon juice, and sugar in a double boiler or in a stainless-steel bowl set on top of a pot with 1 inch of simmering water. (The bowl should not be touching the simmering water but should rest directly above it.) Whisk vigorously at all times until the mixture is thick and creamy, 7 to 8 minutes. Remove from the heat and whisk in the cold butter a piece at a time. Mix in the lemon zest and let cool slightly. Cut out a round of parchment paper and press it onto the surface of the curd so it will not form a skin. Refrigerate for at least 2 hours. (You can also make the lemon curd in advance and keep it refrigerated in a tightly sealed glass container for up to 3 days. Place a round of parchment paper on top of the curd to prevent it from forming a skin.)

2. MAKE THE BATTER: Whisk together the room-temperature butter and the sugar in a large bowl until creamy. Whisk in the 3 eggs, one at a time, until the mixture is light and frothy, 3 to 5 minutes. Whisk in the lemon juice and zest.

3. Combine the flour, baking powder, nutmeg, and salt in a large bowl. Add half of the flour mixture to the egg mixture and fold until smooth, then fold in the second half of the flour mixture.

4. ASSEMBLE AND STEAM THE DUMPLING: *Before assembling the pudding, review the Pudding Basin Setup.*

5. Soak the muslin and the string under running water. Wring them out and set aside.

6. Place the empty pudding basin in the pot. Pour water into the space between the basin and the pot until it's three-quarters of the way up the sides of the basin. Remove the basin and bring the water to a boil over high heat. Reduce heat to low for a gentle simmer.

7. Meanwhile, make sure the interior of the basin is dry before rubbing it with butter and coating it with sugar. If using lemon slices to decorate the pudding, cut the peel off the lemon, then slice the lemon into ¼-inch rounds. Center the largest round of lemon on the bottom of the basin. Arrange 4 or 5 lemon rounds around the centered slice. The surrounding lemon slices should be partly resting on the bottom of the basin and partly climbing up against the basin's side, creating a "cap" for the pudding. Scoop the batter into the basin and wiggle it gently to level it off. Cut out a round of parchment paper and place it on top of the batter. Cover the basin with the damp muslin and secure it tightly with the string. Tie the opposite corners of the muslin into handles over the top of the pudding.

8. Using tongs or a wooden spoon, push a folded cloth, like a standard white cotton napkin, into the simmering water and arrange it to lie flat on the bottom of the pot. Using the cloth handle, carefully lower the basin into the pot, cover, and simmer for at least 1½ hours or up to 2 hours for a pudding that's even richer in flavor and texture. Check the water level every 30 minutes and replenish with boiling water as needed.

9. Remove the pot from the heat. Using a pot holder to grasp the cloth handle, carefully remove the basin from the pot, put it on a folded kitchen towel, and allow the pudding to cool for 5 minutes. Remove the string, cloth, and paper. Unmold by inverting it onto a plate. Slice and serve with a generous topping of lemon curd. The pudding can be refrigerated for up to 3 days. Reheat in a steamer pot or use the Steamer Plate Setup (page 37).

Black Sesame Roll-Ups

Hei Zi Ma Juan (China)

SERVES 4 TO 8 (MAKES 16 DUMPLINGS)

Hei zi ma juan is a mildly sweet dessert or snack dumpling with an inky black color and a pure sesame flavor. This dumpling is steamed in thin sheets, rolled up into a log, and then cut into large, bite-sized pieces. When you bite into a piece of *hei zi ma juan*, you can feel the layers pop softly inside your mouth as you relish the coarse yet tender texture of the ground sesame seeds.

For the Dumplings

- ⅓ cup black sesame seeds (do not substitute with white sesame seeds)
- ⅔ cup sugar
- ¼ cup water chestnut flour or rice flour, preferably from China or Thailand
- ½ cup tapioca flour (tapioca starch)
- Pinch of salt

For Cooking

Toasted sesame oil or a neutral oil, such as grapeseed, to coat the cake pan

Equipment

- Clean spice or coffee grinder
- 2-inch-high steamer rack
- 9-inch square cake pan
- Pot large enough to hold both the rack and the pan when covered

1. Toast the black sesame seeds in a small skillet over medium heat, stirring continuously, for 2 minutes. Immediately move them to a small bowl to cool. Finely grind in the spice grinder.

2. Combine the ground sesame seeds, sugar, water chestnut flour, tapioca flour, and salt in a medium heatproof bowl.

3. Place the steamer rack inside the pot. Keeping the cake pan level is key for such a thin batter, so take the time now to check for any tilts or leanings with your pot or rack, and try to even things out as best you can. Add 1½ inches of water to the pot and bring to a boil over high heat. Meanwhile, rub a little sesame oil around the inside of the cake pan.

4. Heat 1¼ cups water in a small saucepan over medium heat until it is hot to the touch but not close to simmering. Pour the water into the sesame mixture and stir until there are no clumps. Immediately measure out ½ cup and pour it into the prepared cake pan. Wiggle the pan until the batter spreads out evenly.

5. Carefully place the pan on the steamer rack, cover, and steam for 5 minutes. This watery batter will cook up to a texture similar to a firm jelly.

6. Remove the pot from the heat. Carefully lift the pan out of the pot, place it on a folded kitchen towel, and allow the sesame sheet to cool for about 2 minutes, or until cool enough to handle.

7. Working from any side of the pan, use your fingers to nudge an edge free and roll the thin sesame sheet up into a log, jelly-roll style. Next, trim off the uneven ends. Cut the log into 4 equal pieces and place them on a large plate seam side down. Be sure to stir and remix the remaining batter just before measuring out each batch. Serve the *hei zi ma juan* at room temperature. *Hei zi ma juan* can be kept tightly wrapped in the refrigerator for up to 3 days. Allow them to come back to room temperature before serving.

Lemony Lentil-Chard Soup with Bulgur Dumplings

Kibbet Raheb (Lebanon)

SERVES 4 (MAKES ABOUT 32 DUMPLINGS)

Chewy, nutty-tasting bulgur dumplings are what make this lentil soup so unusual. Bulgur is a form of cracked wheat and it will feel grainy and unworkable when you start making the dough, but it comes together beautifully as you gradually work in more flour. Because there is a fair amount of lemon juice in this soup, the darker flavors of the lentils, bulgur, and chard become zesty and vivid, making it as refreshing as it is nourishing.

For the Soup

3 tablespoons olive oil

1 medium yellow onion, chopped fine

2 garlic cloves, chopped very fine

½ cup finely chopped fresh cilantro stems and leaves

⅓ cup fresh lemon juice

1 cup dried brown or green lentils, rinsed

1 small bunch chard, stemmed and cut into 1-inch ribbons

2 teaspoons salt

½ teaspoon freshly ground black pepper

For the Dumplings

¼ cup finely ground bulgur

½ teaspoon salt

¼ cup unbleached all-purpose flour, plus some extra for dusting

1. MAKE THE SOUP: Heat the oil in a large skillet over medium heat. Add the onion and garlic and stir frequently until the onion is soft, about 4 minutes. Remove from the heat and mix in the cilantro. Pour the lemon juice into a bowl. Measure out ⅓ cup of the onion mixture and set aside. Add the rest to the lemon juice, mix well, and set aside.

2. Fill a medium pot with 7 cups water and bring to a boil over high heat. Stir in the lentils, cover, reduce the heat to low, and simmer for 20 minutes. Add the chard, 2 teaspoons salt, and the pepper and cook for 15 minutes longer. Remove from the heat and set aside until you are ready to add the dumplings.

3. MAKE THE DUMPLINGS: While the soup is simmering, place ⅓ cup water in a small saucepan and bring to a boil over high heat. Remove from the heat, stir in the bulgur, cover, and steep until all the water has been absorbed, about 1 minute. Scoop the bulgur into a medium bowl and mix in the ⅓ cup onion mixture and the ½ teaspoon salt. Cover and refrigerate for 15 minutes.

4. Mix 2 tablespoons of the flour into the chilled bulgur mixture and work the dough into one manageable ball. This dough needs to be firm enough to hold its shape when rolled into balls. If the dough is too soft or sticky, work in some of the remaining flour, a little at a time.

5. Line a tray with a kitchen towel and sprinkle with a little flour.

6. Pinch off a very small piece of dough, roll it into a ball about ¾ inch around, dust with flour, and place on the prepared tray. Repeat with the remaining dough.

7. COOK THE DUMPLINGS: Bring the soup back to a simmer over medium heat. Carefully drop the dumplings, a few at a time, into the soup. Stir gently, cover, reduce the heat to low, and cook for 20 minutes. Stir in the lemon and onion mixture just before serving.

Fish Ravioli with a Thinned Cream Sauce

Ravioli di Pesce (Italy)

SERVES 4 TO 6 (MAKES ABOUT 40 DUMPLINGS)

In this recipe, the poaching liquid of the fish is turned into a delicious and light sauce for the dumplings. Sole is a standard choice, but just about any flaky, white-fleshed fish will do. Mixing some chopped anchovies into the filling is a quick way to strengthen the flavor, no matter what fish you use. If filleting a whole fish, be sure to add the head and the bones into the poaching liquid for an even richer flavor.

For the Dough

1½ cups Italian "type 00" pasta flour, or ¾ cup unbleached all-purpose flour mixed with ¾ cup cake flour, plus some extra for dusting

3 large eggs, plus 1 large egg yolk

1 teaspoon olive oil

For the Poaching Liquid

¾ cup white wine

2 teaspoons fresh lemon juice

2 garlic cloves, sliced thin

4 fresh thyme sprigs

3 fresh marjoram sprigs

¼ teaspoon salt

For the Filling

4 small white-fleshed fish fillets, such as sole, flounder, or turbot (about 1 pound)

1 large egg yolk

½ teaspoon grated lemon zest

2 tablespoons finely chopped fresh flat-leaf parsley leaves

½ teaspoon salt

¼ teaspoon freshly ground white pepper

For the Sauce

4 tablespoons (½ stick) unsalted butter, cut into chunks

2 garlic cloves, chopped very fine

2 salt-packed or oil-packed anchovy fillets, rinsed if salt-packed, chopped fine

1 plum tomato, peeled, seeded (see page 21), and coarsely chopped

¼ cup heavy cream

1 tablespoon coarsely chopped fresh flat-leaf parsley leaves

Equipment

2-inch round cookie cutter

Large, wide bowl to hold the dumplings cooked in batches

1. MAKE THE DOUGH: Place about 1¼ cups of the flour in a large bowl and keep the remaining ¼ cup handy. Mix in the eggs and yolk with a fork until all the egg has been absorbed. Work the dough with your hands into one manageable ball. If the dough is wet and sticky, work in some of the remaining flour, a little at a time, until it no longer sticks to your fingers.

2. Place the dough on a flat work surface and knead for 4 to 5 minutes. The dough will be smooth and somewhat firm. Return the dough ball to the bowl and brush the surface with the oil. Cover with a damp towel and let it rest for at least 20 minutes before using.

3. POACH THE FISH: Pour the wine and ¾ cup water into a medium pot or a large skillet with a cover and bring to a boil over high heat. Reduce the heat to low and stir in the lemon juice, sliced garlic, thyme, marjoram, and ¼ teaspoon salt.

4. Slide the fillets into the simmering liquid, cover, and cook for 5 minutes. Carefully remove the fillets from the broth with a slotted spoon or a spatula, place them in a shallow bowl, and set them aside until cool enough to handle. Strain the poaching liquid through a sieve into a bowl, then measure out 1 cup for the sauce.

5. MAKE THE FILLING: Flake apart the fillets. Add the egg yolk, lemon zest, 2 tablespoons parsley, ½ teaspoon salt, and the pepper and mix well with a fork. Cover and keep refrigerated while you roll out the dough.

6. ASSEMBLE THE DUMPLINGS: Line a tray with a kitchen towel and sprinkle with a little flour. Also have ready the dough and the filling.

7. Knead the dough once or twice on a floured surface, divide it into 4 equal pieces, and set 3 of them aside under a kitchen towel. Shape the remaining piece into a ball, then roll it out until it's ¹⁄₁₆ inch thick. (For tips on how to roll dough out thin, see page 33.) Sprinkle with flour if it gets sticky. Let the rolled-out dough relax for a couple of minutes before cutting out rounds.

8. Using the cookie cutter, cut out as many rounds as you can, usually 16 to 20. Scraps cannot be reused because dough rolled out this thin is too dry to recombine.

9. Lay flat 4 to 8 dough rounds. Brush half of them with a little water to make them sticky enough to seal. Place a rounded teaspoon of filling in the center of each dampened round. Top each spoonful of filling with an unbrushed round, creating little sandwiches. Pinch the edges of the rounds together, pushing out any air, and seal. If desired, trim or crimp the edges for a more tailored look. Place the assembled dumplings in a single layer on the prepared tray and keep them covered with a kitchen towel while you work. Once you have assembled the first batch of dumplings, continue with the remaining dough and filling.

10. Cover the tray of assembled dumplings and place them in the refrigerator for 30 to 60 minutes before cooking. Chilling them helps to set the dough, making the dumplings firm and toothsome when cooked instead of puffy and soft.

11. COOK THE DUMPLINGS: Fill a large pot halfway with salted water and bring to a boil over high heat. Reduce the heat to medium for a steady simmer. Gently drop half of the dumplings, a few at a time, into the water. Stir carefully to prevent sticking. Cook until all of them are floating, about 2 to 3 minutes, then cook for 3 minutes longer.

12. Using a slotted spoon, remove the dumplings, place them in the large bowl, and drizzle with a ladle of the cooking liquid to prevent them from sticking. Cook the remaining dumplings, place them in the bowl with another ladle of the cooking liquid, and keep warm.

13. MAKE THE SAUCE AND FINISH THE DUMPLINGS: Melt the butter in a large skillet over medium heat. Stir in the chopped garlic and the anchovies and cook for 1 minute. Carefully and quickly pour the reserved cup of poaching liquid into the pan. Simmer until the sauce has reduced by half, about 5 minutes. Reduce the heat to low, add the tomato, and swirl in the cream.

14. Drain the ravioli and place them in the simmering sauce. Shake the pan until the ravioli are well coated and heated through. Remove from the heat, sprinkle with 1 tablespoon parsley, and serve.

Sticky Rice Dumplings Stuffed with Pork and Shrimp

Bánh It Trán (Vietnam)

SERVES 4 TO 6 (MAKES ABOUT 20 DUMPLINGS)

As with *Bánh Bèo* (recipe follows), these rice flour dumplings balance several flavors, from the savory and sweet pork-and-shrimp filling to the sweet and tart fish sauce they are dipped in. The dough is made with a sweet (glutinous) rice flour that gets very sticky as it cooks, so lining the steamer basket with lettuce leaves is essential.

These dumplings are made using the Bowl Fold (page 45).

For the Filling

¼ cup dried peeled mung beans

10 raw medium shrimp, peeled, deveined, and kept on ice

2 tablespoons grapeseed or other neutral oil

1 large shallot, chopped fine

1 garlic clove, chopped very fine

½ pound boneless pork butt or shoulder, chopped fine

1 teaspoon sugar

¼ teaspoon salt

1 teaspoon fish sauce, preferably from Vietnam

For the Dough

2¼ cups sweet (glutinous) rice flour, preferably from Vietnam or Thailand, plus some extra for dusting

1 cup warm water

For the Topping*

1 tablespoon grapeseed or other neutral oil

2 scallions, sliced thin into rings

1 recipe Sweet, Sour, and Spicy Fish Sauce (recipe follows)

For Cooking and Serving

Soft lettuce leaves, such as Boston, to line the steamer basket and the serving plate

Equipment

8- to 10-quart steamer pot

1. MAKE THE FILLING: Place the mung beans in a small saucepan, pour in enough water to cover them by 1 inch, and bring to a simmer over medium heat. Cover and cook until the beans are very soft, 20 to 30 minutes. Drain, place the beans in a medium bowl, and mash them with a fork until mostly smooth.

2. Finely chop the shrimp and set aside.

3. Heat the 2 tablespoons oil in a large skillet over medium heat. Add the shallot and garlic and stir until the shallot is soft, about 3 minutes. Mix in the mashed mung beans, the chopped shrimp, and the pork. As the pork begins to brown, break up any clumps with a

---

*These amounts are for a full recipe. If you plan on freezing and storing some of the dumplings, reduce the amounts in proportion to the number you are serving.

wooden spoon. Add the sugar, salt, and fish sauce and stir frequently until the pork is golden brown, about 3 minutes. Remove from the heat, scoop into a bowl, and set aside to cool. (You can also make the filling in advance and keep it tightly covered in the refrigerator for up to 2 days.)

4. MAKE THE DOUGH: Place 2 cups of the rice flour in a medium bowl and keep the remaining ¼ cup handy. Pour in the warm water and mix until all the liquid has been absorbed. Knead the dough in the bowl for a minute. This dough needs to be firm enough to hold its shape when rolled into balls. If it is too soft or sticky, work in some of the remaining flour, a little at a time.

5. ASSEMBLE THE DUMPLINGS: *Before assembling the* bánh it trán, *review the Bowl Fold.*

6. Line a tray with a kitchen towel and sprinkle with a little rice flour. Have ready the dough and the filling.

7. Pinch off a small piece of dough and roll it into a ball about 1¼ inches around. Keep the remaining dough covered with a kitchen towel as you work. Use your thumbs to shape it into a bowl about 1 inch deep. This will be a wide bowl that is best supported in the palm of your hand. Place a rounded tablespoon of filling in the center of the dough bowl. Close by pushing and pinching the edges of the dough around and over the filling until the filling is surrounded, pushing out any air. Dab a little water along the edges, if needed, for a better seal. Reroll into a ball, dust with flour, and place on the prepared tray. Continue with the remaining dough and filling.

8. Set aside the number of dumplings that you would like to cook and freeze the rest (see page 36). Keep the dumplings you are planning to cook in the refrigerator on a plate or tray, covered with a kitchen towel, until it's time to steam them.

9. MAKE THE SCALLION TOPPING: Heat the 1 tablespoon oil in a small skillet over medium heat and add the scallions. Stir until the scallions are just beginning to brown, about 1 minute. Immediately remove from the heat, scoop into a bowl, and set aside.

10. STEAM THE DUMPLINGS: Remove the basket from the steamer pot, add 1 inch of water to the pot, and bring to a boil over high heat. Line the basket with lettuce leaves. Arrange as many dumplings in the basket as you can, spacing them about ½ inch apart. Place the basket in the pot, cover, reduce the heat to medium, and steam for 6 to 8 minutes.

11. Remove the pot from the heat. Carefully remove the basket and place it on a folded kitchen towel. Arrange a few lettuce leaves on a plate. Use a spoon or a small spatula to move the dumplings to the prepared plate. Sprinkle fried scallions over each, then drizzle them with a little Sweet, Sour, and Spicy Fish Sauce. Serve immediately while you cook any remaining dumplings.

SWEET, SOUR, AND SPICY FISH SAUCE

MAKES ABOUT ½ CUP

1 garlic clove, chopped coarse

2 small hot red chiles, such as Hanoi Red, cored, seeded, and chopped coarse

2 tablespoons sugar

1 small hot red chile, such as Hanoi Red, stemmed and sliced into thin rings

2 tablespoons rice vinegar or coconut vinegar

1 tablespoon fish sauce, preferably from Vietnam

½ ime or lemon

Equipment

Mortar and pestle

Pound the garlic and the chopped chiles in the mortar with the pestle until well mashed, then scoop it into a small bowl. Add the sugar, chile rings, vinegar, and 2 tablespoons water and stir until the sugar has dissolved. Stir in the fish sauce. Keep in a tightly sealed container for up to 1 month in the refrigerator. Squeeze the lime juice into the sauce just before serving.

Rice and Tapioca Dumplings Topped with Shrimp and Bean Paste

Bánh Bèo (Vietnam)

SERVES 4 (MAKES 20 DUMPLINGS)

It takes very little batter to make 20 of these savory and absolutely delicious dumplings, which resemble small open-faced sandwiches or canapés. Shrimp, shallots, and mung bean paste top these soft, slightly gelatinous dumplings with a superb combination of flavors and textures.

For the Toppings

- ½ pound fresh shrimp, peeled and deveined
- ¼ cup grapeseed or other neutral oil
- ⅓ cup finely chopped shallot
- ⅓ cup dried peeled mung beans
- ¼ teaspoon salt
- 1 recipe Sweet, Sour, and Spicy Fish Sauce (preceding recipe)

- 1 scallion, sliced into thin rings
- 1 to 2 small green chiles, such as a green Hanoi Red, stemmed, seeded if desired, and sliced into thin rings

For the Dumplings

- ⅔ cup white rice flour, preferably from Vietnam or Thailand
- ⅓ cup tapioca flour (tapioca starch)

Equipment

8- to 10-quart steamer pot

Five to ten 2-inch-wide dipping bowls (see page 26)

1. MAKE THE SHRIMP TOPPING: Add ½ inch of water to a small pot and bring to a boil over high heat. Add the shrimp, cover, reduce the heat to low, and cook for 3 to 4 minutes. Drain and place the shrimp under cool running water for a couple minutes. Coarsely chop the shrimp, place in a food processor, and process into a very fine meal, about 4 minutes, scraping down the sides as you go.

2. Heat a medium skillet over low heat. Add the shrimp meal and cook, tossing and stirring continuously, until the shrimp is dry and fluffy but not brown, 4 to 6 minutes, depending on the moisture of the shrimp. Because the shrimp is being cooked without any added fat, some of the shrimp will stick to the pan, but by constantly tossing and scraping the bits off the bottom with a wooden spoon, you should be able to avoid any scorching. Scoop into a bowl and set aside. (You can also make the shrimp topping in advance and keep it tightly covered in the refrigerator for up to 3 days.)

3. MAKE THE SHALLOT OIL AND THE MUNG BEAN TOPPING: Heat the oil in a small saucepan over medium heat. Add shallot and stir frequently until soft, about 4 minutes. Remove from the heat, scoop all of it into a bowl, and set aside.

4. Place the mung beans in a small saucepan and pour in enough water to cover by 1 inch. Bring to a simmer over medium heat. Cover and cook until the beans are very soft, 20 to 30 minutes.

5. Drain the mung beans over a bowl and reserve the cooking liquid. Process the beans into a smooth paste in a food processor, about 3 minutes, scraping down the sides as you go. If the paste is too dry to process smoothly, work in some of the reserved cooking liquid, a little at a time, until you have an extremely smooth paste.

6. Scrape down the sides of the processor bowl and move all the paste onto a kitchen towel. Bring together the ends of the cloth and twist to squeeze out as much of the liquid as you can. The amount of liquid you are squeezing out won't be much and may simply be absorbed by the cloth. Scrape the paste into a small bowl and mix in the salt.

7. Strain the shallot oil through a sieve into a small bowl and place the shallot in another small bowl. Mix 2 tablespoons of the shallot oil into the mung bean paste. The paste should be thick, creamy, and spreadable. If it's crumbly and stiff, mix in a little more oil. Set aside the shallot, the shallot oil, and the mung bean mixture. (You can make these toppings in advance and keep them tightly covered in the refrigerator for up to 12 hours.)

8. MAKE THE BATTER: Combine the rice flour and tapioca flour in a large heatproof bowl. Heat 1½ cups water in a small saucepan over medium heat until it is hot to the touch but not close to simmering. Add the hot water to the flour mixture and whisk until there are no clumps in the batter. This is a very thin batter that will cook up to a texture similar to a smooth, dense jelly.

9. STEAM THE DUMPLINGS: Remove the basket from the steamer pot, add 2 inches of water to the pot, and bring to a boil over high heat. Arrange as many small dipping bowls as you can in the basket. Rewhisk the batter and immediately spoon 1½ tablespoons into each bowl. Carefully place the basket in the pot, cover, and cook for 10 minutes.

10. Remove the pot from the heat. Carefully remove the basket and place it on a folded kitchen towel. Carefully remove the bowls and let the dumplings cool slightly. Slip the dumplings out of the bowls with a butter knife and place them top side up in a single layer on a plate. Once unmolded, they will spread out and become a bit wider. Rewhisk the batter just before cooking the remaining batches.

11. Once all the dumplings have been cooked and plated, top each one with a small dollop of the mung bean paste, and spread it out a bit with the back of a spoon. Now top each one neatly with ½ teaspoon of the shallot and a teaspoon of the shrimp meal. Spoon the shallot oil and the Sweet, Sour, and Spicy Fish Sauce over each dumpling, then sprinkle with scallion and chile rings. Serve at room temperature.

Pork Tamales with Green Olives and Jalapeño

Tamales de Puerco (Mexico)

SERVES 4 TO 6 (MAKES 12 DUMPLINGS)

These extravagant pork tamales from southern Mexico offer a multitude of distinct flavors in a small package. As they cook, the tamales soak in flavors both from the filling and from the leaves used to wrap them. *Hoja santa* leaves, or Mexican pepper leaves, cling to their bodies, adding an herbal, aniselike flavor that is exceptional with pork. *Hoja santa* leaves can be found at Mexican markets, but if they are not available, you can use chard leaves as a substitute. If you do, mix 2 to 3 tablespoons of finely chopped fresh tarragon into the batter to give the tamales an anise flavor comparable to that of *hoja santa*.

These dumplings are wrapped using the Envelope Fold (page 56), but you can also use the Diamond in the Square Fold (page 42) if your banana leaves are brittle or torn.

For the Sauce

4 plum tomatoes

2 to 3 large jalapeño chiles

1 small white onion, chopped coarse

2 garlic cloves, crushed

½ teaspoon salt

2 tablespoons nonhydrogenated lard or a neutral oil, such as grapeseed

For the Filling

1 cup bite-sized pieces of cooked pork (if you are making fresh pork broth for the tamale batter, this will provide you with more than enough meat)

⅓ cup raisins

12 large green olives, pitted

For the Batter

1 recipe Tamale Batter from Fresh Masa (page 188) or from Masa Harina (page 189) made with pork broth

For Assembly

12 *hoja santa* leaves or green chard leaves, stemmed

Fifteen 10 × 12-inch prepared banana leaf rectangles (see page 28)

Twelve 15-inch lengths kitchen string for tying the tamales

Equipment

8- to 10-quart steamer pot

1. MAKE THE SAUCE AND THE FILLING: Preheat the oven to 400°F.

2. Place the tomatoes and the jalapeños on a baking sheet and roast until soft and charred in spots, about 20 minutes. Once they are cool enough to handle, pick or rub off the patches of charred skin as best you can. Trim the tomatoes and the peppers of their tougher stem ends. For a less spicy sauce, core and seed the jalapeños.

3. Pulse tomatoes, jalapeños, onion, and garlic in a food processor until the mixture is light and pulpy. Add the salt and pulse once or twice to combine. You will have about 2 cups of sauce.

4. Heat the lard in a small pot over high heat. Carefully and quickly pour in the tomato mixture. Reduce the heat to medium and simmer until the sauce thickens and darkens in color, 6 to 8 minutes. (You can also make the sauce in advance and keep it refrigerated in a tightly sealed container for up to 3 days.)

5. Pour half of the cooked tomato sauce into a small bowl and set aside to cool. Mix the pork and the raisins into the remaining sauce simmering in the pot and cook for 3 minutes longer. Remove from the heat, scoop into another bowl, and set aside to cool.

6. ASSEMBLE THE TAMALES: *Before assembling the tamales, review the Envelope Fold or the Diamond in the Square Fold.*

7. Line a tray with a kitchen towel. Have ready the batter, tomato sauce, pork and raisin mixture, olives, *hoja santa* leaves, banana-leaf rectangles, and ties.

8. Loosen up the batter by whisking it for 2 to 3 minutes. The consistency should be something similar to a grainy and dense mousse. If the batter is too stiff to whisk easily, mix in some cold water, a little at a time, until it is softer and fluffier.

9. Pick out the best 12 banana-leaf rectangles. Lay flat 1 rectangle, smooth side up. Center a single *hoja santa* leaf, smooth side down, on top of the banana leaf. Place 1 heaping tablespoon of batter in the center of the *hoja santa* leaf and spread it out into a 4-inch square. Place a forkful of the pork, 1 olive, and a spoonful of sauce on top of the batter. Top everything with another heaping tablespoon of batter. Fold over one side. Fold over the opposite side. Fold the ends of the leaf over as tightly as you can to create a neat package. Tie the package in a crisscross pattern to prevent the leaf from unfolding and place the tamale on the lined tray. Repeat until you have 12 tamales.

10. Set aside the number of tamales that you would like to cook and keep the rest frozen for up to 6 months (see page 36).

11. STEAM THE TAMALES: Remove the basket from the steamer pot, add 2 inches of water to the pot, and bring to a boil over high heat. Meanwhile, arrange the packages upright, leaning or wedged loosely against each other in the basket. Ball up and stick in any banana-leaf scraps or parchment paper to keep the tamales propped up if needed. Blanket them with the remaining banana leaves. Place the basket in the pot, cover, reduce the heat to medium, and steam for 1½ hours. Check the water level every 30 minutes and replenish with boiling water as needed. (If steaming frozen tamales, place them directly in the basket and cook them in the steamer pot for 2 hours. Do not allow the tamales to thaw before cooking.)

12. Remove the pot from the heat. Carefully remove the basket and place it on a folded kitchen towel. Let the *tamales de puerco* cool slightly, cut off the strings, and serve. It's best not to open the tamales too soon and to peel back the leaves just before eating so that they stay moist and warm.

The Arm of the Queen Tamale

Brazo de la Reina (Mexico)

SERVES 4 (MAKES 1 DUMPLING)

The inspiration behind this dumpling's curious name becomes apparent when you cut into this tamale to reveal what resembles the cross section of flesh and bone. Masa mixed with *chaya* (tree spinach) and thickened with ground pumpkin seeds surrounds a row of hard-boiled eggs. It's difficult to find *chaya* outside of Mexico, but chard makes a fine substitute. Because of its size, it's best to steam this tamale in a roasting pan fitted with a rack. You can also use a standard-size steamer if you divide the ingredients in half and create two medium-sized tamales.

This dumpling is wrapped using the Candy-Wrapper Shape Using a Leaf (page 57).

For the Sauce

5 plum tomatoes

2 serrano chiles or 1 habanero chile

1 small white onion, chopped coarse

1 teaspoon finely chopped epazote leaves or ¼ teaspoon dried Mexican oregano

½ teaspoon salt

2 tablespoons nonhydrogenated lard or a neutral oil, such as grapeseed

For the Batter

1 cup toasted or raw hulled unsalted pumpkin seeds

1 recipe Tamale Batter from Fresh Masa (page 188) or from Masa Harina (page 189) made with chicken broth

6 large green chard leaves or ½ small bunch spinach, stemmed, hand-wilted (see page 37), and chopped fine

¼ teaspoon salt

For the Filling

4 large hard-boiled eggs, peeled

For Assembly

One 12 × 20-inch prepared banana-leaf rectangle (see page 28), plus a couple of large scraps

Five 16-inch lengths of kitchen string for tying the *brazo de la reina*

Equipment

Clean spice or coffee grinder

1 or 2 racks at least 1 inch high and small enough to fit into the roasting pan but large enough to support the length of the tamale

16-inch roasting pan with cover

1. MAKE THE SAUCE: Preheat the oven to 400°F.

2. Place the tomatoes and the chiles on a small baking sheet and roast until they are soft and charred in spots, about 20 minutes. Once they are cool enough to handle, pick or rub off the patches of charred skin as best you can. Trim the tomatoes and the peppers of their firmer stem ends. For less heat, core and seed the chiles.

3. Pulse the tomatoes, chiles, and onion in a food processor until the mixture is light and pulpy. Add the epazote and the ½ teaspoon salt and pulse once or twice to combine.

4. Melt the lard in a small saucepan over high heat. Carefully and quickly pour in the tomato mixture. Reduce the heat to medium and simmer until the sauce thickens and darkens slightly in color, 6 to 8 minutes. Remove from the heat and set aside. (You can also make the sauce in advance and keep it refrigerated in a tightly sealed container for up to 3 days.)

5. MAKE THE BATTER: If using toasted pumpkin seeds, finely grind them in the spice grinder. If using raw pumpkin seeds, toast them in a large skillet over medium heat, stirring constantly, until they just begin to brown, 2 to 3 minutes. Turn them immediately into a bowl and allow them to cool before grinding.

6. Loosen up the batter by whisking it for about 2 minutes. The proper consistency should be something similar to a grainy and dense mousse. If the batter is too stiff to whisk easily, mix in some cold water, a little at a time, until it is softer and fluffier. Add the chard, ¼ teaspoon salt, and ¾ cup of the ground pumpkin seeds and fold gently until just combined.

7. ASSEMBLE THE TAMALE: *Before assembling the* brazo de la reina, *review the Candy-Wrapper Shape Using a Leaf.*

8. Have ready the sauce, the batter, the eggs, the banana-leaf rectangle, and the ties.

9. Lay flat the banana-leaf rectangle, smooth side up. Arrange half of the batter on one of the longer edges of the leaf, leaving a 1-inch border in the front and a 2-inch border on each side. Arrange the eggs lengthwise in a straight line on top of the batter, making sure they are spaced apart evenly. Gently push down on the eggs until the batter comes halfway up their sides. Spoon the remaining batter over the eggs. Roll the egg-stuffed batter up in the leaf, doing your best not to tear it. Tightly tie the two open ends, then tie 3 strings, spaced apart, around the body of the tamale to secure the seam. Using scissors, trim and neaten up the ends of the leaf.

10. STEAM THE TAMALE: Place one or both racks in the roasting pan and pour in enough water to reach below the rungs. Place over 2 burners and bring to a boil. Place the tamale on the rack and blanket with the banana-leaf scraps. Cover, reduce the heat to medium, and steam for 2½ hours. Check the water level every 30 minutes and replenish with boiling water as needed.

11. Remove the pot from the heat. Using pot holders, grip the tamale at both ends, carefully lift it out of the pan, place it on a folded kitchen towel, and allow it to cool slightly. Meanwhile, reheat the sauce. Move the still-wrapped tamale to a large plate, seam side up. Cut off the strings and peel back the leaf. Pour the sauce over the tamale, sprinkle with the remaining ground pumpkin seeds, and serve. It's best not to open this tamale too soon and to peel back the leaf just before serving so that it stays moist and warm. *Brazo de la reina* can be refrigerated for up to 3 days. Reheat in a steamer pot or use the Steamer Plate Setup (page 37).

Leaf-Wrapped Rice Bundles Stuffed with Chicken and Peanuts

Juanes de Arroz (Peru)

SERVES 4 (MAKES 4 DUMPLINGS)

Everything from pork to fish can be tucked into the center of these rice dumplings, but the most popular versions are stuffed with a big piece of chicken and slices of hard-boiled egg. Olives and tomatoes add a lot of flavor, but are never overpowering. Long-grain rice would be too absorbent, so use medium-grain rice to keep this dish moist and luscious. A traditional *juanes* is wrapped in *bijao* leaves, but they are difficult to find. Banana leaves are an acceptable substitute, which some even prefer because of the particular flavors the banana leaf provides.

These dumplings are wrapped using the Lotus-Leaf Fold (page 54).

For the Filling

2 tablespoons nonhydrogenated lard, olive oil, or a neutral oil such as grapeseed

1 small yellow onion, chopped fine

2 tomatoes, peeled, seeded (see page 21), and chopped fine

1 red *aji* chile, fresh or jarred, chopped fine, or ¼ teaspoon *aji* powder or hot paprika

3 garlic cloves, chopped fine

1 teaspoon ground turmeric

1 teaspoon ground cumin

3 tablespoons finely chopped fresh oregano leaves or 1 tablespoon dried

2 tablespoons coarsely chopped fresh culantro (*recao*) or cilantro leaves

1 tablespoon salt

1 teaspoon freshly ground black pepper

2 whole chicken legs, cut at the joint and trimmed of excess fat

4 large black olives, such as Botija or Kalamata, pitted and cut in half

¼ cup unsalted roasted peanuts, papery skins removed

2 large hard-boiled eggs, peeled and cut in half

For the Rice

1¼ cups medium-grain white rice, lightly rinsed

2 large eggs, beaten

For Assembly

Ten 12×15-inch prepared banana-leaf rectangles (see page 28)

Four 35-inch lengths of kitchen string for tying the *juanes*

1. MAKE THE FILLING AND THE RICE: Heat the lard in a medium pot over high heat. Add the onion and stir frequently until golden brown, about 7 minutes. Stir in the tomatoes, *aji* chiles, garlic, turmeric, and cumin and cook for 2 minutes longer. Pour in 2 cups water and scrape up any sticky bits with a wooden spoon. Stir in the oregano, culantro, salt, and pepper, then arrange the chicken pieces, skin side down, in the pot in one layer. Cover, reduce the heat to low, and simmer for 15 minutes. Turn the chicken over, cover, and cook for 15 minutes longer.

2. Using a slotted spoon or tongs, move the chicken to a bowl. Stir the rice into the simmering sauce, cover, reduce the heat to very low, and cook for 20 minutes.

3. Once the chicken is cool enough to handle, remove the skin. Pull the meat off the bones, tear it into bite-sized pieces, place it back in the bowl, and set aside. Discard the bones.

4. Once the rice has finished cooking, remove the pot from the heat, keep covered, and let it rest for 10 minutes longer. The rice will be just about cooked through. Scoop the rice into a shallow bowl and allow it to cool to room temperature.

5. ASSEMBLE THE DUMPLINGS: *Before assembling the* juanes, *review the Lotus-Leaf Fold, only instead of lotus leaves, you will be using banana leaves.*

6. Line a tray with a kitchen towel and have ready the rice, chicken, olives, peanuts, hard-boiled eggs, banana-leaf rectangles, and ties.

7. Add the beaten eggs to the cooled rice and mix well. Divide the chicken into 4 equal piles. Do the same with the peanuts.

8. Pick out the best 8 leaf rectangles. Lay flat 2 rectangles, smooth side up. Center about a third of the rice on one of the rectangles. Moisten your hands with water and pat the rice into a 5-inch round patty. Arrange 1 pile of chicken over the rice, then add 2 olive halves, 1 pile of the peanuts, and 1 hard-boiled egg half. Top everything with another $2/3$ cup of rice. Gently pat and pack the rice around the filling, shaping it into as neat a pile as you can.

9. Fold one of the longer sides of the rectangle snugly over the pile of rice and filling. Fold the opposite side over just as snuggly. Fold over the ends as firmly as you can, forming a neat package. Center this package, seam side down, on the second rectangle. Using the same folding pattern, wrap the package as tightly as you can. Tie this bundle in a crisscross pattern to prevent the leaves from unfolding. Repeat until you have 4 bundles.

10. COOK THE DUMPLINGS: Place an upside-down plate in a large pot, fill it with 2 inches of water, and bring to a boil over high heat. The plate is there to protect the dumplings from direct heat as they cook. Arrange the bundles in one layer inside the pot. It is fine if they are wedged against each other. The water should just reach the tops of the bundles. Cover, reduce the heat to medium, and simmer for 1 hour. Check the water level every 30 minutes and replenish with boiling water as needed.

11. Remove the pot from the heat. Carefully move the *juanes de arroz* with tongs to a folded kitchen towel to drain. Once the excess water has been drained, place them on a large serving plate. Cut off the strings (unless you are freezing the dumplings), unwrap, and serve. It's best not to open the packages too soon and to peel back the leaves just before eating so that they stay moist and warm. *Juanes* can be refrigerated for up to 3 days or frozen (unopened) for up to 6 months. Reheat them in a steamer pot or use the Steamer Plate Setup (page 37). If re-heating frozen *juanes*, allow them to thaw before steaming.

July

BANANA CUPCAKES
Apam Pisang (Malaysia)..227

PLANTAIN DUMPLINGS IN CHICKEN BROTH
Sopa de Bolitas de Plátano Verde (Puerto Rico)...................................229

"NAPKIN" BREAD DUMPLING WITH CHERRIES
Kirschen Serviettenknödel (Austria) 231

FRESH CORN AND COCONUT "TAMALES"
Pamonhas (Brazil)..233

FRESH CORN AND BASIL "TAMALES"
Humitas (Chile)..235

CABINET PUDDING, A CAKE AND ALMOND COOKIE PUDDING
(England) 237

SWEET AND DARK PEPPERPOT STEW AND DUMPLINGS
(Guyana) 240

BOTTLENECKED PORK AND SHRIMP DUMPLINGS
Shao Mai (China) 242

RICE DUMPLINGS STUFFED WITH PEANUT AND COCONUT
Nuo Mi Ci (China) 245

LIGHTLY SOURED RICE CAKES
Sada Idli (India)...247

Banana Cupcakes

Apam Pisang (Malaysia)

SERVES 4 TO 8 (MAKES 8 DUMPLINGS)

These steamed banana cakes are as good as, if not better than, any baked banana bread we've ever had. They are moist and soft and have just the right amount of sweetness. Malaysia has a luscious pool of bananas to choose from, but the common yellow banana will work perfectly, as long as it is overripe. If you like nuts, you can mix ¼ cup of crushed pecans or walnuts into the batter.

For the Dumplings

- 1 cup unbleached all-purpose flour
- ½ teaspoon baking powder
- Pinch of salt
- 3 medium (very ripe) bananas
- ½ teaspoon baking soda
- 2 large eggs
- 2 ounces hard palm sugar or ¼ cup soft palm sugar or other unrefined sugar (see page 20)
- 1 teaspoon grapeseed or other neutral oil
- ½ cup freshly grated coconut (see page 8), or frozen grated coconut, thawed (optional)

Equipment

- 8- to 10-quart steamer pot
- 8 individual baking cups
- 8 paper baking cups

1. MAKE THE BATTER: Sift the flour, baking powder, and salt through a fine sieve into a medium bowl.

2. Place the bananas in a small bowl and mash with a fork until mostly smooth and gooey (or lumpy if you like a more textured cake). You will have just over 1 cup of mashed banana. Mix in the baking soda and set aside.

3. Whisk the eggs in a large bowl until light and foamy. If using hard palm sugar, chop it into bits and crush it as finely as you can. Add the palm sugar and the oil and continue whisking until the sugar has mostly dissolved.

4. Add the mashed banana to the egg mixture and fold together. Add half of the flour mixture, fold together, then fold in the rest. Do not overmix.

5. STEAM THE DUMPLINGS: Remove the basket from the steamer pot, add 2 inches of water to the pot, and bring to a boil over high heat. Line the individual baking cups with the paper baking cups, then arrange as many lined cups in the basket as you can. Spoon in enough batter to fill each cup to just below the rim. Sprinkle about a tablespoon of coconut on the surface of each filled cup, if desired. Place the basket in the pot, cover, and steam for 20 minutes.

6. Remove the pot from the heat. Carefully remove the basket, place it on a folded kitchen towel, and allow the *apam pisang* to cool slightly. Lift them out of the individual baking cups and arrange them on a plate. Cook any remaining batter. Serve warm or at room temperature.

Plantain Dumplings in Chicken Broth

Sopa de Bolitas de Plátano Verde (Puerto Rico)

SERVES 5 TO 6 (MAKES ABOUT 30 DUMPLINGS)

This Puerto Rican chicken-and-dumpling soup is a classic that delivers sunshiny flavors quite distinct from the other traditional chicken and dumpling dishes in this book, such as the *Sopa de Bolitas de Masa* (April), Chicken Fricot with Dumplings (September), and Chicken and Dumpling Soup (September). The dumplings are made from unripe green plantains, and they are cooked in a chicken broth flavored with a *sofrito* of onions, bell peppers, culantro,* cilantro, and oregano. A generous sprinkling of Parmesan cheese completes this soup.

For the Soup

1 recipe (2 quarts) Chicken Broth with Puerto Rican Flavors (page 394)

2 cups chicken meat from making the broth (optional)

3 tablespoons olive oil

1 recipe *Sofrito* (page 83)

For the Dumplings

3 green (unripe) plantains, peeled (see page 17) and grated into fine strands through the smaller holes of your box grater

3 garlic cloves, chopped very fine

¼ teaspoon salt

⅓ cup unbleached all-purpose flour, plus some extra for dusting

For Serving

3 to 4 tablespoons freshly grated Parmesan cheese

1. MAKE THE SOUP: Pour the chicken broth into a medium pot, add the chicken if desired, and bring to a boil over high heat. Reduce the heat to medium for a steady simmer.

2. Heat the oil in a small saucepan over high heat. Carefully and quickly pour in the *sofrito*. Reduce the heat to medium and simmer, stirring frequently until the mixture thickens and darkens in color, 4 to 5 minutes. Scoop all the *sofrito* into the simmering chicken broth. Cover and cook for 10 minutes.

3. MAKE AND COOK THE DUMPLINGS: Line a tray with a kitchen towel and sprinkle with a little flour.

---

* Culantro (also called long coriander or *recao*) is a leafy green herb. It is similar in flavor to cilantro, only stronger and more pungent. Culantro can be found at some Caribbean and Mexican markets. If it is not available, you can double the amount of cilantro in this recipe.

4. Combine the plantain, garlic, and salt in a medium bowl. Work in some of the flour, a little at a time, until the mixture is firm enough to hold its shape when rolled into balls.

5. Pinch off a small piece of dough, roll it into a ball about 1 inch around, dust with flour, and place it on the prepared tray. Repeat the rolling steps with the remaining dough.

6. Carefully drop the dumplings, a few at a time, into the simmering soup and stir gently. Cook until all of them are floating, 3 to 5 minutes, and then cook for 3 minutes longer. Sprinkle Parmesan over each bowl of soup and serve.

"Napkin" Bread Dumpling with Cherries

Kirschen Serviettenknödel (Austria)

SERVES 4 (MAKES 1 DUMPLING)

This large bread dumpling, like the *Serviettenkloss* (November), is an inspired use of fresh or leftover bread. Mixing the bread cubes with eggs, spices, and fruit creates a new, flavorful loaf, textured with all sorts of nooks and crannies. Chopped plums are traditional, but we found that cherries, preferably fresh ones, will provide spectacular swirls of color while retaining their pulpy bursts of sweetness.

This dumpling is wrapped using the Pudding Bag Fold (page 58).

For the Dumpling

1 cup milk

¾ cup semolina flour

4 tablespoons (½ stick) unsalted butter, cut into chunks

6 cups ½-inch crustless white bread cubes (see page 6)

1 large egg, plus 1 large egg yolk

¼ cup sugar

¼ teaspoon ground cinnamon

¼ teaspoon freshly grated nutmeg

⅛ teaspoon salt

Grated zest of 1 lemon

½ pound fresh sweet cherries, pitted and chopped coarse (about 1 cup)

For Cooking and Serving

Unsalted butter to coat the muslin

1 recipe Cherry Compote (recipe follows) or Cream Sauce (page 94)

Equipment

24-inch square of muslin or white cotton napkin

8-inch length of kitchen string for tying the *Kirschen Serviettenknödel*

1. MAKE THE DOUGH: Heat the milk in a small saucepan over medium heat just until the milk begins to bubble at the sides of the pan. Do not allow the milk to come to a full simmer. Immediately remove from the heat and pour into a large bowl. While the milk is hot, stir in the semolina flour and keep stirring until the mixture is a smooth thick batter. Cover and set aside.

2. Melt half of the butter in a large skillet over medium heat. Add half of the bread cubes and stir occasionally until they are lightly browned, 3 to 4 minutes. Scoop them into a bowl, carefully wipe the pan free of crumbs, brown the remaining bread cubes in the remaining butter, and scoop them into the bowl, and allow them to cool slightly.

3. Beat together the egg and the egg yolk. Stir the semolina batter once or twice and mix in the egg, sugar, cinnamon, nutmeg, salt, and lemon zest. Add the cherries and the toasted bread cubes and work everything together with your hands until the bread is thoroughly coated with the batter. Pack the bread mixture into a ball.

4. ASSEMBLE AND COOK THE DUMPLING: *Before assembling the* Kirschen Serviettenknödel, *review the Pudding Bag Fold.*

5. Fill a large pot halfway with salted water and bring to a boil over high heat. Reduce the heat to medium for a steady simmer.

6. Soak the muslin under running water, wring it out, and spread it out on a flat surface. Rub one side of the damp muslin with butter, leaving a narrow border on all sides. Center the cherry-bread ball on top of the muslin. Gather up the corners of the muslin and arrange the folds neatly, creating a bag. As you collect the muslin and prepare it for tying, leave it slightly baggy so that the dumpling can swell as it cooks. Be certain, however, to grip the muslin low enough to leave no open gaps. Tightly tie the gathered muslin.

7. Carefully lower the wrapped dumpling into the simmering water, cover, and cook for 1 hour. Check the water level halfway through cooking and replenish with boiling water as needed.

8. Remove the *Kirschen Serviettenknödel* with tongs and place it on a folded kitchen towel to cool slightly. Remove the strings, carefully unwrap it, and place it on a cutting board. If there is no naturally flat side, steady the dumpling with a fork and slice off just enough from any side to create a "foot," making it possible for it to sit steadily on a plate without rolling around. Serve warm topped with Cherry Compote or Cream Sauce. *Kirschen Serviettenknödel* is also good the next day, sliced and fried in a little butter or used as the bread for French toast.

CHERRY COMPOTE

MAKES ABOUT 1½ CUPS

1 cup dry white wine or unsweetened white grape juice

2 tablespoons sugar

1 cup fresh sweet cherries, pitted

1 tablespoon fresh lemon juice

Combine the wine and the sugar in a small pot and bring to a boil over high heat. Reduce the heat to medium and simmer, uncovered, until the liquid has reduced by half, about 10 minutes. Remove from the heat, then stir in the cherries and the lemon juice. Cover and steep for 10 minutes, stirring occasionally. Scoop the cherries and all the liquid into a glass bowl or other container and set aside to cool. Once the compote has cooled, cover and keep refrigerated for 6 to 8 hours before serving.

Fresh Corn and Coconut "Tamales"

Pamonhas (Brazil)

SERVES 4 TO 8 (MAKES 16 DUMPLINGS)

These sweet dumplings feature the creamy essence and soft nibble of grated coconut and pulped corn. You can, of course, make them with frozen corn, store-bought grated coconut, and canned coconut milk, but if you want to taste the best *pamonhas* possible, only fresh ingredients will do. These unusual dumplings can be so soft and custardlike that you may need to eat them with a spoon.

These dumplings are wrapped using the Two-Husk Tamale Fold 2 (Long) (page 59).

For the Dumplings

6 large ears of corn with husks

½ cup coarse yellow cornmeal

¾ cup sugar

⅛ teaspoon salt

4 tablespoons (½ stick) unsalted butter, melted

1 cup fresh coconut milk (see page 8) or ⅔ cup canned coconut milk mixed with ⅓ cup water

2 cups freshly grated coconut (see page 8), or frozen grated coconut, thawed

For Serving

4 tablespoons (½ stick) unsalted butter, melted just before serving

Sugar for sprinkling

For Assembly

Sixteen 20-inch lengths of kitchen string for tying the *pamonhas*

Equipment

8- to 10-quart steamer pot

1. MAKE THE BATTER: Remove the husks from the corn and separate them from the silk. Set aside the silk and a handful of the smaller husks for later use. Count out 32 of the largest husks, rinse them, pat them dry, and set aside.

2. Cut the kernels off the cobs over a large clean board or tray to make the kernels easier to collect. You will need 5 cups of kernels.

3. Process the kernels in a food processor until almost smooth, about 3 minutes, scraping down the sides as you go. Pour the pureed corn into a large bowl and mix in the cornmeal, sugar, salt, and melted butter. Mix in just enough coconut milk, a little at a time, to thin the batter out into a consistency that resembles the pureed corn before the dried ingredients were added. Mix in the grated coconut.

4. ASSEMBLE THE DUMPLINGS: *Before assembling the* pamonhas, *review the Two-Husk Tamale Fold 2 (Long). This fold makes it possible to create wrappers for generous portions of batter by overlapping fresh corn husks. Dried husks are typically much larger than fresh husks so there's no need to overlap, but they will slightly alter the flavor of the dumplings.*

5. Line a tray with a kitchen towel and have ready the batter, 32 husks, and ties.

6. Arrange 2 husks, smooth side up, overlapping their wider ends by about 2 inches. Center about ½ cup of batter on top of the overlapping husks. Fold over one side. Fold over the opposite side. Tightly tie the open ends, but leave a little room at each end for the dumpling to expand into while it cooks. Using scissors, trim and neaten up the ends of the package and place it on the tray. Repeat until you have 16 packages.

7. STEAM THE DUMPLINGS: Remove the basket from the steamer pot, add 2 inches of water to the pot, and stir in the reserved corn silk. Bring to a boil over high heat. Meanwhile, arrange the packages upright, leaning, or wedged loosely against each other in the basket. Ball up and stick in any extra husks or parchment paper to keep them propped up if needed. Blanket them with the smaller, reserved husks. Place the basket in the pot, reduce the heat to medium, cover, and steam for 1½ hours. Check the water level every 30 minutes and replenish with boiling water as needed.

8. Remove the pot from the heat. Carefully remove the basket and place it on a folded kitchen towel. Let the *pamonhas* cool slightly, cut off the strings (unless you are freezing the dumplings), and serve topped with melted butter and a sprinkling of sugar. It's best not to open the packages too soon and to peel back the husks just before eating, so that they stay moist and warm. *Pamonhas* can be refrigerated for up to 3 days or frozen (unopened) for up to 6 months (see page 36). Reheat them in a steamer pot or use the Steamer Plate Setup (page 37). If reheating frozen *pamonhas*, allow them to thaw before steaming.

Fresh Corn and Basil "Tamales"

Humitas (Chile)

SERVES 8 TO 16 (MAKES 16 DUMPLINGS)

The only obstacle to making a batch of savory and sweet *humitas* can be finding the appropriate corn. These dumplings are made with a particular type of white, starchy corn not easily found. The solution is to use the freshest corn you can find and to mix in some white cornmeal to boost the starch content. Precooking the dough before it's wrapped in the husks helps to create fluffier dumplings. *Humitas,* flavored with generous amounts of basil, are often served with a *pebre* sauce—an uncooked sauce of herbs, chiles, lime, garlic, and sometimes tomatoes—and a sprinkling of sugar.

These dumplings are wrapped using the Two-Husk Tamale Fold 1 (Wide) (page 55).

For the Sauce

- ⅓ cup finely chopped fresh flat-leaf parsley leaves
- ⅓ cup finely chopped fresh cilantro leaves
- 1 small yellow onion, chopped fine
- 1 garlic clove, chopped fine
- 1 small hot red chile, preferably a red *aji* chile, chopped very fine
- 1 jalapeño chile, chopped very fine
- 3 tablespoons olive oil
- 2 teaspoons red wine vinegar
- 2 tablespoons fresh lime juice
- ¾ teaspoon salt

For the Dumplings

- 6 large ears of corn with husks
- ¾ cup finely ground white cornmeal
- ⅓ cup finely chopped fresh basil leaves
- 1 to 2 jalapeño chiles, cored, seeded, and chopped very fine
- 1 teaspoon baking powder
- 1 tablespoon sugar
- 1 tablespoon salt
- 3 tablespoons unsalted butter, cut into chunks
- 1 large yellow onion, chopped fine

For Assembly

- Sixteen 20-inch lengths of kitchen string for tying the *humitas*

Equipment

- 8- to 10-quart steamer pot

1. MAKE THE SAUCE: Combine all the sauce ingredients in a medium bowl, cover, and set aside while you make the *humitas.* (You can make the sauce in advance and keep it refrigerated in a tightly sealed container for up to 1 week.)

2. MAKE THE DOUGH: Remove the husks from the corn and separate them from the silk. Set aside the silk and a handful of the smaller husks for later use. Count out 32 of the largest husks, rinse them, pat them dry, and set aside.

3. Cut the kernels off the cobs over a large clean board or tray to make the kernels easier to collect. You will need 5 cups of kernels.

4. Process the kernels in a food processor until almost smooth, about 3 minutes, scraping down the sides as you go. Pour the corn into a large bowl and mix in the cornmeal, basil, jalapeño, baking powder, sugar, and 1 tablespoon salt.

5. Melt the butter in a large skillet over medium heat. As the butter melts, add the large onion that's been finely chopped and stir frequently until soft, about 4 minutes. Add the pureed corn mixture and stir continuously until it begins to thicken, pulls away from the sides of the pan, and becomes more of a dough, about 3 minutes. Remove from the heat, scoop into a medium bowl, and set aside to cool.

6. ASSEMBLE THE DUMPLINGS: *Before assembling the* humitas, *review the Two-Husk Tamale Fold 1 (Wide). This fold makes it possible to create wrappers for generous portions of dough by overlapping fresh corn husks. Dried husks are typically much larger than fresh husks so there's no need to overlap, but they will slightly alter the flavor of the dumplings.*

7. Line a tray with a kitchen towel and have ready the 32 husks, the ties, and the cooled dough.

8. Arrange 2 husks, smooth side up, next to each other lengthwise with the widest ends on opposite sides. Overlap the husks by about 1½ inches. Center about ½ cup of dough on top of the overlapping husks. Fold over one side. Fold over the opposite side. Fold the ends of the overlapping husks over as tightly as you can to create a neat package. Tie the package in a crisscross pattern to prevent the husks from unfolding and place it on the tray. Repeat until you have 16 packages.

9. STEAM THE DUMPLINGS: Remove the basket from the steamer pot, add 2 inches of water to the pot, and stir in the reserved corn silk. Bring to a boil over high heat. Meanwhile, arrange the packages upright, leaning or loosely wedged against each other in the basket. Ball up and stick in any extra husks or parchment paper to keep them propped up if needed. Blanket them with the smaller, reserved husks. Place the basket in the pot, cover, reduce the heat to medium, and steam for 1½ hours. Check the water level every 30 minutes and replenish with boiling water as needed.

10. Remove the pot from the heat. Carefully remove the basket and place it on a folded kitchen towel. Let the *humitas* cool slightly, cut off the strings (unless you are freezing them), and serve with the sauce and a sprinkling of sugar. It's best not to open the packages too soon and to peel back the husks just before eating so that they stay moist and warm. *Humitas* can be refrigerated for up to 3 days or frozen (unopened) for up to 6 months (see page 36). Reheat them in a steamer pot or use the Steamer Plate Setup (page 37). If reheating frozen *humitas*, allow them to thaw before steaming.

Cabinet Pudding, a Cake and Almond Cookie Pudding

(England)

This eye-catching steamed pudding is made from layers of sponge cake and almond cookie crumbs. It can be made with cubes of cake, but thin, neatly layered slices create a more spectacular pudding, and that's how it's done here. You can leave the crust on the cake for a marbled appearance or cut it off for a cleaner, tidy look. This pudding can be made with different types of sponge cake or pound cake, such as chocolate and lemon, or any combination of leftovers. Ratafias, sometimes called *almond macaroons,* are light, crisp almond cookies that are easy to make and delicious on their own. Store-bought amaretti cookies make a good substitute.

This dumpling is made using the Pudding Basin Setup (page 43).

For the Dumpling

¼ cup raisins

2 tablespoons unsweetened dried sweet cherries, chopped coarse

1 cup milk

4 large eggs, at room temperature

¼ cup sugar

1 teaspoon Pudding Spice (recipe follows)

Pinch of salt

3 cups ¼-inch slices sponge cake

6 Ratafia Cookies (recipe follows), broken into small pieces (about 1⅓ cups), or 1⅓ cups crushed amaretti cookies

For Cooking and Serving

Unsalted butter and sugar to coat the pudding basin

1 recipe Vanilla Custard Sauce (page 97) or Cherry Compote (page 232)

Equipment

24-inch square of muslin

35-inch lengths of kitchen string

4- to 5-cup pudding basin

Pot large enough to hold the basin when covered

Parchment paper

1. SOAK THE FRUIT: Place the raisins and the cherries in a small bowl, pour in warm water to cover by 1 inch, and set aside for 30 to 60 minutes.

2. MAKE THE CUSTARD: Heat the milk in a small saucepan over medium heat just until bubbles begin to appear along the sides of pan. Do not allow the milk to come to a full simmer. Immediately remove from the heat and set aside.

3. Whisk together the eggs, sugar, spice, and salt in a medium bowl until the sugar has mostly dissolved. Continue whisking the egg mixture while gradually drizzling in the warm milk. Cover the bowl to keep the custard warm while you assemble the pudding.

4. ASSEMBLE AND STEAM THE DUMPLING: *Before assembling the pudding, review the Pudding Basin Setup.*

5. Soak the muslin and the string under running water. Wring them out and set aside. Have ready the cake slices, cherries, raisins, custard, and cookie pieces.

6. Divide the cake into 3 equal piles and the cookie pieces into 2 piles.

7. Place the empty pudding basin in the pot. Pour water into the space between the basin and the pot until it comes three-quarters of the way up the sides of the basin. Remove the basin and set the pot aside.

8. Meanwhile, make sure the interior of the basin is dry before rubbing it with butter and coating it with sugar. Drain the raisins and the cherries, shake off any excess water, and scatter them around the bottom of the basin. Layer 1 pile of cake slices on top of the fruit. Spread 1 pile of cookie pieces on top of the cake, followed by another layer of cake, a second layer of cookie pieces, then a third and final layer of cake. Slowly drizzle the custard evenly over the top. Cut out a round of parchment paper and place it on top of the custard-soaked layers. Cover the basin with the damp muslin and secure it tightly with the string. Tie the opposite corners of the muslin into handles over the top of the pudding. Place the pudding basin in the refrigerator for 30 minutes.

9. Bring the water in the pot to a boil over high heat, then reduce the heat to low for a gentle simmer. Using tongs or a wooden spoon, push a folded cloth, like a standard white cotton napkin, into the water and arrange it to lie flat on the bottom of the pot. Using the cloth handle, carefully lower the basin into the pot, cover, and simmer for at least 1½ hours or up to 2½ hours for a pudding that's even richer in flavor and texture. Check the water level every 30 minutes and replenish with boiling water as needed.

10. Remove the pot from the heat. Using a pot holder to grasp the cloth handle, carefully remove the basin from the pot, put it on a folded kitchen towel, and allow the pudding to cool for 5 minutes. Remove the string, cloth, and paper. Unmold by inverting it onto a plate. Slice and serve with Vanilla Custard Sauce or Cherry Compote. The pudding can be refrigerated for up to 3 days. Reheat in a steamer pot or use the Steamer Plate Setup (page 37).

PUDDING SPICE

2½ tablespoons coriander seeds

1½ tablespoons allspice berries

1 tablespoon whole cloves

One 3-inch cinnamon stick, broken into 2 or 3 pieces

1½ tablespoons ground ginger

1 whole nutmeg, freshly grated

Equipment

Clean spice or coffee grinder

Place the coriander, allspice, cloves, and cinnamon in the spice grinder and grind into a fine powder. Mix in the ginger and nutmeg. Measure out what is needed for your recipe and keep the rest in a tightly sealed glass jar in the refrigerator for up to 6 months.

If substituting ground spices, combine the following amounts. Measure out what is needed for the recipe and follow the storage instructions above.

2 tablespoons ground coriander

1½ tablespoons ground allspice

1 tablespoon ground cloves

1 tablespoon ground cinnamon

2 tablespoons freshly grated nutmeg

RATAFIA COOKIES

MAKES ABOUT 12 COOKIES

2 large egg whites, at room temperature

½ cup superfine sugar (or granulated sugar pulsed in a clean spice or coffee grinder for 1 to 2 minutes)

1 teaspoon almond extract

1 cup freshly ground blanched almonds

1. Preheat the oven to 325°F.

2. Whisk the egg whites in a medium bowl until very light and foamy. Add half of the sugar and the almond extract and continue whisking until the mixture forms soft peaks. Gently fold in the ground almonds and the rest of the sugar.

3. Line a baking sheet with parchment paper. Using a teaspoon, scoop up a well-rounded amount of cookie batter. Use another spoon or your finger to move the batter off the spoon and onto the baking sheet. Continue until the sheet is full, allowing 2 inches between scoops so the cookies can spread out evenly while cooking. Use another baking sheet or work in batches if necessary.

4. Bake until the cookies are golden brown, 25 to 30 minutes. Place the tray on a rack and allow the cookies to cool completely before breaking them into small pieces for the cabinet pudding.

Sweet and Dark Pepperpot Stew and Dumplings

(Guyana)

SERVES 4 TO 6 (MAKES 12 DUMPLINGS)

If you like the winning combination of sweet, sticky barbecue with slices of white bread, this dumpling dish is a chance to experience those flavors and textures in a new way. This extremely rich stew is made with soft, bready dumplings and shows off three different types of meat. Cassareep syrup is essential to the flavor of this particular type of pepperpot, because it's this ingredient that imparts the deeply caramelized barbecue flavor. Both sweet and bitter, it is made of a long-cooked reduction of cassava juice, sugar, and spices. Cassareep looks and behaves like molasses, but it has less of that mineral-rich medicinal flavor and more of a pure burnt sugar taste. It is found at many Caribbean markets.

For the Stew

½ small bunch fresh thyme

1 small cinnamon stick

1 pound beef stew meat, cut into bite-sized pieces

1 pound meaty oxtail pieces

½ pound salt beef or corned beef

2 small pig's feet or 1 pound pig's tail

4 whole cloves, finely crushed, or ½ teaspoon ground cloves

One 3-pound chicken, cut into serving pieces with backbone and skin removed

½ cup cassareep

2 tablespoons light muscovado or other unrefined sugar (see page 20)

1 Scotch bonnet or habanero chile*

Grated zest of 1 lemon

For the Dumplings

1½ cups unbleached all-purpose flour, plus some extra for dusting

¼ cup finely ground white or yellow cornmeal

1½ teaspoons baking powder

2 tablespoons sugar

½ teaspoon freshly grated nutmeg

¼ teaspoon salt

Equipment

Kitchen string for tying the thyme and cinnamon

1. MAKE THE STEW: Tie the thyme and the cinnamon stick together and place them in a medium pot along with the beef stew meat, oxtail, salt beef, pig's feet, and cloves. Pour in 6 cups water and bring to a boil over high heat. Cover, reduce the heat to low, and simmer for 1 hour.

2. Stir in the chicken, cassareep, muscovado sugar, and chile. Cover and simmer for 1 hour longer. (You can also make the stew in advance and keep it refrigerated in a tightly sealed

---

*To ensure safe handling of hot chiles, wear rubber gloves and immediately wash your hands thoroughly afterward.

container for up to 3 days. If the stew is too thick to stir easily, add a little water to thin it out.)

3. MAKE THE DUMPLINGS: Halfway through the chicken's cooking time, place 1¼ cups of the flour in a large bowl and keep the remaining ¼ cup handy. Add the cornmeal, baking powder, sugar, nutmeg, and salt and mix well. Pour in ¾ cup water and stir until all the liquid has been absorbed. Work the dough with your hands into one manageable ball. If the dough is wet and sticky, work in some of the remaining flour, a little at a time, until it no longer sticks to your fingers. Do not overwork the dough. Return the dough to the bowl, cover, and let it rest for 20 minutes.

4. Sprinkle a large plate with a little flour. Place the dough on a floured work surface and divide it into 12 equal pieces. Roll each piece into a ball and place them on the prepared plate.

5. COOK THE DUMPLINGS: Once the stew has simmered for 2 hours, remove the salt beef and the pig's feet with a slotted spoon and place them in a bowl. Remove half of the stew meat and place it in another bowl. The stew's sauce should reach at least two-thirds of the way up the remaining pieces of meat. Stir in a little water if the level of the liquid is too low, then let the stew come back up to a simmer.

6. Drop the dumplings, one by one, into the simmering stew and stir gently. Cover and simmer for 15 minutes.

7. Meanwhile, once the meat is cool enough to handle, tear the salt beef into bite-sized pieces and pull off any bits of meat from the pig's feet. Discard the bones and keep the meat in the bowl. Once the dumplings have finished cooking, mix both the pulled meat and the stew meat back into the stew and warm through. Remove from the heat, stir in the lemon zest, and serve.

Bottlenecked Pork and Shrimp Dumplings

Shao Mai (China)

SERVES 4 TO 8 (MAKES ABOUT 48 DUMPLINGS)

A familiar sight at dim sum parlors and dumpling stalls, *shao mai* are enticing little dumplings shaped like small, crinkly sacklike purses left open just enough to reveal a hint of filling. The filling, made from raw ground pork and shrimp, is mixed so well it takes on a whipped, almost cottony texture. Because the dough needs to be rolled out so thin, these dumplings are a challenge and a real source of pride.

These dumplings are made using the Bottleneck Fold (page 50).

For the Dough

2 cups unbleached all-purpose flour, plus some extra for dusting

1 teaspoon salt

1 large egg

For the Filling

4 dried shiitake or black mushrooms, soaked in hot water to cover for 30 minutes

½ pound lean boneless pork loin, chopped very fine, or coarsely ground pork

½ pound fresh shrimp, peeled, deveined, and chopped very fine

5 to 6 fresh water chestnuts, peeled and chopped fine, or canned water chestnuts, drained and chopped fine

2 tablespoons cornstarch

1 teaspoon sugar

1½ teaspoons salt

¼ teaspoon freshly ground white pepper

1 tablespoon rice wine

2 teaspoons soy sauce

1 teaspoon toasted sesame oil

For Cooking

Soft lettuce leaves, such as Boston, to line the steamer basket

Equipment

3¼-inch round cookie cutter

8- to 10-quart steamer pot

1. MAKE THE DOUGH: Place 1¾ cups of the flour in a large bowl and keep the remaining ¼ cup handy. Add the 1 teaspoon salt and mix well.

2. Whisk the egg with ½ cup water in a small bowl and stir it into the flour mixture until all of the liquid has been absorbed. Work the dough with your hands into one manageable ball. If it is wet and sticky, work in some of the remaining flour, a little at a time, until it no longer sticks to your fingers.

3. Place the dough on a floured surface and knead for 4 to 5 minutes. The dough will be somewhat firm. Return it to the bowl, cover with a damp towel, and let it rest for 30 minutes.

4. MAKE THE FILLING: Drain the mushrooms and squeeze out any excess liquid. Remove and discard the stems and finely chop the mushroom caps. Place the mushrooms in a medium bowl along with the remaining filling ingredients. Mix vigorously with a wooden spoon until the filling has a velvety texture, about 3 minutes. Cover and refrigerate for at least 30 minutes. (You can also make the filling in advance and keep it wrapped tightly in the refrigerator for up to 12 hours.)

5. ASSEMBLE THE DUMPLINGS: *Before assembling the* shao mai, *review the Bottleneck Fold.*

6. Line a tray with a kitchen towel and sprinkle with a little flour. Have ready the dough and the chilled filling.

7. Knead the dough once or twice on a floured surface, divide it into 4 equal pieces, and set 3 of them aside under a kitchen towel. Shape the remaining piece into a ball, then roll it out until it's 1/16 inch thick, even thinner would be ideal. (For tips on how to roll dough out thinly, see page 35.) Take your time and sprinkle with flour if it gets sticky. Let the rolled-out dough relax for a couple minutes before cutting out rounds.

8. Using the cookie cutter, cut out as many rounds as you can, usually 10 to 12. Scraps cannot be reused because dough rolled out this thin is too dry to recombine.

9. Lay flat 1 to 5 dough rounds. Brush each round with a very thin coating of water to make it sticky enough to seal. Place a rounded teaspoon of filling in the center of each round. Gather up the sides of the round, creating a pouch around the filling and leaving an open neck in the center of the gathered dough. Pinch together the creases and pleats that formed naturally while the round was gathered up, without closing the neck. This gives the dumpling a loose and frilly top. Gently squeeze the body of the dumpling until the filling pushes up through the neck a little. Holding the dumpling by the neck, tap its base on your work surface until it is flat enough on the bottom to sit upright. Place on the prepared tray and repeat with the remaining rounds and filling. Keep the dumplings covered with a kitchen towel as you work. Once you have assembled the first batch of dumplings, continue with the remaining dough and filling.

10. Set aside the number of dumplings that you would like to cook and keep the rest frozen for up to 6 months (see page 36).

11. STEAM THE DUMPLINGS: Remove the basket from the steamer pot, add 2 inches of water to the pot, and bring to a boil over high heat. Line the basket with the lettuce leaves and arrange as many dumplings in the basket as you can fit without their touching. Place the basket in the pot, cover, reduce the heat to medium-high, and steam for 20 minutes.

(If steaming frozen *shao mai*, place them directly in the basket and cook them in the steamer pot for 25 minutes. Do not allow the *shao mai* to thaw before cooking.)

12. Remove the pot from the heat. Carefully remove the basket and place it on a folded kitchen towel. Remove the *shao mai* with a spoon or a small spatula and place them on a serving plate. Serve immediately while you cook any remaining *shao mai*.

Rice Dumplings Stuffed with Peanut and Coconut

Nuo Mi Ci (China)

SERVES 4 TO 8 (MAKES 8 DUMPLINGS)

These chewy rice dumplings combine two delights, peanuts and coconut. When these two aromatic ingredients mingle, the peanut's flavor is enhanced. The filling tends to be crumbly, making it tricky to handle when stuffing it into a delicate dough. You can make this step more manageable by mixing some freshly ground peanut butter into the filling. The dumplings are coated in more of the grated coconut, but they would be just as traditional if you choose to coat them in finely crushed peanuts, sesame seeds, or a dusting of snowy potato starch.

These dumplings are made using the Bowl Fold (page 45).

For the Filling

¼ cup freshly grated and dried coconut (see page 8) or unsweetened dried grated coconut

⅔ cup unsalted roasted peanuts, papery skins removed and nuts chopped coarse

⅓ cup sugar

3 tablespoons nonhydrogenated lard or vegetable shortening, at room temperature

For the Dough

2 cups sweet (glutinous) rice flour, preferably from China or Thailand, plus some extra for dusting

2 tablespoons tapioca flour (tapioca starch)

For Coating

¾ cup freshly grated and dried coconut (see page 8) or unsweetened dried grated coconut

Equipment

8- to 10-quart steamer pot

24-inch square of muslin

1. MAKE THE FILLING: Place all the filling ingredients in a medium bowl and mix well.

2. MAKE THE DOUGH: Pour 1 cup water into a small saucepan and bring to a boil over high heat. Combine the rice flour and the tapioca flour in a large heatproof bowl.

3. Measure out ¾ cup of the boiling water and keep the remaining ¼ cup handy. Immediately pour the ¾ cup water into the flour mixture and mix until all the liquid has been absorbed. Let the dough cool slightly.

4. Carefully work the dough with your hands. If this is in any way uncomfortable, let it cool another minute or two, but keep in mind that you need to work with this dough while it is still very, very warm. Knead the dough in the bowl until it is smooth and manageable. If the dough is crumbly or cracking around the edges, work in some of the remaining hot water, a little at a time, until the dough comes together. Cover the dough with a cloth, keeping it warm as you assemble the dumplings.

5. ASSEMBLE THE DUMPLINGS: *Before assembling the* nuo mi ci, *review the Bowl Fold.*

6. Sprinkle a plate with a little rice flour and have ready the filling and the dough.

7. Divide the dough into 8 equal pieces. Roll each piece into a ball and keep them covered with a kitchen towel as you work. Use your thumbs to shape one ball into a bowl, about 1½ inches deep. This will be a wide bowl that is best supported in the palm of your hand. Place 2 tablespoons of filling in the center of the dough bowl. Close by pushing and pinching the edges of the dough around and over the filling until the filling is surrounded, pushing out any air. Dab a little water along the edges, if needed, for a better seal. Reroll into a ball, dust with rice flour, and place on the prepared plate. Repeat with the remaining dough balls and filling.

8. STEAM AND COAT THE DUMPLINGS: Remove the basket from the steamer pot, add 2 inches of water to the pot, and bring to a boil over high heat. Soak the muslin under running water, wring it out, then drape it inside the basket, creating a lining. Arrange the dumplings about ½ inch apart in the basket. Place the basket in the pot, cover, reduce the heat to medium, and steam for 10 minutes.

9. Remove the pot from the heat. Carefully remove the basket, place it on a folded kitchen towel, and allow the dumplings to cool slightly. Meanwhile, spread out the ¾ cup grated coconut on a plate and have ready a small bowl of water.

10. Dip one of your hands into the water, pick up one dumpling, and dampen its entire surface. Place it in the grated coconut, roll it around with your dry hand to coat well, and place on a plate. (Moistening the dumpling allows the coconut to stick more evenly.) Repeat with the remaining dumplings. Serve slightly warm or at room temperature. *Nuo mi ci* can be refrigerated for up to 3 days. Allow them to come back to room temperature before serving.

Lightly Soured Rice Cakes

Sada Idli (India)

SERVES 3 TO 4 (MAKES ABOUT 16 DUMPLINGS)

Sada idli are delicate, slightly tangy rice cakes that are exceptionally useful because they absorb sauces, gravies, soups, or soupy condiments without getting soggy. These popular everyday dumplings are distinctly flavorful because they are made out of a fermented batter of ground rice and *urad dal* (a dried split pea). *Idli* molds—round metal plates with perforated depressions—are usually sold in stacks or "trees" so that as many *idli* as possible can be steamed at once. You can buy *idli* trees at most Indian supermarkets.

For the Dumplings

¾ cup white basmati or other long-grain rice, soaked in plenty of nonchlorinated water, such as distilled or spring water, for 6 to 8 hours

½ cup nonchlorinated water, such as distilled or spring water

¼ cup peeled black gram (*urad dal*), soaked in plenty of nonchlorinated water, such as distilled or spring water, for 2 to 3 hours

¼ teaspoon finely crushed fenugreek seeds (optional)

¼ teaspoon baking soda

1 teaspoon salt

For Cooking and Serving

Grapeseed or other neutral oil to coat the *idli* molds

1 recipe each Vegetable Sambhar and Coconut Chutney (recipes follow)

Equipment

Pot large enough to hold the *idli* tree when covered

Idli tree with 3 or 4 layers

1. MAKE THE BATTER 12 TO 36 HOURS IN ADVANCE: Drain the rice, scoop it into a food processor, and process until it resembles coarse, wet sand, 2 to 3 minutes. Add no more than ¼ cup of the nonchlorinated water and process until the mixture becomes a thick paste, 2 to 3 minutes, scraping down the sides as you go. Scoop into a medium bowl and set aside. Don't rinse out the food processor.

2. Drain the black gram and turn it into the food processor along with the fenugreek, if desired. Pour in the remaining nonchlorinated water and process until the mixture is frothy and slightly gritty, about 2 minutes, scraping down the sides as you go. Pour it into the rice mixture and mix.

3. Cover with a cloth and let the batter ferment in a warm room for 12 to 36 hours. Fermentation takes longer at cooler room temperatures, so allow 36 hours if necessary. When properly fermented, the *idli* batter will expand to take up nearly twice as much room in the bowl and will smell slightly sour.

4. **STEAM THE DUMPLINGS:** Add 1 inch of water to the pot and bring to a boil over high heat. Detach the layers of the *idli* tree and coat each mold with a little oil.

5. Add the baking soda and the salt to the batter and fold gently to combine.

6. Fill each mold with 2 heaping tablespoons of batter. Assemble the *idli* tree and carefully insert it into the pot. Cover, reduce the heat to medium, and steam for 20 minutes.

7. Remove the pot from the heat. Place the *idli* tree on a folded kitchen towel and allow the *idli* to cool slightly. Using a butter knife or a small spatula, unmold them gently and keep warm. Cook the remaining batter and serve with Vegetable Sambhar and Coconut Chutney.

IDLI STUFFED WITH ONION CHUTNEY

Make the Onion Chutney (page 252). Add a small spoonful of the chutney to each *idli* mold before spooning in the *idli* batter and cook as directed.

VEGETABLE SAMBHAR

MAKES 6 CUPS

¾ cup split pigeon peas (*toovar dal* or *toor dal*)

1 teaspoon ground turmeric

1 medium yellow onion, cut into ½-inch squares

5 okra pods, trimmed of their tops and cut into ½-inch rounds (about 1 cup)

3 plum tomatoes, peeled, seeded (see page 21), and chopped coarse

1 small carrot, cut into ½-inch rounds

2 tablespoons Sambhar Powder (recipe follows) or use store-bought

1 teaspoon salt

2 teaspoons tamarind paste

¼ cup coarsely chopped fresh cilantro leaves

1 tablespoon ghee (see page 12) or a neutral oil, such as grapeseed

1½ teaspoons black or brown mustard seeds

½ teaspoon cumin seeds

1 to 2 small dried hot red chiles, such as *lal mirch* or *Kashmiri*, sliced into thin rings

5 to 6 fresh curry leaves

1. Place the split pigeon peas and turmeric in a medium pot, pour in 4 cups water, and bring to a boil over high heat. Reduce the heat to low and simmer, partially covered, until the peas are just breaking apart, about 20 minutes.

2. Add the onion, okra, tomatoes, carrot, *sambhar* powder, salt, and tamarind paste and stir. There should be just enough liquid to cover the vegetables. Add more water if needed. Cover and simmer over low heat until the vegetables are very tender, 20 to 25 minutes.

3. Shortly before the stew has finished cooking, heat the ghee over medium heat and add the mustard seeds, cumin, chiles, and curry leaves. Stir until the mustard seeds begin to crackle, about 2 minutes, then immediately remove from the heat.

4. Once the stew has finished cooking, pour it into a large serving bowl or individual soup bowls. Top with the fried spice mixture and stir just before serving. You can also make the stew in advance and keep it refrigerated in a tightly sealed container for up to 3 days.

SAMBHAR POWDER

MAKES ABOUT ½ CUP

¼ cup coriander seeds

2 tablespoons *chana dal* (a type of dried split chickpea)

1½ tablespoons peeled black gram (*urad dal*)

2 teaspoons cumin seeds

1 teaspoon fenugreek seeds

1 teaspoon black peppercorns

1 to 2 small dried hot red chiles, such as *lal mirch* or *Kashmiri*

10 fresh curry leaves

One 1-inch cinnamon stick or ½ teaspoon ground

Equipment

Clean spice or coffee grinder

1. Combine all the ingredients in a medium skillet over medium heat. (If using ground cinnamon, do not add until after the other ingredients are toasted.) Stir continuously until the spices are lightly browned, about 5 minutes. Scoop the mixture into a small bowl and set aside to cool to room temperature.

2. Once the spice mixture has cooled, grind it in the spice grinder until you have a fine powder. Measure out what you need and keep the rest tightly sealed in a glass container for up to 3 months.

COCONUT CHUTNEY

MAKES ABOUT 2 CUPS

1 tablespoon peeled black gram (*urad dal*)

1 cup freshly grated coconut (see page 8) or frozen grated coconut, thawed

1 teaspoon freshly grated ginger

½ cup warm water

2 teaspoons fresh lemon juice

1 tablespoon coarsely chopped fresh cilantro leaves

¼ teaspoon sugar

¼ teaspoon salt

2 teaspoons ghee (page 12) or a neutral oil, such as grapeseed

¾ teaspoon black or brown mustard seeds

¼ teaspoon cumin seeds

1 small dried hot red chile, such as *lal mirch* or *Kashmiri*, sliced into thin rings

2 to 3 fresh curry leaves

Equipment

Clean spice or coffee grinder

1. Toast the black gram in a small skillet over medium heat, stirring or shaking the pan constantly, until it just begins to brown, about 3 minutes. Immediately scoop the black gram into a small bowl and set aside to cool to room temperature. Once it has cooled, grind it in the spice grinder until you have a coarse powder and set aside.

2. Pulse the coconut and ginger in a food processor until the coconut is very finely chopped. Pour in the warm water and process until you have a moist, gritty paste, about 1 minute. Add the lemon juice, cilantro, sugar, and salt, pulse once or twice to combine, then scoop into a small serving bowl.

3. Heat the ghee over medium heat and add the mustard seeds, cumin, chile, and curry leaves. Stir until the mustard seeds begin to crackle, about 2 minutes, then scoop all the spices and the oil on top of the coconut mixture. Stir everything together when you are ready to serve.

ONION CHUTNEY

MAKES ½ CUP

2 tablespoons ghee (page 12) or a neutral oil such as grapeseed

1 teaspoon peeled black gram (*urad dal*)

1 small dried hot red chile, such as *lal mirch* or *Kashmiri,* split in half

½ teaspoon grated fresh ginger

1 small yellow onion, chopped fine

2 plum tomatoes, peeled, seeded (see page 21), and chopped coarse

¼ teaspoon brown mustard seeds

¼ teaspoon cumin seeds

½ teaspoon tamarind paste or ¼ pitted prune, mashed into a thick paste with ¼ teaspoon lime juice

1 teaspoon jaggery or other unrefined sugar (see page 20)

¼ teaspoon salt

1. Melt half of the ghee in a medium skillet over medium heat. Stir in the black gram, chile, and ginger and cook until the gram begins to brown, about 2 minutes. Add the onion and stir frequently until the onion is lightly browned, about 5 minutes. Mix in the tomatoes and cook for 1 minute longer. Remove from the heat. Scoop into a food processor and pulse until the mixture is light and pulpy.

2. Melt the rest of the ghee in a clean skillet over medium heat. Add the mustard and cumin seeds and stir continuously for 1 minute. Mix in the pureed onion mixture, the tamarind, jaggery, and salt and continue stirring until you have a thick, moist paste, about 3 minutes longer. Remove from the heat, scoop into a bowl, set aside, and allow it to cool to room temperature before using. You can make the chutney in advance and keep it refrigerated in a tightly sealed container for up to 1 week.

August

PEACH AND BERRY GRUNT
(United States) 255

CASSAVA PATTIES WITH GRATED COCONUT
Pichi-Pichi (Philippines) 256

RED PEA SOUP WITH SPINNERS
(Caribbean) 257

LEAF-WRAPPED RICE AND BANANA BUNDLES
Khao Tom Mat (Thailand) 259

WONTONS WITH RED CHILE OIL
Hung You Chao Shou (China) 261

CORN TAMALES STUFFED WITH STRINGY CHEESE AND POBLANO
Tamales de Elote (Mexico) 263

LEAF-WRAPPED BLACK-EYED PEA DUMPLINGS
Moyin-Moyin (Nigeria) 265

LEAF-WRAPPED RICE BUNDLES STUFFED WITH PORK AND BEANS
Bánh Tet (Vietnam) 267

COCONUT-FILLED RICE DUMPLINGS

Modak (India).. 270

TAPIOCA BALLS STUFFED WITH MINCED PORK AND PEANUTS

Sakoo Sai Moo (Thailand)... 272

Peach and Berry Grunt

(United States)

SERVES 4 (MAKES ABOUT 12 DUMPLINGS)

Blueberry Grunt is a classic dessert that often relies on a lot of sugar to compensate for the natural tartness of the berries. By combining the berries with peaches and just a touch of sugar, however, you can emphasize the deep fruity flavors of both without going into sugar shock. You can use milk instead of buttermilk in the dough, but buttermilk adds a tang that goes well with fruit. You can always substitute blackberries or raspberries for the blueberries.

For the Dumplings

- 1 cup unbleached all-purpose flour
- 2 teaspoons sugar
- 2 teaspoons baking powder
- ½ teaspoon salt
- 2 tablespoons cold unsalted butter, cut into bits
- ⅓ cup buttermilk or milk

For the Stew

- 4 ripe but firm peaches, peeled, pitted, and cut into ½-inch slices
- 1 pint (about 2 cups) fresh or frozen blueberries or blackberries
- ⅓ cup honey, preferably raw
- 2 tablespoons fresh lemon juice
- ¼ cup sugar
- ¼ teaspoon ground ginger
- ½ teaspoon ground allspice

For Serving

- 1 recipe Sweetened Whipped Cream (page 94), Cream Sauce (page 94), or vanilla ice cream

Equipment

Large, wide pot or skillet with a cover

1. MAKE THE BATTER: Combine the flour, 2 teaspoons sugar, the baking powder, and salt in a large bowl. Add the butter and work it into the flour mixture with a pastry cutter or 2 butter knives until it looks like a coarse, damp meal. Add the buttermilk and stir until you have a thick, slightly lumpy batter. Do not overmix.

2. MAKE THE STEW AND COOK THE DUMPLINGS: Place all the stew ingredients, along with ¼ cup water, in the large pot. Bring to a simmer over medium heat. Cover, reduce the heat to low, and simmer for 2 minutes. Stir and see if the liquid is level with the fruit. Add some more water if needed.

3. Scoop up a heaping tablespoon of batter. Use another spoon or your finger to move the batter gently off the spoon and on top of the simmering fruit. Drop in spoonfuls of the remaining batter, leaving as much space as you can around each. Cover and simmer for 10 minutes. Uncover and cook for 2 minutes longer. Serve these dumplings with plenty of the fruit and Sweetened Whipped Cream, Cream Sauce, or vanilla ice cream.

Cassava Patties with Grated Coconut

Pichi-Pichi (Philippines)

SERVES 4 TO 6 (MAKES 12 DUMPLINGS)

Pichi-pichi, made from grated cassava, sugar, and pandan water, are something like large, soft gumdrops with a clean, floral flavor. *Pichi-pichi* are typically enjoyed in one of two ways: right out of the steamer, while still warm and soft, or at room temperature, when they're firm on the outside but still quite soft on the inside. No matter their temperature, they're commonly topped or coated with a generous amount of freshly grated coconut.

For the Dumplings

10 fresh or frozen pandan leaves, each folded in half and tied into a knot for easier handling, or ½ teaspoon pandan extract

1 cup finely grated cassava (see page 7)

1 cup sugar

For the Coating

4 cups freshly grated coconut (see page 8) or frozen grated coconut, thawed

Equipment

8- to 10-quart steamer pot

Twelve 2-inch dipping bowls (see page 26)

1. MAKE THE BATTER: Place the knotted pandan leaves and 1¼ cups water in a small saucepan and bring to a boil over high heat. Cover, reduce the heat to low, and simmer for 15 minutes. Measure out 1 cup of the pandan water and allow it to cool to room temperature. If using pandan extract, stir it into 1 cup cool water and set aside.

2. Move the grated cassava onto a kitchen towel. Bring together the ends of the cloth and twist to squeeze out as much liquid as you can. There won't be much liquid, and it may simply be absorbed by the cloth. Place the cassava in a large bowl and break it up a little. Add the sugar and pandan water and mix well.

3. STEAM AND COAT THE DUMPLINGS: Remove the basket from the steamer pot, add 2 inches of water to the pot, and bring to a boil over high heat. Arrange as many dipping bowls in the basket as you can. Spoon enough batter into each bowl to fill them halfway. Place the basket in the pot, cover, and steam for 15 minutes.

4. Remove the pot from the heat. Carefully remove the basket, place it on a folded kitchen towel, and allow the *pichi-pichi* to cool slightly. Meanwhile, spread the coconut out on a large plate. Working while they are still warm, unmold the *pichi-pichi* with a butter knife or a small spatula and place them on the plate of grated coconut. Turn and press all sides into the coconut, then arrange them on a serving plate. Repeat with any remaining batter. Serve warm or at room temperature. *Pichi-pichi* can be refrigerated for up to 3 days. Allow them to come back to room temperature before serving.

Red Pea Soup with Spinners

(Caribbean)

SERVES 6 (MAKES 6 DUMPLINGS)

This Caribbean soup is frequently made with lots of little dumplings, but versions prepared with palm-sized dumplings are more fun to eat. The long slow cooking of the soup dissolves the beans almost completely and makes the soup thick and velvety. Cooking the soup with a whole Scotch bonnet pepper will give a slight sense of heat, but if you want a truly fiery soup, chop up the Scotch bonnet before adding it.

For the Soup

- 1 large smoked ham hock
- 1¼ cups dried red kidney beans, soaked in plenty of water for 6 to 8 hours, or 2½ cups canned, drained and rinsed
- ¾ pound boneless smoked brine-cured (or wet-cured) ham, cut into 6 pieces
- 1 small yellow onion, chopped fine
- 1 medium baking potato, such as russet, peeled and cut into ½-inch cubes
- 1 small tropical yam or sweet potato, peeled and cut into ½-inch cubes
- 1 medium carrot, cut into ½-inch rounds
- 3 fresh thyme sprigs
- 1 Scotch bonnet or habanero chile*
- Salt and freshly ground pepper to taste

For the Dumplings

- 1¼ cups unbleached all-purpose flour, plus some extra for dusting
- ¼ teaspoon salt

1. MAKE THE SOUP: Fill a small saucepan halfway with water and bring to a boil over high heat. Add the ham hock, cover, and cook for 5 minutes, then drain.

2. Place the ham hock in a large pot and pour in 10 cups water. Drain the kidney beans and stir them, along with the ham pieces, into the pot. (If using canned beans, add them later when adding the vegetables.) Bring to a boil over high heat, cover, reduce the heat to medium-low, and cook until the beans are just tender, stirring occasionally, 1½ to 2 hours.

3. Add the onion, potato, yam, carrot, thyme, and chile. Cover and cook for 1 hour longer, stirring occasionally. The vegetables will be very tender and the beans will begin to break apart. Reduce the heat to very, very low to keep the soup hot until it's time to add the dumplings. (You can also make the soup in advance and keep it refrigerated in a tightly sealed container for up to 3 days.)

---

*To ensure safe handling of hot chile peppers, wear rubber gloves and immediately wash your hands thoroughly afterward.

4. MAKE THE DOUGH: While the soup is simmering, place 1 cup of the flour in a medium bowl and keep the remaining ¼ cup handy. Add the salt and mix well. Pour in ⅔ cup water and mix until all the liquid has been absorbed. Work the dough with your hands into one manageable ball. If the dough is wet and sticky, work in some of the remaining flour, a little at a time, until it no longer sticks to your fingers.

5. Place the dough on a floured surface and knead for 3 to 4 minutes. The dough will be soft and stretchy. Return it to the bowl, cover, and let rest for 30 minutes.

6. MAKE THE DUMPLINGS: Line a tray with a kitchen towel and dust with a little flour.

7. Knead the dough once or twice on a floured surface and divide it into 6 equal pieces. Roll each piece into a ball, then pat each ball down into a disk about ½ inch thick. Place the disks on the prepared tray and set aside.

8. FINISH THE SOUP AND COOK THE DUMPLINGS: Remove the ham hock from the soup with tongs or a slotted spoon, place it on a plate, and allow it to cool slightly. Fish out the thyme stems and chile and discard.

9. Return the soup to a simmer over medium heat. Gently drop the dumplings, one by one, into the simmering soup and stir gently to prevent sticking. Cover and simmer for 30 minutes.

10. While the dumplings cook, pull the rind off the ham hock and tear the meat off the bones. Discard the rind and bones. Once the dumplings have finished cooking, return the torn meat to the soup and stir. Sprinkle with salt and pepper and serve.

Leaf-Wrapped Rice and Banana Bundles

Khao Tom Mat (Thailand)

SERVES 4 TO 8 (MAKES 8 DUMPLINGS)

Khao tom mat are always made with whole grains of sweet rice, but you can use any type of banana or substitute a slice of papaya or plantain. Many bananas found in Thailand are not available here, but the small red-skinned ones available in some markets work well, as do the larger, more common yellow ones. As the dumpling cooks, the rice expands and gets sticky and soft around the filling, creating a type of rice cake. Because *khao tom mat* are fashioned with a looser leaf wrap, they have a more yielding and less compact texture than do similar rice dumplings that are more tightly wrapped.

These dumplings are wrapped using the Diamond in the Square Fold (page 42).

For the Rice Mixture

¼ cup dried black turtle beans, soaked in plenty of water for 6 to 8 hours, or ½ cup canned, drained and rinsed

3 pandan leaves, each folded in half and tied into a knot for easier handling, or ¼ teaspoon pandan extract

⅔ cup fresh coconut milk (see page 8) or canned coconut milk

¼ cup sugar

½ teaspoon salt

1 cup medium-grain sweet (glutinous) white rice, preferably from Thailand, rinsed (see page 18) and soaked in plenty of water for 6 to 8 hours

For the Filling

2 very ripe bananas

For Assembly

Eight 8-inch prepared banana-leaf squares (see page 28)

Eight 6-inch prepared banana-leaf squares

Eight 36-inch lengths of kitchen string for tying the *khao tom mat*

Equipment

8- to 10-quart steamer pot

1. COOK THE BEANS 1 TO 1½ HOURS IN ADVANCE: (Skip this step if using canned black turtle beans.) Drain the black turtle beans and place them in a small saucepan. Cover the beans with plenty of water and bring to a simmer over medium heat. Cover, reduce the heat to low, and simmer until the beans are tender, 1 to 1½ hours. Drain and place in a small bowl to cool.

2. COOK THE RICE: Place the knotted pandan leaves in a small pot. Pour in the coconut milk and stir in the sugar and salt. Bring to a simmer over medium-low heat. Immediately cover, reduce the heat to very low, and barely simmer for 15 minutes. If using fresh coconut milk, be careful not to let it come to a boil.

3. Drain the rice. Remove the pandan leaves from the coconut milk and discard. Raise the heat from very low to low, mix in the rice, cover, and simmer for 3 minutes. Uncover and stir the rice until most of the liquid has been absorbed, 1 to 2 minutes. The rice will be firm and undercooked. Scoop into a bowl, mix in the beans, and set aside to cool.

4. ASSEMBLE THE DUMPLINGS: *Before assembling the* khao tom mat, *review the Diamond in the Square Fold.*

5. Line a tray with a kitchen towel and have ready the rice mixture, bananas, banana-leaf squares, and ties.

6. Peel the bananas and split each one into 4 equal pieces by cutting them both crosswise and lengthwise. You will have 8 banana slices.

7. Lay flat 1 large banana-leaf square, smooth side up, then place a smaller leaf square, smooth side up, diagonally on top of the large square. Center 2 rounded tablespoons of the rice mixture on top of the stacked leaves and spread it out into a 4×2-inch rectangle. Gently press a piece of banana into the rice mixture. The length of the banana should not be longer than the 4-inch length of the rice rectangle. Top with 1 tablespoon of the rice mixture. Fold over one corner of the stacked leaves. Fold over the opposite corner. Fold the ends of the leaves over as firmly as you can to create a neat, rectangular package. Tie to secure the folds, place it on the lined tray, and repeat until you have 8 packages.

8. STEAM THE DUMPLINGS: Remove the basket from the steamer pot, add 2 inches of water to the pot, and bring to a boil over high heat. Arrange the packages in the basket, then place the basket in the pot. Cover, reduce the heat to medium, and steam for 1 hour. Check the water level halfway through the cooking and replenish with boiling water as needed.

9. Remove the pot from the heat. Carefully remove the basket and place it on a folded kitchen towel. Let the *khao tom mat* cool slightly, cut off the strings (unless you are freezing the dumplings), and serve. They can also be served at room temperature. It's best not to open the packages too soon, and to peel back the leaves just before eating, so they stay moist and warm. *Khao tom mat* can be refrigerated for up to 3 days or frozen (unopened) for up to 6 months (see page 36). Reheat them in a steamer pot or use the Steamer Plate Setup (page 37). If reheating frozen *khao tom mat*, allow them to thaw before steaming.

Wontons with Red Chile Oil

Hung You Chao Shou (China)

SERVES 4 TO 8 (MAKES ABOUT 36 DUMPLINGS)

Hung you chao shou are tasty pork and cabbage dumplings served in a generous slick of chile oil. The amount of chile recommended here should be just enough to make you break into a gentle sweat, although you could of course use less or more. If it's wonton soup you want, just cook the dumplings in a big pot of simmering water until they float and then immediately add them to a pot of Chicken Broth with Chinese Flavors (page 394).

These dumplings are made using the Curled-Letter Fold (page 60).

For the Filling

- ½ pound (2 to 3 small heads) Shanghai bok choy or baby bok choy, trimmed, chopped fine, and hand-wilted (see page 37)
- ½ pound freshly ground pork
- 2 garlic cloves, chopped very fine
- 1 teaspoon freshly grated ginger
- 2 scallions, sliced into thin rings
- 1 tablespoon soy sauce
- 2 teaspoons rice wine
- 1 teaspoon salt
- ½ teaspoon freshly ground white pepper

For the Dough

- 1 recipe *Sheesh Barak bi Laban* (page 153) dough, preferably made while the filling is being chilled but no more than 1 hour in advance
- Unbleached all-purpose flour for dusting

For the Chile Oil

- ¼ cup grapeseed or other neutral oil
- 2 to 3 teaspoons mild pure ground chile, preferably from China or Korea, or Aleppo pepper flakes
- 1 teaspoon Sichuan peppercorns, finely crushed
- 1 garlic clove, chopped very fine
- 1 tablespoon toasted sesame oil
- ½ teaspoon salt
- 1½ teaspoons rice vinegar

For Serving

- 1 scallion, sliced into thin rings

Equipment

- Large, wide bowl to hold the dumplings cooked in batches

1. MAKE THE FILLING: Scoop the hand-wilted bok choy onto a kitchen towel. Bring together the ends of the cloth and twist to squeeze out as much liquid as you can. Place the bok choy in a medium bowl and mix in all the remaining filling ingredients. Cover and refrigerate for at least 30 minutes but no more than 6 hours.

2. ASSEMBLE THE DUMPLINGS: *Before assembling the wontons, review the Curled-Letter Fold.*

3. Line a tray with a kitchen towel and sprinkle with a little flour. Have ready the dough and the filling.

4. Knead the dough once or twice on a floured surface, divide it into 4 equal pieces, and set 3 of them aside under a kitchen towel. Shape the remaining piece into a blunt log, then roll it out into a 9-inch square. This dough should not be thicker than $1/16$ inch, ideally even thinner. (For tips on how to roll dough out thin, see page 35.) Take your time and sprinkle the dough with flour if it gets sticky. Let the rolled-out dough rest for a couple of minutes.

5. Trim the edges, creating a cleaner square shape. Cut the dough into 3-inch strips, then cut across the strips every 3 inches to make 9 squares. Place the squares in a single layer on the prepared tray. Repeat with the remaining dough pieces, separating layers with kitchen towels. Keep the squares covered as you work. Scraps cannot be reused because dough rolled out this thin is too dry to recombine.

6. Lay flat 1 to 5 dough squares. Brush each with a very thin coating of water to make it sticky enough to seal. Center a rounded teaspoon of the filling on top of each square. Fold one side over the filling, then fold over the opposite side. Now take both ends, pull them together, overlapping them a bit, and pinch to seal. Dab a little water on the ends, if needed, for a better seal. Place the assembled dumplings in a single layer on the prepared tray and keep them covered with a kitchen towel. Continue with the remaining squares and filling.

7. Cover the tray of assembled dumplings and place in the refrigerator for 30 to 60 minutes before cooking. Chilling the dumplings helps to set the dough, making them firm and toothsome when cooked instead of puffy and soft. Set aside the number of dumplings that you would like to cook, and keep the rest frozen for up to 6 months (see page 36).

8. MAKE THE CHILE OIL: Heat the oil, ground chile, Sichuan pepper, the clove of chopped garlic, the sesame oil, and $1/2$ teaspoon salt in a small saucepan over low heat. Cook for 5 minutes and remove from the heat. Pour the flavored oil into a small bowl, stir in the rice vinegar, and set aside. (You can also make the chile oil in advance and keep it refrigerated in a tightly sealed glass container for up to 3 months.)

9. COOK THE DUMPLINGS: Fill a large pot three-quarters of the way with salted water and bring to a boil over high heat. Reduce the heat to medium for a steady simmer.

10. Gently drop up to 20 dumplings, one by one, into the simmering water. Stir carefully and occasionally to prevent sticking. Cook until all of them are floating, then cook for 3 minutes longer. (If cooking frozen wontons, add them directly to the simmering water. Do not allow the dumplings to thaw before cooking.)

11. Using a slotted spoon, remove the dumplings and place them in the large bowl. Drizzle with a ladle of the cooking liquid to prevent sticking. Cook the remaining dumplings and place them in the bowl with another ladle of the cooking liquid.

12. Drain the wontons and place them in a large, shallow serving bowl. Drizzle with the chile oil, sprinkle with the scallion, and serve.

Corn Tamales Stuffed with Stringy Cheese and Poblano

Tamales de Elote (Mexico)

SERVES 4 TO 8 (MAKES 8 DUMPLINGS)

Big handfuls of juicy corn kernels mixed into the batter give *tamales de elote* a fresh corn texture and a delicate juiciness. Strips of Oaxacan cheese and poblano pepper in the center of these tamales add creaminess and a refreshing fruity flavor. If you prefer to leave out the peppers, the cheese alone is a delightful filling.

These dumplings are wrapped using the Two-Husk Tamale Fold 1 (Wide) (page 55).

For the Batter

2 large ears of corn or 1½ cups fresh or frozen corn kernels

1 recipe Tamale Batter from Fresh Masa (page 188) or Tamale Batter from Masa Harina (page 189) made with chicken broth

½ teaspoon salt

For the Filling

½ pound fresh Oaxacan cheese or soft mozzarella cheese, sliced into twenty-four 3-inch-long strips

2 poblano chiles, cored, seeded, and sliced into twenty-four 3-inch-long strips

For Assembly

20 to 25 prepared dried corn husks (see page 28)

Eight 26-inch lengths of kitchen string for tying the tamales

Equipment

8- to 10-quart steamer pot

1. ASSEMBLE THE TAMALES: *Before assembling the tamales, review the Two-Husk Tamale Fold 1 (Wide). This fold makes it possible to create wrappers for generous portions of batter by overlapping the corn husks.*

2. Cut the kernels off the cobs over a large clean board or tray to make the kernels easier to collect. You will need 1½ cups of kernels.

3. Loosen up the batter by whisking it for 2 to 3 minutes. The consistency should be something similar to a grainy and dense mousse. If the batter is too stiff to whisk easily, mix in some cold water, a little at a time, until it is softer and fluffier. Fold the kernels and salt into the batter.

4. Line a tray with a kitchen towel and have ready the batter, strips of cheese and pepper, the husks, and the ties.

5. Pick out the best 16 husks. Arrange 2 husks, smooth side up, next to each other lengthwise with the widest ends on opposite sides. Overlap the husks by about $1^1/_2$ inches. Center 2 heaping tablespoons of the batter on top of the overlapping husks. Arrange 3 strips of cheese and 3 strips of pepper on top of the batter, then spoon another 2 heaping tablespoons of batter on top. Fold over one side. Fold over the opposite side. Fold the ends of the overlapping husks over as tightly as you can to create a neat package. Tie the package in a crisscross pattern to prevent the husks from unfolding and place it on the lined tray. Repeat until you have 8 tamales.

6. Set aside the number of tamales that you would like to cook and keep the rest frozen for up to 6 months (see page 36).

7. STEAM THE TAMALES: Remove the basket from the steamer pot, add 2 inches of water to the pot, and bring to a boil over high heat. Meanwhile, arrange the packages upright, leaning or loosely wedged against each other in the basket. Ball up and stick in any extra husks or parchment paper to keep the tamales propped up if needed. Blanket them with any remaining husks. Place the basket in the pot, reduce the heat to medium, cover, and steam for 2 hours. Check the water level every 30 minutes and replenish with boiling water as needed. (If steaming frozen tamales, place them directly in the basket and cook them in the steamer pot for $2^1/_2$ hours. Do not allow the tamales to thaw before cooking.)

8. Remove the pot from the heat. Carefully remove the basket and place it on a folded kitchen towel. Let the *tamales de elote* cool slightly, cut off the strings, and serve. It's best not to open the tamales too soon and to peel back the husks just before eating so they stay moist and warm.

Leaf-Wrapped Black-Eyed Pea Dumplings

Moyin–Moyin (Nigeria)

SERVES 6 TO 8 (MAKES 16 DUMPLINGS)

These steamed banana-leaf-wrapped dumplings call for you to peel off the papery skins of black-eyed peas. This may sound tiresome, but in fact it's quite easy to do. The result is a batch of savory dumplings that are creamy in texture and, because of the tomato paste, almost salmon-pink in color. These are popular dumplings, sold at markets or directly from stalls, varying according to the addition of shrimp powder or just about any fresh, salted, canned or dried meat or fish. Slices of hard-boiled egg and green peas are often appreciated additions.

These dumplings are wrapped using the Envelope Fold (page 56), but you can also use the Diamond in the Square Fold (page 42) if your banana leaves are brittle or torn.

For the Dumplings

1 cup dried black-eyed peas, soaked in plenty of water for 6 to 8 hours

1 large yellow onion, chopped coarse

2 teaspoons tomato paste

1/2 cup fresh or frozen green peas

1 red or green bell pepper, cored, seeded, and chopped fine

1 teaspoon salt

1/4 to 1/2 teaspoon cayenne

1/2 teaspoon freshly ground black pepper

1 teaspoon shrimp powder (optional)

4 large hard-boiled eggs, peeled and each sliced into 4 rounds

For Assembly

Twenty 8-inch prepared banana leaf squares (see page 28)

Sixteen 24-inch lengths of kitchen string for tying the *moyin-moyin*

Equipment

8- to 10-quart steamer pot

1. **MAKE THE BATTER:** Drain the black-eyed peas and place them in a large bowl. Cover them with water by at least 4 inches. Scoop up handfuls of the black-eyed peas and rub them back and forth gently between your palms. They will split apart as you rub them against each other, loosening their skins. Occasionally swirl the black-eyed peas around in the water so that the loosened skins can float to the top and be skimmed off. Keep rubbing until most of the black-eyed peas have been peeled. Then use your fingers to peel off any remaining skins. Drain the black-eyed peas and pick out any obvious bits of skin.

2. Pulse the onion and the tomato paste in a food processor until the onion is finely chopped. Add the peeled black-eyed peas and pulse until the mixture becomes a grainy batter, scraping down the sides as you go. Drizzle in up to $^1/_4$ cup water, a little at a time, until the batter is just loose enough to spread out evenly within the food processor.

3. Scoop the batter into a medium bowl and stir in the green peas, bell pepper, salt, cayenne, black pepper, and shrimp powder if desired. (You can also make the batter in advance and keep it tightly covered in the refrigerator for up to 8 hours.)

4. ASSEMBLE THE DUMPLINGS: *Before assembling the* moyin-moyin, *review the Envelope Fold.*

5. Line a tray with a kitchen towel and have ready the batter, the sliced eggs, the banana-leaf squares, and the ties.

6. Lay flat 1 banana-leaf square, smooth side up. Center 2 rounded tablespoons of batter on top of the leaf. Gently press a slice of egg into the batter and top with another tablespoon of the batter. Fold over one side. Fold over the opposite side. Fold the ends of the leaf over as tightly as you can to create a neat package. Tie the package in a crisscross pattern to prevent the leaf from unfolding and place it on the lined tray. Repeat until you have 16 packages.

7. STEAM THE DUMPLINGS: Remove the basket from the steamer pot and add 2 inches of water to the pot. Bring the water to a boil over high heat. Meanwhile, arrange the packages in layers within the basket. Blanket them with any remaining banana leaves. Place the basket in the pot, reduce the heat to medium, cover, and steam for 1 hour. Check the water level halfway through the cooking and replenish with boiling water as needed.

8. Remove the pot from the heat. Carefully remove the basket and place it on a folded kitchen towel. Let the *moyin-moyin* cool and set for about 5 minutes, cut off the strings (unless you are freezing the dumplings), and serve. It's best not to open the packages too soon and to peel back the leaves just before eating, so that they stay moist and warm, but they can also be served at room temperature. *Moyin-moyin* can be refrigerated for up to 3 days or frozen for up to 6 months (see page 36). Reheat them in a steamer pot or use the Steamer Plate Setup (page 37). If reheating frozen *moyin-moyin*, allow them to thaw before steaming.

Leaf-Wrapped Rice Bundles Stuffed with Pork and Beans

Bánh Tét (Vietnam)

SERVES 4 TO 8 (MAKES 8 DUMPLINGS)

Along with *Zhong Zi* (September), this recipe is one of the most challenging in the book. It will test your dexterity to overlap the bamboo leaves, fill them with spoonfuls of partially cooked rice and other ingredients, and then wrap them up as tightly as you can. The snug wrapping keeps these savory dumplings, designed for travel without refrigeration, practically sterile for days.

These dumplings are wrapped using the Bamboo-Leaf Fold (page 61).

For the Filling

½ pound boneless pork shoulder, trimmed of skin and excess fat and cut into 8 equal pieces

1 small yellow onion, cut in half and sliced thin

1½ teaspoons sugar

⅛ teaspoon freshly ground black pepper

⅛ teaspoon freshly ground white pepper

2 tablespoons fish sauce, preferably from Vietnam

½ cup dried peeled mung beans

8 small dried shiitake or black mushrooms, soaked in hot water to cover for 30 minutes

1 link Chinese pork sausage (*la chang*), cut diagonally into 8 thin slices

For the Rice

⅔ cup dried black-eyed peas, soaked in plenty of water for 6 to 8 hours, or 1⅓ cups canned, drained and rinsed

1 cup fresh coconut milk (see page 8) or canned coconut milk

2½ cups medium-grain sweet (glutinous) white rice, preferably from Vietnam or

Thailand, rinsed (see page 18) and soaked in plenty of water for 6 to 8 hours

1 teaspoon salt

2 scallions, sliced into thin rings

For Assembly

30 prepared bamboo leaves (see page 28)

Eight 60-inch lengths of kitchen string for tying the *bánh tet*

For Serving

1 recipe Sweet, Sour, and Spicy Fish Sauce (page 214)

1. MARINATE THE PORK 2 TO 6 HOURS IN ADVANCE: Combine the pork, onion, sugar, black pepper, white pepper, and fish sauce in a medium bowl. Cover and refrigerate for 2 to 6 hours.

2. MAKE THE MUNG BEAN FILLING: Place the mung beans in a small saucepan. Pour in 1 cup water and bring to a boil over high heat. Reduce the heat to medium and simmer until the beans are soft, about 30 minutes. Drain off excess water, if any, and return to the stove. Mash the mixture with a potato masher or the back of a wooden spoon into a moist, chunky paste. Remove from the heat, scoop into a bowl, and set aside to cool.

3. COOK THE BLACK-EYED PEAS AND THE RICE: (Skip this step if using canned black-eyed peas.) Drain the black-eyed peas. Place them in a small pot, pour in enough water to cover them by 1 inch, and bring to a boil over high heat. Cover, reduce the heat to low, and simmer until they are just tender but not breaking apart, 20 to 30 minutes. Drain and set aside.

4. Pour the coconut milk into a medium pot and place over medium-low heat. Drain the rice. Once the coconut milk is warm, stir in the rice, black-eyed peas, and salt. If using fresh coconut milk, be careful not to let it come to a boil. Stir and cook until all the coconut milk has been absorbed, about 3 minutes. Remove from the heat and mix in the scallions. Scoop this partially cooked rice mixture into a large bowl and set aside to cool.

5. ASSEMBLE THE DUMPLINGS: *Before assembling the* bánh tet, *review the Bamboo–Leaf Fold. The Bamboo–Leaf Fold uses 2 leaves as a platform for the filling and a third leaf as a cover before all 3 leaves are wrapped and folded around the filling.*

6. Drain the mushrooms and squeeze out any excess water. Remove and discard the stems and slice the mushrooms into ¼-inch strips.

7. Line a tray with a kitchen towel. Have ready the partially cooked rice mixture, the marinated pork, the mung bean mash, mushroom strips, sausage slices, bamboo leaves, and ties.

8. Pick out the best 24 bamboo leaves. Place 2 leaves, smooth side up, lengthwise, and alongside each other, in the palm of your hand. Overlap the leaves by about 1½ inches. Center 3 rounded tablespoons of the rice mixture on top of the overlapped bamboo leaves and spread out into a rectangle about 4 inches long and 2 inches across or about the size of your palm. Scoop up a rounded tablespoon of the mung bean mash and place it over the rice. Arrange 4 to 5 slices of the mushroom over the mung bean mash, then place 1 piece of sausage, 1 piece of pork, and some of the onions on top of the mushrooms. Top everything with 3 more rounded tablespoons of the rice mixture. Lay a third bamboo leaf, smooth side down, on top of the mound. Grip and curl the sides of the overlapped bottom leaves over the top leaf. Fold back the top ends of the leaves. Then fold back the bottom ends of the leaves as firmly as you can to create a neat, tight rectangular package. Wrap and tie the package 4 or 5 times across the width of the dumpling and at least once vertically to prevent the leaves from unfolding. Place the package on the lined tray and repeat until you have 8 packages.

9. COOK THE DUMPLINGS: Stack the packages as evenly as possible in a large pot and pour in enough water to cover. Bring to a boil over high heat. Reduce the heat to medium, cover, and simmer for 2 to 2½ hours. Check the water level every 30 minutes and replenish with just enough boiling water to keep the packages covered.

10. Remove the pot from the heat. Carefully remove the *bánh tet* with tongs, place them on a folded kitchen towel, and allow them to cool slightly. Cut off the strings (unless you are freezing the dumplings) and serve with Sweet, Sour, and Spicy Fish Sauce. It's best not to open the packages too soon and to peel back the leaves just before eating, so that they stay moist and warm. *Bánh tet* can be refrigerated for up to 1 week or frozen (unopened) for up to 6 months (see page 36). Reheat them in a steamer pot or use the Steamer Plate Setup (page 37). If reheating frozen *bánh tet*, allow them to thaw before steaming.

Coconut-Filled Rice Dumplings

Modak (India)

SERVES 4 TO 8 (MAKES ABOUT 20 DUMPLINGS)

The customary dumpling of the lengthy and joyous Ganpati Festival is the supersweet *modak*. Its richness comes from a filling of coconut, sugar, and raisins. Although the sweetness of the filling may be over-the-top, these dumplings are doughy enough to balance out every bite. *Modak* are often presented in a smooth, garlic-bulb shape that can be difficult to master. Luckily, there is a simpler pear shape that is equally acceptable and much easier to manage.

These dumplings are made using the Bowl Fold (page 45).

For the Filling

¼ cup raw or roasted unsalted shelled cashews or pistachios

40 cardamom pods or 1 teaspoon ground cardamom

1 tablespoon ghee (page 12) or a neutral oil, such as grapeseed

1 cup freshly grated coconut (see page 8) or frozen grated coconut, thawed

⅓ cup finely crushed jaggery (about 2½ ounces) or other unrefined sugar (see page 20)

¼ cup raisins or dried currants

Pinch of salt

1 teaspoon rose water mixed with ¼ cup water

For the Dough

1 tablespoon ghee (page 12) or a neutral oil, such as grapeseed

¼ teaspoon salt

1¾ cups white rice flour, preferably from India, plus some extra for dusting

For Cooking and Serving

Ghee or a neutral oil, such as grapeseed, to coat the steamer basket

¼ cup melted ghee for dipping

Equipment

8- to 10-quart steamer pot

1. MAKE THE FILLING: If using raw cashews or pistachios, roast them in a 375°F oven until they just begin to brown, 6 to 8 minutes. Move them immediately into a bowl and cool slightly, then coarsely chop them. If using pistachios, remove their papery skins. If using cardamom pods, split them open in a bowl and collect all of the tiny seeds. You will have about 1 teaspoon.

2. Heat the ghee in a large skillet over medium heat. Add the coconut and stir frequently until lightly browned, about 2 minutes. Mix in the jaggery, then mix in the nuts, cardamom, raisins, and the pinch of salt and cook for 1 minute longer. Pour in the rose water mixture, stir continuously, and cook until most of the liquid has cooked off. The mixture will be sticky and clumpy. Scoop into a bowl and set aside to cool. (You can also make the filling in advance and keep it tightly wrapped in the refrigerator for up to 1 week.)

3. MAKE THE DOUGH: Place the ghee and the $^1/_4$ teaspoon salt in a small saucepan, pour in $1^1/_2$ cups water, and bring to a boil over high heat. Set aside $^1/_4$ cup of the rice flour and add the remaining $1^1/_2$ cups, all at once, to the boiling water. Stir 2 or 3 times to combine, then immediately remove from the heat. Stir vigorously until all the liquid has been absorbed and the dough is a moist, sticky ball. Scoop the dough into a bowl and allow it to cool slightly.

4. Carefully work the dough with your hands. If this is in any way uncomfortable, let it cool for another minute or two, but keep in mind that you need to work with this dough while it is still very, very warm. Work the dough in the bowl until it is a smooth and manageable ball, 2 to 3 minutes. If the dough is wet and sticky, work in some of the reserved rice flour, a little at a time, until the dough no longer sticks to your fingers. Keep the dough warm by covering it with a towel.

5. ASSEMBLE THE DUMPLINGS: *Before assembling the* modak, *review the Bowl Fold.*

6. Line a tray with a kitchen towel and sprinkle with a little rice flour. Also have ready the dough and the filling.

7. Pinch off a small piece of dough and roll it into a ball about $1^1/_2$ inches around. Keep the remaining dough covered with a kitchen towel while you work. Use your thumbs to shape it into a bowl about $1^1/_2$ inches deep. This will be a wide bowl that is best supported in the palm of your hand. Place 1 teaspoon of filling in the center of the dough bowl. Close by pushing and pinching the edges of the dough around and over the filling until the filling is surrounded, pushing out any air. Dab a little water along the edges, if needed, for a better seal. Reroll into a ball and dust with flour. Holding the dumpling in the palm of your hand, gently pinch and pull its top until the shape is more like a pear. Place upright on the prepared tray and gently tap down to create a flat bottom or foot so that it can stand without tipping over. Repeat with the remaining filling and dough.

8. STEAM THE DUMPLINGS: Remove the basket from the steamer pot, add 1 inch of water to the pot, and bring to a boil over high heat. Coat the bottom of the basket with ghee. Arrange as many dumplings in the basket as you can, spacing them about $^1/_2$ inch apart. Place the basket in the pot, cover, reduce the heat to low, and steam for 15 minutes.

9. Remove the pot from the heat. Carefully remove the basket, place it on a folded kitchen towel, and allow the *modak* to cool slightly. Use a spoon or a small spatula to carefully move them onto a plate. Cook any remaining *modak* and serve with melted ghee.

Tapioca Balls Stuffed with Minced Pork and Peanuts

Sakoo Sai Moo (Thailand)

SERVES 4 (MAKES ABOUT 24 DUMPLINGS)

Tapioca pearls mixed throughout the dough of the *sakoo sai moo* give it a distinctively bumpy look not seen in any other dumpling. These translucent pearls also make the dumplings intensely chewy, the better to savor their sweet and spicy pork filling. *Sakoo sai moo* can be tricky to assemble because of the soft and unusually knobby texture of the dough, so give yourself plenty of time. Cooked *sakoo sai moo* are sticky to the touch, but wrapping them in lettuce leaves makes them much easier to serve and eat. Lettuce also adds a refreshing contrast to the mildly spicy filling.

These dumplings are made using the Bowl Fold (page 45).

For the Filling

- 2 tablespoons grapeseed or other neutral oil
- 1 medium yellow onion, chopped very fine
- ½ pound freshly ground pork
- 2 garlic cloves, chopped very fine
- 1½ tablespoons finely chopped hard palm sugar or soft palm sugar or other unrefined sugar (see page 20)
- 1 to 2 small Thai red chiles, such as *prik kee noo*, cored, seeded, and chopped very fine
- ¼ teaspoon freshly ground white pepper

- ¼ cup unsalted roasted peanuts, papery skins removed and nuts chopped coarse
- 1 tablespoon fish sauce, preferably from Thailand
- 3 tablespoons finely chopped fresh cilantro leaves

For the Dough

- 1 cup small tapioca pearls
- 1 cup tapioca flour (tapioca starch), plus some extra for dusting

For the Topping

- 1 teaspoon grapeseed or other neutral oil
- 4 garlic cloves, chopped fine
- 1 to 2 small Thai red or green chiles, such as *prik kee noo*, sliced into thin rings

For Cooking and Serving

Soft lettuce leaves such as Boston or Bibb to line the serving plate and steamer basket, plus 12 additional leaves, torn in half, for wrapping

Equipment

8- to 10-quart steamer pot

1. MAKE THE FILLING: Heat the 2 tablespoons oil in a medium skillet over high heat. Add the onion and stir occasionally until just soft, about 2 minutes. Add the pork and the 2 cloves of chopped garlic and continue to stir until the pork starts to brown, breaking up clumps of pork as you go, about 4 minutes. Mix in the palm sugar, the chopped red chiles, and the white pepper and cook for 1 minute longer. Mix in the peanuts and fish sauce and continue stirring until the pork is golden brown, 2 to 3 minutes. Remove from the heat and stir in the cilantro. Scoop the pork mixture into a bowl and allow it to cool completely. (You can also make the filling in advance and keep it tightly covered in the refrigerator for up to 2 days.)

2. MAKE THE DOUGH: Boil $1^1/_2$ cups water in a small saucepan over high heat. Reduce the heat to medium and stir in the tapioca pearls. Cook for 3 minutes, stirring continuously. Remove from the heat, scoop into a medium bowl, and set aside to cool slightly. The cooked tapioca will set and thicken as it cools. The pearls will be partially cooked through with tiny, still-white centers.

3. Add $^3/_4$ cup of the tapioca flour to the warm tapioca pearls and keep the remaining $^1/_4$ cup handy. Carefully work the mixture with your hands. If this is in any way uncomfortable, let it cool for another minute or two, but keep in mind that you need to work with this dough while it is still very, very warm. Work the dough with your hands into one manageable ball. You can work this dough with all the force needed to incorporate the flour, and you will not crush or break apart the pearls. If the dough is wet and sticky, work in some of the remaining tapioca flour, a little at a time, until it no longer sticks to your fingers.

4. Place the dough on a surface dusted with tapioca flour and knead for 2 minutes. Sprinkle with more tapioca flour if it gets a little sticky. The dough will be soft and very elastic. Place the dough back into the bowl and keep warm by covering it with a towel.

5. ASSEMBLE THE DUMPLINGS: *Before assembling the* sakoo sai moo, *review the Bowl Fold.*

6. Line a tray with a kitchen towel and dust it with tapioca flour. Have ready the dough and the filling.

7. Pinch off a small piece of dough and roll it into a ball about 1 inch around. Keep the remaining dough covered with a kitchen towel as you work. Use your thumbs to shape the ball into a bowl about 1 inch deep. This will be a wide and floppy bowl that is best supported in the palm of your hand. Place a rounded teaspoon of filling in the center of the dough bowl. Close by pushing and pinching the edges of the dough around and over the filling until the filling is surrounded, pushing out any air. Dab a little water along the edges, if needed, for a better seal. Reroll into a ball, dust with tapioca flour, and place on the prepared tray. Repeat with the remaining dough and filling.

8. STEAM THE DUMPLINGS: Line a serving plate with lettuce leaves.

9. Remove the basket from the steamer pot, add 2 inches of water to the pot, and bring to a boil over high heat. Line the bottom of the basket with lettuce leaves. Arrange as many dumplings in the basket as you can, spacing them about $^1/_2$ inch apart. Place the basket in the pot, cover, reduce the heat to low, and steam for 10 minutes. Uncover and steam for 2 minutes longer.

10. MAKE THE TOPPING: While the dumplings steam, heat the 1 teaspoon oil in a small skillet over medium heat and add the 4 cloves of chopped garlic. Cook until the garlic is golden brown, about 2 minutes. Remove from the heat and scoop into a small bowl. Mix in the chile rings.

11. Once the *sakoo sai moo* have finished steaming, remove the steamer pot from the heat. Carefully remove the basket, place it on a folded kitchen towel, and allow the dumplings to cool slightly. Using a spoon or small spatula, carefully move them to the prepared plate. Serve immediately while you cook any remaining *sakoo sai moo*. Serve with a sprinkle of the garlic and chile mixture and the lettuce leaf wrappers.

September

WILD GRAPES AND DUMPLINGS
(United States) 277

BOSTON BROWN BREAD
(United States) 279

CHICKEN FRICOT WITH DUMPLINGS
(Canada) 281

CHICKEN AND DUMPLING SOUP
(United States) 283

BREAD AND SEMOLINA LOAF
Houskové Knedlíky (Czech Republic) 285

OAT AND HONEY PUDDING
(Ireland) 287

GRAHAM POTATO BUNS
(United States) 289

LAYERED APPLE AND BREAD PUDDING
(United States) 291

BEEF AND OYSTER STEW WITH SUET DUMPLINGS
(England) 293

MILD YOGURT SEMOLINA CAKES

Rava Idli (India) 295

BUCKWHEAT DUMPLINGS STUFFED WITH APPLES AND CHEESE

Vareniki s Yablokami (Russia) 297

POTATO DUMPLINGS STUFFED WITH SUGAR-STUFFED PLUMS

Švestkové Knedlíky (Czech Republic).. 299

LEAF-WRAPPED RICE PACKAGES STUFFED WITH PEANUTS AND SAUSAGE

Zhong Zi (China) 301

Wild Grapes and Dumplings

(United States)

SERVES 4 TO 5 (MAKES ABOUT 12 DUMPLINGS)

This brilliantly purple dessert is both warming and refreshing. Like the Peach and Berry Grunt (August), this is a dish of simple cakelike dumplings cooked in a fruit stew. Possum grapes or wild Muscadine are ideal, but if you can't find them, Concord grapes are a fine substitute. Versions of this dumpling dish are found nationwide, especially in Choctaw, Cherokee, and Lenape regions. It can be made with bottled grape juice, but the results are far superior and worth the effort when the dumplings are simmered in freshly squeezed grape juice.

For Cooking

- 4 cups Muscadine or Concord grapes for juicing or 2½ cups unsweetened bottled Concord grape juice
- 4 cups Muscadine or Concord grapes for stewing
- 2 tablespoons honey, preferably raw

For the Dumplings

- 1½ cups unbleached all-purpose flour
- 1 tablespoon baking powder
- ¼ teaspoon salt
- 1½ tablespoons sugar
- 3 tablespoons cold unsalted butter, cut into bits
- ½ cup cold milk

Equipment

Large, wide pot or skillet with cover

1. JUICE THE GRAPES: If making your own juice, place the grapes for juicing in a blender or a food processor and blend into a thin pulp. Strain the juice through a fine sieve into a bowl, pressing down on the pulp with the back of a spoon. Measure out 2½ cups of juice and set aside. If the juice measures less than 2½ cups, add just enough water to make up the difference.

2. Place the grapes for stewing and the honey in the large pot. Pour in the grape juice and set aside.

3. MAKE THE DUMPLINGS: Place 1¼ cups of the flour in a medium bowl and keep the remaining ¼ cup handy. Add the baking powder, salt, and sugar and mix well. Add the butter and work it into the flour mixture with a pastry cutter or 2 butter knives until it looks like a damp cornmeal. Gradually drizzle in the milk, stirring constantly. Work the dough with your hands into one manageable ball. If the dough is wet and sticky, work in some of the remaining flour, a little at a time, until it no longer sticks to your fingers.

4. Place the dough on a floured surface and shape it into a blunt log. Pat the dough into a 4 × 9-inch rectangle. Working along the 9-inch side, cut the dough every ¾ inch. These strips will be quite soft and are best left on the work surface until it's time to put them in the simmering juice.

5. COOK THE DUMPLINGS: Bring the grapes and juice mixture in the pot to a boil over high heat, then reduce the heat to low for a gentle simmer.

6. Gently drop the dough strips into the juice, forming a single layer on top of the grapes. Cover and cook for 15 minutes. Serve these dumplings with generous amounts of grapes and sauce. Serve as is or with vanilla ice cream.

Boston Brown Bread

(United States)

SERVES 4 (MAKES 1 DUMPLING)

Equal parts whole wheat flour, rye flour, and cornmeal give this steamed bread its interesting, complex flavor. You can buy this mixture prepackaged, but it's easy enough to make your own. The brown sugar, raisins, and molasses add a dark sweetness and color. This bread is sweet enough to be a dessert, or it can be used to make traditional tea sandwiches. Slices of leftover Boston brown bread toast beautifully and make great crumbs for parfaits or bread cubes for bread puddings.

This dumpling is made using the Pudding Basin Setup (page 43).

For the Dumpling

¼ cup graham or whole wheat flour

¼ cup rye flour

¼ cup coarse yellow cornmeal

2 teaspoons baking soda

¼ teaspoon salt

¾ cup buttermilk

2 tablespoons molasses

3 tablespoons light muscovado or other unrefined sugar (see page 20)

⅓ cup raisins (optional)

For Cooking and Serving

Unsalted butter and sugar to coat the pudding basin

Unsalted butter or cream cheese for serving

Equipment

24-inch square of muslin

35-inch length of kitchen string

4- to 5-cup pudding basin

Pot large enough to hold the basin when covered

Parchment paper

1. MAKE THE BATTER: Combine the graham flour, rye flour, cornmeal, baking soda, and salt in a large bowl. In another bowl, mix together the buttermilk, molasses, sugar, and raisins, if desired, until the sugar has mostly dissolved. Set both mixtures aside.

2. ASSEMBLE AND STEAM THE DUMPLING: *Before assembling the brown bread, review the Pudding Basin Setup.*

3. Soak the muslin and the string under running water. Wring them out and set aside.

4. Place the empty pudding basin in the pot. Pour water into the space between the basin and the pot until it comes three-quarters of the way up the sides of the basin. Remove the basin and bring the water to a boil over high heat. Reduce the heat to low for a gentle simmer.

5. Meanwhile, make sure the interior of the basin is dry before rubbing it with butter and coating it with sugar. Give the buttermilk mixture a good stir, pour it into the flour mixture, and stir until combined. Do not overmix. Scoop the batter into the basin and give it a gentle shake to level it off. Cut out a round of parchment paper and place it on top of the batter. Cover the basin with the damp muslin and secure it tightly with the string. Tie the opposite corners of the muslin into handles over the top of the brown bread.

6. Using tongs or a wooden spoon, push a folded cloth, such as a standard white cotton napkin, into the simmering water and arrange it to lie flat on the bottom of the pot. Using the cloth handle, carefully lower the basin into the pot, cover, and simmer for at least $1^1/_2$ hours, or up to $2^1/_2$ hours for a pudding that's even richer in flavor and texture. Check the water level every 30 minutes and replenish with boiling water as needed.

7. Remove the pot from the heat. Using a pot holder to grasp the cloth handle, carefully remove the basin from the pot, put it on a folded kitchen towel, and allow the brown bread to cool for 5 minutes. Remove the string, cloth, and paper. Unmold by inverting it onto a plate. Slice and serve with butter or cream cheese. Brown bread can be kept refrigerated for up to 3 days. Reheat in a steamer pot or use the Steamer Plate Setup (page 37).

Chicken Fricot with Dumplings

(Canada)

SERVES 4 TO 6 (MAKES ABOUT 12 DUMPLINGS)

This classic Acadian dish is like most other chicken and dumpling stew recipes in that it requires dropping spoonfuls of biscuitlike dough onto its simmering surface. What makes it distinctive is the use of fresh savory and lots of potatoes. Traditionally, salt pork goes into the base of *fricots*, but if you can't find salt pork, bacon can be substituted, although the flavor will be a bit smoky. Summer savory is a fragrant herb in the mint family, but its aroma and flavor are closer to thyme. It has a milder flavor than winter savory and is much more commonly used for cooking. You can find it fresh at specialty food markets, or dried at most supermarkets.

For the Stew

¼ pound salt pork, cut into ¼-inch cubes

One 3- to 4-pound chicken, skin on, cut into serving pieces

1 medium yellow onion, chopped coarse

2 tablespoons unbleached all-purpose flour

5 black peppercorns

2 large carrots, sliced into 1-inch rounds

3 medium baking potatoes, such as russet, cut into 1-inch cubes

1 tablespoon coarsely chopped fresh summer savory leaves or 1 teaspoon dried

For the Dumplings

1 cup unbleached all-purpose flour

2 teaspoons baking powder

½ teaspoon salt

2 tablespoons cold unsalted butter, cut into bits

¾ cup cold water

1. MAKE THE STEW: Place the salt pork in a large, wide pot over medium heat and stir occasionally until enough fat has melted off to coat the bottom of the pot, about 2 minutes. Add the chicken pieces, skin side down, in one layer and do not turn until the undersides are golden brown, about 8 minutes. Turn and brown the other sides, about 6 minutes longer. Move the chicken with a slotted spoon or tongs to a bowl, leaving behind the bits of salt pork and oily fat. Stir the onions into the fat and cook for 2 minutes. Sprinkle in the 2 tablespoons flour and cook, stirring frequently, until the mixture turns a deep caramel brown, about 8 minutes.

2. Pour in 6 cups water and scrape up any sticky bits off the bottom of the pot with a wooden spoon. Return the chicken pieces and any drippings to the pot. Add the peppercorns. Cover and simmer for 1 hour, stirring occasionally.

3. Take out the chicken with a slotted spoon or tongs and place it in a bowl to cool. Add the carrots, potatoes, and savory to the simmering stew, cover, reduce the heat to low, and cook for 30 minutes longer, stirring occasionally.

4. Meanwhile, prepare the chicken. Once the chicken is cool enough to handle, remove the skin. Pull the meat off the bones, tear it into bite-sized pieces, place the pieces back in the bowl, and discard the bones.

5. Once the vegetables have cooked, mix the chicken back into the stew. Reduce the heat to very, very low to keep the stew hot until it's time to add the dumplings. (You can also make the stew in advance and keep it refrigerated in a tightly sealed container for up to 3 days. If the stew is too thick to stir easily, add a little water to thin it out.)

6. MAKE THE BATTER AND COOK THE DUMPLINGS: Combine the 1 cup flour, baking powder, and salt in a medium bowl. Add the butter and work it into the flour mixture with a pastry cutter or 2 butter knives until it looks like a coarse, damp meal. Pour in the cold water and stir until you have a doughy and slightly lumpy batter. Do not overmix.

7. Scoop up a rounded tablespoon of batter. Use another spoon or your finger to move the batter gently off the spoon and onto the surface of the stew. Drop in the remaining spoonfuls of batter, as close together as possible without touching. Cover and simmer for 10 minutes, then uncover and cook for 5 minutes longer and serve.

Chicken and Dumpling Soup

(United States)

SERVES 4 TO 6 (MAKES ABOUT 50 DUMPLINGS)

The dumplings are the main event in this classic creamy chicken and celery soup. Made from a simple flour and water dough, they are smooth and slippery, which is why they are referred to at times as "slick dumplings." Because they are cooked in the soup, they absorb a lot of flavor and are delicious by themselves, scooped out of the pot as a snack. Cooked celery develops a mild and sweet taste. For an even subtler celery flavor, use the innermost stalks or the heart. If you are looking for a darker, more intense version of chicken and dumplings, try the Chicken Fricot with Dumplings (preceding recipe) or the *Csirke Paprikas Galuskaval* (October).

For the Soup

One 4- to 5-pound chicken, cut into serving pieces, skin removed

1 large yellow onion, chopped coarse

1 garlic clove, chopped coarse

1 fresh rosemary sprig

2 bay leaves

5 celery ribs with leaves, cut into ½-inch pieces

2 teaspoons salt

⅓ cup heavy cream

Salt and freshly ground black pepper to taste

For the Dumplings

1¼ cups unbleached all-purpose flour, plus some extra for dusting

½ teaspoon baking powder

2 teaspoons salt

2 tablespoons cold unsalted butter, cut into bits

½ cup cold water

1. MAKE THE SOUP: Place the chicken, onion, garlic, rosemary, and bay leaves in a large pot. Pour in 2 quarts water and bring to a simmer over medium heat. Mix in the celery and the salt, cover, reduce the heat to low, and simmer for 1 hour. Skim the froth off the surface with a spoon. (You can also make the soup in advance and keep it refrigerated in a tightly sealed container for up to 3 days.)

2. MAKE THE DOUGH: While the soup is simmering, place 1 cup of the flour in a large bowl and keep the remaining ¼ cup handy. Add the baking powder and salt and mix well. Add the butter and work it into the flour mixture with a pastry cutter or 2 butter knives until it looks like a coarse, damp meal. Pour in the cold water and mix until all the liquid has been absorbed. Work the dough with your hands into one manageable ball. If the dough is wet and sticky, work in some of the remaining flour, a little at a time, until it no longer sticks to your fingers.

3. Place the dough on a floured surface and knead for 2 to 3 minutes. Return the dough to the bowl, cover, and refrigerate for 30 minutes.

4. MAKE THE DUMPLINGS: Line a tray with a kitchen towel and sprinkle with a little flour.

5. Place the dough on a floured surface, knead once or twice, and shape into a blunt log. Roll the log out into a 10-inch square about $1/8$ inch thick. Using a sharp knife, cut the dough into 1-inch strips and then cut across the strips at 2-inch intervals. Place the dough rectangles and all the scraps in one layer on the prepared tray.

6. COOK THE DUMPLINGS: Once the soup has simmered for 1 hour, take the chicken pieces out with a slotted spoon or tongs and place them in a bowl to cool. Remove and discard the rosemary stem. Stir the cream into the simmering soup. Reduce the heat to very, very low to keep the soup hot while preparing the chicken.

7. Once the chicken is cool enough to handle, pull the meat off the bones, tear it into bite-sized pieces, place the pieces back in the bowl, and set aside. Discard the bones.

8. Bring the soup to a strong simmer over medium-high heat. Drop the dough rectangles and scraps, a few at a time, into the soup and stir gently. Cover and cook for 10 minutes. Stir in the chicken, sprinkle with salt and pepper to taste, simmer for a minute longer, and serve.

Bread and Semolina Loaf

Houskové Knedlíky (Czech Republic)

SERVES 4 (MAKES 1 DUMPLING)

Traditionally served with roast pork and sauerkraut, *houskové knedlíky* is a foolproof side to any meal that has plenty of sauce, roasted meat, or stewed vegetables. Bits of bread are mixed into a soft semolina dough, creating a glistening, slightly dense loaf. *Houskové knedlíky* can also be sliced and turned into extra-soft French toast the next day, or it can be worked into your favorite bread pudding.

For the Dumplings

2 cups semolina flour, plus some extra for dusting

2 teaspoons baking powder

1½ teaspoons salt

1 large egg, beaten

1¼ cups milk

6 cups ½-inch crustless white bread cubes (see page 6)

1. MAKE THE DOUGH: Line a tray with a smooth kitchen towel and sprinkle with a little semolina flour.

2. Place the semolina flour, baking powder, and salt in a large bowl and mix well. Add the eggs and milk and mix until all the liquid has been absorbed. Don't overmix. You will have a very moist sticky dough.

3. Add 2 cups of the bread cubes and work them into the dough. For those new to this recipe it can feel strange to combine bread into dough, but it will come together as you knead. Continue kneading in the bread cubes, 2 cups at a time, until all the bread has been added. The end result will be a stiff, chunky dough.

4. Shape the dough into a log about 9 inches long. Place on the prepared tray, cover, and rest at room temperature for 30 minutes.

5. COOK THE DUMPLINGS: Fill a large, wide pot halfway with salted water and bring to a boil over high heat. Slide the dumpling gently into the water. Cover, reduce the heat to low, and cook for 15 minutes. Turn over the dumpling, or dumplings, cover, and cook for 10 minutes longer.

6. Carefully lift the *houskové knedlíky* out of the pot with 2 slotted spoons and place on a serving plate. Let rest for 2 to 3 minutes. Serve with roasted meats and sauce. This dumpling is so tender that it's best to slice into it with a taut piece of fine string. *Houskové knedlíky* can be refrigerated for up to 3 days.

Oat and Honey Pudding

(Ireland)

SERVES 4 TO 6 (MAKES 1 DUMPLING)

Most of us tend to eat oatmeal in just one or two ways—cereal and cookies—but this oat and honey pudding is a great alternative to such classics. Steamed oatmeal puddings come in dozens of varieties, but this particular version creates a dense cakelike pudding with the flavors of whole wheat and honey. If you don't want to use cherries, use raisins or any other dried fruit. Because the batter is made with a modest amount of honey, it's nice to drizzle a little extra honey over each slice. The oats in this recipe are not pressed, rolled, or instant. Steel-cut oats are used because of their longer cooking time, sturdy texture, and fresh oatmeal taste.

This dumpling is made using the Pudding Basin Setup (page 43).

For the Dumpling

½ cup steel-cut oats

¼ cup sugar

3 tablespoons honey, preferably raw

4 tablespoons (½ stick) unsalted butter, melted

1 large egg, beaten

1 teaspoon baking powder

⅛ teaspoon salt

¼ teaspoon freshly grated nutmeg

¼ teaspoon ground ginger

½ cup unsweetened dried tart cherries (optional)

½ cup whole wheat flour

For Cooking and Serving

Unsalted butter and sugar to coat the pudding basin

Unsalted butter and honey, preferably raw for serving

Equipment

24-inch square of muslin

35-inch length of kitchen string

4- to 5-cup pudding basin

Pot large enough to hold the basin when covered

Parchment paper

1. MAKE THE BATTER 1 HOUR IN ADVANCE: Bring 2 cups water to a boil in a small pot. Stir in the oats, cover, reduce the heat to low, and simmer, stirring occasionally, until creamy and thick, about 30 minutes. Scoop the oats into a large bowl, set them aside, and cool to room temperature.

2. Once the oats have cooled, add the sugar, honey, the melted butter, egg, baking powder, salt, nutmeg, ground ginger, and cherries and mix well. Fold in some of the whole wheat flour, a little at a time, until the batter just holds its shape when scooped up with a spoon.

3. ASSEMBLE AND STEAM THE DUMPLING: *Before assembling the pudding, review the Pudding Basin Setup.*

4. Soak the muslin and the string under running water. Wring them out and set aside.

5. Place the empty pudding basin in the pot. Pour water into the space between the basin and the pot until it comes three-quarters of the way up the sides of the basin. Remove the basin and bring the water to a boil over high heat. Reduce the heat to low for a gentle simmer.

6. Meanwhile, make sure the interior of the basin is dry before rubbing it with butter and coating it with sugar. Scoop the batter into the basin and wiggle it gently to level it off. Cut out a round of parchment paper and place it on top of the batter. Cover the basin with the damp muslin and secure it tightly with the string. Tie the opposite corners of the muslin into handles over the top of the pudding.

7. Using tongs or a wooden spoon, push a folded cloth, such as a standard white cotton napkin, into the simmering water and arrange it to lie flat on the bottom of the pot. Using the cloth handle, carefully lower the basin into the pot, cover, and simmer for at least $1^1/_2$ hours, or up to $2^1/_2$ hours for a pudding that's even richer in flavor and texture. Check the water level every 30 minutes and replenish with boiling water as needed.

8. Remove the pot from the heat. Using a pot holder to grasp the cloth handle, carefully remove the basin from the pot and put it on a folded kitchen towel, and allow the pudding to cool for 5 minutes. Remove the string, cloth, and paper. Unmold by inverting it onto a plate. Slice and serve, topped with some butter and a spoonful of honey. The pudding can be refrigerated for up to 3 days. Reheat in a steamer pot or use the Steamer Plate Setup (page 37).

Graham Potato Buns

(United States)

SERVES UP TO 9 (MAKES 9 DUMPLINGS)

These steamed graham potato buns are easy to make and are equally marvelous with honey or jam or smothered in a savory sauce. They satisfy cravings for freshly made whole wheat bread and are just right for sandwiches. The potato softens the texture of the graham flour and turns what would otherwise be a dense dough into something spongy and delicate. Leftover mashed potatoes can be used as long as they have only a little butter or milk, but such creamy accents will require the addition of a little more white flour to the dough. For a denser whole wheat steamed bun, try *Ting Momo* (February).

For the Dumplings

¾ cup warm milk

2 teaspoons sugar

1¼ teaspoons active dry yeast (about ½ packet)

½ cup riced or well-mashed potato (about 1 small baking potato)

2 tablespoons grapeseed or other neutral oil

1⅓ cups graham flour

⅔ cup unbleached all-purpose flour, plus some extra for dusting

½ teaspoon salt

For Cooking

Grapeseed or other neutral oil to coat the cake pan

Equipment

2-inch-high steamer rack

9-inch round cake pan

Pot large enough to hold both the rack and the pan when covered

1. PROOF THE YEAST: Pour the milk into a large bowl, stir in the sugar and the yeast, and proof for 15 minutes. The surface should become foamy. If not, start again with a new yeast packet. Mix in the mashed potato and the oil.

2. MAKE THE DOUGH: Combine the graham flour and all-purpose flour in a large bowl. Scoop out and set aside ¼ cup. Add the salt to the mixture that remains and mix well. Pour in the potato and yeast mixture and mix until all the liquid has been absorbed. Work the dough with your hands into one manageable ball. If it is too wet and sticky, work in some of the remaining flour mixture, a little at a time, until it no longer sticks to your fingers.

3. Place the dough on a floured surface and knead for 3 to 5 minutes. The dough will be soft and tacky. Return the dough to the bowl, cover with a kitchen towel, and set aside in a warm and dark place until the dough doubles in size, 1½ to 2 hours. Use the Proofing Pot Setup (page 36) if the temperature of the room is not ideal.

4. MAKE THE DUMPLINGS: Coat the bottom and sides of the cake pan with oil.

5. Punch down the dough, place it on a floured surface, and knead once or twice. Divide the dough into 9 equal pieces. Knead each piece once or twice, then roll into a ball. Once all the dough has been rolled into balls, arrange them evenly within the prepared cake pan. The dough balls should be close enough to just barely touch each other. Cover with a kitchen towel and set aside while preparing the steamer.

6. STEAM THE DUMPLINGS: Place a steamer rack into the pot, add $1^1/_2$ inches of water to the pot, and bring to a boil over high heat. Lower the filled cake pan into the pot. Cover, reduce the heat to medium, and steam for 30 minutes.

7. Remove the pot from the heat, carefully lift the cake pan out of the pot, place it on a folded kitchen towel, and allow the buns to cool slightly. Remove them from the pan individually or as a segmented loaf. Serve warm or at room temperature. Graham potato buns can be refrigerated for up to 3 days or frozen for up to 6 months (see page 36). Reheat them in a steamer pot or use the Steamer Plate Setup (page 37). If reheating frozen buns, allow them to thaw before steaming.

Layered Apple and Bread Pudding

(United States)

SERVES 4 TO 5 (MAKES 1 DUMPLING)

This great apple dessert may have a somewhat sloppy look when turned out of its basin, but once sliced it shows off its layers beautifully and tastes absolutely wonderful. The condensed milk brings a rich, long-cooked flavor to the bread and apples, while coating the basin with dark sugar adds a tempting caramelized coating.

This dumpling is made using the Pudding Basin Setup (page 43).

For the Dumpling

4 cups ½-inch crustless white bread cubes (see page 6)

6 tablespoons (¾ stick) unsalted butter, cut into chunks

4 crisp, tart apples, such as Granny Smith

2 tablespoons light muscovado or other unrefined sugar (see page 20)

¼ teaspoon whole cloves, finely crushed

¼ teaspoon ground ginger

For the Custard Sauce

¾ cup milk

¼ cup sweetened condensed milk

3 large eggs, beaten

3 tablespoons light muscovado or other unrefined sugar

¼ teaspoon ground cinnamon

⅛ teaspoon salt

For Cooking and Serving

Unsalted butter and sugar to coat the pudding basin

1 recipe Vanilla Custard Sauce (page 97), Sweetened Whipped Cream (page 94), or vanilla ice cream

Equipment

24-inch square of muslin

35-inch length of kitchen string

4- to 5-cup pudding basin

Pot large enough to hold the basin when covered

Parchment paper

1. PREPARE THE BREAD AND THE APPLES: Place the bread cubes in a large bowl. Melt 4 tablespoons of the butter in a large skillet, drizzle it over the bread cubes, and toss with your fingers until evenly combined.

2. Peel, core, and slice the apples into thin wedges. Melt the remaining 2 tablespoons butter in a skillet over high heat. Add the apples and stir frequently until lightly browned, about 5 minutes. Mix in the 2 tablespoons sugar, the cloves, and the ginger. Reduce the heat to low and cook until the apples soften and turn golden brown, about 2 minutes longer. Scoop the apples into a bowl and set aside to cool.

3. MAKE THE CUSTARD SAUCE: Combine the milk and the condensed milk in a small saucepan and place over medium heat until it begins to bubble at the sides of the pan. Do not allow it to come to a full simmer. Immediately remove from the heat and set aside.

4. Whisk together the eggs, 3 tablespoons sugar, cinnamon, and salt in a large bowl until smooth. Continue to whisk vigorously while gradually drizzling in the warm milk mixture.

5. ASSEMBLE AND STEAM THE DUMPLING: *Before assembling the pudding, review the Pudding Basin Setup.*

6. Soak the muslin and the string under running water. Wring them out and set aside. Have ready the bread, cooked apples, and custard sauce.

7. Place the empty pudding basin in the pot. Pour water into the space between the basin and the pot until it comes three-quarters of the way up the sides of the basin. Remove the basin and bring the water to a boil over high heat. Reduce the heat to low for a gentle simmer.

8. Meanwhile, make sure the interior of the basin is dry before rubbing it with butter and coating it with sugar. Arrange an overlapping single layer of the apple slices on the bottom of the basin. Divide the rest of the apples into 2 equal piles. Divide the bread cubes into 3 equal piles. Spread 1 pile of bread on top of the apples already in the basin, followed by another layer of apples, a second layer of bread, another layer of apples, and then a final layer of bread. Slowly drizzle the custard sauce evenly over the top. Cut out a round of parchment paper and place it on top of the custard-soaked layers. Cover the basin with the damp muslin and secure it tightly with the string. Tie the opposite corners of the muslin into handles over the top of the pudding. Place it in the refrigerator for 30 to 60 minutes.

9. Using tongs or a wooden spoon, push a folded cloth, such as a standard white cotton napkin, into the simmering water and arrange it to lie flat on the bottom of the pot. Using the cloth handle, carefully lower the basin into the pot, cover, and simmer for at least 2 hours, or up to 3 hours for a pudding that's even richer in flavor and texture. Check the water level every 30 minutes and replenish with boiling water as needed.

10. Remove the pot from the heat. Using a pot holder to grasp the cloth handle, carefully remove the basin from the pot, put it on a folded kitchen towel, and allow the pudding to cool for 5 minutes. Remove the string, cloth, and paper. Unmold by inverting it onto a plate. Slice and serve warm, topped with Vanilla Custard Sauce, Sweetened Whipped Cream, or vanilla ice cream. The pudding can be refrigerated for up to 3 days. Reheat in a steamer pot or use the Steamer Plate Setup (page 37).

Beef and Oyster Stew with Suet Dumplings

(England)

SERVES 4 TO 6 (MAKES 12 DUMPLINGS)

Suet dumplings are a classic pairing with beef and oyster stew. They're best made with unrendered suet, but if you want a subtler suet taste you should render it (see page 12), chill it until firm, rub it into the flour, and then continue with the recipe. Fresh oysters can be found shelled and in tubs at some fish shops, specialty shops, or markets. Be sure to keep all the liquid that comes with the oysters, because you will use it in the stew.

For the Stew

¼ pound bacon, chopped coarse

2 pounds beef stew meat, cut into 2-inch pieces

1 medium yellow onion, chopped coarse

1½ tablespoons unbleached all-purpose flour

1 cup brown ale

1 tablespoon Worcestershire sauce

2 teaspoons tomato paste

6 fresh thyme sprigs or 2 teaspoons dried

½ teaspoon freshly grated mace or nutmeg

½ teaspoon salt

¼ teaspoon freshly ground black pepper

1 quart Beef Broth with British Flavors (page 396)

12 large white button mushrooms

15 large fresh sage leaves, chopped coarse

20 to 25 freshly shucked oysters, undrained (just over 1 cup)

For the Dumplings

1 cup unbleached all-purpose flour

1½ teaspoons baking powder

½ teaspoon salt

¼ cup very finely chopped cold suet

2 tablespoons finely chopped fresh flat-leaf parsley leaves

¾ cup cold water

1. MAKE THE STEW: Place the bacon in a large, wide pot over medium heat and cook, stirring occasionally, until it has rendered enough fat to generously coat the bottom of the pot. Add the beef and stir occasionally until golden brown on all sides, 6 to 8 minutes. Using a slotted spoon, move the beef and the bacon to a bowl, leaving behind the oily fat. Stir the onion into the fat and cook for 2 minutes. Sprinkle in the 1½ tablespoons flour and cook, stirring frequently, until the mixture is a dark, caramel brown, about 8 minutes.

2. Stir the ale into the onion mixture and scrape up the bits from the bottom of the pot with a wooden spoon. Let the mixture come to a simmer and reduce slightly, about 2 minutes. Stir in the Worcestershire sauce, tomato paste, thyme, mace, salt, and pepper. Return the beef, bacon, and any of their drippings back into the pot. Pour in the broth, raise the heat to high, and bring to a boil. Cover, reduce the heat to low, and simmer until the beef is fork-tender, about 2 hours. (You can also make the stew in advance and keep it refrigerated in a tightly sealed container for up to 3 days. Bring the stew back to a simmer before adding the mushrooms, sage, and the oysters. If the stew is too thick to stir easily, add a little water to thin it out.)

3. MAKE THE BATTER: Toward the end of the beef's cooking time, combine the 1 cup flour, baking powder, and salt in a large bowl. Add and rub the suet completely into the flour mixture with your finger, making sure there are no bulky clumps. Mix in the parsley. Pour in the cold water and mix until you have a thick, slightly lumpy batter. Do not overmix. Cover and set aside.

4. FINISH THE STEW AND COOK THE DUMPLINGS: Once the beef has finished cooking, cut the mushrooms into $1/4$-inch slices. Stir the mushrooms and sage into the stew, cover, and simmer for 10 minutes.

5. Stir in the oysters and all of their juices. There should be just enough liquid in the stew to cover the beef. (Mix in a little water if needed. Once the stew returns to a simmer, you can immediately begin to add the dumplings.) Scoop up a heaping tablespoon of batter. Use another spoon or your finger to move the batter gently off the spoon and onto the surface of the stew. Drop remaining spoonfuls of batter as close together as possible without their touching. Cover and simmer for 10 minutes. Uncover and cook for 3 minutes longer. Remove from the heat and serve.

Mild Yogurt Semolina Cakes

Rava Idli (India)

SERVES 4 TO 5 (MAKES ABOUT 20 DUMPLINGS)

Rava idli are nutty, buttery, and quite different from the cleaner-tasting *Sada Idli* (July). The toasting of the dry ingredients, especially the ground semolina, is what makes these dumplings so fragrant and tasty. A little bit of yogurt gives the batter an instant tang that other rice-based *idli* batters develop only after hours (or sometimes days) of natural fermentation, so this batter doesn't need the warmer months to help develop its zingy flavor—the yogurt does the job. Like *sada idli, rava idli* are often served with vegetable sambhar and coconut chutney. *Idli* molds—round metal plates with perforated round depressions—are usually sold in stacks or "trees" so that as many *idli* as possible can be steamed at once. You can buy *idli* trees at most Indian supermarkets.

For the Dumplings

¼ cup peeled black gram *(urad dal)*

½ teaspoon black or brown mustard seeds

½ cup coarsely ground semolina flour *(sooji* or *rava)*

1 cup nonchlorinated water, such as distilled or spring water

½ cup plain whole-milk yogurt

1 teaspoon grated fresh ginger

¼ teaspoon baking soda

1 teaspoon salt

For Cooking and Serving

Grapeseed or other neutral oil to coat the *idli* molds

1 recipe each Vegetable Sambhar (page 249) and Coconut Chutney (page 251)

Equipment

Pot large enough to hold the *idli* tree when covered

Idli tree with 3 or 4 layers

1. **MAKE THE BATTER 4 TO 6 HOURS IN ADVANCE:** Toast the black gram in a small skillet over medium heat, stirring or shaking the pan constantly, until it is lightly browned, about 5 minutes. Place in a small bowl, cover with plenty of water, and soak for 2 to 3 hours.

2. Combine the mustard seeds and the semolina flour in the same skillet and toast over medium heat. Stir the mixture until the semolina is lightly browned, about 3 minutes. Place the mixture in a large bowl and set aside.

3. Drain the black gram and turn it into a food processor. Pour in ¼ cup of the nonchlorinated water and process until the mixture is frothy and slightly gritty, about 2 minutes, scraping down the sides as you go.

4. Add the black gram mixture to the toasted semolina along with the yogurt, ginger, and the rest of the nonchlorinated water and mix well. Cover with a cloth and rest at room temperature for 2 to 3 hours. The batter will swell slightly and look a little softer.

5. STEAM THE DUMPLINGS: Add 1 inch of water to the pot and bring to a boil over high heat. Detach the layers of the *idli* tree and coat each mold with a little oil.

6. Add the baking soda and the salt to the batter and mix gently.

7. Fill each mold with 2 heaping tablespoons of batter. Assemble the *idli* tree and carefully insert it into the pot. Cover, reduce the heat to medium, and steam for 20 minutes.

8. Remove the pot from the heat. Place the *idli* tree on a folded kitchen towel and let the *rava idli* cool slightly. Using a butter knife or a small spatula, unmold them gently and keep warm. Cook the remaining batter, and serve with Vegetable Sambhar and Coconut Chutney.

Buckwheat Dumplings Stuffed with Apples and Cheese

Vareniki s Yablokami (Russia)

SERVES 4 TO 8 (MAKES ABOUT 40 DUMPLINGS)

These dumplings are often stuffed with blueberries or cherries, but because a fair amount of sugar is needed to balance out the natural tartness of such fruit, they can be quite sweet. Apple-filled varieties need less sugar, and they don't overwhelm the more delicate flavors of the farmer cheese. Forcing the cheese through a sieve a few times gives you a much finer curd, and when the curds are tiny they cling to the apple better.

These dumplings are made using the Half-Moon Fold (page 47).

For the Dough

1½ cups light buckwheat flour

½ cup unbleached all-purpose flour, plus some extra for dusting

¼ teaspoon salt

2 large eggs, beaten

For the Filling

1 teaspoon poppy seeds

1 cup soft farmer cheese, drained for 1 hour (see page 23), or 1¼ cups cottage cheese, drained for 4 to 8 hours

1 large egg yolk

1 tablespoon sugar

1 tablespoon fresh lemon juice and ½ teaspoon grated zest

1 large crisp, tart apple, such as Granny Smith or Gala

For Serving

3 tablespoons unsalted butter, melted just before serving

Sour cream and sugar for serving

Equipment

2¾-inch round cookie cutter

Large, wide bowl to hold the dumplings cooked in batches

1. MAKE THE DOUGH: Combine the flours in a large bowl. Scoop out and set aside ¼ cup. Add the salt, eggs, and ¼ cup water to the mixture that remains and mix until all the liquid has been absorbed. Work the dough with your hands into one manageable ball. If the dough is wet and sticky, work in some of the reserved flour mixture, a little at a time, until it no longer sticks to your fingers. Knead the dough in the bowl for 2 to 3 minutes, sprinkling with a little all-purpose flour if it gets sticky. Cover and let it rest for 15 minutes.

2. MAKE THE FILLING: Toast the poppy seeds in a small skillet over medium heat, stirring constantly for 2 minutes. Immediately move them to a small bowl to cool.

3. Hold a fine-mesh sieve over a bowl and push the drained farmer cheese through it with a wooden spoon or a rubber spatula.

4. Combine the cheese, egg yolk, 1 tablespoon sugar, lemon juice, zest, and poppy seeds in a medium bowl. Peel, core, and cut the apple into ¼-inch cubes, then stir it into the cheese mixture.

5. ASSEMBLE THE DUMPLINGS: *Before assembling the* vareniki s yablokami, *review the Half-Moon Fold.*

6. Line a tray with a kitchen towel and sprinkle with a little all-purpose flour. Have ready the dough and the filling.

7. Knead the dough once or twice on a floured surface, then divide it in half. Roll one piece into a ball and roll it out until it's about ⅛ inch thick.

8. Using the cookie cutter, cut out as many rounds as you can, usually 18 to 20. Collect all scraps from around the rounds and put aside under a damp kitchen towel for later use.

9. Lay flat 1 to 5 dough rounds. Brush each round with a very thin coating of water to make it sticky enough to seal. Center a rounded teaspoon of filling on top of each round, fold each neatly in half, pushing out any air, and pinch to seal. Dab a little water along the edges, if needed, for a better seal. Place the assembled dumplings in a single layer on the prepared tray and keep them covered with a kitchen towel while you work. Once you have assembled the first batch of dumplings, continue with the remaining dough and filling. Combine all the dough scraps, knead them into a ball, roll it out, cut out as many rounds as you can, and fill and fold those too.

10. COOK THE DUMPLINGS: Fill a large pot halfway with lightly salted water and bring it to a boil over high heat. Reduce the heat to medium for a steady simmer.

11. Gently drop up to 20 dumplings, a few at a time, into the simmering water. Stir gently to prevent sticking. Cook until all of them are floating, about 3 minutes, then cook for 3 minutes longer.

12. Remove the dumplings with a slotted spoon, place them in the large bowl, and drizzle with a ladle of the cooking liquid to prevent sticking. Cook the remaining dumplings, place them in the bowl with another ladle of the cooking liquid, and keep warm.

13. Drain the *vareniki s yablokami* and place them in a shallow serving bowl. Drizzle with the melted butter, top with spoonfuls of sour cream, sprinkle with sugar, and serve.

Potato Dumplings Stuffed with Sugar-Stuffed Plums

Švestkové Knedlíky (Czech Republic)

SERVES 4 (MAKES ABOUT 20 DUMPLINGS)

Make these dumplings with Italian plums that are perfectly ripe. Overripe plums will break down too much during cooking, while underripe plums will cause you to overcook the dough while you wait for the plums to cook all the way through. Italian plums are small and oval and most often have a deep purple-black skin. Their flesh is sweet and sticky, and when cooked inside a layer of dough they soften into a pulpy jam. A cream topping adds to the experience and is nearly as important to this dish as the plums themselves. Farmer cheese is also a great topping. A generous sprinkling of fried bread crumbs adds crunch and a toasted flavor. If you are new to potato dough, it is delicate, and you might want to first gain experience with a simpler potato dumpling like *Kartoffelklösse* (November) or *Kluski Śląskie* (February).

For the Dough

4 medium baking potatoes, such as russet

1 teaspoon salt

1¼ cups unbleached all-purpose flour, plus some extra for dusting

1 large egg, beaten

For the Filling

½ cup sugar

1½ tablespoons ground cinnamon

20 ripe but firm Italian plums, unpeeled, cut in half, pits removed, and the halves kept together

For Serving

3 tablespoons unsalted butter, melted just before serving

½ cup heavy cream or farmer cheese

¼ cup fried bread crumbs (see page 7)

Equipment

Potato ricer

Large, wide bowl to hold the dumplings cooked in batches

1. MAKE THE DOUGH: Place the potatoes in a small pot, pour in enough water to cover them, and bring to a boil over high heat. Cover, reduce the heat to medium, and simmer until fork-tender, about 30 minutes. Drain and place the potatoes on a folded kitchen towel. Once they're cool enough to handle, peel off their skins, cut them into chunks, and press them through the ricer into a large bowl. Set aside to cool to room temperature.

2. Sprinkle the salt and 1 cup of the flour onto the riced potatoes, keeping the remaining ¼ cup handy. Toss with your fingers until mixed evenly. Add the egg and work the dough with your hands into one manageable ball. If the dough is wet and sticky, work in some of the remaining flour, a little at a time, until it no longer sticks to your fingers.

3. Knead the dough in the bowl for 1 minute. The dough will be smooth, soft, and somewhat delicate.

4. ASSEMBLE THE DUMPLINGS: Combine the sugar and cinnamon in a bowl. Line a tray with a kitchen towel and sprinkle with a little flour. Also have ready the dough and the plums.

5. Pinch off a piece of dough about the size of the plums and roll it into a ball. Place it on a floured surface and pat it out into a flat $3^1/2$-inch round. Place half a plum, skin side down, in the center of the round. Spoon 1 teaspoon of the cinnamon-sugar into the hollow of the plum and top with the other half of the plum, cut side down. Lift the edges of the dough up and around the plum until they meet and gently pinch them enough to seal. Carefully grip the assembled dumpling between both palms and mold the dough by pressing and packing it around the shape of the fruit. Roll the dumpling between your palms to smooth out its look, dust with flour, and place on the prepared tray. Repeat with the remaining dough, plums, and cinnamon-sugar.

6. COOK THE DUMPLINGS: Fill a large pot halfway with salted water and bring to a boil over high heat. Reduce the heat to medium for a steady simmer. Gently drop in up to 10 dumplings. Stir carefully to prevent sticking. Simmer until the dumplings float to the surface, 2 to 3 minutes, then cook for 3 to 4 minutes longer.

7. Remove the dumplings with a slotted spoon, place them in the large bowl, and drizzle with a ladle of the cooking liquid to prevent sticking, and keep warm. Cook the remaining dumplings and place them in the bowl with another ladle of the cooking liquid.

8. Drain the *švestkové knedlíky* and place them in a shallow serving bowl. Drizzle with the melted butter and serve topped with cream or farmer cheese and a sprinkling of fried bread crumbs.

Leaf-Wrapped Rice Packages Stuffed with Peanuts and Sausage

Zhong Zi (China)

SERVES 6 (MAKES 6 DUMPLINGS)

Bamboo leaf–wrapped *zhong zi* are firm packages of sticky rice, stuffed with a variety of fillings, that have been boiled patiently for hours. Wrapping and tying these dumplings tightly gives them their dense, satisfying chew, as well as their ability to remain fresh for days at room temperature. While they are usually wrapped expertly in a pyramid shape, there is a much less complicated fold that works just as well.

These dumplings are wrapped using the Bamboo-Leaf Fold (page 61).

For the Dumplings

2 cups medium-grain sweet (glutinous) white rice, preferably from China or Japan, rinsed and soaked in plenty of water for 2 to 3 hours

1½ tablespoons salt

½ pound pork belly, trimmed of skin, cut into 6 equal pieces, rubbed with 1½ teaspoons salt, covered, and refrigerated for at least 6 hours and up to 1 day

¾ cup raw peanuts, papery skins removed

1 link Chinese pork sausage *(la chang)*, cut into 6 equal pieces (optional)

For Assembly

20 prepared bamboo leaves (see page 28)

Six 60-inch lengths of kitchen string for tying the *zhong zi*

For Serving

Soy sauce

1. ASSEMBLE THE DUMPLINGS: *Before assembling the* zhong zi, *review the Bamboo-Leaf Fold.*

2. Drain the rice, place it in a medium bowl, and mix in the salt.

3. Line a tray with a kitchen towel and have ready the salted rice, pork, peanuts, sausage, if desired, bamboo leaves, and ties.

4. Divide the peanuts into 6 equal piles.

5. Pick out the best 18 bamboo leaves. Place 2 bamboo leaves, smooth side up, lengthwise, and alongside each other, in the palm of your hand. Overlap the leaves by about 1½ inches. Center 3 heaping tablespoons of rice on top of the overlapped bamboo leaves and spread out into a rectangle 4 inches long by 2 inches across or about the size of your palm. Place 1 piece of pork, 1 pile of peanuts, and a slice of sausage over the rice and top everything with 3 more heaping tablespoons of rice. Lay a third bamboo leaf, smooth side down, on top of the mound. Grip and curl the sides of the overlapped bottom leaves over the top leaf. Fold back the top ends of the leaves. Then fold back the bottom ends of the leaves as firmly as you can to create a neat, tight rectangular package. Wrap and tie the package 4 or 5 times across the width of the dumpling and at least once vertically to prevent the leaves from unfolding. Place the package on the large plate or tray and continue until you have 6 packages.

6. COOK THE DUMPLINGS: Stack the packages as evenly as possible in a large pot and fill with enough water to cover. Bring to a boil over high heat. Reduce the heat to medium, cover, and simmer for 2 to 2$^1/_2$ hours. Check the water level every 30 minutes and replenish with just enough boiling water to keep the dumplings covered.

7. Remove the pot from the heat. Carefully remove the *zhong zi* with tongs and place them on a folded kitchen towel to cool slightly. Cut off the strings (unless you are freezing the dumplings) and serve with soy sauce. They can also remain wrapped and be served later at room temperature. It's best not to open the packages too soon and to peel back the leaves just before eating so that they stay moist. *Zhong zi* can be refrigerated for up to 3 days or frozen (unopened) for up to 6 months (see page 36). Reheat them in a steamer pot or use the Steamer Plate Setup (page 37). If reheating frozen *zhong zi*, allow them to thaw before steaming.

October

NO-FUSS POTATO DUMPLINGS
Pyzy (Poland) 305

SPICED CARROT PUDDING
(England) 307

COLLARD GREENS WITH CORN DUMPLINGS
(United States) 309

CHICKEN PAPRIKA WITH DUMPLINGS
Csirke Paprikas Galuskaval (Hungary) 311

BEAN SOUP WITH TINY DUMPLINGS
Csipetke (Hungary) 313

CHICKPEA "FISH" IN A SPICY ONION SAUCE
Yeshimbra Asa (Ethiopia) 315

BACON AND SAGE ROLY-POLY
(England) 318

DAIKON CAKE
Luo Bo Gao (China) 320

CHEDDAR CHEESE AND POTATO PIEROGI
(United States) 322

LENTIL AND ONION PIEROGI
Pierogi z Soczewicą (Poland) 324

POTATO "TAMALES" STUFFED WITH CHICKEN AND JALAPEÑO
Paches de Papa (Guatemala) 326

BEEF-STUFFED PLANTAIN BALLS IN A CASSAVA-CORN SOUP
Caldo de Bolas (Ecuador)... 328

No-Fuss Potato Dumplings

Pyzy (Poland)

SERVES 4 TO 8 (MAKES ABOUT 40 DUMPLINGS)

Because they are dense, *pyzy* are typically smaller than other potato dumplings. Their small size ensures that they cook quickly and completely, leaving no uncooked centers. Raw potato oxidizes and turns gray after grating so you will notice a deepening in the color of the dough as it's handled and rolled into balls. If this gray color does not appeal to you, know that the dumplings will lighten during cooking. These sticky dumplings are served smothered in fried bread crumbs, sautéed onions, or bits of bacon.

For the Dumplings

3 medium baking potatoes, such as russet

½ teaspoon salt

½ cup unbleached all-purpose flour, plus some extra for dusting

1 large egg yolk

For the Topping

4 strips bacon, chopped coarse

1 small yellow onion, chopped fine

Salt and freshly ground black pepper to taste

1. MAKE THE DOUGH: Place one of the potatoes in a small saucepan, pour in enough water to cover, and bring to a boil over high heat. Cover, reduce the heat to medium, and simmer until fork-tender, about 30 minutes. Drain and place the potato on a folded kitchen towel. Once it's cool enough to handle, peel off its skin and put the flesh into a large bowl. Mash until mostly smooth.

2. Peel the 2 remaining potatoes and finely grate them onto a kitchen towel. Bring together the ends of the cloth and twist to squeeze out as much of the potato juice as you can. Do this step in batches if it seems more effective.

3. Add the grated potato to the mashed potato. Sprinkle the salt and ¼ cup of the flour over the potato, keeping the remaining ¼ cup handy, and toss gently with your fingers until well combined. Add the egg yolk. Using your hands work the crumbly mixture into a dough, about 2 minutes. This dough needs to be firm enough to hold its shape when rolled into balls. If the dough is too soft or sticky, work in some of the remaining flour, a little at a time. Cover and refrigerate until you are ready to roll the dumplings.

4. COOK THE BACON AND THE ONION: Place the bacon in a small skillet over medium heat and cook, stirring occasionally, until it has rendered enough fat to generously coat the bottom of the pan. Mix in the onion and raise the heat to high. Cook, stirring frequently, until both the bacon and the onion are golden brown, about 5 minutes. Scoop everything, including the drippings, into a small bowl and set aside.

5. MAKE AND COOK THE DUMPLINGS: Line a tray with a kitchen towel and sprinkle with a little flour.

6. Pinch off a small piece of dough and roll it into a ball about 1 inch around, dust with flour, and place it on the prepared tray. Repeat with the remaining dough.

7. Fill a large pot three-quarters of the way with salted water and bring to a boil over high heat. Reduce the heat to medium for a steady simmer. Carefully drop the dumplings, a few at a time, into the water. Cook until all of them are floating, about 2 minutes, then cook for 3 minutes longer.

8. Remove the *pyzy* with a slotted spoon and place in a shallow serving bowl. Top them with the bacon and onion mixture and all of its drippings, sprinkle with salt and pepper, and serve.

Spiced Carrot Pudding

(England)

SERVES 4 TO 5 (MAKES 1 DUMPLING)

Many steamed puddings use a good amount of a particular spice blend called Pudding Spice. This spice mixture works exceptionally well in this carrot pudding. Grated white potato mimics the texture of the grated carrot and keeps the pudding from getting too sweet. Bread crumbs bind all the ingredients together and give the pudding a cakelike texture.

This dumpling is made using the Pudding Basin Setup (page 43).

For the Dumpling

- 1 cup coarse fresh crustless white bread crumbs (see page 6)
- 1 cup unbleached all-purpose flour
- 1/3 cup light muscovado or other unrefined sugar (see page 20)
- 2 teaspoons baking powder
- 2 teaspoons Pudding Spice (page 239)
- 1/4 teaspoon salt
- 1/2 cup very finely chopped cold suet or 4 tablespoons (1/2 stick) unsalted butter, frozen, coarsely grated, and kept cold
- 1 medium baking potato, such as russet
- 1 medium carrot
- 1/2 cup dark raisins
- 1 large egg, beaten
- 1/4 cup cold milk

For Cooking and Serving

Unsalted butter and sugar to coat the pudding basin

- 1 recipe Vanilla Custard Sauce (page 97) or vanilla ice cream

Equipment

24-inch square of muslin

35-inch length of kitchen string

4- to 5-cup pudding basin

Pot large enough to hold the basin when covered

Parchment paper

1. MAKE THE BATTER: Combine the bread crumbs, flour, sugar, baking powder, pudding spice, and salt in a large bowl. Mix in the suet by gently breaking apart any clumps while working it through the bread crumb mixture. If using butter, work it into the bread crumb mixture with a pastry cutter or 2 butter knives until it looks like a damp meal.

2. Peel the potato and grate it through the medium holes of your grater onto a kitchen towel. Bring together the ends of the cloth and twist to squeeze out as much of the juice as you can. Do this step in batches if it seems more effective.

3. Peel the carrot and grate it through the medium holes of your grater. Mix the potato and the carrot into the bread crumb mixture.

4. Set aside 2 handfuls of the raisins to line the bottom of the pudding basin. Mix the remaining raisins into the bread crumb and carrot mixture. Mix in the egg. Stir in just enough milk, a little at a time, to create a very moist batter.

5. ASSEMBLE AND STEAM THE DUMPLING: *Before assembling the pudding, review the Pudding Basin Setup.*

6. Rinse the muslin and the string under cool running water. Wring them out and set aside.

7. Place the empty pudding basin in the pot. Pour water into the space between the basin and the pot until it comes three-quarters of the way up the sides of the basin. Remove the basin and bring the water to a boil over high heat. Reduce the heat to low for a gentle simmer.

8. Meanwhile, make sure the interior of the basin is dry before rubbing it with butter and coating it with sugar. Scatter the reserved raisins around the bottom of the basin. Scoop the batter into the basin and smooth out its surface using wet fingers. Cut out a round of parchment paper and place it on top of the batter. Cover the basin with the damp muslin and secure it tightly with the string. Tie the opposite corners of the muslin into handles over the top of the pudding.

9. Using tongs or a wooden spoon, push a folded cloth, such as a standard white cotton napkin, into the simmering water and arrange it to lie flat on the bottom of the pot. Using the cloth handle, carefully lower the basin into the pot, cover, and simmer for at least $1^1/_2$ hours, or up to $2^1/_2$ hours for a pudding that's even richer in flavor and texture. Check the water level every 30 minutes and replenish with boiling water as needed.

10. Remove the pot from the heat. Using a pot holder to grasp the cloth handle, carefully remove the basin from the pot, put it on a folded kitchen towel, and allow the pudding to cool for 5 minutes. Remove the string, cloth, and paper. Unmold by inverting it onto a plate. Slice and serve with Vanilla Custard Sauce or vanilla ice cream. The pudding can be refrigerated for up to 3 days. Reheat in a steamer pot or use the Steamer Plate Setup (page 37).

Collard Greens with Corn Dumplings

(United States)

SERVES 4 (MAKES ABOUT 16 DUMPLINGS)

These cornmeal dumplings are not as creamy as *Sopa de Bolitas de Masa* (April) or as dense as *Soupe aux Miques et aux Choux* (November), instead they are chewy and breadlike. This dish starts with the fat from rendered salt pork, but a few strips of bacon will flavor everything just as well. If collard greens are not available, kale works and doesn't need blanching.

For the Stew

2 pounds collard greens

1/4 pound salt pork, half lean and half fat, cut into 4 equal pieces

1/4 teaspoon cayenne

2 teaspoons sugar

For the Dumplings

1 cup white cornmeal

1/4 teaspoon salt

Unbleached all-purpose flour for dusting

1. MAKE THE STEW: Fill a medium pot halfway with water and bring to a boil over high heat. Remove the stalks from the middle of each collard leaf, then cut the leaves into 1-inch ribbons. Stir the cut greens into the boiling water, cover, and cook for 2 minutes. Drain and set aside.

2. Place the salt pork in the same pot over medium heat. Cook, stirring occasionally, until at least 1 tablespoon of fat has melted off the pork, about 5 minutes. Carefully remove the pork with tongs and place on a small plate. Pour the rendered fat into a bowl and set aside.

3. Return the pork to the pot. Mix in the collard greens, cayenne, sugar, and 3 cups water. Bring to a boil over high heat. Cover, reduce the heat to low, and simmer for 1 1/2 hours, stirring occasionally. (You can also make the stew in advance and keep it refrigerated in a tightly sealed container for up to 3 days.)

4. MAKE THE DUMPLINGS: Place 1/2 cup water in a small saucepan and bring to a boil over high heat. Measure out 1/4 cup of the cornmeal and set aside. Place the remaining cornmeal, the salt, and the reserved pork fat in a medium bowl. Meanwhile, place 3/4 cup of the cornmeal in a medium heatproof bowl and keep the remaining 1/4 cup handy. Rub the fat evenly throughout the cornmeal with your fingers. Pour in the boiling water and mix with a fork until all the liquid has been absorbed.

5. Carefully work the dough with your hands. If this is in any way uncomfortable, let it cool for another minute or two, but keep in mind that you need to work with this dough while it is still very, very warm. Knead the dough in the bowl until it is smooth and manageable. This dough needs to be firm enough to hold its shape when rolled into balls. If it is too soft or sticky, work in some of the remaining cornmeal, a little at a time.

6. Line a tray with a kitchen towel and sprinkle with a little flour.

7. Pinch off a small piece of dough and roll it into a ball about $1\frac{1}{4}$ inches around, dust with flour, and place it on the prepared tray. Repeat with the remaining dough. Cover with a cloth and set aside.

8. COOK THE DUMPLINGS: Once the greens have cooked for $1\frac{1}{2}$ hours, check the broth level. There should be enough to come halfway up the greens. Stir in a little water if needed. Drop the dumplings onto the surface of the greens, spacing them apart evenly. Cover and cook for 30 minutes longer. Serve these dumplings with a generous amount of greens and a piece of pork.

Chicken Paprika with Dumplings

Csirke Paprikas Galuskaval (Hungary)

SERVES 4 (MAKES ABOUT 16 DUMPLINGS)

Csirke paprikas galuskaval is a saucy batch of chicken and dumplings flavored with paprika, tomatoes, and cloves. Unlike Chicken and Dumpling Soup (September), this is an intense dish to which the dumplings bring balance by breaking up the concentrated flavors. Browning the chicken adds a lot of body and is a crucial step. If the chicken is browned too lightly or not at all, the stew will lose its savory, smoky personality. *Csirke paprikas galuskaval* is tasty enough by itself, but it's often served with pickled vegetables.

For the Stew

2 tablespoons unsalted butter

One 3- to 4-pound chicken, cut into serving pieces

1 small yellow onion, chopped fine

3 garlic cloves, chopped fine

1 tablespoon sweet paprika

3 whole cloves

4 plum tomatoes, peeled, seeded (see page 21), and chopped fine

1 teaspoon salt

1/2 teaspoon freshly ground black pepper

2 green bell peppers, cored and sliced into 1/4-inch rings

1/4 cup sour cream (optional)

For the Dumplings

1 1/2 cups unbleached all-purpose flour

1 teaspoon salt

1 large egg, beaten

2 tablespoons unsalted butter, melted

1. MAKE THE STEW: Melt the butter in a large, wide pot over medium heat. Add the chicken pieces in one layer and do not stir until the undersides are dark golden brown, 8 to 10 minutes. Turn the chicken pieces over and brown the other side, about 8 minutes longer. Using a slotted spoon or tongs, move the chicken to a plate, leaving behind the buttery fat. Place the onion, garlic, paprika, and cloves in the pot. Stir frequently until the onion just begins to soften, about 4 minutes. Mix in the tomatoes, salt, and pepper and scrape up any sticky bits from the bottom of the pot with a wooden spoon. If there is not enough sauce to coat the bottom of the pot, add no more than 1/2 cup water.

2. Return the chicken pieces and any drippings to the pot. Cover, reduce the heat to low, and simmer for 30 minutes, turning the chicken pieces over halfway through the cooking. There may not appear to be enough liquid, but the chicken will release additional juices as it cooks.

3. Turn the chicken pieces over one more time, stir in the green peppers, cover, and cook for 10 minutes longer. Reduce the heat to very, very low to keep the chicken and sauce hot while making the dumplings. (You can also make the stew in advance and keep it refrigerated in a tightly sealed container for up to 3 days.)

4. MAKE AND COOK THE DUMPLINGS: Fill a large pot halfway with salted water and bring to a boil over high heat. Reduce the heat to medium for a steady simmer.

5. Combine the flour and the salt in a medium bowl. Add the egg, melted butter, and $3/4$ cup water and mix well. You will have a very moist, sticky dough.

6. Scoop up a rounded teaspoon of dough. Use another spoon or your finger to move the dough gently off the spoon and into the simmering water. Drop in spoonfuls of the remaining dough, leaving as much space as you can around each. Stir gently to prevent sticking. Cook until all of them are floating, about 2 minutes, then cook for 3 minutes longer.

7. Reserve 1 cup of the cooking liquid, drain the dumplings, and stir them gently into the chicken stew. Raise the heat to medium and heat through for 1 to 2 minutes. If the stew is too thick, stir in some of the reserved cooking liquid. Remove from the heat, swirl in the sour cream, if desired, and serve.

Bean Soup with Tiny Dumplings

Csipetke (Hungary)

SERVES 4 (MAKES ABOUT 80 DUMPLINGS)

This dumpling soup can make use of whatever you might find in your kitchen, but the must-have components are beans, paprika, a zesty topping like sour cream or vinegar, and, of course, lots of tiny dumplings. Don't be intimidated by the number of dumplings required for this soup. They are quick to make and need only be roughly shaped. This soup typically uses a blend of hot and sweet paprika. You can increase the amount of hot paprika for a spicier soup, or you can choose to use only the sweet paprika.

For the Soup

- 4 pounds meaty beef bones, such as rib, shank, or neck
- 2 tablespoons nonhydrogenated lard or a neutral oil, such as grapeseed
- 1 small yellow onion, chopped fine
- 1 tablespoon sweet paprika
- $1/8$ to $1/4$ teaspoon hot paprika or cayenne
- 2 tablespoons unbleached all-purpose flour
- $1/2$ cup dried speckled beans, such as pinto or speckled dark kidney, soaked in plenty of water for 6 to 8 hours or 1 cup canned, drained and rinsed

- 2 large carrots, cut into 1-inch rounds
- 3 large parsnips, cut into 1-inch rounds
- 1 green bell pepper, cored and cut into $1/2$-inch strips
- $1 1/2$ teaspoons salt
- $1/4$ cup sour cream

For the Dumplings

- $1/2$ cup unbleached all-purpose flour, plus some extra for dusting
- $1/2$ teaspoon salt
- 1 large egg, beaten

1. MAKE THE SOUP: Place the beef bones in a large pot with 2 quarts water and bring to a boil over high heat. Cover, reduce the heat to low, and cook for $1 1/2$ hours. Skim the froth off the surface with a spoon.

2. Meanwhile, melt the lard in a medium skillet over medium heat. Add the onion and stir frequently until soft, about 4 minutes. Stir in the sweet and hot paprika and the 2 tablespoons flour and cook for 2 minutes longer. Scoop into a small bowl and set aside to cool.

3. Once the broth has finished cooking, use a slotted spoon or tongs to move the bones to a bowl to cool slightly. Add the beans to the broth, cover, and simmer for 20 minutes. Add the carrots, parsnips, green pepper, $1 1/2$ teaspoons salt, and the cooked onion mixture. Pull off any bits of meat from the bones, place it back in the bowl, and discard the bones. Add the meat back to the broth. Cover and cook until the beans are tender, 45 to 60 minutes longer, depending on the bean used. (If using canned beans, add them 20 minutes before the vegetables have finished cooking.) (You can also make the soup in advance and keep it refrigerated in a tightly sealed container for up to 3 days. If the soup is too thick to stir easily, add a little water to thin it out.)

4. MAKE THE DOUGH: While the soup is simmering, place the $1/2$ cup flour in a medium bowl. Scoop out 2 tablespoons of the flour and set aside. Mix in the $1/2$ teaspoon salt. Add the egg and mix until all the liquid has been absorbed. Work the dough with your hands into one manageable ball. If the dough is wet and sticky, work in some of the remaining flour, a little at a time, until it no longer sticks to your fingers. Knead the dough in the bowl for 4 to 5 minutes, cover, and let it rest at room temperature for 30 minutes.

5. MAKE AND COOK THE DUMPLINGS: Line a tray with a kitchen towel and sprinkle with a little flour.

6. Knead the dough once or twice on a floured surface, shape it into a ball, then roll it out until it's about $1/8$ inch thick. Cut the sheet of dough in half. Pick up one half and pinch off small pieces, about the size of a dime, and place them in one layer on the prepared tray. Repeat with the remaining half.

7. Move half of the dough pieces onto a plate, slide them into the simmering soup, and stir gently to prevent sticking. Using the plate, quickly add the remaining dough pieces to the soup, stir, cover, and simmer for about 5 minutes. Remove from the heat and allow the soup to cool slightly. Stir in the sour cream and serve.

Chickpea "Fish" in a Spicy Onion Sauce

Yeshimbra Asa (Ethiopia)

SERVES 4 (MAKES ABOUT 36 DUMPLINGS)

These simple chickpea flour dumplings are baked first, and then, as they simmer in a thick, spicy sauce, they develop their distinctively toothsome texture. The spices in the dish are full and heady and fill the house with a wonderfully warm aroma. Some of the spices and herbs that go into this dish may require more than one shopping trip, but all of the other ingredients are commonplace. Some specialty food markets carry premixed packages of *berbere* spice, which is convenient if some of the individual ingredients are not available. This dish is traditionally served with *injera* bread, an Ethiopian flat bread made from teff, but you can serve it with your favorite soft flat bread.

For the Dumplings

1 cup chickpea flour, plus some extra for dusting

½ teaspoon salt

2 tablespoons grapeseed or other neutral oil

For the Sauce

2 large yellow onions, chopped fine

⅓ cup grapeseed or other neutral oil

2 fresh hot green chiles, such as jalapeño or Anaheim, seeded and chopped fine

4 garlic cloves, chopped very fine

1 tablespoon *Berbere* Spice (recipe follows) or use store-bought

1 teaspoon salt

½ cup red wine (optional)

1 tablespoon tomato paste

Equipment

Fish-shaped cookie cutter about 1 inch long or any other cutter about that size

1. MAKE THE DUMPLINGS: Preheat the oven to 350°F.

2. Combine the chickpea flour and ½ teaspoon salt in a medium bowl. Add the 2 tablespoons oil, pour in ¼ cup water, and mix until all the liquid has been absorbed. Knead the dough in the bowl until all the loose flour has been worked into the dough. The dough will be smooth and very firm but still soft enough to shape.

3. Shape the dough into a ball, place it on a work surface lightly dusted with chickpea flour, then roll it out until just under ¼ inch thick. Sprinkle with a little chickpea flour if it gets sticky. Using the cookie cutter, cut out as many fish shapes as you can, usually 24 to 30. Combine the scraps of dough, roll them out, and cut out as many more chickpea fish as you can.

4. Place the chickpea fish on an ungreased baking sheet and bake until golden brown, about 15 minutes. Once cooked, place them in a bowl and pour in enough cold water to cover. Allow them to soak while you make the sauce, but no longer than 15 minutes. (You can bake the chickpea fish up to 1 week in advance and keep them in a cool, dry place. Do not soak them in water until you are ready to cook them in the sauce.)

5. MAKE THE SAUCE AND COOK THE DUMPLINGS: While the chickpea fish are soaking, pulse the onions in a food processor 4 or 5 times to release their juices, but don't puree. Heat the ⅓ cup oil in a medium pot over high heat. Add the pulped onion and the chiles and stir until the mixture is golden brown, 6 to 7 minutes. Mix in the garlic, *Berbere* Spice, and 1 teaspoon salt and cook for 2 minutes longer. Stir in the wine, if desired, and 2 cups water and bring to a simmer. Stir in the tomato paste. Drain the soaked chickpea fish, add them to the sauce, and stir gently to coat. Cover, reduce the heat to low, and simmer for 15 minutes.

6. Uncover the pot, raise the heat to medium, and continue to cook, stirring occasionally, 2 to 3 minutes. Remove from the heat and serve as is or with *injera* bread or your favorite soft flat bread.

BERBERE SPICE

2 teaspoons cumin seeds

2 teaspoons carom seeds (*ajwain*)

1 teaspoon rue seeds

1 teaspoon cardamon seeds

6 whole cloves

10 allspice berries

2 tablespoons crumbled mildly spicy dried red chile, such as New Mexican

1/2 teaspoon cayenne

1 teaspoon ground ginger

1 tablespoon dried holy basil leaves

Equipment

Clean spice or coffee grinder

1. Toast the cumin, carom, rue, cardamom, cloves, and allspice in a small skillet over medium heat until the seeds are lightly browned, about 3 minutes. Scoop the mixture into a small bowl.

2. In the same skillet, toast the red chile, cayenne, and ground ginger, stirring constantly, about 2 minutes. Scoop it into the bowl with the other toasted spices and allow to cool.

3. Place the cooled spice mixture and the holy basil in the spice grinder and process into a fine powder. Measure out what is needed for the recipe and refrigerate the rest in a tightly sealed glass container for up to 6 months.

If substituting ground spices, combine the following amounts in a skillet over medium heat. Toast, stirring constantly, about 3 minutes. Scoop immediately into a bowl to cool. Measure out what is needed for the recipe and follow the storage instructions above.

2 teaspoons ground cumin

2 teaspoons ground carom seeds (*ajwain*)

1 teaspoon rue powder

1 teaspoon ground cardamom

1/4 teaspoon ground cloves

3/4 teaspoon ground allspice

2 tablespoons crumbled mildly spicy dried red chiles, such as New Mexican

1/2 teaspoon cayenne

1 teaspoon ground ginger

1 tablespoon dried holy basil leaves

Bacon and Sage Roly-Poly

(England)

SERVES 4 (MAKES 1 DUMPLING)

This is a dumpling for bacon lovers. A sheet of soft dough, covered with a layer of chewy back bacon, leeks, and sage, is rolled up and steamed. Back bacon, taken from the loin of the pig, is much leaner. The leeks add an aromatic lightness and moisture. Served with mustard or spiked with steak sauce, this dumpling is a good side with beef or vegetables.

This dumpling is made using the Jelly-Roll Shape (page 41) and then wrapped using the Candy-Wrapper Shape Using a Cloth (page 51).

For the Dough

2 cups unbleached all-purpose flour, plus some extra for dusting

1 tablespoon baking powder

1/2 teaspoon salt

1/2 cup very finely chopped cold suet or 4 tablespoons (1/2 stick) unsalted butter, frozen, coarsely grated, and kept cold

3/4 cup cold water

For the Filling

3/4 pound raw back bacon (Irish bacon) or raw brine-cured ham, chopped coarse

2 medium leeks, white and light green parts only, rinsed clean and chopped fine

1/4 cup coarsely chopped fresh flat-leaf parsley leaves

25 fresh sage leaves, cut crosswise into thin ribbons

1/2 teaspoon freshly ground black pepper

For Cooking

Unsalted butter to coat the muslin

Equipment

24-inch square of muslin or white cotton napkin

Two 5-inch and one 20-inch lengths of kitchen string

16-inch roasting pan with a cover

1 or 2 racks at least 1 inch high, small enough to fit into the roasting pan but large enough to support the 14-inch roly-poly

1. MAKE THE DOUGH: Measure out 1/4 cup of the flour and set aside. Place the remaining flour, the baking powder, and salt in a large bowl and mix well. Mix in the suet, gently breaking apart any clumps while working it through the flour mixture. If using butter, work it into the flour using a pastry cutter or 2 butter knives until the mixture looks like a damp, coarse meal.

2. Drizzle in the cold water and work the dough with your hands into one manageable ball. If the dough is wet and sticky, work in some of the remaining flour, a little at a time, until it no longer sticks to your fingers. Knead the dough in the bowl for about 1 minute. Cover and refrigerate for 30 minutes.

3. ASSEMBLE THE DUMPLING: *Before assembling the bacon and sage roly-poly, review the Jelly-Roll Shape and the Candy-Wrapper Shape Using a Cloth.*

4. Combine all the filling ingredients in a bowl.

5. Soak the muslin under running water, wring it out, and set it aside.

6. Place the chilled dough on a floured surface. Shape the dough into a blunt log. Roll it out into a 9 × 14-inch rectangle about $1/8$ inch thick. Sprinkle with flour if it gets sticky. Scatter the filling mixture over the top of the dough, leaving a narrow border on all sides. Starting with one of the longer sides, begin to roll up the dough, pinching the ends to seal as you go. Pinch and press the far edge of the dough along the length of the log to seal.

7. Spread out the muslin on a flat surface and rub it generously with butter, leaving a narrow border on all sides. Place the log, seam side down, along one edge of the prepared muslin. Roll up the log in the muslin. The muslin should be slightly baggy so the log can swell while it cooks. Tie the 2 open ends with the shorter strings, then tie the longer string around the body of the wrapped log to secure the seam. Once it's been wrapped and tied, place it on a large plate and refrigerate for 15 minutes. (You can also assemble the dumpling in advance and keep it tightly wrapped in the refrigerator for up to 8 hours.)

8. STEAM THE DUMPLING: Place one rack or both racks in the roasting pan and pour in enough water to come up just below the rungs. Place over 2 burners and bring to a boil over high heat. Place the wrapped log on the rack. Cover, reduce the heat to medium, and steam for 2 hours. Check the water level every 30 minutes and replenish with boiling water as needed.

9. Remove the pot from the heat. Carefully lift the bacon and sage roly-poly out of the pot, place it on a folded kitchen towel, and allow it to drain and cool slightly. Remove the strings, unwrap, slice, and serve.

Daikon Cake

Luo Bo Gao (China)

SERVES 6 TO 8 (MAKES 2 DUMPLINGS)

Luo bo gao is a dim sum dish made with daikon, or winter radish. Daikon is juicy like an apple, is shaped like a large white carrot, and has a smooth radish flavor. To make the batter for *luo bo gao* you need to cook the daikon, break it down, and mellow out its flavor while concentrating its essence. You can eat this dumpling fresh from the steamer, but it's most popular sliced and lightly seared for a crispy skin.

For the Dumplings

2 cups white rice flour, preferably from China or Thailand

¼ cup wheat starch

1 teaspoon salt

½ teaspoon freshly ground white pepper

10 to 12 small or medium dried shrimp, soaked in hot water to cover for 30 minutes

1 pound daikon radish

1 link Chinese pork sausage (*la chang*), chopped very fine (about ⅔ cup)

3 scallions, chopped fine

For Cooking and Serving

Grapeseed or other neutral oil to coat the cake pans and the skillet

Oyster sauce or hot sauce

Equipment

2-inch-high steamer rack

Two 9-inch round cake pans

Pot large enough to hold both the rack and cake pan when covered

1. MAKE THE BATTER: Combine the rice flour, wheat starch, salt, and pepper in a large bowl and set aside. Drain and finely chop the shrimp.

2. Peel the daikon and grate it through the small holes of your grater onto a kitchen towel. Bring together the ends of the cloth and twist to squeeze out as much liquid as you can into a bowl. Measure out the collected juices and add enough water to the juice to make 3½ cups.

3. Pour the daikon juice and water mixture into a medium pot. Add the grated daikon and bring to a boil over high heat. Cover, reduce the heat to low, and simmer for 5 minutes. Mix in the sausage, scallions, and chopped shrimp, cover, and cook for 5 minutes longer. Remove from the heat. Slowly add the rice flour mixture and whisk continuously until free of most large lumps. The batter will be thick and sticky and a little lumpy.

4. STEAM THE DUMPLINGS: Place the steamer rack in the pot, add 1½ inches of water to the pot, and bring to a boil over high heat.

5. Brush both cake pans with a little oil and divide the batter between the 2 pans. Dip a spoon into cool water and use the back of the spoon to smooth out the surface of the batter.

6. Carefully place one of the filled pans on the steamer rack, cover, and steam for 40 minutes. The other filled pan should be covered and left sitting at room temperature while the first one cooks, or it can be cooked simultaneously in another pot.

7. Remove the pot from the heat. Carefully lift the pan out of the pot, place it on a folded kitchen towel, and allow the *luo bo gao* to cool to room temperature. Repeat with the other filled cake pan.

8. Unmold the *luo bo gao* and gently turn it onto a cutting board. Cut each dumpling into 8 equal slices. (Do not slice the *luo bo gao* if you are planning on serving it later. They can be refrigerated, tightly wrapped, for up to 3 days. Slice and fry just before serving.)

9. When ready to serve, coat a large skillet with oil and heat over medium heat. Carefully place the slices of *luo bo gao* in the pan and cook until their bottoms are crispy and golden brown, about 4 minutes. Turn them over to brown the other sides. Serve with a side of oyster sauce or hot sauce.

Cheddar Cheese and Potato Pierogi

(United States)

SERVES 4 TO 8 (MAKES ABOUT 40 DUMPLINGS)

The combination of potato and Cheddar has been a popular pierogi filling for generations, especially in the Great Lakes region. Extra-sharp Cheddar is the type used here, but any other type, except mild, will work just as well. Like other time-honored pierogi recipes, this one includes caramelized onion in the filling.

These dumplings are made using the Half-Moon Fold (page 47).

For the Filling

2 medium baking potatoes, such as russet

2 tablespoons unsalted butter or bacon fat

1 small yellow onion, chopped fine

1/4 pound extra-sharp Cheddar cheese, grated coarse (about 1 heaping cup)

1 large egg yolk

1 teaspoon salt (omit if using bacon fat)

1/2 teaspoon freshly ground black pepper

For the Dough

1 recipe *Pierogi z Kaszą Gryczaną* (page 127) dough, preferably made no more than 2 hours in advance

Unbleached all-purpose flour for dusting

For Serving*

4 tablespoons (1/2 stick) unsalted butter, melted just before serving

1/2 cup sour cream

1/4 cup finely chopped fresh chives

Equipment

2 1/2-inch round cookie cutter

Large, wide bowl to hold the dumplings cooked in batches

1. MAKE THE FILLING: Place the potatoes in a small pot, pour in enough water to cover, and bring to a boil over high heat. Cover, reduce the heat to medium, and simmer until fork-tender, about 30 minutes. Drain the potatoes and place them on a folded kitchen towel. Once they are cool enough to handle, peel off their skins, place the flesh in a large bowl, and mash until mostly smooth.

2. Melt the 2 tablespoons butter in a medium skillet over medium heat. Add the onion and stir frequently until golden brown, about 8 minutes. Mix the onion into the mashed potatoes and set aside to cool.

3. Add the Cheddar cheese, egg yolk, salt, and pepper to the cooled potato mixture and mix well.

---

* These amounts are for a full recipe. If you plan on freezing and storing some of the dumplings, reduce the amounts in proportion to the number you are serving.

4. ASSEMBLE THE DUMPLINGS: *Before assembling the pierogi, review the Half-Moon Fold.*

5. Line a tray with a kitchen towel and sprinkle with a little flour. Have ready the dough and the filling.

6. Knead the dough once or twice on a floured surface, divide it into 4 equal pieces, then set 3 of them aside under a kitchen towel. Shape the remaining piece into a ball and roll it out until it's about ⅛ inch thick. Sprinkle with flour if it gets sticky.

7. Using the cookie cutter, cut out as many rounds as you can, usually 8 to 10. Collect all scraps from around the rounds and put them aside under a damp kitchen towel for later use.

8. Lay flat 1 to 5 dough rounds. Brush each round with a very thin coating of water to make it sticky enough to seal. Center a rounded teaspoon of filling on top of each round, fold each neatly in half, pushing out any air, and pinch to seal. Dab a little water along the edges, if needed, for a better seal. Place the assembled dumplings in a single layer on the prepared tray and keep them covered with a kitchen towel while you work. Once you have assembled the first batch of dumplings, continue with the remaining dough and filling. Combine all the dough scraps, knead them into a ball, roll it out, cut out as many rounds as you can, and fill and fold those too.

9. Cover the tray of assembled dumplings and place in the refrigerator for 30 to 60 minutes before cooking. Chilling them helps to set the dough, making the dumplings firm and toothsome when cooked instead of puffy and soft. Set aside the number of dumplings that you would like to cook and keep the rest frozen for up to 6 months (see page 36).

10. COOK THE DUMPLINGS: Fill a large pot halfway with salted water and bring it to a boil over high heat. Reduce the heat to medium for a steady simmer.

11. Gently drop up to 20 dumplings, a few at a time, into the simmering water. Stir gently to prevent sticking. Cook until all of them are floating, about 3 minutes, then cook for 2 minutes longer. (If cooking frozen pierogi, add them directly to the simmering water and increase the cooking time by 1 minute. Do not allow the pierogi to thaw before cooking.)

12. Remove the dumplings with a slotted spoon, place them in the large bowl, and drizzle with a ladle of the cooking liquid to prevent sticking. Cook the remaining dumplings and place them in the bowl with another ladle of the cooking liquid.

13. Drain the pierogi and place them in a large, shallow serving bowl. Drizzle the dumplings with melted butter, spoon sour cream over the top, sprinkle with chives, and serve.

Lentil and Onion Pierogi

Pierogi z Soczewiçą (Poland)

SERVES 4 TO 8 (MAKES ABOUT 40 DUMPLINGS)

If you've never made pierogi before, this is a great recipe for beginners. *Pierogi z soczewiça* are on the small side, and the filling is easy to work with. If you like the idea of lentils as a filling, *Ravioli di Zucca e Lenticchie* (November) is another recipe that uses them brilliantly.

These dumplings are made using the Half-Moon Fold (page 47).

For the Filling

- ½ cup dried green lentils, rinsed
- 4 tablespoons (½ stick) unsalted butter, cut into chunks
- 1 large yellow onion, chopped fine
- ½ teaspoon salt
- ¼ teaspoon freshly ground black pepper

For the Dough

- 1 recipe *Pierogi z Kaszą Gryczaną* (page 127) dough, preferably made no more than 2 hours in advance
- Unbleached all-purpose flour for dusting

For Serving*

- 4 tablespoons (½ stick) unsalted butter, melted just before serving
- Sour cream
- ½ cup fried bread crumbs (see page 7)

Equipment

- 2½-inch round cookie cutter
- Large, wide bowl to hold the dumplings cooked in batches

1. MAKE THE FILLING: Fill a small pot halfway with water and bring to a boil over high heat. Add the lentils, cover, reduce the heat to low, and simmer until the lentils are soft and starting to break apart, about 45 minutes. Drain the lentils over a bowl so you can reserve ½ cup of the cooking liquid. Place the lentils in a medium bowl and mash them as roughly or as finely as you like. Set aside and allow them to cool to room temperature.

2. Melt the butter in a large skillet over medium heat. Add the onion and stir frequently until golden brown, about 8 minutes. Mix in the mashed lentils, salt, and pepper and stir for 2 to 3 minutes longer. Drizzle in a little of the reserved cooking liquid if the mixture begins to stick to the bottom of the pan. Don't add more cooking liquid than you need, because the mixture should be thick enough to hold its shape when scooped up with a spoon. Remove from the heat, scoop back into the bowl, and set aside to cool.

3. ASSEMBLE THE DUMPLINGS: *Before assembling the pierogi, review the Half-Moon Fold.*

---

*These amounts are for a full recipe. If you plan on freezing and storing some of the dumplings, reduce the amounts in proportion to the number you are serving.

4. Line a tray with a kitchen towel and sprinkle with a little flour. Also have ready the dough and the filling.

5. Knead the dough once or twice on a floured surface, divide it into 4 equal pieces, then set 3 of them aside under a kitchen towel. Shape the remaining piece into a ball, and roll it out until it's about $1/8$ inch thick. Sprinkle with flour if it gets sticky.

6. Using the cookie cutter, cut out as many rounds as you can, usually 8 to 10. Collect all the scraps from around the rounds and put them aside under a damp kitchen towel for later use.

7. Lay flat 1 to 5 dough rounds. Brush each round with a very thin coating of water to make it sticky enough to seal. Place a rounded teaspoon of filling in the center of each round, fold each round neatly in half, pushing out any air, and pinch to seal. Dab a little water along the edges, if needed, for a better seal. Place the assembled dumplings in a single layer on the prepared tray and keep them covered with a kitchen towel while you work. Once you have assembled the first batch of dumplings, continue with the remaining dough and filling. Combine all the dough scraps, knead them into a ball, roll it out, cut out as many rounds as you can, and fill and fold those too.

8. Cover the tray of assembled dumplings and place in the refrigerator for 30 to 60 minutes before cooking. Chilling them helps to set the dough, making the dumplings firm and toothsome when cooked instead of puffy and soft. Set aside the number of dumplings that you would like to cook and keep the rest frozen for up to 6 months (see page 36).

9. COOK THE DUMPLINGS: Fill a large pot halfway with salted water and bring to a boil over high heat. Reduce the heat to medium for a steady simmer.

10. Gently drop up to 20 dumplings, a few at a time, into the simmering water. Stir gently to prevent sticking. Cook until all of them are floating, about 3 minutes, then cook for 2 minutes longer. (If cooking frozen pierogi, add them directly to the simmering water and increase the cooking time by 1 minute. Do not allow the pierogi to thaw before cooking.)

11. Using a slotted spoon, remove the dumplings, place them in the large bowl, and drizzle with a ladle of the cooking liquid to prevent sticking. Cook the remaining dumplings and place them in the bowl with another ladle of the cooking liquid.

12. Drain the pierogi and place them in a large, shallow serving bowl. Drizzle the dumplings with melted butter, spoon sour cream over the top, sprinkle with fried bread crumbs, and serve.

Potato "Tamales" Stuffed with Chicken and Jalapeño

Paches de Papa (Guatemala)

SERVES 4 TO 8 (MAKES 8 DUMPLINGS)

Mixing mashed potatoes into a batch of highly flavored masa harina batter creates an extraordinary background for chicken. These dumplings require a fair amount of work, but they're a whole meal in one package, and a wonderfully memorable one at that. Because the potato-masa batter is made with a roasted tomatillo, tomato, and jalapeño sauce, the chicken needs nothing more than a little salt before being stuffed—with some additional chiles—into small mounds of the batter.

These dumplings are wrapped using the Envelope Fold (page 56), but you can also use the Diamond in the Square Fold (page 42) if your banana leaves are brittle or torn.

For the Sauce

6 tomatillos, papery husks removed and fruit rinsed

3 plum tomatoes

1 small red bell pepper

2 jalapeño chiles

1 dried chipotle chile, toasted and finely ground

1 teaspoon achiote (*annatto*) powder

½ teaspoon salt

For the Batter

2 medium baking potatoes, such as russet

1½ cups masa harina

1 teaspoon salt

2 tablespoons nonhydrogenated lard or a neutral oil, such as grapeseed

½ cup warm water

For the Filling

2 boneless, skinless chicken breasts or thighs, cut into 8 equal pieces and sprinkled with ½ teaspoon salt

4 jalapeño chiles, cored, cut in half lengthwise, and seeded

For Assembly

Twelve 10-inch prepared banana-leaf squares (see page 28)

Eight 24-inch lengths of kitchen string for tying the *paches*

Equipment

Electric hand mixer

8- to 10-quart steamer pot

1. MAKE THE SAUCE: Preheat the oven to 400°F.

2. Poke a small hole with a knife into each tomatillo, tomato, bell pepper, and both of the jalapeños and place them on an ungreased baking sheet. Roast until soft and charred in spots, about 20 minutes. Once they are cool enough to handle, pick or rub off as best you can the patches of charred skin. Trim the tomatillos, tomatoes, and peppers of their tougher stem ends. For less heat, core and seed the jalapeños.

3. Pulse all the roasted ingredients in a food processor until the mixture is pulpy and mostly smooth. Add the ground chipotle, achiote powder, and ½ teaspoon salt and pulse 2 or 3 times to combine. You will have about 2 cups of sauce. (You can make the sauce in advance and keep it refrigerated in a tightly sealed container for up to 3 days.)

4. MAKE THE BATTER: Place the potatoes in a small pot, pour in enough water to cover, and bring to a boil over high heat. Cover, reduce the heat to medium, and simmer until fork-tender, about 30 minutes. Drain and place them on a folded kitchen towel. Once they are cool enough to handle, peel off their skins and put the flesh into a medium bowl. Mash the potatoes into small chunks and set aside.

5. Place the masa harina, 1 teaspoon salt, and $1^1/_2$ cups of the sauce in a large bowl. Whip with the hand mixer at medium speed until combined. Add the lard, raise the mixing speed to high, and continue to whip until the batter is very light and fluffy, about 10 minutes. Scrape down the sides as you go. If the batter is dry and separating into crumbs, add some of the warm water, one spoonful at a time, and whip until the mixture is smooth and even. Add the chunky mashed potatoes and fold until well mixed.

6. ASSEMBLE THE DUMPLINGS: *Before assembling the* paches de papa, *review the Envelope Fold.*

7. Line a tray with a kitchen towel and have ready the chicken, halved jalapeños, batter, remaining sauce, banana-leaf squares, and ties.

8. Pick out the best 8 leaf squares. Lay flat 1 square, smooth side up. Put 2 rounded tablespoons of the batter in the center of the square and spread out into a rectangle about 3×5 inches. Arrange a piece of chicken and a jalapeño half on top of the batter, then drizzle with a tablespoon of sauce. Top with another rounded tablespoon of the batter. Fold over one side. Fold over the opposite side. Fold the ends of the leaf over as tightly as you can to create a neat package. Tie the package in a crisscross pattern to prevent the leaf from unfolding and place it on the lined tray. Repeat until you have 8 packages.

9. STEAM THE DUMPLINGS: Remove the basket from the steamer pot, add 2 inches of water to the pot, and bring to a boil over high heat. Meanwhile, arrange the packages upright, leaning or loosely wedged against each other in the basket. Ball up and stick in a couple of extra leaf squares or parchment paper to keep them propped up if needed. Blanket them with the remaining banana leaves. Place the basket in the pot, cover, reduce the heat to medium, and steam for $1^1/_2$ hours. Check the water level every 30 minutes and replenish with boiling water as needed.

10. Remove the pot from the heat. Carefully remove the basket and place it on a folded kitchen towel. Let the *paches de papa* cool slightly, cut off the strings unless you are freezing the dumplings, and serve. It's best not to open the packages too soon and to peel back the leaves just before eating, so that they stay moist and warm. Keep any extra *paches de papa* refrigerated for up to 3 days or frozen (unopened) for up to 6 months. Reheat them in a steamer pot or use the Steamer Plate Setup (page 37). If reheating frozen *paches de papa*, allow them to thaw before steaming.

Beef-Stuffed Plantain Balls in a Cassava-Corn Soup

Caldo de Bolas (Ecuador)

SERVES 4 TO 6 (MAKES ABOUT 12 DUMPLINGS)

Caldo de bolas is an extremely rich dumpling soup that glows because of the addition of achiote or *annatto*, small red seeds that are known for their vivid color. These plantain dumplings, stuffed with ground beef and raisins, are a pleasure to bite into, but they are just as good broken apart in the soup. It takes practice to handle plantain dough deftly, because it is rather soft and sticky, but the large size of these dumplings makes the process a bit easier.

These dumplings are made using the Bowl Fold (page 45).

For the Soup

4 pounds meaty beef bones, such as rib, shank, or neck

2 tablespoons grapeseed or other neutral oil

1 small yellow onion, chopped fine

1 green bell pepper, cored and chopped fine

1/2 teaspoon achiote powder (*annatto*)

6 plum tomatoes, peeled, seeded (see page 21), and chopped fine

2 pounds cassava, prepared (see page 7) and cut into 2-inch chunks

2 ears of corn, cut into 1-inch rounds

2 teaspoons salt

1 teaspoon freshly ground black pepper

For the Filling

2 tablespoons grapeseed or other neutral oil

1/4 pound ground beef

2 tablespoons raisins

1 small yellow onion, chopped fine

1 green bell pepper, cored and chopped fine

1 small carrot, chopped fine

1/2 teaspoon achiote powder (*annatto*)

1/2 teaspoon salt

1/4 teaspoon freshly ground black pepper

2 large hard-boiled eggs, peeled and each cut into 6 pieces

For the Dough

3 ripe plantains (skins should be yellow with some black spots)

1/4 teaspoon salt

Unbleached all-purpose flour for dusting

1. MAKE THE SOUP: Place the bones and 3 quarts water in a large pot and bring to a boil over high heat. Cover, reduce the heat to low, and simmer for 2 hours. Skim the froth off the surface with a spoon. (You can also make this broth in advance and keep it refrigerated in a tightly sealed container for up to 3 days.)

2. MAKE THE FILLING: While the broth is simmering, heat 1 tablespoon of the oil in a medium skillet over medium heat. Add the ground beef and stir, breaking up any clumps as the beef begins to brown. Add the raisins and cook until they begin to plump up a bit and the beef is golden brown, about 3 minutes. Remove from the heat, scoop into a bowl, and set aside.

3. Heat the remaining tablespoon of oil in the same skillet and add the onion, green pepper, carrot, and achiote. Stir occasionally until the onion is soft, about 4 minutes. Stir in the beef mixture, the $1/2$ teaspoon salt, and the $1/4$ teaspoon pepper and cook for 3 minutes longer. Remove from the heat, scoop the mixture into a bowl, and allow it to cool to room temperature.

4. MAKE THE DOUGH: Peel the plantains, add them whole to the simmering broth, and cook for 3 minutes. Immediately remove them with a slotted spoon and put them in a large bowl, add the $1/4$ teaspoon salt, and mash until slightly lumpy but evenly textured. Shape the mashed plantain into one manageable ball. Work in a little water if the plantain ball is crumbly, or a little all-purpose flour if it's too sticky to handle. Return to the bowl, cover, and set aside.

5. FINISH THE SOUP: Heat the oil in a medium skillet over medium heat. Add the onion, green pepper, and achiote. Stir occasionally until the onion is soft, about 4 minutes. Add the tomatoes and cook for 2 minutes longer. Remove from the heat, scoop into a bowl, and set aside.

6. Once the soup has cooked for 2 hours, remove the bones using a slotted spoon or tongs and discard. Return the heat to medium, stir in the cassava, corn, 2 teaspoons salt, 1 teaspoon pepper, and the cooked onion mixture, and simmer for 15 minutes longer. Reduce the heat to very, very low to keep the soup hot while assembling the dumplings.

7. ASSEMBLE THE DUMPLINGS: *Before assembling the dumplings for* caldo de bolas, *review the Bowl Fold.*

8. Line a tray with a kitchen towel and sprinkle with a little flour. Have ready the dough, beef filling, and eggs.

9. Pinch off a small piece of dough and roll it into a ball about $1^1/2$ inches around. Use your thumbs to shape the ball into a bowl about $1^1/2$ inches deep. This will be a wide bowl that is best supported in the palm of your hand. Sprinkle with flour if it gets a little sticky. Place a heaping teaspoon of the beef filling and one egg piece into the center of the dough bowl. Close by pushing and pinching the edges of the dough around and over the filling until the filling is surrounded, pushing out any air. Dab a little water along the edges, if needed, for a better seal. Reroll into a ball, dust with flour, and place on the prepared tray. Continue with the remaining dough, filling, and eggs.

10. COOK THE DUMPLINGS: Bring the soup back to a simmer over medium heat. Carefully lower the dumplings, one by one, into the soup. Cook uncovered until the dumplings float to the top of the soup, about 10 minutes. Cover, cook for 2 minutes longer, and serve.

November

DUMPLINGS AND COCKY'S JOY
(Australia) 333

"NAPKIN" BREAD DUMPLING
Serviettenkloss (Germany) 334

TURKEY STEW WITH STUFFING DUMPLINGS
(United States) 336

CRANBERRY PUDDING
(United States) 338

LORD RANDALL'S PUDDING, AN APRICOT DESSERT
(England) 341

STICKY TOFFEE PUDDING
(England) 343

POTATO DUMPLINGS WITH CROUTON CENTERS
Kartoffelklösse (Germany) 345

COUNTRY CABBAGE SOUP WITH LARGE CORNMEAL DUMPLINGS
Soupe aux Miques et aux Choux (France) 347

PHILADELPHIA PEPPERPOT SOUP WITH DUMPLINGS
(United States) 349

LARGE BEEF- AND SPINACH-FILLED DUMPLINGS IN A BEEF BROTH
Maultaschen (Germany) 351

DUMPLINGS STUFFED WITH PEARS, FIGS, AND CHOCOLATE
Cialzons alla Frutta (Italy).. 354

PUMPKIN AND LENTIL RAVIOLI WITH BROWNED BUTTER AND ROSEMARY
Ravioli di Zucca e Lenticchie (Italy)... 356

"LITTLE EAR" DUMPLINGS STUFFED WITH MUSHROOMS IN A BEET SOUP
Borshch z Vushka (Russia) 359

Dumplings and Cocky's Joy

(Australia)

SERVES 4 TO 6 (MAKES ABOUT 12 DUMPLINGS)

Sometimes called "Dampers and Cocky's Joy," these ridiculously good dumplings are like glazed doughnuts minus the frying. Big spoonfuls of soft, eggy dough are cooked in a pot of sugar syrup known as Cocky's Joy, an affectionate term for golden syrup. A similarly wonderful dumpling dish from Canada, *grand-père,* is made with maple syrup, but we think that the deep caramel taste of the golden syrup and muscovado sugar is outstanding.

For the Syrup

1/2 cup golden syrup

1/2 cup light muscovado or other unrefined sugar (see page 20)

4 tablespoons (1/2 stick) unsalted butter, cut into chunks

For the Dumplings

1 cup unbleached all-purpose flour

2 teaspoons baking powder

1 tablespoon sugar

1/4 teaspoon salt

4 tablespoons (1/2 stick) cold unsalted butter, cut into bits

2 large eggs

1/4 cup milk

Equipment

Large, wide pot or skillet with a cover

1. MAKE THE SYRUP: Pour 1 1/2 cups water into the large pot. Stir in the golden syrup, muscovado sugar, and butter and bring to a boil over high heat. Reduce the heat to very, very low and cover to keep the syrup hot while you make the batter.

2. MAKE THE BATTER: Combine the flour, baking powder, sugar, and salt in a medium bowl. Add the butter and work it into the flour mixture with a pastry cutter or 2 butter knives until the mixture looks like a coarse, damp meal.

3. Whisk the eggs and milk together in small bowl. Pour the egg mixture into the flour mixture and mix until all the liquid has been absorbed and you have a thick, slightly lumpy batter. Do not overmix. This batter should not sit around. Once mixed, it should be dropped immediately into the syrup.

4. COOK THE DUMPLINGS: Scoop up a heaping tablespoon of batter. Use another spoon or your finger to move the batter gently off the spoon and into the syrup. Drop in spoonfuls of the remaining batter, leaving as much space as you can around each. You will get 10 to 12 dumplings. Cover, raise the heat to medium, and cook for 10 minutes. Uncover and cook for 5 minutes longer.

5. Carefully scoop up the dumplings with a slotted spoon and serve with a generous helping of the hot syrup. These dumplings are great as is or topped with vanilla ice cream.

"Napkin" Bread Dumpling

Serviettenkloss (Germany)

SERVES 4 TO 6 (MAKES 1 LARGE DUMPLING)

Serviettenkloss is a rich bread dumpling cooked in the shape of a log. Traditionally wrapped up in a napkin or a cloth, it can be opened at the table and torn from at will. If you let it cool a bit, it will stiffen up and be easier to slice into nice-looking rounds. This dumpling is a great way to create a fresh side dish out of day-old bread and is especially wonderful when served up with anything sauce laden.

This dumpling is wrapped using the Pudding Bag Fold (page 58).

For the Dumpling

6 tablespoons (¾ stick) unsalted butter, cut into 6 equal pieces

1 medium yellow onion, chopped coarse

9 cups 1-inch crustless white bread cubes (see page 6)

6 large eggs

½ cup milk

2 teaspoons salt

2 tablespoons finely chopped fresh flat-leaf parsley leaves

For Cooking

Unsalted butter to coat the muslin

Equipment

24-inch square of muslin or a white cotton napkin

One 10-inch length of kitchen string

1. MAKE THE BREAD MIXTURE: Melt 2 tablespoons of the butter in a large skillet over medium heat. Add the onion and stir frequently until soft, about 4 minutes. Scoop the onion into a large bowl. Melt another 2 tablespoons of the butter in the same skillet, add half of the bread cubes, and toss and stir until all sides are lightly browned, 7 to 8 minutes. Add them to the onion. Brown the remaining bread cubes with the last 2 tablespoons of butter, add them to the onion, and allow them to cool slightly.

2. In another bowl, whisk together the eggs, milk, and salt. Pour the egg mixture over the bread cubes and onion, and add the parsley. Using your hands, toss and turn the mixture until all of the bread has been coated and the onion is mixed throughout. Cover and refrigerate for 45 minutes.

3. Firmly gather and pack the bread mixture into a ball. Work in a little more milk or water if it is not sticking together.

4. ASSEMBLE AND COOK THE DUMPLING: *Before assembling the* serviettenkloss, *review the Pudding Bag Fold.*

5. Fill a large, deep pot halfway with salted water and bring to a boil over high heat. Reduce the heat to medium for a steady simmer.

6. Meanwhile, soak the muslin under running water, wring it out, and spread it out on a flat surface. Rub one side of the damp muslin with butter, leaving a narrow border on all sides. Center the bread cube ball on top of the muslin. Gather up the corners of the muslin and arrange the folds neatly, creating a bag. As you collect the muslin and prepare it for tying, leave it slightly baggy so that the dumpling can swell as it cooks. Be certain, however, to grip the muslin low enough to leave no open gaps. Tie the gathered muslin tightly.

7. Carefully lower the wrapped dumpling into the simmering water, cover, and cook for 35 minutes.

8. Remove the *Serviettenkloss* with tongs, place it on a folded kitchen towel, and allow it to drain and cool slightly. Remove the string, carefully unwrap the dumpling, and place it on a cutting board. If there is no naturally flat side, steady the dumpling with a fork and slice off just enough from any side to create a "foot," making it possible for it to sit on a plate steadily. Serve warm with your favorite meaty stew or sauce. Use forks to tear the dumpling into serving-size portions. *Serviettenkloss* can be kept tightly wrapped in the refrigerator for up to 3 days.

Turkey Stew with Stuffing Dumplings

(United States)

SERVES 4 (MAKES 8 DUMPLINGS)

This fast, delicious recipe takes leftovers from a typical Thanksgiving dinner and turns them into a vibrant and plentiful stew. The dumplings, made from bread-based stuffing, are the main attraction in this dish. If you don't have enough stuffing left over, you can make up the difference with bread cubes or bread crumbs. Better yet, plan to make extra stuffing the day before, because this dish may even outshine the impressive meal from the previous night.

For the Dumplings

2 cups cooked (bread or corn bread) stuffing

1 large egg, beaten

1/2 cup unbleached all-purpose flour, plus some extra for dusting

For the Stew

2 tablespoons grapeseed or other neutral oil

1 small yellow onion, chopped fine

1 garlic clove, chopped fine

2 tablespoons unbleached all-purpose flour

3 cups Chicken Broth (page 394)

3 cups bite-sized pieces of cooked turkey

2 pounds sweet potatoes, pumpkin, squash, or a combination, peeled and cut into 1-inch chunks (about 4 cups)

1 teaspoon tomato paste

1/2 teaspoon salt

1/4 teaspoon freshly ground black pepper

6 fresh sage leaves, sliced crosswise into thin ribbons

1. MAKE THE DOUGH: Place the stuffing in a large bowl and break it up into loose bits with your fingers. Add the egg and 1/4 cup of the flour, keeping the remaining 1/4 cup handy, and mix well, being careful not to squish the stuffing into a paste. This mixture needs to be firm enough to hold its shape when rolled into balls. If it is too soft or sticky, work in some of the remaining flour, a little at a time. Cover and refrigerate for 15 minutes.

2. Line a tray with a kitchen towel and sprinkle with a little flour.

3. Divide the dough into 8 equal pieces. Roll each piece into a ball, dust it lightly with flour, and place on the prepared tray.

4. COOK THE DUMPLINGS: Fill a medium pot halfway with salted water and bring to a boil over high heat. Reduce the heat to medium for a steady simmer. Gently drop the dumplings, one by one, into the water. Cook until all of them are floating, 2 to 3 minutes, then cook for 2 minutes longer.

5. Using a slotted spoon, remove the dumplings, place them in a large bowl, and drizzle with a ladle of the cooking liquid to prevent sticking.

6. MAKE THE STEW: Heat the oil in a large, wide pot over medium heat. Add the onion and stir frequently until just soft, about 2 minutes. Add the garlic and the 2 tablespoons flour and stir until the mixture is golden brown, about 5 minutes.

7. Pour in the broth, scrape up any sticky bits from the bottom of the pot with a wooden spoon, and bring to a boil over high heat. Stir in the turkey meat, sweet potatoes, tomato paste, salt, and pepper. Cover, reduce the heat to low, and simmer for 5 minutes, stirring occasionally.

8. Uncover and arrange the dumplings evenly on top of the stew. Cover and simmer for 5 minutes longer. Remove the pot from the heat, stir in the sage, and serve.

Cranberry Pudding

(United States)

SERVES 4 TO 6 (MAKES 1 DUMPLING)

A good cranberry pudding is moist and dense, with plenty of tart, juicy cranberries. Molasses is what gives this pudding its dark chocolate color and a subtle caramel flavor. Serve it with a spoonful of Caramel Sauce or save some for the next day to enjoy with a hot cup of tea or coffee.

This dumpling is made using the Pudding Basin Setup (page 43).

For the Sweetened Cranberries

¼ cup fresh orange juice

¼ cup light muscovado or other unrefined sugar (see page 20)

1¾ cups fresh or frozen cranberries

¼ teaspoon ground cinnamon

For the Batter

4 tablespoons (½ stick) unsalted butter, at room temperature

⅓ cup light muscovado or other unrefined sugar (see page 20)

2 large eggs, plus 1 large egg yolk, at room temperature

1 tablespoon molasses

1 teaspoon grated orange zest

¾ cup unbleached all-purpose flour

½ teaspoon baking powder

¼ teaspoon baking soda

¼ teaspoon salt

For Cooking and Serving

Unsalted butter and sugar to coat the pudding basin

1 recipe Caramel Sauce (recipe follows) or powdered sugar

Equipment

24-inch square of muslin

35-inch length of kitchen string

4- to 5-cup pudding basin

Pot large enough to hold the basin when covered

Parchment paper

1. PREPARE THE CRANBERRIES: Pour the orange juice into a small pot, mix in the ¼ cup muscovado sugar, the cranberries, and the cinnamon and bring to a simmer over medium heat. Cook, stirring occasionally, until about half of the cranberries burst open, about 4 minutes. Remove from the heat, scoop the berries and the juice into a small bowl, and set aside to cool.

2. MAKE THE BATTER: Place the butter and the ⅓ cup muscovado sugar in a large bowl and whisk until most of the sugar has dissolved. Whisk in the eggs, egg yolk, molasses, and orange zest until the mixture is smooth and frothy, 3 to 4 minutes.

3. Combine the flour, baking powder, baking soda, and salt in a medium bowl.

4. ASSEMBLE AND STEAM THE DUMPLING: *Before assembling the pudding, review the Pudding Basin Setup.*

5. Soak the muslin and the string under running water. Wring them out and set aside. Have ready the egg mixture, flour mixture, and the cranberries.

6. Place the empty pudding basin in the pot. Pour water into the space between the basin and the pot until it comes three-quarters of the way up the sides of the basin. Remove the basin and bring the water to a boil over high heat. Reduce the heat to low for a gentle simmer.

7. Meanwhile, make sure the interior of the basin is dry before rubbing it with butter and coating it with sugar. Scatter $1/2$ cup of the cranberries around the bottom of the basin. Mix the rest of the cranberries and all of their juices into the egg mixture. Fold the flour mixture into the egg and cranberry mixture. Do not overmix. Scoop the batter into the basin and wiggle it gently to level it off. Cut out a round of parchment paper and place it on top of the batter. Cover the basin with the damp muslin and secure it tightly with the string. Tie the opposite corners of the muslin into handles over the top of the pudding.

8. Using tongs or a wooden spoon, push a folded cloth, such as a standard white cotton napkin, into the simmering water and arrange it to lie flat on the bottom of the pot. Using the cloth handle, carefully lower the basin into the pot, cover, and simmer for at least $1^1/2$ hours, or up to $2^1/2$ hours for a pudding that's even richer in flavor and texture. Check the water level every 30 minutes and replenish with boiling water as needed.

9. Remove the pot from the heat. Using a pot holder to grasp the cloth handle, carefully remove the basin from the pot, put it on a folded kitchen towel, and allow the pudding to cool for 5 minutes. Remove the string, cloth, and paper. Unmold by inverting it onto a plate. Slice and serve with Caramel Sauce or a dusting of powdered sugar. The pudding can be refrigerated for up to 3 days. Reheat in a steamer pot or use the Steamer Plate Setup (page 37).

CARAMEL SAUCE

MAKES ABOUT 1 CUP

    1 cup sugar
    1/2 teaspoon fresh lemon juice
    3/4 cup heavy cream
    2 tablespoons dark rum (optional)

1. Combine the sugar, 1/2 cup water, and the lemon juice in a small pot and bring to a boil over high heat. Continue to boil without stirring until the syrup turns light amber in color, about 10 minutes. Meanwhile, heat the heavy cream in a small saucepan over high heat. Stir continuously until the cream just begins to bubble along the sides of the pot.

2. Once the syrup turns light amber in color, reduce the heat to low and simmer until the syrup darkens to a golden amber color, about 1 minute longer. (If using a candy thermometer, the temperature of the syrup should be around 340°F.) Immediately remove from the heat and set aside to cool slightly. Whisk the syrup vigorously while you drizzle in the hot cream. The sauce may bubble and splatter at first but will settle once some of the cream has been added. Continue to whisk until all the cream is added and you have a thick, smooth sauce. Stir in the rum, if desired, and serve warm. You can also make the sauce up to 3 days in advance and keep it refrigerated in a tightly sealed container. Reheat the sauce over medium heat until warm, stirring constantly.

Lord Randall's Pudding, an Apricot Dessert

(England)

SERVES 4 TO 6 (MAKES 1 DUMPLING)

This is a moist apricot and orange pudding that is tangy and sweet. As with all dried fruits, it is best to buy all-natural dried apricots that are firm and dark. The ones preserved with sulfur dioxide are too soft, and their flavors seem to melt away during cooking. You can find all-natural dried apricots at health food stores and specialty shops.

This dumpling is made using the Pudding Basin Setup (page 43).

For the Dumpling

¾ cup unbleached all-purpose flour

½ teaspoon baking soda

¼ teaspoon baking powder

Pinch of salt

6 tablespoons (¾ stick) unsalted butter, at room temperature

½ cup light muscovado or other unrefined sugar (see page 20)

1 large egg, beaten

3 tablespoons milk

½ cup orange marmalade, preferably dark

½ cup all-natural unsweetened dried apricots, chopped fine

For Cooking and Serving

Unsalted butter and sugar to coat the pudding basin

½ cup honey, preferably raw, or orange marmalade for serving

Equipment

24-inch square of muslin

35-inch length of kitchen string

4- to 5-cup pudding basin

Pot large enough to hold the basin when covered

Parchment paper

1. MAKE THE BATTER: Combine the flour, baking soda, baking powder, and salt in a small bowl.

2. Place the butter and the sugar in a large bowl and whisk until the sugar has mostly dissolved. Add the egg and the milk and whisk until the mixture is very smooth and creamy, about 5 minutes. Add the flour mixture in small batches to the egg mixture, whisking constantly. Once the last batch of flour has been whisked in, fold in the marmalade and apricots.

3. ASSEMBLE AND STEAM THE DUMPLING: *Before assembling the pudding, review the Pudding Basin Set-Up.*

4. Soak the muslin and the string under running water. Wring them out and set aside.

5. Place the empty pudding basin in the pot. Pour water into the space between the basin and the pot until it comes three-quarters of the way up the sides of the basin. Remove the basin and bring the water to a boil over high heat. Reduce the heat to low for a gentle simmer.

6. Meanwhile, make sure the interior of the basin is dry before rubbing it with butter and coating it with sugar. Scoop the batter into the basin and wiggle it gently to level it off. Cut out a round of parchment paper and place it on top of the batter. Cover the basin with the damp muslin and secure it tightly with the string. Tie the opposite corners of the muslin into handles over the top of the pudding.

7. Using tongs or a wooden spoon, push a folded cloth, such as a standard white cotton napkin, into the simmering water and arrange it to lie flat on the bottom of the pot. Using the cloth handle, carefully lower the basin into the pot, cover, and simmer for at least 2 hours or up to 4 hours for a pudding that's even richer in flavor and texture. Check the water level every 30 minutes and replenish with boiling water as needed.

8. Remove the pot from the heat. Using a pot holder to grasp the cloth handle, carefully remove the basin from the pot, put it on a folded kitchen towel, and allow the pudding to cool for 5 minutes. Remove the string, cloth, and paper. Unmold by inverting it onto a plate. Slice and serve with some honey or more of the orange marmalade. The pudding can be kept refrigerated for up to 3 days. Reheat in a steamer pot or use the Steamer Plate Setup (page 37).

Sticky Toffee Pudding

(England)

SERVES 4 TO 6 (MAKES 1 DUMPLING)

Sticky toffee pudding is a traditional sponge pudding enriched by a date paste mixed throughout the batter. The dates add stickiness, moisture, and color, as well as flavors similar to caramel, chocolate, and molasses. You can use any kind of date, but if you are using dates that are more fibrous than the super-soft medjool, add one more teaspoon of water to the paste. You can turn this into a fig pudding by simply substituting figs for the dates.

This dumpling is made using the Pudding Basin Setup (page 43).

For the Date Paste

1/3 cup finely chopped medjool dates

1/3 cup warm water

1/2 teaspoon baking soda

For the Sauce

1/2 cup heavy cream

1/2 cup light muscovado or other unrefined sugar (see page 20)

2 tablespoons unsalted butter, cut into chunks

For the Batter

1 cup unbleached all-purpose flour

1 teaspoon baking powder

Pinch of salt

6 tablespoons (3/4 stick) unsalted butter, at room temperature

1/2 cup sugar

2 large eggs, plus 2 large egg yolks, at room temperature

1/4 teaspoon vanilla extract

For Cooking

Unsalted butter and sugar to coat the pudding basin

Equipment

24-inch square of muslin

35-inch length of kitchen string

4- to 5-cup pudding basin

Pot large enough to hold the basin when covered

Parchment paper

1. PREPARE THE DATE PASTE: Mix the dates, warm water, and baking soda in a small bowl and set aside.

2. MAKE THE SAUCE: Pour the cream into a small saucepan and stir in the muscovado sugar. Add the 2 tablespoons of butter and bring to a gentle simmer over low heat. Stir continuously until the sauce turns a golden brown, 8 to 10 minutes. Remove from the heat, cover, and keep warm.

3. MAKE THE BATTER: Combine the flour, baking powder, and salt in a small bowl.

4. Place the 6 tablespoons butter and the sugar in a large bowl and whisk until most of the sugar has dissolved. Whisk in the eggs and the egg yolks one at a time. Continue whipping until the mixture is light and airy, about 5 minutes. Mix in the vanilla extract. Add the flour mixture in small batches to the egg mixture, whisking constantly. Once the last batch of flour mixture has been whisked in, fold in the date mixture.

5. ASSEMBLE AND STEAM THE DUMPLING: *Before assembling the pudding, review the Pudding Basin Setup.*

6. Soak the muslin and the string under running water. Wring them out and set aside. Have ready the batter and the warm sauce.

7. Place the empty pudding basin in the pot. Pour water into the space between the basin and the pot until it comes three-quarters of the way up the sides of the basin. Remove the basin and bring the water to a boil over high heat. Reduce the heat to low for a gentle simmer.

8. Meanwhile, make sure the interior of the basin is dry before rubbing it with butter and coating it with sugar. Pour about half of the sauce into the basin, generously coating the bottom. Scoop the batter into the basin and wiggle it gently to level it off. Cut out a round of parchment paper and place it on top of the batter. Cover the basin with the damp muslin and secure it tightly with the string. Tie the opposite corners of the muslin into handles over the top of the pudding.

9. Using tongs or a wooden spoon, push a folded cloth, such as a standard white cotton napkin, into the simmering water and arrange it to lie flat on the bottom of the pot. Using the cloth handle, carefully lower the basin into the pot, cover, and simmer for at least $1^1/2$ hours, or up to $2^1/2$ hours for a pudding that's even richer in flavor and texture. Check the water level every 30 minutes and replenish with boiling water as needed.

10. Remove the pot from the heat. Using a pot holder to grasp the cloth handle, carefully remove the basin from the pot, put it on a folded kitchen towel, and allow the pudding to cool for 5 minutes. Remove the string, cloth, and paper. Carefully unmold by inverting it onto a plate. Reheat the rest of the sauce over medium heat, whisking it back together if it has separated. Slice the pudding and serve with a drizzle of the warm sauce. The pudding can be refrigerated for up to 3 days. Reheat in a steamer pot or use the Steamer Plate Setup (page 37).

Potato Dumplings with Crouton Centers

Kartoffelklösse (Germany)

SERVES 4 (MAKES 16 DUMPLINGS)

The crouton centers of these potato dumplings—a buttery and chewy surprise to bite into—lessen the cooking time of these generously sized dumplings. Dusting the uncooked dumplings in flour forms a skin that helps to hold them together as you slide them into the simmering water. These dumplings can be served as a simple side with butter, or more ambitiously, with a roasted meat dish such as sauerbraten.

For the Dough

 2 medium baking potatoes, such as russet

½ teaspoon salt

½ teaspoon freshly grated nutmeg

¾ cup unbleached all-purpose flour, plus some extra for dusting

 1 large egg yolk

 1 tablespoon finely chopped fresh flat-leaf parsley leaves

 3 strips bacon, cooked crisp and crumbled (optional)

For the Bread Cube Center

 1 tablespoon unsalted butter

Sixteen ½-inch crustless white bread cubes (see page 6)

1. MAKE THE DOUGH: Place the potatoes in a small pot, pour in enough water to cover them, and bring to a boil over high heat. Cover, reduce the heat to medium, and simmer until fork-tender, about 30 minutes. Drain and place the potatoes on a folded kitchen towel. Once they are cool enough to handle, peel off their skins and put the flesh into a large bowl. Mash until mostly smooth.

2. Add the salt, nutmeg, and ½ cup of the flour to the potato, keeping the remaining ¼ cup of flour handy. Toss with your fingers until well mixed. Add the egg yolk, parsley, and bacon and work the mixture into a soft dough, about 2 minutes. This dough needs to be firm enough to hold its shape when rolled into balls. If it is too soft or sticky, work in some of the remaining flour, a little at a time.

3. PREPARE THE BREAD CUBES: Line a plate with paper towels.

4. Melt the butter in a large skillet over medium heat. Add the bread cubes and toss and stir continuously until lightly browned, 3 to 4 minutes. Spread the bread cubes out on the prepared plate to cool.

5. MAKE AND COOK THE DUMPLINGS: Line a tray with a kitchen towel and sprinkle with a little flour. Have ready the dough and the bread cubes.

6. Pinch off a small piece of dough and roll it into a ball about $1^1/_2$ inches around. Sprinkle with flour if it gets sticky. Press a hole halfway into the dough ball with your thumb. Push a bread cube into the hole and close by pushing the edges of the dough over the bread cube until it is surrounded, pushing out any air. Reroll into a ball, dust with flour, and place on the prepared tray. Repeat with the remaining dough and bread cubes.

7. Fill a large pot halfway with salted water and bring to a boil over high heat. Reduce the heat to medium for a steady simmer.

8. Carefully drop the dumplings, one by one, into the simmering water. Stir carefully to prevent sticking. Cook until all of them are floating, about 3 minutes, then cook for 5 minutes longer. Serve with your favorite stew or sauce.

Country Cabbage Soup with Large Cornmeal Dumplings

Soupe aux Miques et aux Choux (France)

SERVES 4 (MAKES 4 DUMPLINGS)

These large cornmeal dumplings create a pleasing balance of textures in this chunky cabbage soup. Standard cornmeal can be too coarse and tough for this dumpling, while corn flour is too fine and will create a dumpling that is much too dense. Standard or stone-ground cornmeal can be used if you first grind it into a finer meal with a few pulses in a spice grinder.

For the Soup

1 pound unsmoked country ham, rinsed and cut into 4 equal pieces

½ small bunch fresh flat-leaf parsley

8 to 10 fresh thyme sprigs

2 to 3 bay leaves

1 large yellow onion, chopped coarse

4 large carrots, cut into 1-inch rounds

5 celery ribs, cut into 1-inch pieces

1 small Savoy or green cabbage, quartered, cored, and cut into 1-inch strips

3 tablespoons unsalted butter, cut into chunks

3 tablespoons unbleached all-purpose flour

For the Dumplings

1½ cups unbleached all-purpose flour

1½ cups stone-ground white cornmeal, ground very fine in a clean spice or coffee grinder

1 teaspoon salt

2 tablespoons rendered duck fat or other animal fat like nonhydrogenated lard or chicken fat

Equipment

Clean spice or coffee grinder

Kitchen string for tying the herbs

Colander lined with 4 to 6 layers of cheesecloth

1. MAKE THE SOUP: Place the ham and 3 quarts water in a large pot and bring to a boil over high heat. Cover, reduce the heat to low, and simmer for 1 hour. Skim the froth off the surface with a spoon.

2. Once the broth has simmered for 1 hour, tie the parsley, thyme, and bay leaves in a tight bundle. Add the herb bundle, the onion, carrots, and celery. Cover and simmer for 30 minutes longer. (You can also make the soup in advance and keep it refrigerated in a tightly sealed container for up to 3 days.)

3. Once the celery and carrots have simmered for 30 minutes, remove them and some of the onion from the broth using a slotted spoon, divide evenly between two bowls, and set aside. Discard the herb bundle. Strain the broth into a large bowl through a cheesecloth-lined colander. Return the soup to the pot. Place over very, very low heat, keeping it hot while you make and cook the dumplings.

4. MAKE AND COOK THE DUMPLINGS: Fill another large pot halfway with water and bring to a boil over high heat.

5. Place 1¹/₄ cups of the flour in a large bowl and keep the remaining ¹/₄ cup handy. Mix in the cornmeal and the salt. Add the duck fat and use your fingers to rub it evenly throughout the flour mixture until it resembles a coarse, damp meal.

6. Pour 1 cup water into the flour mixture and mix until all the liquid has been absorbed. Work the dough with your hands into one manageable ball. The dough should be firm and slightly dry. If the dough is sticky, work in some of the remaining flour, a little at a time. Knead the dough in the bowl for 1 to 2 minutes. Cut the dough into 4 equal pieces and roll each piece into a ball.

7. Add all 4 dumplings to the boiling water. These dumplings will sink at first but will float to the surface as they cook. Cover, reduce the heat to medium, and simmer for 15 minutes. Turn the dumplings over, cover, and cook for 15 minutes longer. Once you turn the dumplings over, add the cabbage to the broth, cover, raise the heat to medium, and simmer for 15 minutes.

8. FINISH THE SOUP: Meanwhile, melt the butter in a large skillet over medium heat. Add 1 bowl of the vegetables, stir occasionally, and cook for 3 to 5 minutes. Sprinkle the flour across the vegetables and continue stirring and cooking for about 3 minutes. Immediately spoon the sautéed vegetables back into the broth. The second bowl of vegetables can be served as a side or saved for another meal.

9. Once the dumplings have finished cooking, use a slotted spoon to immediately move them form their cooking liquid to the soup. Cover, cook for 10 minutes longer over medium heat, and serve.

Philadelphia Pepperpot Soup with Dumplings

(United States)

SERVES 4 TO 6 (MAKES ABOUT 30 DUMPLINGS)

Philadelphia pepperpot soup is a traditional tripe soup that's more often than not filled with soft dumplings that add even more character to the "squidgy" texture of the tripe. Most tripe sold has already been blanched and often bleached. If you want a more intense or natural tripe soup, you can buy fresh tripe and blanch it yourself for a short time as it is done here. Like most soups, this one improves after a day of resting in the refrigerator. If making the soup in advance, add the dumplings after the soup has been reheated.

For the Soup

- 1½ pounds honeycomb or pocket beef tripe, well rinsed and cut into 3 or 4 equal pieces
- 2 tablespoons grapeseed or other neutral oil
- 2 leeks, white and light green parts only, rinsed clean and chopped fine
- 1 large green bell pepper, cored and cut into ½-inch squares
- 2 tablespoons unbleached all-purpose flour
- 1 recipe (2 quarts) Beef Broth with American Flavors (page 397)
- 1 teaspoon salt
- ¼ teaspoon freshly ground black pepper
- 1 large boiling potato, such as Yukon Gold, peeled and cut into ½-inch cubes
- 2 tablespoons finely chopped fresh marjoram leaves or 2 teaspoons dried
- ¼ cup heavy cream (optional)

For the Dumplings

- 1¼ cups unbleached all-purpose flour, plus some extra for dusting
- ½ teaspoon baking powder
- 1 teaspoon salt
- 2 tablespoons cold unsalted butter, cut into bits
- ½ cup cold water

1. MAKE THE SOUP 3 HOURS IN ADVANCE: Place the tripe in a small pot, cover with water by about 2 inches, and bring to a boil over high heat. Cover, reduce the heat to low, and simmer for 1 hour. Drain and rinse the tripe under cold running water until cool enough to handle. Cut the tripe into ½-inch squares and set aside. The tripe will be squishy but firm enough to cut.

2. Heat the oil in a large pot over medium heat. Add the leeks and the green pepper and cook, stirring frequently, until the leeks are lightly browned, about 5 minutes. Mix in the 2 tablespoons flour and cook for 2 minutes longer.

3. Pour in the beef broth and scrape up any sticky bits from the bottom of the pot with a wooden spoon. Add the tripe, salt, and pepper. Cover and simmer for 2 hours. (You can also make the soup in advance and keep it refrigerated in a tightly sealed container for up to 3 days.)

4. MAKE THE DOUGH: While the soup simmers, place 1 cup of the flour in a medium bowl and keep the remaining ¼ cup handy. Add the baking powder and the salt and mix well.

Add the butter to the flour mixture and work them together with a pastry cutter or 2 butter knives until the mixture looks like a damp, coarse meal. Pour in the cold water and mix until all the water has been absorbed. Work the dough with your hands into one manageable ball. If the dough is wet and sticky, work in some of the remaining flour, a little at a time, until it no longer sticks to your fingers.

5. Place the dough on a floured surface and knead for 3 to 4 minutes. The dough will be somewhat firm and elastic. Return the dough to the bowl, cover, and refrigerate for 30 minutes.

6. MAKE AND COOK THE DUMPLINGS: Shortly before the soup has finished cooking, line a tray with a kitchen towel and sprinkle with a little flour.

7. Pinch off a small piece of dough and roll it into a ball about 1 inch around. Dust with a little flour and place it on the prepared tray. Repeat with the remaining dough. Keep the dumplings in a single layer on the tray. Cover and refrigerate until it is time to add the dumplings.

8. Once the soup has cooked for 2 hours, add the potatoes and marjoram, cover, and cook for 15 minutes. Drop the dumplings, a few at a time, into the soup and stir gently. Cover and simmer for 10 minutes longer. Remove the pot from the heat, stir in the cream, if desired, and serve.

Large Beef- and Spinach-Filled Dumplings in a Beef Broth

Maultaschen (Germany)

SERVES 4 TO 6 (MAKES ABOUT 24 DUMPLINGS)

The meat and vegetable filling in these large soup dumplings has a surprisingly creamy consistency created by the addition of soaked bread. They are rewarding to make, comforting to eat, and spectacular to serve.

For the Dough

2½ cups unbleached all-purpose flour, plus some extra for dusting

3 large eggs, beaten

1 teaspoon grapeseed or other neutral oil

For the Filling

3 cups ½-inch crustless white bread cubes (see page 6)

⅓ cup milk or water

¼ cup finely chopped bacon or a neutral oil, such as grapeseed

1 small yellow onion, chopped fine

1 garlic clove, chopped fine

½ pound freshly ground beef

½ teaspoon freshly grated nutmeg

1 small bunch spinach, stemmed, hand-wilted (see page 37), and chopped fine, or ½ cup frozen spinach, thawed and chopped fine

¼ cup finely chopped fresh flat-leaf parsley

1 large egg yolk

1 teaspoon salt

For the Broth*

1 recipe (2 quarts) Beef Broth with German Flavors (page 397)

1 teaspoon salt

Equipment

3-inch round cookie cutter

1. MAKE THE DOUGH: Place 2¼ cups of the flour in a large bowl and keep the remaining ¼ cup handy. Add the eggs, oil, and 1 tablespoon water and mix until all the liquid has been absorbed. Work the dough with your hands into one manageable ball. If the dough is wet and sticky, work in some of the remaining flour, a little at a time, until it no longer sticks to your fingers.

2. Place the dough on a floured surface and knead for 4 to 5 minutes. The dough will be somewhat firm. Return the dough ball to the bowl, cover, and let it rest for at least 30 minutes but no more than 1 hour.

---

*These amounts are for a full recipe. If you plan on freezing and storing some of the dumplings, reduce the amounts in proportion to the number you are serving.

3. MAKE THE FILLING: Place the bread cubes in a large bowl and pour in the milk. Work and squish the mixture until all the bread cubes become pulpy bits. Pick up handfuls of the mixture, squeeze out any excess milk into a small bowl, and place the bread pulp in another bowl. Discard the excess milk and set the bread pulp aside.

4. Place the bacon in a large skillet over medium heat. Once enough bacon fat has melted to coat the pan, about 3 minutes, raise the heat to high and add the onion. Stir frequently until the bacon is lightly browned, about 5 minutes. Mix in the garlic and beef, breaking up clumps as the meat begins to brown. Stir until the beef is golden brown, about 3 minutes. Mix in the nutmeg and remove from the heat, letting the mixture cool slightly in the pan. Scoop it into a food processor, add the spinach, and pulse until the beef is finely minced, scraping down the sides as you go. Scoop it into a large bowl, then mix in the bread pulp, parsley, egg yolk, and salt. Cover and refrigerate for 30 to 60 minutes before assembling the dumplings.

5. ASSEMBLE THE DUMPLINGS: Line a tray with a kitchen towel and sprinkle with a little flour. Have ready the dough and the filling.

6. Knead the dough once or twice on a floured surface, divide it into 4 equal pieces, and set 3 of them aside under a kitchen towel. Shape the remaining piece into a ball, then roll it out until it's ¹/₁₆ inch thick. (For tips on how to roll dough out thin, see page 35.) Sprinkle with flour if it gets sticky. Let the rolled-out dough relax for a couple of minutes before cutting out rounds.

7. Using the cookie cutter, cut out as many rounds as you can, usually 10 to 12. Scraps cannot be reused because dough rolled out this thin is too dry to recombine.

8. Set apart 4 to 6 dough rounds and brush half of them with a little water to make them sticky enough to seal. Place a rounded tablespoon of filling in the center of each dampened round. Top each spoonful of filling with an unbrushed round, creating little sandwiches. Pinch the edges of the rounds together, pushing out any air, and seal. Dab a little water along the edges, if needed, for a better seal. If desired, trim or crimp the edges for a more tailored look. Place the assembled dumplings in a single layer on the prepared tray and keep them covered with a kitchen towel while you work. Once you have assembled the first batch of dumplings, continue with the remaining dough and filling.

9. Cover the tray of assembled dumplings and place in the refrigerator for 30 to 60 minutes before cooking. Chilling them helps to set the dough, making the dumplings firm and toothsome when cooked instead of puffy and soft. Set aside the number of dumplings that you would like to cook and keep the rest frozen for up to 6 months (see page 36).

10. COOK THE DUMPLINGS: Pour the broth into a medium pot and bring to a boil over high heat. Stir in the salt and reduce the heat to medium for a steady simmer.

11. Gently drop half of the dumplings, one by one, into the broth. Stir carefully to prevent sticking. Cook until all of them are floating, 2 to 3 minutes, then cook for 3 minutes longer. (If cooking frozen *maultaschen,* add them directly to the simmering broth and increase the cooking time by 2 minutes. Do not allow the *maultaschen* to thaw before cooking.)

12. Using a slotted spoon, remove the *maultaschen* and lay them on a plate and drizzle them with a couple of spoonfuls of the broth to prevent sticking. Cook the remaining *maultaschen.* Once the second batch has finished cooking, return the first batch to the broth, stir to warm through, and serve.

Dumplings Stuffed with Pears, Figs, and Chocolate

Cialzons alla Frutta (Italy)

SERVES 4 TO 5 (MAKES ABOUT 20 DUMPLINGS)

Cialzons are large Italian dumplings stuffed with an elaborate and impressive combination of ingredients that can include fresh and dried fruits, meats, herbs, chocolate, and cheese. Some recipes are quite savory, while others, like this one, are on the sweeter side. If you can't get dried pears, you can use dried apples or prunes instead.

These dumplings are made using the Half-Moon Fold (page 47).

For the Filling

⅓ cup red wine

4 all-natural dried golden figs, cut into raisin-sized bits

2 all-natural dried pear halves, cut into raisin-sized bits

⅓ cup raisins

⅓ cup whole-milk ricotta, drained (see page 23) for 4 to 8 hours

⅛ teaspoon ground cinnamon

⅛ teaspoon freshly grated nutmeg

1 tablespoon sugar

Pinch of salt

2 tablespoons finely chopped fresh flat-leaf parsley leaves or mint leaves

2 tablespoons finely grated dark chocolate

For the Dough

1 recipe *Ravioli di Pesce* (page 209) dough, preferably made while the filling is being chilled but no more than 1 hour in advance

Unbleached all-purpose flour for dusting

For the Sauce*

4 tablespoons (½ stick) unsalted butter, cut into chunks

Equipment

5-inch round cookie cutter

Large, wide bowl to hold the dumplings cooked in batches

1. MAKE THE FILLING: Pour the wine into a small saucepan and bring to a boil over high heat. Remove from the heat and stir in the figs, pears, and raisins. Let the fruit soak for 15 minutes, drain, place in a bowl, and set aside.

2. Hold a fine-mesh sieve over a large bowl and push the ricotta through 2 or 3 times with a rubber spatula. Mix in the soaked and drained fruit and the rest of the filling ingredients. Cover and refrigerate for 30 to 60 minutes before assembling the dumplings.

3. ASSEMBLE THE DUMPLINGS: *Before assembling the* cialzons, *review the Half-Moon Fold.*

---

* This is for a full recipe. If you plan on freezing and storing some of the dumplings, reduce the amount in proportion to the number you are serving.

4. Line a tray with a kitchen towel and sprinkle with a little flour. Have ready the dough and the filling.

5. Knead the dough once or twice on a floured surface, divide it into 4 equal pieces, and set 3 of them aside under a kitchen towel. Shape the remaining piece into a ball, then roll it out until it's $1/16$ inch thick. (For tips on how to roll dough out thin, see page 35.) Sprinkle with flour if it gets sticky. Let the rolled out dough relax for a couple of minutes before cutting out rounds.

6. Using the cookie cutter, cut out as many rounds as you can, usually 4 to 5. Scraps cannot be reused because dough rolled out this thin is too dry to recombine.

7. Lay flat 1 to 5 dough rounds. Brush each round with a very thin coating of water to make them sticky enough to seal. Center a rounded tablespoon of filling on top of each round, fold each neatly in half, pushing out any air, and pinch to seal. Dab a little water along the edges, if needed, for a better seal. Place the assembled dumplings in a single layer on the prepared tray and keep them covered with a kitchen towel while you work. Once you have assembled the first batch of dumplings, continue with the remaining dough and filling.

8. Cover the tray of assembled dumplings and place in the refrigerator for 30 to 60 minutes before cooking. Chilling them helps to set the dough, making the dumplings firm and toothsome when cooked instead of puffy and soft. Set aside the number of dumplings that you would like to cook and keep the rest frozen for up to 6 months (see page 36).

9. COOK THE DUMPLINGS: Fill a large pot halfway with salted water and bring it to a boil over high heat. Reduce the heat to medium for a steady simmer. Gently drop half of the dumplings, one by one, into the water. Stir carefully to prevent sticking. Cook until all of them are floating, 3 to 4 minutes, then cook for 3 minutes longer. (If cooking frozen *cialzons*, add them directly to the simmering water and increase the cooking time by 2 minutes. Do not allow the *cialzons* to thaw before cooking.)

10. Remove the *cialzons* with a slotted spoon, place them in the large bowl, and drizzle them with a ladle of the cooking liquid to prevent sticking. Cook the remaining *cialzons* and place them in the bowl with another ladle of the cooking liquid.

11. MAKE THE SAUCE AND FINISH THE DUMPLINGS: Melt the butter slowly in a large skillet over low heat without browning. Once the butter has melted completely, raise the heat to medium and cook until the butter turns a dark caramel brown, about 3 minutes, swirling the butter around occasionally. Drain the *cialzons,* turn them into the butter, toss gently to coat and warm through, about 1 minute, and serve.

Pumpkin and Lentil Ravioli with Browned Butter and Rosemary

Ravioli di Zucca e Lenticchie (Italy)

SERVES 4 (MAKES ABOUT 60 DUMPLINGS)

We use butternut squash in this recipe, but any hard, sweet orange-fleshed squash will do without any loss of flavor or texture. This filling may look quite dry in the bowl, but it cooks up soft and succulent inside the dumplings. The crushed amaretti cookies add more of a nutty flavor than a sugary touch, but you can reduce the number of cookies if you like.

These dumplings are made using the Half-Moon Fold (page 47).

For the Filling

1 small butternut squash, split lengthwise with the seeds scooped out (about 2 pounds)

¼ cup dried green lentils, rinsed

7 small amaretti cookies, coarsely crushed

½ cup freshly grated Parmesan cheese

⅛ teaspoon ground cinnamon

⅛ teaspoon freshly grated nutmeg

½ teaspoon salt

¼ teaspoon freshly ground black pepper

⅔ cup coarse dry crustless white bread crumbs (see page 6)

For the Dough

1 recipe *Ravioli di Pesce* (page 209) dough, preferably made while the filling is being chilled but no more than 1 hour in advance

Unbleached all-purpose flour for dusting

For the Sauce*

4 tablespoons (½ stick) unsalted butter, cut into chunks

1 fresh rosemary sprig

1 garlic clove, chopped very fine

Salt and freshly ground black pepper to taste

Equipment

2½-inch round cookie cutter

Large, wide bowl to hold the dumplings cooked in batches

1. MAKE THE FILLING: Preheat the oven to 375°F.

2. Roast the butternut squash, flesh side down, on a lightly oiled baking sheet until soft, about 30 minutes.

---

* These amounts are for a full recipe. If you plan on freezing and storing some of the dumplings, reduce the amounts in proportion to the number you are serving.

3. Meanwhile, fill a small saucepan halfway with water and bring to a boil over high heat. Add the lentils, cover, reduce the heat to low, and simmer until tender, about 30 minutes. Drain, mash lightly with a fork while still in the pot, and set aside.

4. Remove the squash from the oven and set it aside until it's cool enough to handle. Scoop the flesh out of the skin, place it in a medium bowl, and mash until mostly smooth.

5. Move the squash onto a kitchen towel. Bring together the ends of the cloth and twist to squeeze out as much liquid as you can. The amount of liquid you are squeezing out won't be much and may simply be absorbed by the cloth. Put the squash back into the bowl. Mix in the amaretti, Parmesan, cinnamon, nutmeg, salt, and pepper. Add the lentils and the bread crumbs and fold just a few times to make a purposely uneven mixture. Cover and refrigerate for 30 to 60 minutes before assembling the dumplings.

6. ASSEMBLE THE DUMPLINGS: *Before assembling the ravioli, review the Half-Moon Fold.*

7. Line a tray with a kitchen towel and sprinkle with a little flour. Also have ready the dough and the filling.

8. Knead the dough once or twice on a floured surface, divide it into 4 equal pieces, and set 3 of them aside under a kitchen towel. Shape the remaining piece into a ball, then roll it out until it's $1/16$ inch thick. (For tips on how to roll dough out thin, see page 35.) Sprinkle with flour if it gets sticky. Let the rolled-out dough relax for a couple of minutes before cutting out rounds.

9. Using the cookie cutter, cut out as many rounds as you can, usually 12 to 15. Scraps cannot be reused because dough rolled out this thin is too dry to recombine.

10. Lay flat 1 to 5 dough rounds. Brush each round with a very thin coating of water to make them sticky enough to seal. Center a rounded teaspoon of filling on top of each round, fold each neatly in half, pushing out any air, and pinch to seal. Dab a little water along the edges, if needed, for a better seal. Place the assembled dumplings in a single layer on the prepared tray and keep them covered with a kitchen towel while you work. Once you have assembled the first batch of dumplings, continue with the remaining dough and filling.

11. Cover the tray of assembled dumplings and place in the refrigerator for 30 to 60 minutes before cooking. Chilling them helps to set the dough, making the dumplings firm and toothsome when cooked instead of puffy and soft. Set aside the number of dumplings that you would like to cook and keep the rest frozen for up to 6 months (see page 36).

12. COOK THE DUMPLINGS: Fill a large pot halfway with salted water and bring to a boil over high heat. Reduce the heat to medium for a steady simmer.

13. Gently drop half of the dumplings, a few at a time, into the simmering water. Stir carefully to prevent sticking. Cook until all of them are floating, 2 to 3 minutes, then cook for 3 minutes longer. (If cooking frozen ravioli, add them directly to the simmering water and increase the cooking time by 1 minute. Do not allow the ravioli to thaw before cooking.)

14. Using a slotted spoon, remove the dumplings, place them in the large bowl, and drizzle with a ladle of the cooking liquid to prevent sticking. Cook the remaining dumplings and place them in the bowl with another ladle of the cooking liquid.

15. **MAKE THE SAUCE AND FINISH THE DUMPLINGS:** Melt the butter in a small saucepan over low heat. Once the butter has melted completely, raise the heat to medium and add the rosemary and garlic. Cook until the butter and garlic turn a deep chestnut brown, about 3 minutes, then discard the rosemary.

16. Drain the ravioli, turn them into the butter, and toss gently to coat and warm through, about 1 minute. Sprinkle with salt and pepper and serve.

"Little Ear" Dumplings Stuffed with Mushrooms in a Beet Soup

Borshch z Vushka (Russia)

SERVES 4 TO 6 (MAKES ABOUT 64 DUMPLINGS)

These savory, thin-skinned dumplings are very tiny, but they are served in big numbers per portion (12 to 20) and are well worth the care and patience required to prepare them. Few soup recipes call for such a generous serving of filled dumplings, which makes this soup a natural choice for celebrations. The combination of fresh and dried mushrooms gives the filling both intensity and lightness. The dumplings can be cooked in water and then added to the soup or cooked directly in the soup, giving it a slight starchy cloudiness and a more cohesive flavor.

These dumplings are made using the Belly-Button Fold (page 49).

For the Soup*

2½ pounds meaty beef bones, such as rib, shank, or neck

1 pound beef brisket, cut into 4 equal pieces

2 bay leaves

2 teaspoons salt

1 teaspoon black peppercorns

3 large carrots, cut into 1-inch rounds

2 large parsnips, peeled and cut into 1-inch rounds

1 large beet, peeled and cut into 1-inch pieces

1 small green cabbage, cored and cut into 1½-inch chunks

3 plum tomatoes, peeled, seeded (see page 21), and crushed, or 3 canned plum tomatoes, drained and crushed (about ¾ cup)

For the Filling

½ ounce dried mushrooms, preferably porcini, soaked in 1 cup hot water for 30 minutes

3 tablespoons grapeseed or other neutral oil

1 small yellow onion, chopped very fine

5 ounces fresh mushrooms, preferably porcini, chopped very fine

¾ teaspoon salt

¼ teaspoon freshly ground black pepper

For the Dough

1 recipe *Shao Mai* (page 242) dough, preferably made while the soup is simmering but no more than 1 hour in advance

Unbleached all-purpose flour for dusting

Equipment

Colander lined with 4 to 6 layers of cheesecloth

Large, wide bowl to hold the dumplings cooked in batches

1. MAKE THE SOUP 2 HOURS IN ADVANCE: Place the beef bones, brisket, bay leaves, 2 teaspoons salt, and peppercorns in a large pot. Pour in 10 cups water and bring to a boil over

---

*These amounts are for a full recipe. If you plan on freezing and storing some of the dumplings, reduce the amounts in proportion to the number you are serving.

high heat. Cover, reduce the heat to low, and simmer for $1^1/_2$ hours. Skim the froth off the surface with a spoon.

2. Remove the pot from the heat. Remove the bones and the brisket with a slotted spoon or tongs and place them in a bowl to cool. Strain the broth into a medium pot through the cheesecloth-lined colander and skim off any remaining fat. Return the broth to a simmer over medium heat, stir in the carrots, parsnips, and beet, cover, and cook for 30 minutes.

3. While the vegetables are cooking, tear the brisket into bite-sized pieces and place them back in the bowl. Pull any meat off the bones, discard the bones, and add the meaty bits back to the bowl. Once the vegetables have finished cooking, stir in the meat, cabbage, and tomatoes. Cover and simmer for 15 minutes longer. Remove from the heat and set aside. (You can also make the soup in advance and keep it refrigerated in a tightly sealed container for up to 3 days. Bring the soup to a simmer before adding the dumplings.)

4. MAKE THE FILLING: Fish out the soaked mushrooms with your fingers, squeezing the excess liquid back into the bowl. Set the liquid aside and finely chop the mushrooms. Strain and reserve all the soaking liquid.

5. Heat the oil in a large skillet over medium heat. Add the onion and cook, stirring frequently, until soft, about 4 minutes. Add the soaked mushrooms, the fresh mushrooms, the $^3/_4$ teaspoon salt, and the ground pepper and stir until the mushrooms are golden brown, about 4 minutes. Pour in the reserved soaking liquid from the mushrooms. Cook, stirring continuously, until most of the liquid has cooked off, about 2 minutes. Scoop the mushroom mixture into a bowl and set aside to cool.

6. ASSEMBLE THE DUMPLINGS: *Before assembling the* vushka, *review the Belly-Button Fold, only you will be using dough squares instead of the rounds shown in the illustrations.*

7. Line a tray with a kitchen towel and sprinkle with a little flour. Have ready the dough and the filling.

8. Knead the dough once or twice on a floured surface, divide it into 4 equal pieces, and set 3 of them aside under a kitchen towel. Shape the remaining piece into a blunt log, then roll it out into an 8-inch square. This dough should not be thicker than $^1/_{16}$ inch, even thinner would be ideal. (For tips on how to roll dough out thin, see page 35.) Take your time and dust with flour if it gets sticky. Let the rolled-out dough relax for a couple of minutes.

9. Trim the edges to create a cleaner square shape, cut the dough into 2-inch strips, then cut across the strips every 2 inches to form 16 squares. Place the squares in a single layer on the prepared tray. Keep the squares covered with a kitchen towel as you work. Scraps cannot be reused because dough rolled out this thin is too dry to recombine.

10. Lay flat 1 to 5 dough squares. Brush each square with a very thin coating of water to make it sticky enough to seal. Place a rounded teaspoon of filling in the center of each square, fold each diagonally into a triangle, pushing out any air, and pinch to seal. Pick up one of the triangles and join and pinch the ends together behind the "belly" of the dumpling. Dab a little water on the ends, if needed, for a better seal. Repeat with the remaining triangles. Place the assembled dumplings in a single layer on the prepared tray and keep them covered with a kitchen towel while you work. Once you have assembled the first batch of dumplings, continue with the remaining dough and filling.

11. Cover and place the tray of assembled dumplings in the refrigerator for 30 to 60 minutes before cooking. Chilling them helps to set the dough, making the dumplings firm and toothsome when cooked instead of puffy and soft. Set aside the number of dumplings that you would like to cook and keep the rest frozen for up to 6 months (see page 36).

12. COOK THE DUMPLINGS: Fill a large pot three-quarters of the way full with salted water and bring to a boil over high heat. If cooking the *vushka* in the soup, bring the soup to a steady simmer over medium heat.

13. Gently drop a few dozen *vushka*, a few at a time, into the simmering water. Stir carefully to prevent sticking. Cook until all of them are floating, 2 to 3 minutes, then cook for 3 minutes longer. (If cooking frozen *vushka*, add them directly to the simmering water and increase the cooking time by 1 minute. Do not allow the *vushka* to thaw before cooking.)

14. Using a slotted spoon, remove the dumplings, place them in the large bowl, and drizzle with a ladle of the cooking liquid to prevent sticking. Cook the remaining dumplings and place them in the bowl with another ladle of the cooking liquid.

15. Bring the soup to a simmer over medium heat. Drain all the *vushka* and stir them into the soup. Cook for 1 minute to warm through and serve.

December

ROOT VEGETABLE BREAD DUMPLINGS
Zöldséggombóc (Hungary) 365

CLOOTIE DUMPLING
(Scotland) 367

STARCHY COCONUT STEW WITH SLIPPERY RICE BALLS
Guinataan at Bilo-Bilo (Philippines) 369

GUAVA DUFF
(Bahamas) 371

POTATO DUMPLINGS WITH CABBAGE LAYERS
Káposztás Gombóc (Hungary) 374

JOHN IN THE SACK
Jan in de Zak (Holland) 376

CLASSIC CHRISTMAS PUDDING
(England) 378

CHOCOLATE TAMALES
Tamales de Chocolate (Mexico) 380

SIBERIAN MEAT DUMPLINGS
Pelmeni (Russia) 382

CHESTNUT RAVIOLI WITH SAGE BUTTER SAUCE
Ravioli di Castagne (Italy) 384

CHICKEN-FILLED DUMPLINGS IN AN ESCAROLE SOUP
Cappelletti in Brodo (Italy) 387

DUMPLINGS STUFFED WITH "STEWED" BREAD CRUMBS
Anolini di Parma (Italy) 390

Root Vegetable Bread Dumplings

Zöldséggombóc (Hungary)

SERVES 4 TO 6 (MAKES ABOUT 30 DUMPLINGS)

This is a good winter dumpling that is chock full of winter vegetables, although they can be made year-round with other seasonally available vegetables. Serve these with your favorite meat, bean, or mushroom dish any time you have a good amount of day-old bread just begging to be put to good use.

For the Vegetable Mixture

2 tablespoons unsalted butter, cut into chunks

½ small yellow onion, chopped fine

1 medium carrot, cut into ¼-inch cubes

1 large parsnip, peeled and cut into ¼-inch cubes

1 small turnip or kohlrabi, peeled and cut into ¼-inch cubes

4 large cremini mushrooms, chopped fine

1 teaspoon salt

1 teaspoon sweet paprika

2 tablespoons finely chopped fresh flat-leaf parsley

For the Dough

4 cups ½-inch crustless white bread cubes (see page 6)

⅔ cup milk

1 large egg, beaten

⅓ cup unbleached all-purpose flour, plus some extra for dusting

½ teaspoon salt

½ cup coarse dry crustless white bread crumbs (see page 6)

For Serving

6 tablespoons (¾ stick) unsalted butter, melted just before serving

Salt and freshly ground black pepper

Sour cream

Equipment

Large, wide bowl to hold the dumplings cooked in batches

1. COOK THE VEGETABLE MIXTURE: Melt the 2 tablespoons butter in a small pot over medium heat. Add the onion and stir just until it begins to soften, about 2 minutes. Add the carrot, parsnip, turnip, mushrooms, 1 tablespoon salt, and the paprika and cook, stirring continuously, for 3 minutes. Stir in ½ cup water, cover, and simmer for 15 minutes longer. Stir occasionally, adding a little more water if the mixture begins to look a little dry.

2. Uncover and stir until all the remaining liquid has evaporated and the mixture begins to brown lightly. Remove the pot from the heat, stir in the parsley, scoop the mixture into a shallow bowl, and allow it to cool slightly.

3. MAKE THE DOUGH: Place the bread cubes in a large bowl and pour in the milk. Work the milk into the bread with your hands, squishing with your fingers until the bread becomes a relatively smooth paste. Mix in the egg, flour, and ½ teaspoon salt, then mix in the warm vegetable mixture and the bread crumbs. Cover and refrigerate for 20 to 30 minutes.

4. MAKE THE DUMPLINGS: Line a tray with a kitchen towel and sprinkle with a little flour.

5. Using wet hands, pinch off a small piece of dough and roll it into a ball about 1¼ inches around. Dust with a little flour and place on the prepared tray. Repeat with the remaining dough.

6. COOK THE DUMPLINGS: Fill a large pot halfway with salted water and bring to a boil over high heat. Reduce the heat to medium for a steady simmer.

7. Gently drop half the balls, a few at a time, into the simmering water. Stir carefully to prevent the dumplings from sticking. Cook until all of them are floating, about 8 minutes, then cook for 3 minutes longer.

8. Remove the dumplings with a slotted spoon, place them in the large bowl, and drizzle with a ladle of the cooking liquid to prevent sticking. Cook with the remaining dumplings and place them in the bowl with another ladle of the cooking liquid.

9. Drain the dumplings and move them to a wide serving bowl. Drizzle the melted butter over the dumplings, sprinkle with salt and pepper, and serve with a side of sour cream.

Clootie Dumpling

(Scotland)

SERVES 4 (MAKES 1 DUMPLING)

Clootie, a Scottish word for "cloth," is also the name of this rich, fruity dumpling that is cooked in a cloth. It's a type of fruitcake, similar to Classic Christmas Pudding (December), and a traditional holiday treat. Some may appreciate the taste and texture of the *clootie* dumpling more than the Christmas Pudding, because the ratio of batter to fruit is more even. The Christmas Pudding has much more fruit and fat, and is made with a dense bread batter, making it extremely intense. Some unwrap and "dry" the *clootie* dumpling for a few minutes in a hot oven, giving its floury skin a slight crunch.

This dumpling is wrapped using the Pudding Bag Fold (page 58).

For the Dumpling

⅔ cup raisins

⅓ cup currants

1¼ cups unbleached all-purpose flour

¼ cup very fine chopped cold suet or
   2 tablespoons unsalted butter, frozen,
   coarsely grated, and kept cold

¼ cup muscovado or other unrefined sugar
   (see page 20)

½ teaspoon baking soda

¼ teaspoon baking powder

1 teaspoon Pudding Spice (page 239)

Pinch of salt

1 large egg, beaten

1 tablespoon treacle or molasses

⅓ cup buttermilk

1 crisp, tart apple, such as Granny Smith

For Cooking and Serving

Unsalted butter and unbleached all-purpose flour
   to coat the muslin

1 recipe Vanilla Custard Sauce (page 97) or
   Cream Sauce (page 94) or vanilla ice cream

Equipment

Heatproof rack or plate, small enough to fit in a
   large pot

24-inch square of muslin

12-inch length of kitchen string for tying the
   clootie dumpling

1. MAKE THE BATTER: Place the raisins and the currants in a small bowl, pour in enough warm water to cover by 1 inch, and soak for 15 to 20 minutes.

2. Meanwhile, place the rack or an upside-down plate in a medium pot, fill it two-thirds of the way with water, and bring to a boil over high heat. The rack or plate is there to protect the dumpling from direct heat by preventing it from sinking to the bottom of the pot. This dumpling floats while it cooks in boiling water, but it will sink for a few minutes when first placed in the pot. It can also settle to the bottom during cooking if the water level falls below halfway up the sides of the dumpling.

3. Place the flour in a large bowl. Add the suet and mix it throughout the flour, breaking apart any clumps. If using butter, rub it into the flour until the mixture looks like a coarse, damp meal. Mix in the sugar, baking soda, baking powder, Pudding Spice, and salt.

4. Whisk together the egg, treacle, and buttermilk in a small bowl. Pour it into the flour mixture and stir just until you have a moist, sticky batter. Do not overmix.

5. Peel and core the apple and coarsely grate it over a plate to collect its juices. Drain the raisins and currants, stir them into the batter along with the grated apple and its juices, and set aside.

6. ASSEMBLE THE DUMPLING: *Before assembling the* clootie *dumpling, review the Pudding Bag Fold.*

7. Soak the muslin under running water, wring it out, and spread it out on a flat surface. Rub one side of the damp muslin with butter, leaving a narrow border on all sides, and coat with flour. Center the batter on top of the muslin. (You may find it easier to assemble the dumpling by using a bowl as a supportive mold for the cloth before filling it with batter.) Gather up the corners of the muslin and arrange the folds neatly, creating a bag. As you collect the muslin and prepare it for tying, leave it slightly baggy so that the dumpling can swell as it cooks. Be certain, however, to grip the muslin low enough to leave no open gaps. Tie the gathered muslin tightly.

8. COOK THE DUMPLING: Carefully lower the wrapped dumpling into the boiling water, cover, and cook for 2 hours. Check the water level every 30 minutes. Add more boiling water if there is not enough to reach at least halfway up the dumpling.

9. Remove the dumpling with tongs, place it on a folded kitchen towel to drain, unwrap, and let it rest for a couple of minutes. If there is no naturally flat side, steady the dumpling with a fork and slice off just enough from any side to create a "foot," making it possible for it to sit steadily on a plate. Serve warm with Vanilla Custard Sauce, Cream Sauce, or vanilla ice cream. The *clootie* dumpling can be refrigerated for up to 3 days. Reheat in a steamer pot or use the Steamer Plate Setup (page 37).

Starchy Coconut Stew with Slippery Rice Balls

Guinataan at Bilo-Bilo (Philippines)

SERVES 4 TO 8 (MAKES ABOUT 20 DUMPLINGS)

The term *guinataan* refers to any dish that is stewed in coconut milk, and *bilo-bilo* means "ball ball," which in this recipe refers to small, chewy rice flour dumplings. Jackfruit is one of the exceptional ingredients in this dish, but it's difficult to find fresh and carries a slight metallic taste when canned. Dried jackfruit is the next best thing once it has been soaked in warm water until soft. The *ube* yam, found either fresh or frozen at many Philippine markets, will tint the stew with a purple hue. If you are unable to find jackfruit or *ube* yam, this creamy and coconutty dessert is still worth making, and you can compensate by just adding more of the other ingredients.

For the Stew

6 cups fresh coconut milk (see page 8) or two and a half 14-ounce cans coconut milk mixed with 2 cups water

½ cup sugar

¼ cup small tapioca pearls

½ pound sweet potato, peeled and cut into 1-inch cubes

½ pound taro, peeled and cut into 1-inch cubes

½ pound fresh or thawed frozen *ube* yam, peeled and cut into 1-inch pieces

1 yellow plantain, peeled and cut into 1-inch rounds

½ pound jackfruit, seeded and cut into 1-inch pieces, or ¼ pound dried jackfruit, soaked in hot water to cover for 30 minutes, drained and cut into 1-inch pieces

For the Dumplings

1¼ cups sweet (glutinous) rice flour, preferably from the Philippines or Thailand, plus some extra for dusting

½ cup warm water

1. **MAKE THE COCONUT STEW:** Pour the coconut milk into a medium pot and bring to a simmer over medium-low heat. Immediately reduce the heat to low for a gentle simmer. If using fresh coconut milk, be sure not to let it come to a boil or it will separate into what looks like a superfine curdle and you will have to start over. Stir in the sugar and tapioca and cook for 1 minute. Add the sweet potato, taro, *ube*, plantain, and jackfruit, cover, and simmer for 20 to 25 minutes, or until the sweet potato just begins to soften. Stir occasionally while it simmers.

2. **MAKE THE DUMPLINGS:** While the stew cooks, line a tray with a kitchen towel and sprinkle with a little rice flour.

3. Place 1 cup of the rice flour in a medium bowl and keep the remaining ¼ cup handy. Pour in the warm water and mix until a smooth ball forms. Knead the dough in the bowl for a minute. This dough needs to be firm enough to hold its shape when rolled into balls. If it is too soft or sticky, work in some of the remaining flour, a little at a time.

4. Pinch off a small piece of dough and roll it into a ball about 1 inch around. Dust with a little rice flour and place on the prepared tray. Repeat with the remaining dough.

5. COOK THE DUMPLINGS: Once the stew has finished simmering for 20 to 25 minutes, carefully drop the rice balls, a few at a time. Cover and simmer for 10 minutes longer, stirring occasionally. Remove from the heat, cool slightly, and serve. *Guinataan* can be refrigerated for up to 3 days. Reheat before serving.

Guava Duff

(Bahamas)

SERVES 4 TO 6 (MAKES 1 DUMPLING)

Take one bite of this layered, steamed cake and you'll immediately notice the big fruity taste of the guava. If you're not familiar with guava, you will be delighted by its sweet berrylike flavor, reminiscent of passionfruit. This recipe uses guava paste, a condensed and sweetened fruit preserve, which can be found at many supermarkets.

This dumpling is made using the Jelly-Roll Shape (page 41) and then steamed using the Pudding Basin Setup (page 43).

For the Dough

1¼ cups unbleached all-purpose flour

1 teaspoon baking soda

½ teaspoon baking powder

⅛ teaspoon salt

4 tablespoons (½ stick) unsalted butter, at room temperature

¼ cup sugar

1 teaspoon fresh lemon juice

1 large egg, at room temperature, beaten

For the Filling

8 ounces guava paste, chopped coarse (about 1 cup)

For Cooking and Serving

Unsalted butter and sugar to coat the pudding basin

1 recipe Hard Sauce (recipe follows)

Equipment

24-inch square of muslin

35-inch length of kitchen string

4- to 5-cup pudding basin

Pot large enough to hold the basin when covered

Parchment paper

1. MAKE THE DOUGH: Place 1 cup of the flour in a medium bowl and keep the remaining ¼ cup handy. Add the baking soda, baking powder, and salt and mix well.

2. Place the butter, sugar, and lemon juice in a large bowl and whisk until the sugar has mostly dissolved. Add the egg and continue whisking until the mixture is light and airy, about 3 minutes.

3. Add half of the flour mixture to the egg mixture and stir until combined, then mix in the second half. Gently work the dough in the bowl into one manageable ball. Do not overwork the dough. If the dough is sticky, work in some of the remaining flour, a little at a time, until it no longer sticks to your fingers. Cover and refrigerate for 30 minutes.

4. MAKE THE FILLING: While the dough is chilling, place the guava paste with 2 tablespoons water in a double boiler or in a stainless-steel bowl set on top of a pot filled with 1 inch of simmering water. (The bowl should not be touching the water but should rest directly above it.) Stir vigorously until the guava paste has melted and you have a very thick, smooth sauce, 3 to 4 minutes. Remove from the heat and set aside to cool.

5. ASSEMBLE AND STEAM THE GUAVA DUFF: *Before assembling the guava duff, review the Jelly-Roll Shape and the Pudding Basin Setup.*

6. Soak the muslin and the string under running water. Wring them out and set aside. Have ready the dough and the filling.

7. Place the empty pudding basin in the pot. Pour water into the space between the basin and the pot until it comes three-quarters of the way up the sides of the basin. Remove the basin and bring the water to a boil over high heat. Reduce the heat to low for a gentle simmer.

8. Meanwhile, make sure the interior of the basin is dry before rubbing it with butter and coating with sugar.

9. Place the dough on a floured surface, shape it into a blunt log, then roll it out into an 8 × 12-inch rectangle about ¼ inch thick. Sprinkle with flour if it gets sticky. Spread the guava sauce on top of the dough rectangle, leaving a narrow border on all sides. Starting with one of the longer sides, begin to roll up the dough, pinching the ends to seal as you go. Pinch and press the far edge of the dough along the length of the log to seal. Pull together and press the ends of the log together to make a doughnut shape, then gently lift and place it in the prepared pudding basin. Cut out a round of parchment paper and place it on top of the log. Cover the basin with the damp muslin and secure it tightly with the string. Tie the opposite corners of the muslin into handles over the top of the pudding.

10. Using tongs or a wooden spoon, push a folded cloth, such as a standard white cotton napkin, into the simmering water and arrange it to lie flat on the bottom of the pot. Using the cloth handle, carefully lower the basin into the pot, cover, and simmer for at least 1½ hours, or up to 2½ hours for a pudding that's even richer in flavor and texture. Check the water level every 30 minutes and replenish with boiling water as needed.

11. Remove the pot from the heat. Using a pot holder to grasp the cloth handle, carefully remove the basin from the pot, put it on a folded kitchen towel, and allow the guava duff to cool for 5 minutes. Remove the string, cloth, and paper. Unmold by inverting it onto a plate. Slice and serve with a generous helping of the Hard Sauce. Guava duff can be refrigerated for up to 3 days. Reheat in a steamer pot or use the Steamer Plate Setup (page 37).

HARD SAUCE

MAKES ABOUT ½ CUP

3 tablespoons unsalted butter, at room temperature

⅓ cup superfine sugar (or granulated sugar pulsed
   in a clean spice or coffee grinder for 1 to 2 minutes)

1 tablespoon brandy or dark rum

Place the butter and sugar in a small bowl and whisk until the sugar has mostly dissolved and the mixture is light and creamy. Slowly whisk in the brandy or rum until combined. Scoop into a small serving dish and chill until solid, about 30 minutes, before using. Hard sauce can be made in advance and kept tightly wrapped in the refrigerator for up to 1 week.

Potato Dumplings with Cabbage Layers

Káposztás Gombóc (Hungary)

SERVES 4 (MAKES 16 DUMPLINGS)

We love these tasty cabbage dumplings. The potato dough is soft and savory, the shredded cabbage sweet and somewhat crunchy. These dumplings are great with a little oil or butter, but here we finish them under a hot broiler with some melted cheese on top. A good sprinkling of fried bread crumbs (see page 7) can be added for a crispy crunch no matter how you serve them. A sharper-tasting version of this dumpling can be made with the same amount of sauerkraut or a combination of sauerkraut and fresh cabbage.

These dumplings are made using the Jelly-Roll Shape (page 41).

For the Filling

3 tablespoons grapeseed or other neutral oil

1 medium yellow onion, chopped fine

¾ pound green cabbage (about ½ small cabbage), cored, cut into wedges, sliced very thin, and hand-wilted (see page 37)

½ teaspoon sweet paprika

½ teaspoon sugar

¼ teaspoon salt

For the Dough

2 medium baking potatoes, such as russet

½ teaspoon salt

1 cup unbleached all-purpose flour, plus some extra for dusting

2 tablespoons unsalted butter, melted

1 large egg, beaten

For Cooking

¼ teaspoon freshly grated nutmeg

2 cups grated Swiss cheese, preferably Emmenthaler

Equipment

Potato ricer

Large, wide bowl to hold the cooked dumplings

8-inch square or similar-size baking pan

1. MAKE THE FILLING: Heat the oil in a large skillet over medium heat. Add the onion and cook, stirring frequently, until soft, about 4 minutes. Add the cabbage, paprika, sugar, and ¼ teaspoon salt and stir until the mixture has browned slightly, about 8 minutes. Remove from the heat, spread the cabbage mixture out on a plate, and allow it to cool to room temperature.

2. MAKE THE DOUGH: Meanwhile, place the potatoes in a small pot, pour in enough water to cover, and bring to a boil over high heat. Cover, reduce the heat to medium, and simmer until fork-tender, about 30 minutes. Drain the potatoes and place on a folded kitchen towel. Once they are cool enough to handle, peel off their skins, cut them into chunks, and press through the ricer into a large bowl.

3. Sprinkle the ½ teaspoon salt and ¾ cup of the flour over the potato, keeping the remaining ¼ cup handy. Toss together with your fingers until mixed evenly. Add the butter and egg and work the dough with your hands until it comes together and is no longer crumbly. This is a delicate dough that needs to be firm enough to be rolled out. If the dough is too soft or sticky, work in some of the remaining flour, a little at a time. Knead the dough in the bowl for 1 minute.

4. ASSEMBLE THE DUMPLINGS: *Before assembling the* káposztás gombóc, *review the Jelly-Roll Shape.*

5. Line a tray with a kitchen towel and sprinkle with a little flour. Have ready the dough and the filling.

6. Divide the dough in half. Place one piece on a floured surface, shape it into a blunt log, then roll it out into a 7×10-inch rectangle about ¼ inch thick. Sprinkle with flour if it gets sticky. Scatter the cabbage mixture on top of the dough rectangle, leaving a narrow border on all sides. Lightly press the mixture into the surface of the dough. Starting with one of the longer sides, begin to roll up the dough, pinching the ends to seal as you go. Pinch and press the far edge of the dough along the length of the log to seal. Repeat with the second half of the dough and the remaining filling.

7. Cut the doughy ends off both logs with a serrated knife (about a ½ inch off each end) then cut each log into 8 equal pieces. Lightly press the 2 cut sides of one piece into a shallow pile of all-purpose flour. Roll the slice into a ball while using just enough pressure to push and pack the layers closer together. Place on the prepared tray and repeat with the remaining slices.

8. COOK THE DUMPLINGS: Fill a large pot halfway with salted water and bring to a boil over high heat. Reduce the heat to low for a gentle simmer. Gently drop the dumplings, one by one, into the water, stirring occasionally to prevent sticking. Cook until the dumplings float to the surface, about 3 minutes, then cook for 2 minutes longer.

9. Remove the dumplings with a slotted spoon, place them in the large bowl, and allow them to cool slightly.

10. BROIL THE DUMPLINGS: Turn on the broiler and lightly coat the baking pan with oil.

11. Arrange the dumplings in one snug layer in the pan. Sprinkle with the nutmeg and grated cheese. Place under the broiler, cook until the cheese is bubbly and golden brown, 3 to 5 minutes, and serve.

John in the Sack

Jan in de Zak (Holland)

SERVES 4 TO 6 (MAKES 1 DUMPLING)

This steamed bread is soft, slightly sweet, and modestly dotted with bits of raisins and candied citrus rind. It's delicious as a side to a savory meal or as a sweet snack with jam. Leftovers can be sliced and used to make excellent French toast. Because the dough rises for the second time inside the "sack," it's important to leave plenty of room for it to expand. Some recipes finish the bread by placing it in the oven just long enough to form a crust, but we prefer it soft inside and out.

This dumpling is wrapped using the Pudding Bag Fold (page 58).

For the Dumpling

¼ cup warm water, preferably nonchlorinated, such as distilled or spring water

¼ teaspoon light muscovado or other unrefined sugar (see page 20)

1¼ teaspoons active dry yeast (about ½ packet)

2 cups unbleached all-purpose flour

½ teaspoon salt

1 large egg, beaten

½ cup milk, lukewarm

1 tablespoon unsalted butter, melted

½ cup raisins

¼ cup very finely chopped candied lemon peel

For Cooking

Unsalted butter to coat the muslin

Equipment

24-inch square of muslin

10-inch length of kitchen string

8- to 10-quart steamer pot

1. PROOF THE YEAST: Pour the warm water into a small bowl, stir in the sugar and the yeast, and proof for 15 minutes. The surface should become foamy. If not, start again with a new yeast packet.

2. MAKE THE DOUGH: Place 1¾ cups of the flour in a large bowl and keep the remaining ¼ cup handy. Add the yeast mixture, salt, egg, milk, and butter and mix until all the liquid has been absorbed. Work the dough with your hands into one manageable ball. If the dough is sticky, work in some of the remaining flour, a little at a time, until it no longer sticks to your fingers.

3. Place the dough on a floured surface and knead for 3 to 5 minutes. Return the dough to the bowl, cover with a damp kitchen towel, and set aside in a warm, dark place until the dough doubles in size, 1½ to 2 hours. Use the Proofing Pot Setup (page 36) if the temperature of the room is not ideal.

4. While the dough is rising, place the raisins in a small bowl, pour in enough warm water to cover by 1 inch, and set aside.

5. Punch down the dough, place it on a floured surface, knead once or twice, then pat it out into a 12-inch round. Drain the raisins, shaking off any excess water, and scatter them across the dough round. Do the same with the lemon peel. Fold the dough in half so that it encloses the fruit, then fold the dough in half one more time. Knead until all the raisins and the lemon have been worked throughout the dough and the dough is smooth and elastic, 3 to 4 minutes. If pieces of fruit begin to spill out, just work them back into the dough.

6. ASSEMBLE THE DUMPLING: *Before assembling the* Jan in de zak, *review the Pudding Bag Fold.*

7. Soak the muslin under running water, wring it out, and spread it out on a flat surface. Rub one side of the damp muslin with butter, leaving a narrow border on all sides. Center the dough ball on top of the muslin. Gather up the corners of the muslin and arrange the folds neatly, creating a bag. As you collect the muslin and prepare it for tying, leave it very baggy so that the dumpling will have enough room to rise. Be certain, however, to grip the muslin low enough to leave no open gaps. Tie the gathered muslin tightly, return the wrapped dough to the bowl, and place again in a warm, dark place (or back into the proofing pot) and allow the dough to expand and fill out the cloth, 1 to 2 hours.

8. STEAM THE DUMPLING: Remove the basket from the steamer pot, add 2 inches of water to the pot and bring to a boil over high heat. Place the wrapped dough in the basket. Place the basket in the pot, cover, reduce the heat to medium, and cook for 2 hours. Check the water level every 30 minutes and replenish with boiling water as needed.

9. Remove the pot from the heat. Carefully remove the basket and place it on a folded kitchen towel. Remove the *Jan in de zak*, place it on a plate, unwrap, and allow it to cool slightly. Serve warm or at room temperature. *Jan in de zak* can be refrigerated for up to 3 days.

Classic Christmas Pudding

(England)

SERVES 12 (MAKES 1 DUMPLING)

This pudding is often made months in advance and aged either at room temperature or in the refrigerator until Christmas. It may be soaked in liquor during the aging process, basted with it periodically, or simply left to develop its flavors on its own. For those of us who are not disciplined enough to take care of a pudding for weeks or months, rest assured that a Christmas pudding that's cooked and eaten on the same day is still extremely delicious and just as proper. This recipe requires an 8- to 10-hour cooking time.

This dumpling is made using the Pudding Basin Setup (page 43).

For the Dumpling

1 crisp, tart apple, such as Granny Smith

1 cup dried currants

2 cups raisins

½ cup finely chopped candied lemon peel

½ cup finely chopped candied orange peel

1 cup amber ale

2 tablespoons brandy or dark rum

8 tablespoons (1 stick) unsalted butter, at room temperature

⅔ cup light muscovado or other unrefined sugar (see page 20)

1 tablespoon treacle or molasses

6 large eggs, at room temperature, beaten

2 cups coarse fresh crustless white bread crumbs (see page 6)

¼ cup unbleached all-purpose flour

1 tablespoon Pudding Spice (page 239)

⅛ teaspoon salt

½ pound very finely chopped cold suet or 4 tablespoons (½ stick) unsalted butter, frozen, coarsely grated, and kept cold

For Cooking and Serving

Unsalted butter and sugar to coat the pudding basin

1 recipe Vanilla Custard Sauce (page 97) or Hard Sauce (page 373)

Equipment

24-inch square of muslin

40-inch length of kitchen string

10- to 12-cup pudding basin

Pot large enough to hold the basin when covered

Parchment paper

1. MAKE THE PUDDING MIXTURE 24 TO 72 HOURS IN ADVANCE: Peel and core the apple and coarsely grate it over a large bowl. Add the currants, raisins, and candied lemon and orange peels. Stir in the ale and brandy. Cover and soak at room temperature for 6 to 8 hours. Stir the fruit occasionally for even soaking.

2. Place the butter, muscovado sugar, and treacle in another large bowl and whisk vigorously until most of the sugar has dissolved. Continue whisking while slowly pouring in the eggs.

3. Combine the bread crumbs, flour, Pudding Spice, and salt in another large bowl. Add the suet and mix it throughout the bread crumb mixture while breaking apart any clumps. If using butter, rub it into the bread crumb mixture until it looks like coarse cornmeal. Pour in the butter and egg mixture and the soaked fruit along with its liquid. Using your hands, mix until combined. Cover and refrigerate overnight for up to 3 days.

4. Remove the mixture from the refrigerator. Firmly compress it into a ball with your hands. If the mixture is not sticking together, work in a little more ale or bandy. If liquid has collected in the bowl, add a little more flour and work everything back into the mixture.

5. ASSEMBLE AND STEAM THE DUMPLING: *Before assembling the pudding, review the Pudding Basin Setup.*

6. Soak the muslin and the string under running water. Wring them out and set aside.

7. Place the empty pudding basin in the pot. Pour water into the space between the basin and the pot until it comes three-quarters of the way up the sides of the basin. Remove the basin and bring the water to a boil over high heat. Reduce the heat to low for a gentle simmer.

8. Meanwhile, make sure the interior of the basin is dry before rubbing it with butter and coating it with sugar. Scoop the pudding mixture into the basin without packing it down and smooth out the surface using wet fingers. Cut out a round of parchment paper and place it on top of the pudding mixture. Cover the basin with the damp muslin and secure it tightly with the string. Tie the opposite corners of the muslin into handles over the top of the pudding.

9. Using tongs or a wooden spoon, push a folded cloth, such as a standard white cotton napkin, into the simmering water and arrange it to lie flat on the bottom of the pot. Using the cloth handle, carefully lower the basin into the pot, cover, and simmer for at least 8 to 10 hours. Check the water level every 30 minutes and replenish with boiling water as needed.

10. Remove the pot from the heat. Using a pot holder to grasp the cloth handle, carefully remove the basin from the pot, put it on a folded kitchen towel, and allow the pudding to cool for 10 minutes. Remove the string, cloth, and paper. Unmold by inverting it onto a plate. Slice and serve hot with Vanilla Custard Sauce or Hard Sauce. If eating the pudding within 2 weeks, allow it to cool completely, and keep it tightly wrapped in the refrigerator. Reheat the pudding in a steamer pot or use the Steamer Plate Setup (page 37). If you are aging the pudding, allow it to cool completely, and wrap it tightly in plastic wrap and refrigerate for up to 3 months. Brush the pudding with ale or brandy twice a week, if you like, and rewrap tightly. To cook, steam it for 2 to 3 hours in a steamer pot or use the Steamer Plate Setup (page 37).

Chocolate Tamales

Tamales de Chocolate (Mexico)

SERVES 4 TO 8 (MAKES 16 DUMPLINGS)

The combination of lime-treated corn and Mexican chocolate creates an unusually light yet satisfyingly rich chocolate dessert. Like *Tamales Dulces* (May), *Tamales de Chocolate* can be enhanced with bits of fruit or nuts added to the filling. Pecans are an especially excellent addition, but be sure to toast them lightly beforehand.

These dumplings are wrapped using the Single-Husk Tamale Fold (page 53).

For the Batter

⅔ cup nonhydrogenated vegetable shortening, at room temperature

2 cups masa harina

⅓ cup cocoa powder

⅔ cup sugar

1 teaspoon baking powder

⅛ teaspoon salt

½ cup warm water

For the Filling

6 ounces Mexican chocolate, such as Ibarra, chopped fine (about 1 cup)

For Assembly

20 to 25 prepared dried corn husks (see page 28)

Sixteen 12-inch lengths of kitchen string for tying the tamales

8- to 10-quart steamer pot

Equipment

Electric hand mixer

1. MAKE THE BATTER: Whip the shortening in a medium bowl with the hand mixer at medium speed until light and glossy, about 5 minutes.

2. Combine the masa harina, cocoa powder, sugar, baking powder, and salt in a large mixing bowl.

3. Pour the warm water into the masa harina mixture and mix with the hand mixer at low speed. Raise the speed to high and mix in the shortening one spoonful at a time. Continue to mix at high speed until the batter is very light and fluffy, about 10 minutes. Cover and set aside for 30 minutes. (You can also make the batter 1 day in advance and keep it refrigerated in a tightly sealed container.)

4. ASSEMBLE THE TAMALES: *Before assembling the tamales, review the Single-Husk Tamale Fold.*

5. Line a tray with a kitchen towel and have ready the batter, chocolate, the husks, and the ties.

6. Loosen up the batter by whisking it for 2 to 3 minutes. The consistency should be something similar to a grainy and dense mousse. If the batter is too stiff to whisk easily, mix in some cold water, a little at a time, until it is softer and fluffier.

7. Pick out the best 16 husks. Lay flat 1 husk, smooth side up. Center 2 rounded tablespoons of the batter on top of the husk and spread it out to the right until it forms a rectangle about 4 × 2½ inches. Place 1 tablespoon of the Mexican chocolate on top of the left half of the rectangle only. Fold the right side of the husk over, sandwiching the filling between the two layers of the batter. Then fold the left side of the husk over the top. Fold the ends of the husk over as firmly as you can to create a neat rectangular package. Tie the package in a crisscross pattern to prevent the husk from unfolding and place on the lined tray. Repeat until you have 16 tamales.

8. Set aside the number of tamales that you would like to cook and keep the rest frozen for up to 6 months (see page 36).

9. STEAM THE TAMALES: Remove the basket from the steamer pot, add 2 inches of water to the pot, and bring to a boil over high heat. Meanwhile, arrange the tamales upright, leaning or loosely wedged against each other in the basket. Ball up and stick in any extra husks or parchment paper to keep the tamales propped up if needed. Blanket the tamales with the remaining husks. Place the basket in the pot, reduce the heat to medium, cover, and steam for 1½ hours. Check the water level every 30 minutes and replenish with boiling water as needed. (If steaming frozen tamales, place them directly in the basket and cook them in the steamer pot for 2 hours. Do not allow the tamales to thaw before cooking.)

10. Remove the pot from the heat. Carefully remove the basket and place it on a folded kitchen towel. Let the tamales cool slightly, cut off the strings, and serve. It's best not to open the tamales too soon and to peel back the husks just before eating so that they stay moist and warm.

Siberian Meat Dumplings

Pelmeni (Russia)

SERVES 6 TO 8

Pelmeni are traditionally made in large batches and left outside to freeze during the frigid Russian winters. Storing these meat dumplings outdoors, on the porch or in the yard, made them readily available whenever a quick meal, or an addition to a meal, was needed. The fact that these dumplings were frozen before being cooked added a characteristic firmness to the dough. In keeping with this tradition, this recipe calls for the dumplings to be frozen solid before cooking. They are usually served in a mushroom or beef broth or a buttery mustard sauce (recipe below) and lots of freshly cracked black pepper.

For the Dough

- 4 cups unbleached all-purpose flour, plus some extra for dusting
- 1 teaspoon salt
- 2 large eggs, beaten

For the Filling

- 1 small yellow onion, chopped fine
- ½ pound freshly ground beef

- ¼ pound freshly ground pork
- 2 garlic cloves, chopped very fine
- 1 teaspoon salt
- ½ teaspoon freshly ground black pepper

For the Sauce*

- 6 tablespoons (¾ stick) unsalted butter
- 3 tablespoons dark brown mustard

- 3 tablespoons distilled white vinegar
- ¼ teaspoon salt
- Freshly ground black pepper to taste

Equipment

- 2-inch round cookie cutter
- Large, wide bowl to hold the dumplings cooked in batches

1. MAKE THE DOUGH: Place 3¾ cups of the flour in a large bowl and keep the remaining ¼ cup handy. Add the 1 teaspoon salt and mix well. Add the eggs and 1½ cups water and mix until all the liquid has been absorbed. Work the dough with your hands into one manageable ball. If the dough is sticky, work in some of the remaining flour, a little at a time, until it no longer sticks to your fingers.

2. Place the dough on a floured surface and knead for 4 to 5 minutes. Return the dough ball to the bowl, cover with a kitchen towel, and let rest for 30 minutes.

3. MAKE THE FILLING: Pulse the onion in a food processor once or twice to break it down slightly. Place it in a small bowl, mix in the remaining filling ingredients, and set aside.

---

*These amounts are for a full recipe. If you plan on freezing and storing some of the dumplings, reduce the amounts in proportion to the number you are serving.

4. ASSEMBLE THE DUMPLINGS: Line a tray with a kitchen towel and sprinkle with a little flour. Have ready the dough and the filling.

5. Knead the dough once or twice on a floured surface, divide it into 8 equal pieces, and set 7 of them aside under a kitchen towel. Shape the remaining piece into a ball, then roll it out until it's $1/16$ inch thick, even thinner would be ideal. (For tips on how to roll dough out thin, see page 35.) Take your time and sprinkle with flour if it gets sticky. Let the rolled-out dough relax for a couple of minutes before cutting out rounds.

6. Using the cookie cutter, cut out as many rounds as you can, usually 28 to 30. Place the rounds in a single layer on the prepared tray. Repeat with the remaining dough pieces. Keep the rounds covered with a kitchen towel as you work. Scraps cannot be reused because dough rolled out this thin is too dry to recombine.

7. Lay flat 4 to 8 dough rounds. Brush half of them with a very thin coating of water to make them sticky enough to seal. Place $1/2$ teaspoon of filling in the center of each dampened round. Top each spoonful of filling with an unbrushed round, creating little sandwiches. Pinch together the edges, pushing out any air, and seal. If desired, trim the edges for a more tailored look. Place the assembled dumplings in a single layer on the prepared tray and keep them covered with a kitchen towel while you work. Once you have assembled the first batch of dumplings, continue with the remaining dough and filling.

8. Cover the tray of assembled dumplings and place in the freezer until they are completely frozen, 3 to 4 hours. Pick out the number of dumplings that you want to cook and keep the rest frozen for up to 6 months (see page 36).

9. COOK THE DUMPLINGS: Fill a large pot halfway with salted water, place over high heat, and bring to a boil. Reduce the heat to medium for a steady simmer.

10. Gently drop a few dozen of the frozen dumplings, a few at a time, into the simmering water. Stir carefully to prevent sticking. Cook until all of them are floating, 3 to 4 minutes, then cook for 4 minutes longer.

11. Remove the *pelmeni* with a slotted spoon, place them in the large bowl, and drizzle with a ladle of the cooking liquid to prevent sticking. Cook any remaining *pelmeni* and place them in the bowl with another ladle of the cooking liquid. Keep them warm while you make the sauce.

12. MAKE THE SAUCE AND FINISH THE DUMPLINGS: Melt the butter in a small saucepan over medium heat. Do not brown. Immediately pour the butter into a large serving bowl and whisk in the mustard, vinegar, and $1/4$ teaspoon salt. Drain the *pelmeni* and add them to the sauce. Toss gently to coat and serve with freshly ground black pepper.

Chestnut Ravioli with Sage Butter Sauce

Ravioli di Castagne (Italy)

SERVES 4 TO 6 (MAKES ABOUT 60 DUMPLINGS)

These dumplings are a tradition at Christmas in Italy, and they do a magnificent job of showing off the chestnut's delicate texture and nutty flavor. First the chestnuts are simmered and peeled, a task that is satisfying and sweet smelling. Then they are combined with prosciutto, apple, crushed amaretti cookies, and cinnamon. Dried or canned chestnuts can also be used in this recipe, but they are not nearly as wonderful as fresh chestnuts.

These dumplings are made using the Half-Moon Fold (page 47).

For the Filling

10 large chestnuts

¼ cup finely chopped prosciutto (about 4 thin slices)

¼ cup whole-milk ricotta

3 tablespoons freshly grated Parmesan cheese

1 amaretti cookie, finely crushed (optional)

1 teaspoon fresh lemon juice plus ½ teaspoon grated zest

⅛ teaspoon ground cinnamon

Pinch of freshly grated nutmeg

¼ teaspoon salt

⅛ teaspoon freshly ground black pepper

½ small crisp, tart apple, such as Granny Smith

For the Dough

1 recipe *Ravioli di Pesce* (page 209) dough, preferably made while the filling is being chilled, but no more than 1 hour in advance

Unbleached all-purpose flour for dusting

For the Sauce*

4 tablespoons (½ stick) unsalted butter, cut into chunks

8 to 10 fresh sage leaves

Salt and freshly ground black pepper

Equipment

2½-inch round cookie cutter

Large, wide bowl to hold the dumplings cooked in batches

1. MAKE THE FILLING: Fill a small pot halfway with water and bring to a boil over high heat. Cut a ½-inch slit into the shell of each chestnut and drop them into the water. Cover, reduce the heat to low, and simmer for 1 hour. Drain the chestnuts, place them in a small bowl, and allow them to cool slightly.

2. Once the chestnuts are cool enough to handle, peel off their shells and skins and pick out any discolored pieces. Crush the chestnuts in a medium mixing bowl with a potato masher

---

*These amounts are for a full recipe. If you plan on freezing and storing some of the dumplings, reduce the amounts in proportion to the number you are serving.

until just slightly chunky. Mix in the proscuitto, ricotta, Parmesan, amaretti crumbs, lemon juice, lemon zest, cinnamon, nutmeg, salt, and pepper.

3. Peel, core, and finely grate the apple. Add it to the chestnut mixture and gently toss with your fingers until everything is mixed evenly. Cover and refrigerate for 30 to 60 minutes before assembling the dumplings.

4. ASSEMBLE THE DUMPLINGS: *Before assembling the ravioli, review the Half-Moon Fold.*

5. Line a tray with a kitchen towel and sprinkle with a little flour. Have ready the dough and the filling.

6. Knead the dough once or twice on a floured surface, divide it into 4 equal pieces, and set 3 of them aside under a kitchen towel. Shape the remaining piece into a ball, then roll it out until it's $1/16$ inch thick. (For tips on how to roll dough out thin, see page 35.) Sprinkle with flour if it gets sticky. Let the rolled-out dough relax for a couple of minutes before cutting out rounds.

7. Using the cookie cutter, cut out as many rounds as you can, usually 12 to 15. Scraps cannot be reused because dough rolled out this thin is too dry to recombine.

8. Lay flat 1 to 5 dough rounds. Brush each round with a very thin coating of water to make it sticky enough to seal. Center a rounded teaspoon of filling on top of each round, fold each neatly in half, pushing out any air, and pinch to seal. Dab a little water along the edges, if needed, for a better seal. Place the assembled dumplings in a single layer on the prepared tray and keep them covered with a kitchen towel while you work. Once you have assembled the first batch of dumplings, continue with the remaining dough and filling.

9. Cover the tray of assembled dumplings and place in the refrigerator for 30 to 60 minutes before cooking. Chilling them helps to set the dough, making the dumplings firm and toothsome when cooked instead of puffy and soft. Set aside the number of dumplings that you would like to cook and keep the rest frozen for up to 6 months (see page 36).

10. COOK THE DUMPLINGS: Fill a large pot halfway with salted water and bring it to a boil over high heat. Reduce the heat to medium for a steady simmer.

11. Gently drop up to 20 dumplings, a few at a time, into the simmering water and stir gently to prevent sticking. Cook until all of them are floating, 2 to 3 minutes, then cook for 3 minutes longer. (If cooking frozen ravioli, add them directly to the simmering water and increase the cooking time by 1 minute. Do not allow the ravioli to thaw before cooking.)

12. Using a slotted spoon, remove the dumplings, place them in the large bowl, and drizzle with a ladle of the cooking liquid to prevent sticking. Cook the remaining dumplings and place them in the bowl with another ladle of the cooking liquid. Reserve 1 cup of the cooking liquid for the sauce.

13. MAKE THE SAUCE AND FINISH THE DUMPLINGS: Melt the butter in a large skillet over low heat without browning. Once the butter has melted completely, raise the heat to medium and stir in the sage. Cook until the butter and the sage just begin to brown, about 2 minutes. Carefully and quickly pour the reserved cup of pasta water. Continue simmering until the sauce has been reduced by half, about 5 minutes.

14. Drain the ravioli and turn them into the pan. Toss and stir for 1 minute to warm through, sprinkle with salt and pepper, and serve.

Chicken-Filled Dumplings in an Escarole Soup

Cappelletti in Brodo (Italy)

SERVES 4 TO 6 (MAKES ABOUT 80 DUMPLINGS)

This popular Christmas soup is filled with tiny, savory dumplings and silky shreds of chopped escarole. The body of these dumplings comes from chicken, but it is the bits of cured meat or sausage that makes them distinctively lavish. Mortadella, a pork sausage similar to bologna, is added in this recipe, along with a small amount of fresh pork. It takes time and planning to make them, a project made easier by the help of family and friends.

These dumplings are made using the Belly-Button Fold (page 49).

For the Filling

2 tablespoons unsalted butter, cut into chunks

1 small skinless chicken breast with bones

¼ pound boneless pork loin

¼ pound mortadella

½ cup freshly grated Parmesan cheese

1 large egg, beaten

2 tablespoons finely chopped fresh flat-leaf parsley leaves

¼ teaspoon salt

¼ teaspoon freshly ground black pepper

For the Dough

1 recipe *Ravioli di Pesce* (page 209) dough, preferably made while the filling is being chilled, but no more than 1 hour in advance

Unbleached all-purpose flour for dusting

For the Soup*

1 recipe (2 quarts) Beef and Chicken Broth (page 398)

1 small head escarole, trimmed and cut into 1-inch pieces

1 teaspoon salt

Equipment

2-inch round cookie cutter

Large, wide bowl to hold the dumplings cooked in batches

1. MAKE THE FILLING: Place the butter and 1 cup water in a small pot and bring to a boil over high heat. Add the chicken and pork, cover, reduce the heat to low, and simmer for 5 minutes. Flip the chicken and pork over, cover, and cook for 5 minutes longer. Drain and place the meat in a medium bowl.

2. Once the meat is cool enough to handle, pull the chicken meat off the bones and discard the bones. Chop the chicken and the pork into very fine pieces and return it to the bowl. Finely chop

---

*The amounts are for a full recipe. If you plan on freezing and storing some of the dumplings, reduce the amounts in proportion to the number you are serving.

the mortadella and mix it into the chopped meat. Mix in the Parmesan, egg, parsley, ¼ teaspoon salt, and pepper. Cover and refrigerate for 30 to 60 minutes before assembling the dumplings.

3. ASSEMBLE THE DUMPLINGS: *Before assembling the* cappelletti, *review the Belly-Button Fold.*

4. Line a tray with a kitchen towel and sprinkle with a little flour. Have ready the dough and the filling.

5. Knead the dough once or twice on a floured surface, divide it into 4 equal pieces, and set 3 of them aside under a kitchen towel. Shape the remaining piece into a ball, then roll it out until it's ¹⁄₁₆ inch thick. This dough should not be thicker than ¹⁄₁₆ inch, even thinner would be ideal. (For tips on how to roll dough out thin, see page 35.) Take your time and sprinkle with flour if it gets sticky. Let the rolled-out dough relax for a couple of minutes before cutting out rounds.

6. Using the cookie cutter, cut out as many rounds as you can, usually 16 to 20. Scraps cannot be reused, because dough is rolled out this thin is too dry to recombine.

7. Lay flat 1 to 5 dough rounds. Brush each round with a very thin coating of water to make it sticky enough to seal. Place a rounded teaspoon of filling in the center of each round, then fold each round neatly in half, pushing out any air, and pinch to seal. Pick up one of the half-moons and join and pinch its ends together behind the base or "belly" of the dumpling. Dab a little water on the ends, if needed, for a better seal. Repeat with the remaining half-moons. Place the assembled dumplings in a single layer on the prepared tray and keep them covered with a kitchen towel. Once you have assembled the first batch of dumplings, continue with the remaining dough and filling.

8. Cover the tray of assembled dumplings and place in the refrigerator for 30 to 60 minutes before cooking. Chilling them helps to set the dough, making the dumplings firm and toothsome when cooked instead of puffy and soft. Set aside the number of dumplings that you would like to cook and keep the rest frozen for up to 6 months (see page 36).

9. COOK THE DUMPLINGS: Pour the broth into a medium pot and bring to a boil over high heat. Stir in the escarole and 1 teaspoon salt, cover, reduce the heat to very low, and keep at a bare simmer until the dumplings are ready to be added.

10. Fill a large pot halfway with salted water and bring to a boil over high heat. Reduce the heat to medium for a steady simmer.

11. Gently drop a few dozen *cappelletti* into the simmering water. Stir carefully to prevent sticking. Cook until all of them are floating, 2 to 3 minutes, then cook for 3 minutes longer.

(If cooking frozen *cappelletti*, add them directly to the simmering water and increase the cooking time by 1 minute. Do not allow the *cappelletti* to thaw before cooking.)

12. Using a slotted spoon, remove the dumplings, place them in the large bowl, and drizzle with a ladle of the cooking liquid to prevent sticking. Cook any remaining dumplings and place them in the bowl with another ladle of the cooking liquid.

13. Drain the *cappelletti* and add them to the hot soup. Cook for 1 minute to warm through and serve.

Dumplings Stuffed with "Stewed" Bread Crumbs

Anolini di Parma (Italy)

SERVES 4 TO 8 (MAKES ABOUT 50 DUMPLINGS)

Inside these small pockets of dough is a creamy filling of bread crumbs that have been soaked in a super-rich beef broth. *Stracotto* is meat that is slow roasted until it is well beyond fork-tender. For these dumplings, the roasting process can go on all day with the idea being to sacrifice the edibleness of the meat in order to create a lush and concentrated sauce. A more accommodating cooking time of 2½ to 3 hours will still provide you with a delicious sauce for your bread crumbs and will also leave the meat perfectly cooked and ready to be eaten in subsequent meals.

For the Stracotto Sauce

- 4 tablespoons (½ stick) unsalted butter, cut into chunks
- 2 pounds beef rump roast
- 1 medium carrot, chopped coarse
- 1 celery rib, chopped coarse
- ¼ cup red wine
- 6 cups Beef and Chicken Broth (page 398)
- 1 teaspoon tomato paste

For the Filling

- 3 cups coarse fresh crustless white bread crumbs (see page 6)
- ½ cup freshly grated Parmesan cheese
- ¼ teaspoon freshly ground black pepper

For the Dough

- 1 recipe *Ravioli di Pesce* (page 209) dough, preferably made while the filling is being chilled, but no longer than 1 hour in advance
- Unbleached all-purpose flour for dusting

For the Soup*

- 1 recipe (2 quarts) Beef and Chicken Broth
- 1 teaspoon salt

Equipment

- Large, wide bowl to hold the dumplings cooked in batches

1. MAKE THE SAUCE FOR THE FILLING 3 TO 8 HOURS IN ADVANCE: Melt the butter in a medium pot over medium-high heat. Add the rump roast and cook until its underside has browned, 5 to 6 minutes. Turn the beef and brown the other sides, 3 to 4 minutes longer on each side. Carefully move the meat to a bowl, leaving the buttery fat behind. Add the carrot and celery to the pot and cook for 3 minutes, stirring occasionally. Pour in the wine and scrape up any bits from the bottom of the pot with a wooden spoon. Return the beef and any of its drippings back into the pot and pour in 4 cups of the broth. Cover, reduce the heat to low, and simmer for 2½ to 3 hours. Turn the meat every half hour and pour in ½ cup of the

---

*These amounts are for a full recipe. If you plan on freezing and storing some of the dumplings, reduce the amounts in proportion to the number you are serving.

remaining broth each time. (You can cook the beef for up to 8 hours for an even richer, more intensely flavored sauce. Meat that is cooked this long will be dry, have very little flavor, and should be discarded.)

2. Remove the meat and the vegetables, place in a bowl, and set aside to cool. Strain the sauce into a pan, stir in the tomato paste, and place over medium heat. Simmer, uncovered, until the sauce reduces to about ⅓ cup, 10 to 15 minutes. Remove it from the heat and allow it to cool slightly. (You can also make the sauce in advance and keep it refrigerated in a tightly sealed container for up to 1 week. Warm the sauce slightly before adding it to the bread crumbs.)

3. MAKE THE FILLING: Place 2½ cups of the bread crumbs in a medium bowl and keep the remaining ½ cup handy. Drizzle the warm sauce over the bread crumbs and stir until all the liquid has been absorbed. This mixture is just thick enough to hold its shape when scooped up with a spoon. If it is too wet, mix in some of the remaining bread crumbs, a little at a time. Mix in the Parmesan and the pepper. Cover and refrigerate for 30 to 60 minutes before assembling the dumplings.

4. ASSEMBLE THE DUMPLINGS: Line a tray with a kitchen towel and sprinkle with a little flour. Have ready the dough and the filling.

5. Knead the dough once or twice on a floured surface, divide it into 4 equal pieces, and set 3 of them aside under a kitchen towel. Shape the remaining piece into a blunt log, then roll it out into a 10-inch square. This dough should not be thicker than 1/16 inch, even thinner would be ideal. (For tips on how to roll dough out thin, see page 35.) Take your time and sprinkle with flour if it gets sticky. Let the rolled-out dough relax for a couple of minutes.

6. Trim the rounded edges, creating a cleaner square shape. Cut the dough into 2-inch strips, then cut again going across the strips every 2 inches to form 25 squares. Place the squares in a single layer on the prepared tray. Keep the squares covered with a kitchen towel as you work. Scraps cannot be reused because dough rolled out this thin is too dry to recombine.

7. Lay flat 4 to 8 dough squares. Brush half of them with a very thin coating of water to make them sticky enough to seal. Place a rounded teaspoon of filling in the center of each dampened square. Top each spoonful of filling with an unbrushed square, lining up the corners to create little sandwiches. Pinch the edges of the squares together, pushing out any air, and seal. Dab a little water along the edges, if needed, for a better seal. You can trim or crimp the edges for a more tailored look. Place the assembled dumplings in a single layer on the prepared tray and keep them covered with a kitchen towel while you continue to fill the remaining squares. Once you have assembled the first batch of dumplings, continue with the remaining dough and filling.

8. Cover the tray of assembled dumplings and place in the refrigerator for 30 to 60 minutes before cooking. Chilling them helps to set the dough, making the dumplings firm and toothsome when cooked instead of puffy and soft. Set aside the number of dumplings that you would like to cook and keep the rest frozen for up to 6 months (see page 36).

9. COOK THE DUMPLINGS: Pour the 2 quarts of broth into a medium pot, stir in the salt, and bring to a boil over high heat. Cover, reduce the heat to very low, and keep at a gentle simmer until the dumplings are added.

10. Fill a large pot halfway with salted water and bring to a boil over high heat. Reduce the heat to medium for a steady simmer. Gently drop a few dozen dumplings, a few at a time, into the water. Stir carefully to prevent sticking. Cook until all of them are floating, 2 to 3 minutes, then cook for 3 minutes longer. (If cooking frozen *anolini,* add them directly to the simmering water and increase the cooking time by 1 minute. Do not allow the *anolini* to thaw before cooking.)

11. Using a slotted spoon, remove the dumplings, place them in the large bowl, and drizzle with a ladle of the cooking liquid to prevent sticking. Cook the remaining dumplings and place them in the bowl with another ladle of the cooking liquid.

12. Drain the *anolini* and turn them into the simmering broth. Cook for 1 minute to warm through and serve.

Broths

CHICKEN BROTH WITH VARIATIONS..394

PORK BROTH WITH VARIATIONS...395

BEEF BROTH WITH VARIATIONS...396

BEEF AND CHICKEN BROTH..398

Chicken Broth

MAKES ABOUT 2 QUARTS WITH 5 TO 6 CUPS SHREDDED MEAT

One 4- to 5-pound chicken, cut into serving pieces, skin removed, and trimmed of excess fat

2 teaspoons salt

2 teaspoons black peppercorns

1. Place the chicken, salt, and peppercorns in a large pot. Pour in 10 cups water and bring it to a boil over high heat. Cover, reduce the heat to low, and simmer for 2 hours. Skim the froth off the surface with a spoon.

2. Remove from the heat, take out the chicken pieces with a slotted spoon or tongs, and place them in a bowl to cool. Strain the broth through a sieve and skim off the fat. Chilling the broth makes removing the fat easier.

3. Once the chicken is cool enough to handle, pull the meat off the bones and tear it into bite-sized pieces. Discard the bones. Measure out enough broth or chicken for your chosen recipe and keep the rest refrigerated for up to 3 days or frozen for up to 6 months.

With Mexican Flavors

Add the following when adding the chicken:

1 white onion, unpeeled and quartered

3 garlic cloves, unpeeled and crushed

With Puerto Rican Flavors

Add the following when adding the chicken:

1 yellow onion, unpeeled and quartered

2 green bell peppers, cored and quartered

4 fresh *culantro (recao)* stems

With Chinese Flavors

Add the following when adding the chicken:

2 large carrots, unpeeled and cut into large pieces

1 small head napa cabbage, cut into 1-inch ribbons

Pork Broth

4 to 5 pounds boneless pork shoulder or butt meat, cut into large serving-size pieces

2 teaspoons salt

2 teaspoons black peppercorns

1. Place the pork, salt, and peppercorns in a large pot. Pour in 10 cups water and bring to a boil over high heat. Cover, reduce the heat to low, and simmer for 3 hours. Skim the froth off the surface with a spoon.

2. Remove from the heat, take out the pork pieces with a slotted spoon or tongs, and place in a bowl to cool. Strain the broth through a sieve and skim off the fat. Chilling the broth makes removing the fat easier.

3. Once the pork is cool enough to handle, pull the meat off the bones and tear it into bite-sized pieces. Discard the bones. Measure out enough broth or pork for your chosen recipe and keep the rest refrigerated for up to 3 days or frozen for up to 6 months.

With Mexican Flavors

Add the following when adding the pork:

1 white onion, unpeeled and quartered

3 garlic cloves, unpeeled and crushed

Beef Broth

3 pounds lean beef stew meat, such as rump or brisket, cut into serving-size pieces

3 pounds meaty beef bones, such as shank, rib, or neck

2 teaspoons salt

2 teaspoon black peppercorns

1. Place the stew meat, beef bones, salt, and peppercorns in a large pot. Pour in 3 quarts water and bring it to a boil over high heat. Cover, reduce the heat to low, and simmer for 3 to 4 hours. Skim the froth off the surface with a spoon.

2. Remove from the heat, take out the beef pieces with a slotted spoon or tongs, and place them in a bowl to cool. Strain the broth through a sieve and skim off the fat. Chilling the broth makes removing the fat easier.

3. Once the beef is cool enough to handle, pull the meat off the bones and tear into bite-sized pieces. Discard the bones. Measure out enough broth or beef for your chosen recipe and keep the rest refrigerated for up to 3 days or frozen for up to 6 months.

With British Flavors

Add the following when adding the beef:

1 large yellow onion, unpeeled and quartered

1 leek, rinsed clean and cut into large pieces

3 carrots, unpeeled and cut into large pieces

3 celery ribs, unpeeled and cut into large pieces

3 fresh thyme sprigs

½ bunch fresh flat-leaf parsley

1 bay leaf

3 whole cloves

With Hungarian Flavors

Add the following when adding the beef:

1 large yellow onion, unpeeled and quartered

3 carrots, unpeeled and cut into large pieces

3 parsnips, unpeeled and cut into large pieces

1 kohlrabi, quartered

1 celery root, unpeeled and cut into large pieces

2 garlic cloves, crushed

½ bunch fresh flat-leaf parsley

With German Flavors

Add the following when adding the beef:

2 leeks, rinsed clean and cut into large pieces

1 small yellow onion, unpeeled and quartered

2 celery ribs, cut into large pieces

3 carrots, unpeeled and cut into large pieces

3 small parsnips, unpeeled and cut into large pieces

1 small celery root or turnip, unpeeled and cut into large pieces

½ bunch fresh flat-leaf parsley

With American Flavors

Add the following when adding the beef:

3 pounds meaty beef bones

1 medium onion, unpeeled and quartered

2 carrots, unpeeled and cut into large pieces

2 celery ribs, cut into large pieces

½ bunch fresh flat-leaf parsley

5 to 6 fresh thyme sprigs

Beef and Chicken Broth

MAKES ABOUT 2 QUARTS WITH 5 TO 6 CUPS SHREDDED MEAT

1 pound lean beef stew meat, such as rump or brisket, cut into serving-size pieces

2 pounds meaty beef bones, such as shank, rib, or neck

2 pounds chicken (about ½ chicken), cut into serving pieces, skin removed, and trimmed of excess fat

2 teaspoons salt

1 small yellow onion, unpeeled and quartered

1 large carrot, unpeeled and cut into large pieces

1 celery rib, cut into large pieces

2 plum tomatoes, quartered

1 bay leaf

½ bunch fresh flat-leaf parsley

2 teaspoons black peppercorns

1. Place all the ingredients in a large pot with 3 quarts water. Bring it to a boil over high heat, cover, reduce the heat to low, and simmer for 3 to 4 hours. Skim the froth off the surface with a spoon.

2. Remove from the heat, take out the beef and chicken pieces with a slotted spoon or tongs, and place them in a bowl to cool. Strain the broth through a sieve and skim off the fat. Chilling the broth makes removing the fat easier.

3. Once the chicken and beef are cool enough to handle, pull the meat off the chicken bones and tear it into bite-sized pieces. Discard the bones. Pull the beef apart into bite-sized pieces. Measure out enough broth or meat for your chosen recipe and keep the rest refrigerated for up to 3 days or frozen for up to 6 months.

Acknowledgments

We would like to thank our agent, Stacey Glick, of Dystel & Goderich Literary Management, and our editor, Stephanie Fraser, both of whom saw this book over more than a few impressive hurdles. We also thank our families, Yee Fan Chu, Rose Ng, Amanda Lovatt, and Jennifer, Jim, Henry, and Molly Romeo. We are forever grateful to Susan Friedland for believing in the possibilities of dumplings and to Harriet Bell and Maureen O'Brien for shepherding the pages within this book. A special thank you to Lorie Young, Christine Benton, Ann Cahn, Kris Tobiassen, and everyone at HarperCollins for all of their hard work and care and for transforming our manuscript into a book. Special thanks to Brandon Harman and Eli Schmidt for all they did to bring the beauty of dumplings to the page. Our appreciation and gratitude to Jeffra and Yash Nandan, Ann and Herman Silverman, Lindsay de Jongh, Stephanie Sugawara, Jon Cohen, Amy Holman, Edward and Tina Baluyut, Ted Calamia, Bill Callahan, Celeste Carrasco, Christine Carroll, Joanne Chan, Connie Chiang, Jonas Damon and Joann Rha, the Dillworth clan, Dong Pui Chun, Marilyn Fein, Dorie Greenspan, Gepsie Harvey, Karen Heaselgrave, Dr. Steven Herman, Nancy Hruska, Amanda and Julie Johns, Anuree Kengrian, Margaret Kornberg, Huy Voun Lee and Seiji Ikuta, Ruth Leiman, Li Gui Hua, Fredrik Larsson and James Anthony, Lorenzo, Kathleen Masterson, the Molly clan, Gita Nandan, Kelly Notaras, Sue Ling Ng, Gail O'Hara, Steve Pilgrim, Bertha Rogers, Linda Rosciano, Alexandra Rowley, Jenny Silverman, Shannon Sinclair, Tiana and Kenny Tang, Wanda Tantayopin, Dianna and Hao Hui Wang, Adam and Illaria Woodward, Ruiqiang Wu and Guichan Mo, and Qiling Wu.

Dumplings by Region and Country

NORTH AND WEST EUROPE

Bacon and Sage Roly-Poly (England) 318

Beef and Oyster Stew with Suet Dumplings (England)..293

Cabinet Pudding, a Cake and Almond Cookie Pudding (England)..............................237

Canary Pudding with Lemon Curd (England) 203

Chocolate Bread Crumb Pudding (England) 92

Classic Christmas Pudding (England) 378

Clootie Dumpling (Scotland) 367

Country Cabbage Soup with Large Cornmeal Dumplings,
   Soupe aux Miques et aux Choux (France) 347

John in the Sack, *Jan in de Zak* (Holland).. 376

Lord Randall's Pudding, an Apricot Dessert (England) 341

Matzo Balls in a Beef Broth, *Fleischsuppe mit Matzoknepfle* (France)................................ 143

Oat and Honey Pudding (Ireland)..287

Potato Dumplings Stuffed with Ham, *Kroppkakor* (Sweden).. 103

Spiced Carrot Pudding (England) 307

Sticky Toffee Pudding (England) 343

ITALY

Chestnut Gnocchi with Walnut Sauce, *Gnocchi di Castagne con Salsa di Noci* 107

Chestnut Ravioli with Sage Butter Sauce, *Ravioli di Castagne* 384

Chicken-Filled Dumplings in an Escarole Soup, *Cappelletti in Brodo* 387

Dumplings Stuffed with Pears, Figs, and Chocolate, *Cialzons alla Frutta* 354

Dumplings Stuffed with "Stewed" Bread Crumbs, *Anolini di Parma* 390

Fish Ravioli with a Thinned Cream Sauce, *Ravioli di Pesce* 209

Potato Gnocchi, *Gnocchi di Patate* 76

"Priest Stranglers" with Brown Butter and Sage, *Strangolapreti* 74

Pumpkin and Lentil Ravioli with Browned Butter and Rosemary,
    Ravioli di Zucca e Lenticchie 356

Semolina Dumplings with Butter and Cheese Sauce, *Frascatelli* 65

Tiny Gnocchi and Cranberry Bean Stew, *Pisarei e Faso* 118

CENTRAL AND EASTERN EUROPE

Bean Soup with Tiny Dumplings, *Csipetke* (Hungary) 313

Bread and Semolina Loaf, *Houskové Knedlíky* (Czech Republic) 285

Butter-Tossed Spaetzle, *Spätzle* (Germany) 67

Cauliflower Soup with Buttery Bread Crumb Dumplings, *Květáková Polévka s Knedlíky*
    (Czech Republic) 121

Chicken Paprika with Dumplings, *Csirke Paprikas Galuskaval* (Hungary) 311

Kasha and Mushroom Pierogi, *Pierogi z Kaszą Gryczaną* (Poland) 127

Large Beef- and Spinach-Filled Dumplings in a Beef Broth, *Maultaschen* (Germany) 351

Lentil and Onion Pierogi, *Pierogi z Soczewicą* (Poland) 324

Marrow Dumplings in Beef Broth, *Markklösschensuppe* (Germany) 79

Milk-Steamed Buns with Vanilla Custard Sauce, *Dampfnudeln* (Germany) 95

Mushroom-Asparagus Bread Dumplings in a Mushroom Sauce,
    Schwammerl Knödel mit Spargel (Austria) 173

"Napkin" Bread Dumpling, *Serviettenkloss* (Germany) 334

"Napkin" Bread Dumpling with Cherries, *Kirschen Serviettenknödel* (Austria) 231

No-Fuss Potato Dumplings, *Pyzy* (Poland) 305

Potato and Dumpling Boil-Up, *Kartoffeln mit Mehlknödel* (Germany) 68

Potato Dumplings Stuffed with Sugar-Stuffed Plums, *Švestkové Knedlíky* (Czech Republic) 299

Potato Dumplings with Cabbage Layers, *Káposztás Gombóc* (Hungary) 374

Potato Dumplings with Crouton Centers, *Kartoffelklösse* (Germany) 345

Root Vegetable Bread Dumplings, *Zöldséggombóc* (Hungary) 365

Silesian Potato Dumplings with Mushroom Sauce, *Kluski Śląskie* (Poland) 105

RUSSIA

Buckwheat Dumplings Stuffed with Apples and Cheese, *Vareniki s Yablokami* 297
"Little Ear" Dumplings Stuffed with Mushrooms in a Beet Soup, *Borshch z Vushka* 359
Siberian Meat Dumplings, *Pelmeni* 382
Spoon-Dropped Semolina Dumplings, *Kletski* 90

AFRICA

Chickpea "Fish" in a Spicy Onion Sauce, *Yeshimbra Asa* (Ethiopia) 315
Leaf-Wrapped Black-Eyed Pea Dumplings, *Moyin-Moyin* (Nigeria) 265
Pounded Cassava Dumpling, *Fufu* (West Africa) 171

THE MIDDLE EAST AND CENTRAL ASIA

Chive-Stuffed Dumplings with Tomato Sauce and Minted Yogurt, *Ashak* (Afghanistan) 145
Cloud-Shaped Bread Buns, *Ting Momo* (Tibet) 99
Lemony Lentil-Chard Soup with Bulgur Dumplings, *Kibbet Raheb* (Lebanon) 207
Oven-Simmered Lamb-Filled Dumplings with Minted Yogurt, *Manti* (Turkey) 156
Spicy Lamb-Filled Dumplings in a Thick Yogurt Soup, *Sheesh Barak bi Laban* (Lebanon) 153
Wheat Dumplings Stuffed with Beef and Onion, *Sha Momo* (Tibet) 151
Wheat Dumplings Stuffed with Turmeric-Stained Potatoes, *Shogo Momo* (Tibet) 148

EAST ASIA

Black Sesame Cupcakes, *Kurogoma Mushipan* (Japan) 165
Black Sesame Roll-Ups, *Hei Zi Ma Juan* (China) 205
Bottlenecked Pork and Shrimp Dumplings, *Shao Mai* (China) 242
Daikon Cake, *Luo Bo Gao* (China) 320
Dumplings Stuffed with Pork and Cabbage, *Mandu* (Korea) 159
Leaf-Wrapped Rice Packages Stuffed with Chicken and Bamboo Shoots, *Nuo Mi Ji* (China) 192
Leaf-Wrapped Rice Packages Stuffed with Peanuts and Sausage, *Zhong Zi* (China) 301
New Year's Day Soup with Pounded Rice Dumplings, *Ozoni* (Japan) 86
Panfried Dumplings Stuffed with Chicken and Mushrooms, *Jiao Zi* (China) 110
Pounded Rice Dumplings, *Mochi* (Japan) 84
Pounded Rice Dumplings Stuffed with Strawberries, *Ichigo Daifuku* (Japan) 190
Rice Dumplings Stuffed with Peanut and Coconut, *Nuo Mi Ci* (China) 245
Rice Dumplings Stuffed with Pork and Kohlrabi, *Fen Guo* (China) 130
Slippery Rice Balls in Cabbage-Radish Soup, *Tang Yuan* (China) 169
Small Mushroom Buns, *Xiang Gu Baozi* (China) 181
Small Pork Buns, *Zhu Rou Baozi* (China) 179

Steamed Bread Loaves Stuffed with Sticky Fried Rice, *Nuo Mi Juan* (China) 101

Steamed Bread Rolls, *Mantou* (China) 72

A Wealth of Steamed Rice Muffins, *Fot Gao* (China) 71

Wontons with Red Chile Oil, *Hung You Chao Shou* (China) 261

INDIA AND SOUTHEAST ASIA

Banana Cupcakes, *Apam Pisang* (Malaysia) 227

Cassava Patties with Grated Coconut, *Pichi-Pichi* (Philippines) 256

Chickpea Dumplings in Tomato Sauce, *Chana Vada ki Tomatochi Bhaji* (India) 125

Chickpea Squares Topped with Mustard Seeds and Spiced Oil, *Khaman Dhokla* (India) 137

Cockles with Rice Dumplings in a Spicy Coconut Sauce, *Kube Mutli* (India) 123

Coconut and Rice Columns with Chickpea Curry, *Puttu Kadala* (India) 176

Coconut-Filled Rice Dumplings, *Modak* (India) 270

Flattened Rice Dumplings with Grated Coconut and Anise Sugar, *Palitao* (Philippines) 197

Leaf-Wrapped Rice and Banana Bundles, *Khao Tom Mat* (Thailand) 259

Leaf-Wrapped Rice Bundles Stuffed with Pork and Beans, *Bánh Tet* (Vietnam) 267

Lightly Soured Rice Cakes, *Sada Idli* (India) 247

Mild Yogurt Semolina Cakes, *Rava Idli* (India) 295

Nine-Layer Coconut Tapioca Cake, *Khanom Chan* (Thailand) 139

Rice and Tapioca Dumplings Topped with Shrimp and Bean Paste, *Bánh Bèo* (Vietnam) 215

Salty-Sweet Bean Puddings with Coconut Cream Topping, *Khanom Thuay* (Thailand) 141

Starchy Coconut Stew with Slippery Rice Balls, *Guinataan at Bilo-Bilo* (Philippines) 369

Sticky Rice Dumplings Stuffed with Pork and Shrimp, *Bánh It Trán* (Vietnam) 212

Sweet Potato Dumplings with a Melted Sugar Center, *Onde-Onde* (Malaysia) 115

Tapioca Balls Stuffed with Minced Pork and Peanuts, *Sakoo Sai Moo* (Thailand) 272

Taro Balls in a Sweet Coconut Soup, *Bua Loi Phuak* (Thailand) 201

AUSTRALIA

Dumplings and Cocky's Joy 333

CANADA AND UNITED STATES

Boston Brown Bread (United States) 279

Cheddar Cheese and Potato Pierogi (United States) 322

Chicken and Dumpling Soup (United States) 283

Chicken Fricot with Dumplings (Canada) 281

Collard Greens with Corn Dumplings (United States) 309

Cranberry Pudding (United States) 338

Graham Potato Buns (United States) 289

Layered Apple and Bread Pudding (United States)......................................291
Leaf Bread, a Fresh Corn "Tamale" (United States and Canada) 199
Peach and Berry Grunt (United States)......................................255
Philadelphia Pepperpot Soup with Dumplings (United States)......................349
Spiced Gingerbread (United States) 70
Steamed Corn Bread (United States)......................................114
Turkey Stew with Stuffing Dumplings (United States) 336
Wild Grapes and Dumplings (United States) 277

MEXICO AND CENTRAL AMERICA

The Arm of the Queen Tamale, *Brazo de la Reina* (Mexico) 220
Chocolate Tamales, *Tamales de Chocolate* (Mexico) 380
Corn Tamales Stuffed with Stringy Cheese and Poblano, *Tamales de Elote* (Mexico) 263
Masa Ball Soup, *Sopa de Bolitas de Masa* (Mexico) 135
Pineapple-Pecan Tamales, *Tamales Dulces* (Mexico)......................184
Pork Tamales with Green Olives and Jalapeño, *Tamales de Puerco* (Mexico).....................217
Potato "Tamales" Stuffed with Chicken and Jalapeño, *Paches de Papa* (Guatemala).................326
Tamales Stuffed with Chicken and Tomatillo Sauce, *Tamales de Pollo* (Mexico)..................186

THE CARIBBEAN

Boiled Fish with Okra and Dumplings (Caribbean)......................167
Cassava "Tamales" Stuffed with Pork and Chickpeas, *Pasteles de Yuca* (Puerto Rico)...............81
Guava Duff (Bahamas)......................................371
Plantain Dumplings in Chicken Broth, *Sopa de Bolitas de Plátano Verde* (Puerto Rico) 229
Red Pea Soup with Spinners (Caribbean) 257
Sweet and Dark Pepperpot Stew and Dumplings (Guyana) 240

SOUTH AMERICA

Beef-Stuffed Plantain Balls in a Cassava-Corn Soup, *Caldo de Bolas* (Ecuador)...................328
Fresh Corn and Basil "Tamales," *Humitas* (Chile) 235
Fresh Corn and Coconut "Tamales," *Pamonhas* (Brazil) 233
Leaf-Wrapped Rice Bundles Stuffed with Chicken and Peanuts, *Juanes de Arroz* (Peru)...............222

Dumplings by Type

Dropped—Dumplings for which the batter or a dough is spooned and dropped into boiling water or into a simmering soup, stew, or sauce.

Butter-Tossed Spaetzle, *Spätzle* (Germany)..67

Chicken Fricot with Dumplings (Canada)...281

Chicken Paprika with Dumplings, *Csirke Paprikas Galuskaval* (Hungary) 311

Chickpea Dumplings in Tomato Sauce, *Chana Vada ki Tomatochi Bhaji* (India)............125

Dumplings and Cocky's Joy (Australia)...333

Matzo Balls in a Beef Broth, *Fleischsuppe mit Matzoknepfle* (France).....................143

Peach and Berry Grunt (United States)...255

Potato and Dumpling Boil-Up, *Kartoffeln mit Mehlknödel* (Germany)......................68

Spoon-Dropped Semolina Dumplings, *Kletski* (Russia)..90

Contained—Dumplings for which the dough or batter is steamed in a container, such as a pudding basin or cake pan.

Banana Cupcakes, *Apam Pisang* (Malaysia)..227

Black Sesame Cupcakes, *Kurogoma Mushipan* (Japan) 165

Black Sesame Roll-Ups, *Hei Zi Ma Juan* (China)..205

Boston Brown Bread (United States)..279

Cabinet Pudding, a Cake and Almond Cookie Pudding (England)............................237

Canary Pudding with Lemon Curd (England) 203

Cassava Patties with Grated Coconut..256

Chickpea Squares Topped with Mustard Seeds and Spiced Oil, *Khaman Dhokla* (India) 137

Chocolate Bread Crumb Pudding (England) 92

Classic Christmas Pudding (England) 378

Coconut and Rice Columns with Chickpea Curry, *Puttu Kadala* (India) 176

Cranberry Pudding (United States) 338

Daikon Cake, *Luo Bo Gao* (China) 320

Guava Duff (Bahamas) 371

Layered Apple and Bread Pudding (United States) 291

Lightly Soured Rice Cakes, *Sada Idli* (India) 247

Lord Randall's Pudding, an Apricot Dessert (England) 341

Mild Yogurt Semolina Cakes, *Rava Idli* (India) 295

Nine-Layer Coconut Tapioca Cake, *Khanom Chan* (Thailand) 139

Oat and Honey Pudding (Ireland) 287

Rice and Tapioca Dumplings Topped with Shrimp and Bean Paste, *Bánh Bèo* (Vietnam) 215

Salty-Sweet Bean Puddings with Coconut Cream Topping, *Khanom Thuay* (Thailand) 141

Spiced Carrot Pudding (England) 307

Spiced Gingerbread (United States) 70

Steamed Corn Bread (United States) 114

Sticky Toffee Pudding (England) 343

A Wealth of Steamed Rice Muffins, *Fot Gao* (China) 71

Pounded—Dumplings for which a starch or a grain is first boiled or steamed, then pounded in a mortar.

New Year's Day Soup with Pounded Rice Dumplings, *Ozoni* (Japan) 86

Pounded Cassava Dumpling, *Fufu* (West Africa) 171

Pounded Rice Dumplings, *Mochi* (Japan) 84

Pounded Rice Dumplings Stuffed with Strawberries, *Ichigo Daifuku* (Japan) 190

Rolled (solid)—Dumplings for which the dough is shaped by hand or rolled out and cut before they are steamed or boiled.

Bean Soup with Tiny Dumplings, *Csipetke* (Hungary) 313

Beef and Oyster Stew with Suet Dumplings (England) 293

Boiled Fish with Okra and Dumplings (Caribbean) 167

Bread and Semolina Loaf, *Houskové Knedlíky* (Czech Republic) 285

Cauliflower Soup with Buttery Bread Crumb Dumplings, *Kvétáková Polévka s Knedlíky* (Czech Republic) 121

Chestnut Gnocchi with Walnut Sauce, *Gnocchi di Castagne con
Salsa di Noci* (Italy) 107

Chicken and Dumpling Soup (United States)..283

Chickpea "Fish" in a Spicy Onion Sauce, *Yeshimbra Asa* (Ethiopia)........................315

Cloud-Shaped Bread Buns, *Ting Momo* (Tibet) 99

Cockles with Rice Dumplings in a Spicy Coconut Sauce, *Kube Mutli* (India) 123

Collard Greens with Corn Dumplings (United States)..309

Country Cabbage Soup with Large Cornmeal Dumplings,
Soupe aux Miques et aux Choux (France) 347

Flattened Rice Dumplings with Grated Coconut and Anise Sugar, *Palitao*
(Philippines)..197

Graham Potato Buns (United States) 289

Lemony Lentil-Chard Soup with Bulgur Dumplings, *Kibbet Raheb* (Lebanon) 207

Marrow Dumplings in Beef Broth, *Markklösschensuppe* (Germany)...........................79

Masa Ball Soup, *Sopa de Bolitas de Masa* (Mexico) 135

Milk-Steamed Buns with Vanilla Custard Sauce, *Dampfnudeln* (Germany) 95

No-Fuss Potato Dumplings, *Pyzy* (Poland)..305

Philadelphia Pepperpot Soup with Dumplings (United States)...................................349

Plantain Dumplings in Chicken Broth, *Sopa de Bolitas de Plátano
Verde* (Puerto Rico) 229

Potato Dumplings with Cabbage Layers, *Káposztás Gombóc* (Hungary)....................374

Potato Gnocchi, *Gnocchi di Patate* (Italy) 76

"Priest Stranglers" with Brown Butter and Sage, *Strangolapreti* (Italy) 74

Red Pea Soup with Spinners (Caribbean) 257

Root Vegetable Bread Dumplings, *Zöldséggombóc* (Hungary) 365

Semolina Dumplings with Butter and Cheese Sauce, *Frascatelli* (Italy)......................65

Silesian Potato Dumplings with Mushroom Sauce, *Kluski Śląski* (Poland).................105

Slippery Rice Balls in Cabbage-Radish Soup, *Tang Yuan* (China)............................169

Starchy Coconut Stew with Slippery Rice Balls, *Guinataan at
Bilo-Bilo* (Philippines)..369

Steamed Bread Rolls, *Mantou* (China) 72

Sweet and Dark Pepperpot Stew and Dumplings (Guyana) 240

Taro Balls in a Sweet Coconut Soup, *Bua Loi Phuak* (Thailand) 201

Tiny Gnocchi and Cranberry Bean Stew, *Pisarei e Faso* (Italy) 118

Turkey Stew with Stuffing Dumplings (United States) 336

Wild Grapes and Dumplings (United States) 277

Stuffed—Dumplings for which a dough is stuffed with a filling before they are steamed or boiled.

Beef-Stuffed Plantain Balls in a Cassava-Corn Soup, *Caldo de Bolas* (Ecuador).............................. 328

Bottlenecked Pork and Shrimp Dumplings, *Shao Mai* (China) 242

Buckwheat Dumplings Stuffed with Apples and Cheese,
   Vareniki s Yablokami (Russia) 297

Cheddar Cheese and Potato Pierogi (United States).. 322

Chestnut Ravioli with Sage Butter Sauce, *Ravioli di Castagne* (Italy)........................... 384

Chicken-Filled Dumplings in an Escarole Soup, *Cappelletti in Brodo* (Italy)................. 387

Chive-Stuffed Dumplings with Tomato Sauce and Minted Yogurt,
   Ashak (Afghanistan) 145

Coconut-Filled Rice Dumplings, *Modak* (India)..270

Dumplings Stuffed with Pears, Figs, and Chocolate, *Cialzons alla*
   Frutta (Italy)..354

Dumplings Stuffed with Pork and Cabbage, *Mandu* (Korea) 159

Dumplings Stuffed with "Stewed" Bread Crumbs, *Anolini di Parma* (Italy)...............390

Fish Ravioli with a Thinned Cream Sauce, *Ravioli di Pesce* (Italy) 209

Kasha and Mushroom Pierogi, *Pierogi z Kaszą Gryczaną* (Poland) 127

Large Beef- and Spinach-Filled Dumplings in a Beef Broth, *Maultaschen*
   (Germany)..351

Lentil and Onion Pierogi, *Pierogi z Soczewicą* (Poland) 324

"Little Ear" Dumplings Stuffed with Mushrooms in a Beet Soup,
   Borshch z Vushka (Russia)...359

Oven-Simmered Lamb-Filled Dumplings with Minted Yogurt, *Manti* (Turkey)...............156

Panfried Dumplings Stuffed with Chicken and Mushrooms, *Jiao Zi* (China) 110

Potato Dumplings Stuffed with Ham, *Kroppkakor* (Sweden)................................103

Potato Dumplings Stuffed with Sugar-Stuffed Plums,
   Švestkové Knedlíky (Czech Republic)..299

Potato Dumplings with Crouton Centers, *Kartoffelklösse* (Germany)...................... 345

Pumpkin and Lentil Ravioli with Browned Butter and Rosemary,
   Ravioli di Zucca e Lenticchie (Italy) 356

Rice Dumplings Stuffed with Peanut and Coconut, *Nuo Mi Ci* (China)...................... 245

Rice Dumplings Stuffed with Pork and Kohlrabi, *Fen Guo* (China) 130

Siberian Meat Dumplings, *Pelmeni* (Russia) 382

Small Mushroom Buns, *Xiang Gu Baozi* (China)...181

Small Pork Buns, *Zhu Rou Baozi* (China) 179

Spicy Lamb-Filled Dumplings in a Thick Yogurt Soup, *Sheesh Barak bi Laban* (Lebanon) 153

Steamed Bread Loaves Stuffed with Sticky Fried Rice, *Nuo Mi Juan* (China) 101

Sticky Rice Dumplings Stuffed with Pork and Shrimp, *Bánh It Trán* (Vietnam)........................... 212

Sweet Potato Dumplings with a Melted Sugar Center, *Onde-Onde* (Malaysia)................115

Tapioca Balls Stuffed with Minced Pork and Peanuts,
   Sakoo Sai Moo (Thailand)... 272

Wheat Dumplings Stuffed with Beef and Onion, *Sha Momo* (Tibet)..................151
Wheat Dumplings Stuffed with Turmeric-Stained Potatoes,
    Shogo Momo (Tibet)..................148
Wontons with Red Chile Oil, *Hung You Chao Shou* (China)..................261

Wrapped—Dumplings for which the batter or dough is wrapped in a cloth or leaf before they are steamed or boiled.

The Arm of the Queen Tamale, *Brazo de la Reina* (Mexico) 220
Bacon and Sage Roly-Poly (England)..................318
Cassava "Tamales" Stuffed with Pork and Chickpeas,
    Pasteles de Yuca (Puerto Rico) 81
Chocolate Tamales, *Tamales de Chocolate* (Mexico) 380
Clootie Dumpling (Scotland)..................367
Corn Tamales Stuffed with Stringy Cheese and Poblano,
    Tamales de Elote (Mexico)..................263
Fresh Corn and Basil "Tamales," *Humitas* (Chile) 235
Fresh Corn and Coconut "Tamales," *Pamonhas* (Brazil) 233
John in the Sack, *Jan in de Zak* (Holland)..................376
Leaf Bread, a Fresh Corn "Tamale" (United States and Canada) 199
Leaf-Wrapped Black-Eyed Pea Dumplings, *Moyin-Moyin* (Nigeria) 265
Leaf-Wrapped Rice and Banana Bundles, *Khao Tom Mat* (Thailand)..................259
Leaf-Wrapped Rice Bundles Stuffed with Chicken and Peanuts,
    Juanes de Arroz (Peru)..................222
Leaf-Wrapped Rice Bundles Stuffed with Pork and Beans, *Bánh Tet* (Vietnam)..................267
Leaf-Wrapped Rice Packages Stuffed with Chicken and Bamboo Shoots,
    Nuo Mi Ji (China) 192
Leaf-Wrapped Rice Packages Stuffed with Peanuts and Sausage,
    Zhong Zi (China)..................301
Mushroom-Asparagus Bread Dumplings in a Mushroom Sauce,
    Schwammerl Knödel mit Spargel (Austria) 173
"Napkin" Bread Dumpling, *Serviettenkloss* (Germany) 334
"Napkin" Bread Dumpling with Cherries, *Kirschen Serviettenknödel* (Austria)..................231
Pineapple-Pecan Tamales, *Tamales Dulces* (Mexico)..................184
Pork Tamales with Green Olives and Jalapeño, *Tamales de Puerco* (Mexico)..................217
Potato "Tamales" Stuffed with Chicken and Jalapeño,
    Paches de Papa (Guatemala)..................326
Tamales Stuffed with Chicken and Tomatillo Sauce,
    Tamales de Pollo (Mexico)..................186

Vegetarian Dumplings

Banana Cupcakes, *Apam Pisang* (Malaysia) 227

Black Sesame Cupcakes, *Kurogoma Mushipan* (Japan) 165

Black Sesame Roll-Ups, *Hei Zi Ma Juan* (China) 205

Boston Brown Bread (United States) 279

Bread and Semolina Loaf, *Houskové Knedlíky* (Czech Republic) 285

Buckwheat Dumplings Stuffed with Apples and Cheese,
   Vareniki s Yablokami (Russia) 297

Butter-Tossed Spaetzle, *Spätzle* (Germany) 67

Cabinet Pudding, a Cake and Almond Cookie Pudding (England) 237

Canary Pudding with Lemon Curd (England) 203

Cassava Patties with Grated Coconut, *Pichi–Pichi* (Philippines) 256

Cauliflower Soup with Buttery Bread Crumb Dumplings,
   Kvétáková Polévka s Knedlíky (Czech Republic) 121

Cheddar Cheese and Potato Pierogi (United States) 322

Chestnut Gnocchi with Walnut Sauce, *Gnocchi di*
   Castagne con Salsa di Noci (Italy) 107

Chickpea Dumplings in Tomato Sauce, *Chana Vada ki Tomatochi Bhaji* (India) 125

Chickpea "Fish" in a Spicy Onion Sauce, *Yeshimbra Asa* (Ethiopia) 315

Chickpea Squares Topped with Mustard Seeds and Spiced Oil,
  Khaman Dhokla (India) 137
Chocolate Bread Crumb Pudding (England) 92
Chocolate Tamales, *Tamales de Chocolate* (Mexico) 380
Cloud-Shaped Bread Buns, *Ting Momo* (Tibet) 99
Coconut and Rice Columns with Chickpea Curry, *Puttu Kadala* (India)......176
Coconut-Filled Rice Dumplings, *Modak* (India) 270
Cranberry Pudding (United States) 338
Dumplings Stuffed with Pears, Figs, and Chocolate, *Cialzons alla*
  Frutta (Italy) 354
Flattened Rice Dumplings with Grated Coconut and Anise Sugar,
  Palitao (Philippines) 197
Fresh Corn and Basil "Tamales," *Humitas* (Chile) 235
Fresh Corn and Coconut "Tamales," *Pamonhas* (Brazil) 233
Graham Potato Buns (United States) 289
Guava Duff (Bahamas) 371
John in the Sack, *Jan in de Zak* (Holland).......................................376
Kasha and Mushroom Pierogi, *Pierogi z Kaszą Gryczaną* (Poland) 127
Layered Apple and Bread Pudding (United States)............................291
Leaf Bread, a Fresh Corn "Tamale" (United States and Canada) 199
Leaf-Wrapped Black-Eyed Pea Dumplings, *Moyin-Moyin* (Nigeria) 265
Leaf-Wrapped Rice and Banana Bundles, *Khao Tom Mat* (Thailand)......259
Lemony Lentil-Chard Soup with Bulgur Dumplings,
  Kibbet Raheb (Lebanon) 207
Lentil and Onion Pierogi, *Pierogi z Soczewicą* (Poland) 324
Lightly Soured Rice Cakes, *Sada Idli* (India) 247
Lord Randall's Pudding, an Apricot Dessert (England)......................341
Mild Yogurt Semolina Cakes, *Rava Idli* (India) 295
Milk-Steamed Buns with Vanilla Custard Sauce, *Dampfnudeln* (Germany) 95
Mushroom-Asparagus Bread Dumplings in a Mushroom Sauce,
  Schwammerl Knödel mit Spargel (Austria) 173
"Napkin" Bread Dumpling, *Serviettenkloss* (Germany) 334
Nine-Layer Coconut Tapioca Cake, *Khanom Chan* (Thailand) 139
No-Fuss Potato Dumplings, *Pyzy* (Poland)......................................305
Oat and Honey Pudding (Ireland)..287
Peach and Berry Grunt (United States)..255
Pineapple-Pecan Tamales, *Tamales Dulces* (Mexico)........................184
Potato and Dumpling Boil-Up, *Kartoffeln mit Mehlknödel* (Germany)......68
Potato Dumplings Stuffed with Sugar-Stuffed Plums,
  Švestkové Knedlíky (Czech Republic)..299
Potato Dumplings with Cabbage Layers, *Káposztás Gombóc* (Hungary)......374

Potato Dumplings with Crouton Centers, *Kartoffelklösse* (Germany)..345

Pounded Rice Dumplings, *Mochi* (Japan)...84

Pounded Rice Dumplings Stuffed with Strawberries, *Ichigo Daifuku* (Japan) 190

"Priest Stranglers" with Brown Butter and Sage, *Strangolapreti* (Italy) 74

Rice Dumplings Stuffed with Peanut and Coconut, *Nuo Mi Ci* (China).................................245

Root Vegetable Bread Dumplings, *Zöldséggombóc* (Hungary) 365

Salty-Sweet Bean Puddings with Coconut Cream Topping,
    Khanom Thuay (Thailand) 141

Semolina Dumplings with Butter and Cheese, *Frascatelli* (Italy)..65

Silesian Potato Dumplings with Mushroom Sauce, *Kluski Śląski* (Poland)................................. 105

Small Mushroom Buns, *Xiang Gu Baozi* (China).. 181

Spiced Gingerbread (United States) 70

Spoon-Dropped Semolina Dumplings, *Kletski* (Russia)..90

Starchy Coconut Stew with Slippery Rice Balls, *Guinataan at*
    Bilo-Bilo (Philippines).. 369

Steamed Bread Rolls, *Mantou* (China) 72

Steamed Corn Bread (United States).. 114

Sticky Toffee Pudding (England) 343

Sweet Potato Dumplings with a Melted Sugar Center, *Onde-Onde* (Malaysia)................................ 115

Taro Balls in a Sweet Coconut Soup, *Bua Loi Phuak* (Thailand) 201

A Wealth of Steamed Rice Muffins, *Fot Gao* (China) 71

Wheat Dumplings Stuffed with Turmeric-Stained Potatoes,
    Shogo Momo (Tibet).. 148

Wild Grapes and Dumplings (United States) 277

Index

A

Almond(s)
 Cookie and Cake Pudding (Cabinet Pudding), 237–38
 Ratafia Cookies, 239
Anolini di Parma (Dumplings Stuffed with "Stewed" Bread Crumbs), 390–92
Apam Pisang (Banana Cupcakes), 227–28
Apple and Bread Pudding, Layered, 291–92
Apples and Cheese, Buckwheat Dumplings Stuffed with, 297–98
Apricot Dessert (Lord Randall's Pudding), 341–42
Ashak (Chive-Stuffed Dumplings with Tomato Sauce and Minted Yogurt), 145–47
Asparagus-Mushroom Bread Dumplings in a Mushroom Sauce, 173–75

B

Bacon and Sage Roly-Poly, 318–19
Bamboo-Leaf Fold, 61
Bamboo leaves, about, 28–29
Bamboo Shoots and Chicken, Leaf-Wrapped Rice Packages Stuffed with, 192–94
Banana and Rice Bundles, Leaf-Wrapped, 259–60
Banana Cupcakes, 227–28
Banana leaves, about, 28
Bánh Bèo (Rice and Tapioca Dumplings Topped with Shrimp and Bean Paste), 215–16
Bánh Ít Trán (Sticky Rice Dumplings Stuffed with Pork and Shrimp), 212–13
Bánh Tet (Leaf-Wrapped Rice Bundles Stuffed with Pork and Beans), 267–69

Basil and Fresh Corn "Tamales," 235–36
Bean(s). *See also* Chickpea(s)
 canned, rinsing, 5
 Cranberry, Stew, Tiny Gnocchi and, 118–20
 Paste and Shrimp, Rice and Tapioca Dumplings Topped with, 215–16
 and Pork, Leaf-Wrapped Rice Bundles Stuffed with, 267–69
 Pounded Rice Dumplings Stuffed with Strawberries, 190–91
 for recipes, 5
 Red Pea Soup with Spinners, 257–58
 Soup with Tiny Dumplings, 313–14
Beef
 Bean Soup with Tiny Dumplings, 313–14
 Broth, 396
 Broth, Chicken and, 398
 Broth, Large Beef- and Spinach-Filled Dumplings in, 351–53
 Broth, Marrow Dumplings in, 79–80
 Broth, Matzo Balls in a, 143–44
 Broth with American Flavors, 397
 Broth with British Flavors, 396
 Broth with German Flavors, 397
 Broth with Hungarian Flavors, 396
 Dumplings Stuffed with "Stewed" Bread Crumbs, 390–92
 "Little Ear" Dumplings Stuffed with Mushrooms in a Beet Soup, 359–61
 and Onion, Wheat Dumplings Stuffed with, 151–52
 Oxtail Sauce, 78

Beef (*continued*)
 and Oyster Stew with Suet Dumplings, 293–94
 Philadelphia Pepperpot Soup with Dumplings, 349–50
 Potato Gnocchi with Oxtail Sauce, 77
 Siberian Meat Dumplings, 382–83
 -Stuffed Plantain Balls in a Cassava-Corn Soup, 328–29
 Sweet and Dark Pepperpot Stew and Dumplings, 240–41
 vegetarian substitutes for, 33
Beet Soup, "Little Ear" Dumplings Stuffed with Mushrooms in a, 359–61
Belly-Button Fold, 49
Berbere Spice, 317
Berry(ies)
 Cranberry Pudding, 338–39
 and Peach Grunt, 255
 Pounded Rice Dumplings Stuffed with Strawberries, 190–91
 for recipes, 13
Black-Eyed Pea Dumplings, Leaf-Wrapped, 265–66
Borshch z Vushka ("Little Ear" Dumplings Stuffed with Mushrooms in a Beet Soup), 359–61
Boston Brown Bread, 279–80
Bottleneck Fold, 50
Bowl Fold, 45
Brazo de la Reina (The Arm of the Queen Tamale), 220–21
Bread Crumb(s)
 Dumplings, Buttery, Cauliflower Soup with, 121–22
 frying, 7
 Marrow Dumplings in Beef Broth, 79–80
 preparing, 6
 Pudding, Chocolate, 92–93
 "Stewed," Dumplings Stuffed with, 390–92
Bread cubes
 Bread and Semolina Loaf, 285–86
 Layered Apple and Bread Pudding, 291–92
 Mushroom-Asparagus Bread Dumplings in a Mushroom Sauce, 173–75
 "Napkin" Bread Dumpling, 324–25
 "Napkin" Bread Dumplings with Cherries, 231–32
 Potato Dumplings with Crouton Centers, 345–46
 preparing, 6
 "Priest Stranglers" with Brown Butter and Sage, 74–75
 Root Vegetable Bread Dumplings, 365–66
Bread(s). *See also* Bread Crumb(s); Bread cubes
 Boston Brown, 279–80
 Buns, Cloud-Shaped, 99–100
 buying, for dumplings, 6
 Corn, Steamed, 114
 John in the Sack, 376–77
 removing crust from, 6
 Rolls, Steamed, 72–73
 Stuffing Dumplings, Turkey Stew with, 336–37

Broth
 Beef, 396
 Beef, Large Beef- and Spinach-Filled Dumplings in, 351–53
 Beef, Marrow Dumplings in, 79–80
 Beef, with American Flavors, 397
 Beef, with British Flavors, 396
 Beef, with German Flavors, 397
 Beef, with Hungarian Flavors, 396
 Beef and Chicken, 398
 Chicken, 394
 Chicken, with Chinese Flavors, 394
 Chicken, with Mexican Flavors, 394
 Chicken, with Puerto Rican Flavors, 394
 Pork, 395
 Pork, with Mexican Flavors, 395
Brown slab sugar, about, 20
Bua Loi Phuak (Taro Balls in a Sweet Coconut Soup), 201–2
Buckwheat Dumplings Stuffed with Apples and Cheese, 297–98
Bulgur Dumplings, Lemony Lentil–Chard Soup with, 207–8
Butter
 clarified (ghee), 12
 for recipes, 12
 -Tossed Spaetzle, 67

C
Cabbage
 Layers, Potato Dumplings with, 374–75
 "Little Ear" Dumplings Stuffed with Mushrooms in a Beet Soup, 359–61
 and Pork, Dumplings Stuffed with, 159–61
 -Radish Soup, Slippery Rice Balls in, 169–70
 Soup, Country, with Large Cornmeal Dumplings, 347–48
 Tofu and Mushroom Mandu, 161
 varieties, for recipes, 7
 Wontons with Red Chile Oil, 261–62
Cake, Coconut Tapioca, Nine-Layer, 139–40
Cake and Almond Cookie Pudding (Cabinet Pudding), 237–38
Caldo de Bolas (Beef-Stuffed Plantain Balls in a Cassava-Corn Soup), 328–29
Canary Pudding with Lemon Curd, 203–4
Candy-Wrapper Shape Using a Cloth, 51
Candy-Wrapper Shape Using a Leaf, 57
Cappelletti in Brodo (Chicken-Filled Dumplings in an Escarole Soup), 387–89
Caramel Sauce, 340
Carrot Pudding, Spiced, 307–8
Cassava
 buying and preparing, 7
 -Corn Soup, Beef-Stuffed Plantain Balls in a, 328–29
 Dumplings, Pounded, 171–72

Patties with Grated Coconut, 256
and Plantain Fufu, 172
"Tamales" Stuffed with Pork and Chickpeas,
81–83
Cauliflower Soup with Buttery Bread Crumb
Dumplings, 121–22
Chana Vada ki Tomatochi Bhaji (Chickpea Dumplings
in Tomato Sauce), 125–26
Chard
The Arm of the Queen Tamale, 220–21
-Lentil Soup, Lemony, with Bulgur Dumplings,
207–8
Cheese
and Apples, Buckwheat Dumplings Stuffed with,
297–98
and Butter Sauce, Semolina Dumplings with,
65–66
Cheddar, and Potato Pierogi, 322–23
Masa Ball Soup, 135–36
Potato Dumplings with Cabbage Layers, 374–75
Stringy, and Poblano, Corn Tamales Stuffed with,
263–64
Cherries, "Napkin" Bread Dumplings with, 231–32
Cherry Compote, 232
Chestnut Gnocchi with Walnut Sauce, 107–8
Chestnut Ravioli with Sage Butter Sauce, 384–86
Chicken
and Bamboo Shoots, Leaf-Wrapped Rice Packages
Stuffed with, 192–94
Broth, 394
Broth, Beef and, 398
Broth, Plantain Dumplings in, 229–30
Broth with Chinese Flavors, 394
Broth with Mexican Flavors, 394
Broth with Puerto Rican Flavors, 394
and Dumpling Soup, 283–84
-Filled Dumplings in an Escarole Soup, 387–89
Fricot with Dumplings, 281–82
Groundnut Soup, 172
and Jalapeño, Potato "Tamales" Stuffed with,
326–27
and Mushrooms, Panfried Dumplings Stuffed
with, 110–12
New Year's Day Soup with Pounded Rice Dump-
lings, 86–87
Paprika with Dumplings, 311–12
and Peanuts, Leaf-Wrapped Rice Bundles Stuffed
with, 222–24
Sweet and Dark Pepperpot Stew and Dumplings,
240–41
and Tomatillo Sauce, Tamales Stuffed with, 186–87
vegetarian substitutes for, 34
Chickpea(s)
Curry, Coconut and Rice Columns with, 176–77
Dumplings in Tomato Sauce, 125–26
"Fish" in a Spicy Onion Sauce, 315–16
and Pork, Cassava "Tamales" Stuffed with, 81–83

Squares Topped with Mustard Seeds and Spiced
Oil, 137–38
Chile(s)
Corn Tamales Stuffed with Stringy Cheese and
Poblano, 263–64
Pork Tamales with Green Olives and Jalapeño,
217–19
Potato "Tamales" Stuffed with Chicken and
Jalapeño, 326–27
for recipes, 14
Red, Oil, Wontons with, 261–62
Sofrito, 83
Sweet, Sour, and Spicy Fish Sauce, 214
Chive-Stuffed Dumplings with Tomato Sauce and
Minted Yogurt, 145–47
Chocolate
Bread Crumb Pudding, 92–93
Pears, and Figs, Dumplings Stuffed with, 354–55
Tamales, 380–81
Christmas Pudding, Classic, 378–79
Chutney, Coconut, 251
Chutney, Onion, 252
Cialzons alla Frutta (Dumplings Stuffed with Pears,
Figs, and Chocolate), 354–55
Clootie Dumpling, 367–69
Cloud-Shaped Bread Buns, 99–100
Cockles with Rice Dumplings in a Spicy Coconut
Sauce, 123–24
Cocky's Joy, Dumplings and, 333
Coconut
Chutney, 251
cracking open, 8
cream, canned, buying, 9
cream, fresh, collecting, 9
Cream Topping, Salty-Sweet Bean Puddings with,
141–42
Curry Masala, 178
-Filled Rice Dumplings, 270–71
and Fresh Corn "Tamales," 233–34
Grated, and Anise Sugar, Flattened Rice Dumplings with, 197–98
grated, buying, 9
Grated, Cassava Patties with, 256
grated, drying in oven, 8
grating meat of, 8
milk
canned, buying and using, 9
cooking with, 9–10
fresh, preparing, 8–9
made from second pressing, 9
scooping cream layer from, 9
and Peanut, Rice Dumplings Stuffed with, 245–46
removing meat from, 8
and Rice Columns with Chickpea Curry, 176–77
Sauce, Spicy, Cockles with Rice Dumplings in a,
123–24
Soup, Sweet, Taro Balls in a, 201–2

Coconut (*continued*)
    Stew, Starchy, with Slippery Rice Balls, 369–70
    Sweet Potato Dumplings with a Melted Sugar
        Center, 115–16
    Tapioca Cake, Nine-Layer, 139–40
Collard Greens with Corn Dumplings, 309–10
Cookies, Ratafia, 239
Corn. *See also* Cornmeal
    Bread, Steamed, 114
    -Cassava Soup, Beef-Stuffed Plantain Balls in a,
        328–29
    flour, about, 10
    Fresh, and Basil "Tamales," 235–36
    Fresh, and Coconut "Tamales," 233–34
    fresh, for recipes, 10
    husks, about, 28
    Leaf Bread, a Fresh Corn "Tamale," 199–200
    Tamales Stuffed with Stringy Cheese and Poblano,
        263–64
Cornmeal
    buying and storing, 10
    Collard Greens with Corn Dumplings, 309–10
    Dumplings, Large, Country Cabbage Soup with,
        347–48
    Fresh Corn and Basil "Tamales," 235–36
    Fresh Corn and Coconut "Tamales," 233–34
    Leaf Bread, a Fresh Corn "Tamale," 199–200
    Steamed Corn Bread, 114
Cranberry Pudding, 338–39
Cream Sauce, 94
Csipetke (Bean Soup with Tiny Dumplings), 313–14
Csirke Paprikas Galuskaval (Chicken Paprika with
        Dumplings), 311–12
Cupcakes, Banana, 227–28
Cupcakes, Black Sesame, 165–66
Curled-Letter Fold, 60
Curry, Chickpea, Coconut and Rice Columns with,
        176–77

D
Daikon radish
    Daikon Cake, 320–21
    Slippery Rice Balls in Cabbage-Radish Soup,
        169–70
Dampfnudeln (Milk-Steamed Buns with Vanilla
        Custard Sauce), 95–96
Dates
    Sticky Toffee Pudding, 343–44
Demerara sugar, about, 20
Diamond in the Square Fold, 42
Dumpling dough
    cutting, 35–36
    leftover, uses for, 34
    proofing, 36
    rolling out, 35
Dumpling folds
    Bamboo-Leaf, 61

Belly-Button, 49
Bottleneck, 50
Bowl, 45
Candy-Wrapper Shape Using a Cloth, 51
Candy-Wrapper Shape Using a Leaf, 57
Curled-Letter, 60
Diamond in the Square, 42
Envelope, 56
Fan-Knot, 44
Half-Moon, 47
Jelly-Roll Shape, 41
Lotus-Leaf, 54
Pinched-Top, 52
Pleated Half-Moon, 46
Pudding Bag, 58
Pudding Basin Setup, 43
Single-Husk Tamale, 53
Standing Half-Moon, 48
Two-Husk Tamale 1 (Wide), 55
Two-Husk Tamale 2 (Long), 59
Dumplings
    boiling and simmering, 36
    cooked, reheating, 37
    definition of, 2
    fillings, leftover, uses for, 34–35
    resting and firming up (setting), 37
    testing cooking method for, 36
    testing for doneness, 37
    uncooked, freezing, 36

E
Eggs
    The Arm of the Queen Tamale, 220–21
    buying, for recipes, 10
    Leaf-Wrapped Black-Eyed Pea Dumplings,
        265–66
Envelope Fold, 56
Equipment
    baking cups, 26
    baking sheet (tray), 26
    box grater, 26
    brush, 26
    dipping bowls, 26
    electric coffee grinder, 26–27
    food processor, 27
    gnocchi board, 27
    kitchen string, 27
    kitchen tongs, 27
    kitchen towels, 27
    leaves and corn husks, 27–29
    metal ruler, 29
    mortar and pestle, 29
    muslin, 29–30
    parchment paper, 30
    potato ricer, 30
    pots and pans, 31–32
    pudding basin, 30

roasting pan fitted with a rack, 30
round cookie cutters, 30–31
scissors, 31
slotted spoon, 31
steamer pot (or multicook pot), 31
steamer racks and collapsible steamers, 32
wooden dowel rolling pin, 32
Escarole Soup, Chicken-Filled Dumplings in an,
    387–89

F
Fan-Knot Fold, 44
Fats and oils
    butter, 12
    cooking oils, 12
    lard, 11
    suet, 11–12
Fen Guo (Rice Dumplings Stuffed with Pork and
    Kohlrabi), 130–31
Figs, Pears, and Chocolate, Dumplings Stuffed with,
    354–55
Fish
    Boiled, with Okra and Dumplings, 167–68
    dried or salted, for recipes, 13
    fresh, for recipes, 13
    New Year's Day Soup with Pounded Rice Dump-
        lings, 86–87
    Ravioli with a Thinned Cream Sauce, 209–11
    vegetarian substitutes for, 34
Fish sauce, about, 14
Fish Sauce, Sweet, Sour, and Spicy, 214
Fleischsuppe mit Matzoknepfle (Matzo Balls in a Beef
    Broth), 143–44
Flour, 22–23. *See also specific flour types*
Folds. *See* Dumpling folds
Fot Gao (A Wealth of Steamed Rice Muffins), 71
Frascatelli (Semolina Dumplings with Butter and
    Cheese Sauce), 65–66
Fruits. *See also specific fruits*
    dried, for recipes, 13–14
    fresh, for recipes, 13
Fufu, Cassava and Plantain, 172
Fufu (Pounded Cassava Dumplings), 171–72

G
Ghee, preparing, 12
Ginger, fresh, about, 14–15
Gingerbread, Spiced, 70
Gnocchi, Potato, with Oxtail Sauce, 77
Gnocchi, Tiny, and Cranberry Bean Stew, 118–20
Gnocchi di Castagne con Salsa di Noci (Chestnut
    Gnocchi with Walnut Sauce), 107–8
Gnocchi di Patate (Potato Gnocchi), 76–77
Golden syrup
    about, 20
    Dumplings and Cocky's Joy, 333
Graham Potato Buns, 289–90

Grapes, Wild, and Dumplings, 277–78
Grapeseed oil, about, 12
Greens. *See also* Cabbage; Spinach
    The Arm of the Queen Tamale, 220–21
    Chicken-Filled Dumplings in an Escarole Soup,
        387–89
    Collard, with Corn Dumplings, 309–10
    hand-wilting, 37
    Lemony Lentil–Chard Soup with Bulgur Dump-
        lings, 207–8
Guava Duff, 371–72
Guinataan at Bilo-Bilo (Starchy Coconut Stew with
    Slippery Rice Balls), 369–70

H
Half-Moon Fold, 47
Half-Moon Fold, Pleated, 46
Half-Moon Fold, Standing, 48
Ham
    Potato Dumplings Stuffed with, 103–4
    Red Pea Soup with Spinners, 257–58
Hard Sauce, 373
Hei Zi Ma Juan (Black Sesame Roll-Ups), 205–6
Herbs. *See also specific herbs*
    hand-wilting, 37
    for recipes, 15
Honey, for recipes, 21
Houskové Knedlíky (Bread and Semolina Loaf),
    285–86
Humitas (Fresh Corn and Basil "Tamales"), 235–36
Hung You Chao Shou (Wontons with Red Chile Oil),
    261–62

I
Ichigo Daifuku (Pounded Rice Dumplings Stuffed
    with Strawberries), 190–91
Idli, Rava (Mild Yogurt Semolina Cakes), 295–96
Idli, Sada (Lightly Soured Rice Cakes), 247–48
Idli Stuffed with Onion Chutney, 248

J
Jaggery, about, 20
Jan in de Zak (John in the Sack), 376–77
Jelly-Roll Shape, 41
Jiao Zi (Panfried Dumplings Stuffed with Chicken
    and Mushrooms), 110–12
Juanes de Arroz (Leaf-Wrapped Rice Bundles Stuffed
    with Chicken and Peanuts), 222–24

K
Káposztás Gombóc (Potato Dumplings with Cabbage
    Layers), 374–75
Kartoffelklösse (Potato Dumplings with Crouton
    Centers), 345–46
Kartoffeln mit Mehlknödel (Potato and Dumpling
    Boil-Up), 68–69
Kasha and Mushroom Pierogi, 127–29

Khaman Dhokla (Chickpea Squares Topped with Mustard Seeds and Spiced Oil), 137–38

Khanom Chan (Nine-Layer Coconut Tapioca Cake), 139–40

Khanom Thuay (Salty-Sweet Bean Puddings with Coconut Cream Topping), 141–42

Khao Tom Mat (Leaf-Wrapped Rice and Banana Bundles), 259–60

Kibbet Raheb (Lemony Lentil–Chard Soup with Bulgur Dumplings), 207–8

Kirschen Serviettenknödel ("Napkin" Bread Dumplings with Cherries), 231–32

Kletski (Spoon-Dropped Semolina Dumplings), 90–91

Kluski Śląskie (Silesian Potato Dumplings with Mushroom Sauce), 105–6

Kohlrabi and Pork, Rice Dumplings Stuffed with, 130–31

Kroppkakor (Potato Dumplings Stuffed with Ham), 103–4

Kube Mutli (Cockles with Rice Dumplings in a Spicy Coconut Sauce), 123–24

Kurogoma Mushipan (Black Sesame Cupcakes), 165–66

Květáková Polévka s Knedlíky (Cauliflower Soup with Buttery Bread Crumb Dumplings), 121–22

L

Lamb-Filled Dumplings
  Oven-Simmered, with Minted Yogurt, 156–58
  Spicy, in a Thick Yogurt Soup, 153–55

Lard, rendering, 11

Lard, vegetarian substitutes for, 34

Leaf Bread, a Fresh Corn "Tamale," 199–200

Legumes. *See also* Lentil(s)
  Leaf-Wrapped Black-Eyed Pea Dumplings, 265–66
  Vegetable Sambhar, 249

Lemon Curd, Canary Pudding with, 203–4

Lemony Lentil–Chard Soup with Bulgur Dumplings, 207–8

Lentil(s)
  -Chard Soup, Lemony, with Bulgur Dumplings, 207–8
  and Onion Pierogi, 324–25
  and Pumpkin Ravioli with Browned Butter and Rosemary, 356–58

Lotus-Leaf Fold, 54

Lotus leaves, about, 29

Luo Bo Gao (Daikon Cake), 320–21

M

Mandu, Tofu and Mushroom, 161

Mandu (Dumplings Stuffed with Pork and Cabbage), 159–61

Manti (Oven-Simmered Lamb-Filled Dumplings with Minted Yogurt), 156–58

Mantou (Steamed Bread Rolls), 72–73

Markklösschensuppe (Marrow Dumplings in Beef Broth), 79–80

Masa
  about, 10
  Ball Soup, 135–36
  Chocolate Tamales, 380–81
  Fresh, Tamale Batter from, 188
  Fresh, 188–89
  harina, about, 10
  Harina, Tamale Batter from, 189
  Pineapple-Pecan Tamales, 184–85
  Potato "Tamales" Stuffed with Chicken and Jalapeño, 326–27

Masala, Coconut Curry, 178

Matzo Balls in a Beef Broth, 143–44

Maultaschen (Large Beef- and Spinach-Filled Dumplings in Beef Broth), 351–53

Meat. *See also* Beef; Lamb; Pork
  buying, for recipes, 16
  chopping fine, 16
  salted, cured, smoked, or dried, 16
  vegetarian substitutes for, 33

Milk-Steamed Buns with Vanilla Custard Sauce, 95–96

Mochi (Pounded Rice Dumplings), 84–85

Modak (Coconut-Filled Rice Dumplings), 270–71

Molasses, for recipes, 20

Moyin-Moyin (Leaf-Wrapped Black-Eyed Pea Dumplings), 265–66

Muscovado sugar, about, 20

Mushroom(s)
  -Asparagus Bread Dumplings in a Mushroom Sauce, 173–75
  Buns, Fresh, 183
  Buns, Small, 181–83
  and Chicken, Panfried Dumplings Stuffed with, 110–12
  and Kasha Pierogi, 127–29
  "Little Ear" Dumplings Stuffed with, in a Beet Soup, 359–61
  Sauce, Silesian Potato Dumplings with, 105–6
  selecting, for recipes, 16–17
  and Tofu Mandu, 161

N

"Napkin" Bread Dumpling, 324–25

"Napkin" Bread Dumplings with Cherries, 231–32

Nuo Mi Ci (Rice Dumplings Stuffed with Peanut and Coconut), 245–46

Nuo Mi Ji (Leaf-Wrapped Rice Packages Stuffed with Chicken and Bamboo Shoots), 192–94

Nuo Mi Juan (Steamed Bread Loaves Stuffed with Sticky Fried Rice), 101–2

Nuts. *See also* Peanut(s)
  Cabinet Pudding, a Cake and Almond Cookie Pudding, 237–38

Chestnut Gnocchi with Walnut Sauce, 107–8
Chestnut Ravioli with Sage Butter Sauce, 384–86
Coconut-Filled Rice Dumplings, 270–71
Pineapple-Pecan Tamales, 184–85
Ratafia Cookies, 239

O

Oat and Honey Pudding, 287–88
Oil, grapeseed, 12
Okra and Dumplings, Boiled Fish with, 167–68
Olives, Green, and Jalapeño, Pork Tamales with, 217–19
Onde-Onde (Sweet Potato Dumplings with a Melted Sugar Center), 115–16
Onion(s)
    Chutney, 252
    Chutney, Idli Stuffed with, 248
    hand-wilting, 37
    and Lentil Pierogi, 324–25
    for recipes, 17
    Sauce, Spicy, Chickpea "Fish" in a, 315–16
Oxtail Sauce, 78
Oyster and Beef Stew with Suet Dumplings, 293–94
Ozoni (New Year's Day Soup with Pounded Rice Dumplings), 86–87

P

Paches de Papa (Potato "Tamales" Stuffed with Chicken and Jalapeño), 326–27
Palitao (Flattened Rice Dumplings with Grated Coconut and Anise Sugar), 197–98
Palm sugar, about, 20
Pamonhas (Fresh Corn and Coconut "Tamales"), 233–34
Pandan leaves, about, 15
Pandan Water, 117
Panela, about, 20
Pasta flour, about, 22
Pasteles de Yuca (Cassava "Tamales" Stuffed with Pork and Chickpeas), 81–83
Peach and Berry Grunt, 255
Peanut butter
    Groundnut Soup, 172
Peanut(s)
    and Chicken, Leaf-Wrapped Rice Bundles Stuffed with, 222–24
    and Coconut, Rice Dumplings Stuffed with, 245–46
    and Minced Pork, Tapioca Balls Stuffed with, 272–74
    and Sausage, Leaf-Wrapped Rice Packages Stuffed with, 301–2
Pears, Figs, and Chocolate, Dumplings Stuffed with, 354–55
Pecan-Pineapple Tamales, 184–85
Pelmeni (Siberian Meat Dumplings), 382–83
Peppercorns, about, 14

Peppercorns, Sichuan, about, 15
Peppers. *See also* Chile(s)
    Chicken Paprika with Dumplings, 311–12
    Sofrito, 83
Pichi-Pichi (Cassava Patties with Grated Coconut), 256
Pierogi, Cheddar Cheese and Potato, 322–23
Pierogi z Kaszą Gryczaną (Kasha and Mushroom Pierogi), 127–29
Pierogi z Soczewicą (Lentil and Onion Pierogi), 324–25
Pinched-Top Fold, 52
Pineapple-Pecan Tamales, 184–85
Pisarei e Faso (Tiny Gnocchi and Cranberry Bean Stew), 118–20
Plantain(s)
    about, 17
    Balls, Beef-Stuffed, in a Cassava-Corn Soup, 328–29
    and Cassava Fufu, 172
    Dumplings in Chicken Broth, 229–30
    green, peeling, 17
Pleated Half-Moon Fold, 46
Plums, Sugar-Stuffed, Potato Dumplings Stuffed with, 299–300
Pork. *See also* Ham; Sausage(s)
    Bacon and Sage Roly-Poly, 318–19
    and Beans, Leaf-Wrapped Rice Bundles Stuffed with, 267–69
    Broth, 395
    Broth with Mexican Flavors, 395
    Buns, Small, 179–80
    and Cabbage, Dumplings Stuffed with, 159–61
    and Chickpeas, Cassava "Tamales" Stuffed with, 81–83
    and Kohlrabi, Rice Dumplings Stuffed with, 130–31
    Minced, and Peanuts, Tapioca Balls Stuffed with, 272–74
    and Shrimp, Sticky Rice Dumplings Stuffed with, 212–13
    and Shrimp Dumplings, Bottlenecked, 242–44
    Siberian Meat Dumplings, 382–83
    Slippery Rice Balls in Cabbage-Radish Soup, 169–70
    vegetarian substitutes for, 33
    Wontons with Red Chile Oil, 261–62
Potato(es)
    baking (russet), about, 18
    boiling (Yukon Gold and red-skinned), about, 18
    Buns, Graham, 289–90
    and Cheddar Cheese Pierogi, 322–23
    Chestnut Gnocchi with Walnut Sauce, 107–8
    cooked, peeling, 18
    and Dumpling Boil-Up, 68–69
    Dumplings, No-Fuss, 305–6
    Dumplings, Silesian, with Mushroom Sauce, 105–6
    Dumplings Stuffed with Ham, 103–4

Potato(es) (*continued*)
    Dumplings Stuffed with Sugar-Stuffed Plums,
        299–300
    Dumplings with Cabbage Layers, 374–75
    Dumplings with Crouton Centers, 345–46
    Gnocchi, 76–77
    Gnocchi with Oxtail Sauce, 77
    grated raw, working with, 18
    riced, compared with mashed, 18
    Sweet, Dumplings with a Melted Sugar Center,
        115–16
    "Tamales" Stuffed with Chicken and Jalapeño,
        326–27
    Turmeric-Stained, Wheat Dumplings Stuffed
        with, 148–50
Poultry. *See also* Chicken; Turkey
    buying, 18
"Priest Stranglers" with Brown Butter and Sage, 74–75
Prune Sauce, Steamed Buns Cooked in, 98
Pudding Bag Fold, 58
Pudding Basin Setup, 43
Puddings, steamed
    Bean, Salty-Sweet, with Coconut Cream Topping,
        141–42
    Cabinet, a Cake and Almond Cookie Pudding,
        237–38
    Canary, with Lemon Curd, 203–4
    Carrot, Spiced, 307–8
    Chocolate Bread Crumb, 92–93
    Christmas, Classic, 378–79
    Clootie Dumpling, 367–69
    Cranberry, 338–39
    Layered Apple and Bread, 291–92
    Lord Randall's, an Apricot Dessert, 341–42
    Oat and Honey, 287–88
    Sticky Toffee, 343–44
Pumpkin and Lentil Ravioli with Browned Butter
    and Rosemary, 356–58
Pumpkin seeds
    The Arm of the Queen Tamale, 220–21
Puttu Kadala (Coconut and Rice Columns with
    Chickpea Curry), 176–77
Pyzy (No-Fuss Potato Dumplings), 305–6

R
Radish. *See* Daikon radish
Raisins
    Classic Christmas Pudding, 378–79
    Clootie Dumpling, 367–69
    John in the Sack, 376–77
    Pineapple-Pecan Tamales, 184–85
    Spiced Carrot Pudding, 307–8
Rava Idli (Mild Yogurt Semolina Cakes), 295–96
Ravioli di Castagne (Chestnut Ravioli with Sage
    Butter Sauce), 384–86
Ravioli di Pesce (Fish Ravioli with a Thinned Cream
    Sauce), 209–11

Ravioli di Zucca e Lenticchie (Pumpkin and Lentil
    Ravioli with Browned Butter and Rosemary),
    356–58
Rice. *See also* Rice flour
    and Banana Bundles, Leaf-Wrapped, 259–60
    basmati, about, 19
    Bundles, Leaf-Wrapped, Stuffed with Chicken and
        Peanuts, 222–24
    Bundles, Leaf-Wrapped, Stuffed with Pork and
        Beans, 267–69
    Cakes, Lightly Soured, 247–48
    and Coconut Columns with Chickpea Curry,
        176–77
    Dumplings, Cockles with, in a Spicy Coconut
        Sauce, 123–24
    Dumplings, Pounded, 84–85
    Dumplings, Pounded, New Year's Day Soup with,
        86–87
    Dumplings, Pounded, Stuffed with Strawberries,
        190–91
    Muffins, Steamed, A Wealth of, 71
    Packages, Leaf-Wrapped, Stuffed with Chicken
        and Bamboo Shoots, 192–94
    Packages, Leaf-Wrapped, Stuffed with Peanuts
        and Sausage, 301–2
    rinsing, 19
    sticky, about, 19
    Sticky Fried, Steamed Bread Loaves Stuffed with,
        101–2
    varieties, for recipes, 18–19
Rice flour
    buying, for recipes, 19
    Coconut-Filled Rice Dumplings, 270–71
    Flattened Rice Dumplings with Grated Coconut
        and Anise Sugar, 197–98
    Rice and Tapioca Dumplings Topped with Shrimp
        and Bean Paste, 215–16
    Rice Dumplings Stuffed with Peanut and Coconut,
        245–46
    Rice Dumplings Stuffed with Pork and Kohlrabi,
        130–31
    Slippery Rice Balls in Cabbage-Radish Soup,
        169–70
    Starchy Coconut Stew with Slippery Rice Balls,
        369–70
    Sticky Rice Dumplings Stuffed with Pork and
        Shrimp, 212–13

S
Sada Idli (Lightly Soured Rice Cakes), 247–48
Sage
    and Bacon Roly-Poly, 318–19
    and Brown Butter, "Priest Stranglers" with,
        74–75
    Butter Sauce, Chestnut Ravioli with, 384–86
Sakoo Sai Moo (Tapioca Balls Stuffed with Minced
    Pork and Peanuts), 272–74

Salt, for recipes, 19
Sambhar Powder, 250
Sauces
    Caramel, 340
    Cream, 94
    Hard, 373
    Oxtail, 78
    Prune, 98
    Soy-Vinegar, 112
    Vanilla Custard, 97
Sausage(s)
    Daikon Cake, 320–21
    and Peanuts, Leaf-Wrapped Rice Packages Stuffed
        with, 301–2
    Steamed Bread Loaves Stuffed with Sticky Fried
        Rice, 101–2
Schwammerl Knödel mit Spargel (Mushroom-
        Asparagus Bread Dumplings in a Mushroom
        Sauce), 173–75
Semolina
    about, 22
    and Bread Loaf, 285–86
    Dumplings, Spoon-Dropped, 90–91
    Dumplings with Butter and Cheese Sauce, 65–66
    Yogurt Cakes, Mild, 295–96
Serviettenkloss ("Napkin" Bread Dumpling), 324–25
Sesame (seeds)
    Black, Cupcakes, 165–66
    Black, Roll-Ups, 205–6
Sha Momo (Wheat Dumplings Stuffed with Beef and
        Onion), 151–52
Shao Mai (Bottlenecked Pork and Shrimp Dump-
        lings), 242–44
Sheesh Barak bi Laban (Spicy Lamb–Filled Dump-
        lings in a Thick Yogurt Soup), 153–55
Shellfish. *See also* Shrimp
    Beef and Oyster Stew with Suet Dumplings,
        293–94
    Cockles with Rice Dumplings in a Spicy Coconut
        Sauce, 123–24
    vegetarian substitutes for, 34
Shogo Momo (Wheat Dumplings Stuffed with
        Turmeric-Stained Potatoes), 148–50
Shrimp
    and Bean Paste, Rice and Tapioca Dumplings
        Topped with, 215–16
    dried or salted, about, 13
    and Pork, Sticky Rice Dumplings Stuffed with,
        212–13
    and Pork Dumplings, Bottlenecked, 242–44
Single-Husk Tamale Fold, 53
Sofrito, 83
Sopa de Bolitas de Masa (Masa Ball Soup), 135–36
Sopa de Bolitas de Plátano Verde (Plantain Dumplings
        in Chicken Broth), 229–30
Soupe aux Miques et aux Choux (Country Cabbage Soup
        with Large Cornmeal Dumplings), 347–48

Soups. *See also* Broth; Stews
    Bean, with Tiny Dumplings, 313–14
    Beet, "Little Ear" Dumplings Stuffed with
        Mushrooms in a, 359–61
    Cabbage, Country, with Large Cornmeal Dump-
        lings, 347–48
    Cabbage-Radish, Slippery Rice Balls in, 169–70
    Cassava-Corn, Beef-Stuffed Plantain Balls in a,
        328–29
    Cauliflower, with Buttery Bread Crumb Dump-
        lings, 121–22
    Chicken and Dumpling, 283–84
    Coconut, Sweet, Taro Balls in a, 201–2
    Escarole, Chicken-Filled Dumplings in an, 387–89
    Groundnut, 172
    Lentil-Chard, Lemony, with Bulgur Dumplings,
        207–8
    Masa Ball, 135–36
    Matzo Balls in a Beef Broth, 143–44
    New Year's Day, with Pounded Rice Dumplings,
        86–87
    Philadelphia Pepperpot, with Dumplings, 349–50
    Plantain Dumplings in Chicken Broth, 229–30
    Red Pea, with Spinners, 257–58
    Thick Yogurt, Spicy Lamb-Filled Dumplings in a,
        153–55
Sour cream, for recipes, 23
Soy sauce, about, 15
Soy-Vinegar Sauce, 112
Spätzle (Butter-Tossed Spaetzle), 67
Spice mixtures
    Berbere Spice, 317
    Coconut Curry Masala, 178
    Pudding Spice, 239
    Sambhar Powder, 250
Spices, for recipes, 14–15
Spices, grinding, 15
Spinach
    and Beef-Filled Dumplings in Beef Broth, 351–53
    "Priest Stranglers" with Brown Butter and Sage,
        74–75
Squash. *See* Pumpkin
Standing Half-Moon Fold, 48
Stews
    Beef and Oyster, with Suet Dumplings, 293–94
    Chicken Fricot with Dumplings, 281–82
    Chicken Paprika with Dumplings, 311–12
    Cockles with Rice Dumplings in a Spicy Coconut
        Sauce, 123–24
    Coconut, Starchy, with Slippery Rice Balls,
        369–70
    Coconut and Rice Columns with Chickpea Curry,
        176–77
    Collard Greens with Corn Dumplings, 309–10
    Cranberry Bean, Tiny Gnocchi and, 118–20
    Pepperpot, Sweet and Dark, and Dumplings,
        240–41

Stews (*continued*)
  Turkey, with Stuffing Dumplings, 336–37
  Vegetable Sambhar, 249
Sticky Toffee Pudding, 343–44
Strangolapreti ("Priest Stranglers" with Brown Butter
    and Sage), 74–75
Strawberries, Pounded Rice Dumplings Stuffed with,
    190–91
Stuffing Dumplings, Turkey Stew with, 336–37
Suet
  Dumplings, Beef and Oyster Stew with, 293–94
  raw, chopping, 11
  rendering, 12
  vegetarian substitutes for, 34
Sugar, types of, 20
Švestkové Knedlíky (Potato Dumplings Stuffed with
    Sugar-Stuffed Plums), 299–300
Sweet Potato Dumplings with a Melted Sugar
    Center, 115–16
Syrup. *See* Golden syrup

T
Tamale, The Arm of the Queen, 220–21
Tamale Batter from Fresh Masa, 188
Tamale Batter from Masa Harina, 189
Tamale Fold, Single-Husk, 53
Tamale Fold, Two-Husk 1 (Wide), 55
Tamale Fold, Two-Husk 2 (Long), 59
Tamales de Chocolate (Chocolate Tamales), 380–81
Tamales de Elote (Corn Tamales Stuffed with Stringy
    Cheese and Poblano), 263–64
Tamales de Pollo (Tamales Stuffed with Chicken and
    Tomatillo Sauce), 186–87
Tamales de Puerco (Pork Tamales with Green Olives
    and Jalapeño), 217–19
Tamales Dulces (Pineapple-Pecan Tamales), 184–85
Tang Yuan (Slippery Rice Balls in Cabbage-Radish
    Soup), 169–70
Tapioca
  Balls Stuffed with Minced Pork and Peanuts,
    272–74
  Coconut Cake, Nine-Layer, 139–40
  flour, about, 7
  pearls, about, 7
  and Rice Dumplings Topped with Shrimp and
    Bean Paste, 215–16
Taro Balls in a Sweet Coconut Soup, 201–2
Ting Momo (Cloud-Shaped Bread Buns), 99–100
Tofu and Mushroom Mandu, 161
Tomatillo(s)
  Potato "Tamales" Stuffed with Chicken and
    Jalapeño, 326–27
  Sauce and Chicken, Tamales Stuffed with, 186–87
Tomato(es)
  The Arm of the Queen Tamale, 220–21
  peeling and seeding, 21

Sauce, Chickpea Dumplings in, 125–26
Sauce and Minted Yogurt, Chive-Stuffed Dump-
    lings with, 145–47
Treacle, about, 20
Turbinado sugar, about, 20
Turkey Stew with Stuffing Dumplings, 336–37
Two-Husk Tamale Fold 1 (Wide), 55
Two-Husk Tamale Fold 2 (Long), 59

V
Vanilla Custard Sauce, 97
Vareniki s Yablokami (Buckwheat Dumplings Stuffed
    with Apples and Cheese), 297–98
Vegetable(s). *See also specific vegetables*
  Root, Bread Dumplings, 365–66
  Sambhar, 249

W
Walnut Sauce, Chestnut Gnocchi with, 107–8
Water
  boiling, replenishing cooking pot with, 22
  cooking water, uses for, 22
  for recipes, 21–22
Wheat
  Dumplings Stuffed with Beef and Onion,
    151–52
  Dumplings Stuffed with Turmeric-Stained
    Potatoes, 148–50
  flours, for wheat-based dumplings, 22
Whipped Cream, Sweetened, 94
Whole wheat flour, about, 22
Wontons with Red Chile Oil, 261–62

X
Xiang Gu Baozi (Small Mushroom Buns), 181–83

Y
Yeshimbra Asa (Chickpea "Fish" in a Spicy Onion
    Sauce), 315–16
Yogurt
  Minted, and Tomato Sauce, Chive-Stuffed
    Dumplings with, 145–47
  Minted, Oven-Simmered Lamb-Filled Dumplings
    with, 156–58
  Semolina Cakes, Mild, 295–96
  strained, preparing, 23
  strained (Greek), buying, 23
  Thick, Soup, Spicy Lamb–Filled Dumplings in a,
    153–55

Z
Zhong Zi (Leaf-Wrapped Rice Packages Stuffed with
    Peanuts and Sausage), 301–2
Zhu Rou Baozi (Small Pork Buns), 179–80
Zöldséggombóc (Root Vegetable Bread Dumplings),
    365–66